ROBERT PRESTHUS, Ph.D., University of Chicago, is University Professor of Political Science at York University, Canada. He previously taught at the University of Oregon, Cornell University, Michigan State University, and University of Southern California. Dr. Presthus, well-known internationally for his work in organizational and political behavior, has lectured at universities throughout Europe and has written for academic journals both here and abroad. Editor of *Administrative Science Quarterly* for a decade, he is widely recognized for his research in organizations, community power structure, and interest group interaction with political elites.

Sixth Edition

PUBLIC ADMINISTRATION

ROBERT PRESTHUS

YORK UNIVERSITY

THE RONALD PRESS COMPANY · NEW YORK

Library of Congress Catalog Card Number: 74–22545
PRINTED IN THE UNITED STATES OF AMERICA

To the Memory of John McDonald Pfiffner

Preface

This standard textbook for the introductory course in public administration covers both the basic substantive areas of the field and their political environment. Extensively revised, the Sixth Edition provides a new focus on the vital role of officials in the policy-making process. In stressing public policy, the text discusses citizen participation, community control, the rise and fall of planning-programming-budgeting systems, and labor-management relations in public service. New developments in systems analysis, computer technology, and the policy sciences are all viewed as instruments of official policy-making. The author's original research brings fresh insights into the role of the bureaucracy in the policy-making process. Materials are included from all levels of government—local, state, and federal. American public administration is treated critically, providing deeper understandings of a vital and growing element in our national life. Examples of parallel problems in the British system are also discussed, for contrast and comparison.

This Sixth Edition then provides a broad-gauged appraisal of public administration. It presents a balanced synthesis of the political-economic environment of public administration and its major functional areas.

This Sixth Edition of *Public Administration* builds on the highly successful approach originally developed by John M. Pfiffner, and refined in later editions in collaboration with the present author. The dedication to this book endeavors to express this indebtedness to the late Dr. Pfiffner.

I should like to acknowledge here my deep gratitude to Dan Butler, my research assistant, for his invaluable aid in preparing this edition. Professors Vaughan Blankenship and Raymond Pomerleau were especially helpful in discussing with the author new and emerging trends in the study of public administration. My thanks are also due to those colleagues who took the time and trouble to write concerning specific aspects of the book. Finally, I am once again indebted to Sara and Robin for accepting the neglect that inevitably attends research and writing.

ROBERT PRESTHUS

Ontario, Canada
April, 1975

Contents

PART II

I

THE STUDY AND CONTEXT OF PUBLIC ADMINISTRATION

1

Public Administration: Definitions and Approaches

Public administration may be defined as the art and science of designing and carrying out public policy As the scale and complexity of government increased, civil servants assumed a larger role in policy-making, in addition to their traditional—and still major—role of implementing policies designed by their elected masters. The area of administrative regulation provides a useful example. Legislators charged with ordering the conditions of participation in many economic sectors found it necessary to delegate considerable authority to administrators to "fill in the details" of regulatory policy. In the process, administrators assumed discretionary powers that tended in a simpler era to remain in the hands of elected representatives. For such reasons, the study of public administration today assigns a vital role in policy-making to higher administrators.

SOME PARAMETERS OF THE FIELD

It is still true, however, that the public bureaucracy is most often an *instrument*. Most civil servants are occupied largely with carrying out policies set down by elected officials in the executive and legislative branches, and by their politically appointed superiors in the administrative hierarchy. Certainly, the "big" decisions, such as Vietnam, NATO, policy in the Mid-East, and price and wage controls in the domestic arena, are designed and rationalized by elected officials and interest group elites, largely in business, the mass media, and labor. The bureaucracy's primal role is to implement such policies.

Nevertheless, if one defines "policy-making" broadly to mean the exercise of discretion, it is clear that officials throughout the civil service often use their own judgment and expertise in the disposition of particular cases. Over time, the collective effect is to shape precedent in a given area, and this often becomes established policy. Although the question is far from settled, it is easy to overestimate the policy initiative of even higher permanent civil servants. While they possess such political resources as expertise and experience, they do not usually displace more decisive resources such as demonstrated achievement in the "real" world of business and law,[1] nor political power in its decisive electoral sense.

Public administration is also concerned with the institutional framework of government, its socioeconomic and political milieu, and the behavior of the individuals who man the bureaucratic machine. Although the field has traditionally focused upon such major substantive areas as organization, finance, and personnel, books such as the present one have also been concerned with so-called informal patterns of behavior which occur in spite of the efforts of organization to provide a structure which, in Herbert Simon's words, controls the "decisional premises" of its members. Organizations, of course, have certain explicit goals and methods that provide the essential reason for their existence, and to some extent, they attempt to fit individuals into this prior framework. The analysis of how individuals attempt to restructure these premises becomes a field of study in itself, often called organizational behavior, and pursued mainly by social psychologists and sociologists. Essentially, for historical and disciplinary reasons, political scientists have tended to focus upon the institutional and legal aspects of public administration. With some exceptions, they have often been concerned mainly with the formal aspects—the manifest goals—of public organizations.

Environment of Public Administration

It seems useful to begin by defining administration generically as a common social process involving certain common activities.[2] These ac-

---

[1] For the advantaged status and selection criteria of high-level appointed executives, see Stanley David, Dean Mann, and Jameson Doig, *Men Who Govern* (Washington, D. C.: Brookings Institution, 1967).

[2] Perhaps a more practical definition of "public administration" is what is contained in this book.

tivities, which usually include policy-making, programming, staffing, budgeting, and supervision, may be seen in most forms of private administration as well. Indeed, to some extent, the differences between private and public administration come to rest largely in the *environment* of each sector.

Public administration may be defined as that aspect of administration occurring under the formal aegis of governments at every level. This condition has significant operational consequences—some restrictive, others liberating. On the restrictive side, public administration often labors under a negative image among advantaged social groups whose "balance of payments" between their contributions to government via taxes and their benefits received may seem unfavorable. Public administration, too, is often charged with assuming responsibility for problem areas only when these have become greatly aggravated. Such intrinsically "unprofitable" areas include urban renewal, shoring up the national economy in times of unemployment, regulating the activities of private sectors, insuring American firms against nationalization in developing countries, etc.

Another restrictive aspect of public administration, not shared by the private sector, is the lesser relevance of quantitative standards of personal and collective achievement and effectiveness. A common example is the lack of the profit criterion, which over the long run and with many exceptions, tends to provide one viable criterion for evaluating the performance of private organizations and administration. There is, of course, some question whether such quantitative standards should be relevant in the field of public administration, which is charged with carrying out large social functions to which criteria of profit and loss and economic viability do not apply. On the other hand, both the language and the self-impressions of higher civil servants are much influenced by the industrial model. The majority of high level appointed officials are recruited from business, industry, and the prestigious law firms who work closely with them.

On the positive side, public administration enjoys several distinct advantages. One of these surely is its virtually unlimited sources of revenue. In a rich society such as the United States, most governments enjoy vast revenues from taxation which enable them to assume and to launch in a rather fulsome manner virtually any program that seems worth undertaking. Obviously, both state and local governments are presently under considerable financial stress, but for the federal government and over the long haul, the generalization is probably accurate. At the same time, of course, a very large proportion of these revenues are

ploughed back into the private system in the forms of subsidies for
virtually every sector of the economy.

The Benefits of Legitimacy

Despite the drama and dislocations of the 1960–1970's, plus the Watergate scandal, government and public administration also probably retain
considerable legitimacy among wide sectors of the public. This condition
may often be negative in that laws and administrative discretion are
accepted reluctantly, perhaps in the category of necessary evils. Nevertheless, compared with most private organizations and administration,
it seems generally fair to say that the governmental apparatus enjoys
some special respected position in mass public opinion as the major
representative of the "public interest." [3] The image of politics and administration as *careers,* concerned essentially with personal power, security, and deference for those who play such roles, is probably not widely
held among members of the public at large. So, despite many reservations, it seems appropriate to say that government retains a certain
monopoly of legitimacy among many citizens. How long this appreciation can withstand onslaughts such as those provided by Watergate
is, of course, a serious question.

Such judgments suggest that public administration probably differs
mainly from private administration in its normative and environmental
aspects, rather than in its technical apparatus and the organizational
structures and methods used to carry out its objectives. Indeed, the
dichotomy posed here between "private" and "public" sectors of administration is to some extent merely an analytical convenience, which
tends to distort reality somewhat. It will be shown in the following
analysis that private interest groups play a sustained, integrated and
influential role in public policy-making in the United States. To a large
extent, as Arthur Bentley put it, "groups create government and then
they use it." [4] Governmental policy is essentially the product of cooperation, compromise, and conflict between substantively relevant
groups, legislators, and higher officials in the bureaucracy.[5] The direc-

---

[3] From time to time, we shall note certain bench-mark issues that merit discussion
by students. The concept of the public interest is among the most critical. Is it
merely an honorific spook, as some observers insist, or is it an operational guide to
administrative behavior?

[4] *The Process of Government,* edited by Peter Odegard (Cambridge, Mass.: Harvard Unievrsity Press, 1967), p. 270.

[5] Robert Presthus, *Elites in the Policy Process* (New York and London: Cambridge
University Press, 1974). For example, three-quarters of all interest group leaders
(N-1,405) in the U. S. and Canada *disagree* that legislators are their competitors in
a struggle to shape government policy (p. 166). Theirs is less a Hobbesian world
than a cooperative commonwealth.

tion and the inspiration for many public programs is provided by interest groups representing the various private sectors of society. Nevertheless, this symbiotic relationship between government and the private sector must be overlooked at times in order to fully analyze the public sector which is our primary focus.

THE STUDY OF PUBLIC ADMINISTRATION

Because public administration is a generalized human activity concerned with ordering the men and materials required to achieve collective social ends, it has drawn widely from the various social sciences. However, it is impossible to gain any adequate perspective of the field without tracing its backgrounds in the area of political science. The emphasis has often been legal, historical, and normative. Traditionally, the analysis of the field has reflected certain dominant contemporary trends in political science, which is usually recognized as the parent discipline of the field. Each of these trends tends to be superseded as analytical tools and fashions change. At any given time, however, the discipline constitutes an amalgam of all such styles, as parts of each are retained in each new wave of revision.

The Institutional Approach

Perhaps the earliest approach to public administration may be designated as the legal and institutional approach. Largely based on the legal rights and obligations of government, this approach tended to emphasize formal relationships and the separation of powers among the three branches of government. Policy and administration were often dichotomized, with the assumption that the role of administrators was almost entirely confined to merely carrying out policy designed by the formal political arms of government. This approach was not very much concerned with methodological questions and its generalizations were often based upon formal analyses of organizational structure and the constitutional delegation of authority and responsibility to the three major sectors of American government.

A major emphasis of this earlier approach was upon the normative question of responsibility. The focus was often upon the ways and means of keeping public administration responsible to the elected branches of government and to the average citizen. To some extent during the early twentieth century, public administration was considered part of public law rather than the independent specialty it has become today. Responsibility, of course, remains a vital question.

The Structural Approach

A second vantage point for the study of public administration may be called the structural approach. This approach, which was much influenced by scientific management and the success of American corporations, tended to focus upon organizational structure and personnel management, augmented by a great deal of concern with financial and legal controls of administration and administrators. To some extent the role of the individual and of so-called informal organization was neglected. It was assumed that the individual in making his employment bargain agreed, tacitly at least, to fit himself into the ongoing system.

This approach has sometimes been criticized for not relating public administration to its political environment and for not emphasizing adequately the fact that organizations are composed of human beings and when decisions are made, they are, in the last analysis, made by individuals. There is some tendency to reify organizations, to assume that they have a life distinct from the activities and norms of the individuals who comprise them. Indeed, this approach is sometimes called the "organization without people" approach. There is probably some tendency for the assumptions that underlie the structural approach to gain a new lease on life from the contemporary interest in the use of computer techniques, policy sciences, programming planning and budgeting, and related technical mechanisms which make it possible to exercise greater rationality, control, and evaluation in policy determination and its outcomes. These new emphases will be considered in detail in subsequent chapters.

In terms of the disciplinary bases of the structural approach, it is probably safe to say that the major reliance was upon traditional political theory, political science, and public law in both its administrative and constitutional aspects. Perhaps the only other discipline which played a very significant role was industrial engineering which brought to the study of administration—particularly in large-scale government operations which were in many ways quite similar to those found in the private sector—innovations concerning the rationalization of production, as seen in the industrial production line, and in some governmental munitions plants, the introduction of stop watches and time and motion studies associated with the name of Taylor. The co-optation of other social science disciplines awaited mainly the development of what may be called the third avenue to the study of public administration, namely the behavioral approach.

The Behavioral Approach

The behavioral approach has sometimes been called the "people without organizations" approach because of its tendency to de-emphasize the manifest goals and larger purposes of organizations in favor of intensive analyses of their internal environment, the motivation of the individuals who man the administrative apparatus, and what may be called the "informal aspects" of public administration. In contrast to earlier approaches, the behavioral approach tends to focus quite strongly on methodological problems, the use of survey analysis to determine organizational "reality," and a concern with the human aspects of administration and decision-making.[6] Its advocates often feel that not very much is known about the actual operational process in public administration, and until such knowledge becomes more established at a higher level of validity, it is perhaps premature to be mainly concerned with the normative aspects of what public administration "should" be doing. Instead, the behavioral approach attempts to build descriptive and analytical generalizations about organizations and administration.[7] Like all intellectual processes, it is based upon certain assumptions, including the fact that there is order and consistency in administrative processes, or at least in the human actions that are believed to lie at the center of public administration. One of its normative assumptions is that it is possible to build an administrative science through careful research on organizations and the behavior of those who work in them.

The difference between the behavioral approach and the earlier approaches is probably most dramatically apparent in the extent to which observers trained in sociology and psychology have made impressive contributions to this field.[8]

The Post-Behavioral Approach

The study of public administration has moved somewhat away from its concern with legal–historical, structural, and behavioral aspects of the

---

[6] For an extended discussion of this orientation, see Robert Presthus, *Behavioral Approaches to Public Administration* (University: University of Alabama Press, 1965).

[7] For a very useful critique that differentiates various approaches within a behavioral context, see Charles Perrow, *Complex Organizations: A Critical Essay* (Glenview, Ill.: Scott, Foresman, 1972).

[8] Among many others, see S. P. Kilpatrick *et al., The Image of the Federal Service* (Washington, D. C.: Brookings Institution, 1964); L. Warner *et al., The American Federal Executive* (New Haven, Conn.: Yale University Press, 1963); Philip Selznick, *T.V.A. and the Grass Roots* (Berkeley: University of California Press, 1949); and Peter Blau, *The Dynamics of Bureaucracy* (Chicago: University of Chicago Press, 1955).

field to a focus upon what may be called advocacy, the prescriptive analysis of policy, and the role of administrators in policy-making. To some extent, this latter orientation to the field has tended to aggravate its traditional empiricism. Meanwhile, some observers are calling rather fervently for full-scale advocacy by administrators. Civil servants and those who study the field are urged to "take a stand" and become active proponents of certain kinds of governmental programs. Students are encouraged to take a consciously normative posture toward public administration and its uses. Clearly, such preferences are affected strongly by contemporary governmental policy, in this case by the somewhat truncated concern of federal political elites with aid to the cities and to poor and minority elements of American society.

This approach, which may be characterized as post-behavorial, obviously appeals to many people who are disenchanted with some of the obvious inadequacies and distorted priorities of the existing governmental and economic systems. Certainly, it has many admirable aspects. At the same time certain dysfunctions exist, not the least of which is the common failure to distinguish between analysis and advocacy. When scholars become advocates, the systematic development of a field probably suffers. As Max Weber put it, "Academic prophecy . . . will create only fanatical sects." [9]

An attending danger of the post-behavior emphasis is that any given individual may be misled as to the extent of influence he can have in changing the existing social and economic structure, with attending discontents. It may be that students, especially, should be provided with a realistic analysis of the occupational field in which they propose to invest their career and energy. Following Weber's admonition, they should probably distinguish between their personal role as activists and the enduring cultural conditions of American public administration, business, and politics which provide the milieu in which such careers will necessarily be worked out. The consequence of advocacy for scholarship and perhaps for policy influence in the long run is surely clear in the cases of recent presidential advisers regarding foreign policy, and particularly Vietnam, where academic cold warriors have been directly involved. Would anyone today ask these talented men for a disinterested appraisal of the shape and consequences of American policy in Southeast Asia? More important, perhaps, any future role they might play is negated by their association with this particular policy.

[9] From Max Weber, edited and translated by H. H. Gerth and C. W. Mills (New York: Oxford University Press, 1946), p. 155.

They are no longer disinterested in the judicial sense of the term. While science can systematically analyze and understand normative judgments, according to their consistency with explicit ends, the fusion of the role of analysis and advocacy is a different matter. Science can, as Max Weber says, "assist politicians in becoming aware of the ultimate standards of values which they do not make explicit to themselves, or which they must pre-suppose in order to be logical . . . but whether the person expressing these value judgments *should* adhere to these ultimate standards is his personal affair; it involves will and conscience, not empirical knowledge." [10]

Science, in effect, is a *vocation* in the service and knowledge of theoretical clarification of facts. Great scholars have at times played both this role and the role of advocate, but they were apparently able to consciously separate these inapposite roles. Given the world trend toward irrationality and the decline of scientific authority, it seems questionable that men in universities, some of which provide one of the few remaining sanctuaries of disinterest in modern society, should be pleading for advocacy in the field of public administration. Obviously, such strictures do not apply to practitioners, consultants, and members of the governmental elite whose role is often one of advocacy.

A related orientation toward public administration is a new concern with the *outcomes* of governmental policy. Heretofore, the *process* of policy-making has received more scholarly attention, although there are notable exceptions. This, of course, is a valuable and appropriate role for disinterested analysis. The early editions of this book, for example, were explicitly concerned with the analysis of the consequences of regulatory policy, the assumptions of bureaucratic structure and rationality, and the guarantee of public accountability among those charged with shaping and carrying out governmental programs. In another context, however, the policy sciences' orientation is quite traditional in its attempts once again to prescribe the conditions under which practitioners might become more effective in shaping and carrying out public policies. In this sense, the current trend is an extrapolation of Herbert Simon's early work,[11] but with an even more pragmatic, consultative orientation. This is especially true of such schemes as program budgeting and the attempt to assign weights to particular aspects of governmental services, using social indicators. These programs will be discussed in

[10] *Max Weber on the Methodology of the Social Sciences,* edited by E. Shils and H. Gerth (New York: Free Press, 1949), p. 54.
[11] *Administrative Behavior* (New York: The Macmillan Co., 1957).

detail later; at the moment we are concerned with outlining contemporary trends in the study of public administration, one of which is a new emphasis upon bureaucratic policy-making, to which we turn in the next chapter.

2

Policy: Toward a Conceptual Understanding

The concept of "policy" is central to the study of public administration, its sub-fields, and related disciplines. Public administration, in its most basic sense, involves the coordination and mobilization of individual and group efforts with a view toward the implementation of public policy. Accordingly, the student of public policy-making must seek first to determine the meaning and implications of the term "policy" before undertaking an examination of the policy process itself or of the specific content of policy. Definitions of "policy" are many and varied, ranging from the simplistic to the hopelessly recondite. They differ from each other regarding divergent conceptions of the nature and functioning of political and administrative structures found among observers in the discipline. Individual definitions of the term often fail to transcend the limitations of the particular analytical framework from which they are derived. Indeed, one of the most persistent problems in the field seems to be the tendency of many observers to treat policy, both theoretically and operationally, as a product of the study of decisional processes (i.e., as a dependent variable rather than as an autonomous or independent variable).

13

WHAT IS POLICY?

Some definitions of the term "policy" in past and current usage are outlined first, followed by a definition of the concept as it is used in the following discussions. In its most fundamental sense, a policy is a salient choice made by an individual or group of individuals that explains, justifies, guides, or outlines a certain course of action, real or contemplated. A policy differs from a decision largely in scope or magnitude. A policy usually establishes a framework according to which individual, particular decisions can be made. In some cases, a policy is an aggregation of smaller decisions, the cumulative result of incremental choices and actions. Often, of course, policies are the consequence of drift and inertia. The whole burden of contemporary policy analysis is to limit this condition.

Seen analytically, the term "policy" is free from any invidious connotation that may be associated with the word "political." [1] One can speak of personal policies, business policies, club policies, school policies, etc., without introducing any more sophisticated political element than that which is normally involved in any social or interpersonal relationship.

Some years ago Lasswell and Kaplan presented a systematic definition of the term which seems applicable to many areas of the social and behavioral sciences:

> Policy is a projected program of goal values and practices: *policy process* is the formulation, promulgation, and application of identifications, demands, and expectations concerning the future interpersonal relations of the self. [2]

Theodore Lowi emphasized the importance of the concept of coercion in thinking about policy. He treats policy as "deliberate coercion" or, in other words, statements intended to delineate the purpose, means, subject, and objects of the exercise of coercion within the context of power relationships in organizational structures. [3] Charles Lindblom prefers a more general meaning which, simply stated, defines policy as any output of any decision-maker, [4] while Bauer characterizes policy as a "course-setting involving decisions of the widest ramifications and longest time perspective in the life of an organization." [5] Carl Friedrich empha-

[1] Daniel Lerner and Harold D. Lasswell, eds., *The Policy Sciences: Recent Developments in Scope and Methods* (Stanford: Stanford University Press, 1951), p. 5.

[2] Harold D. Lasswell and Abraham Kaplan, *Power and Society: A Framework for Political Inquiry* (New Haven: Yale University Press, 1950), p. 71.

[3] "Decision Making versus Policy Making: Toward an Antidote for Technocracy" in *Public Administration Review*, Vol. 30 (May/June 1970), p. 315.

[4] Cited in *Ibid.*, p. 317.

[5] *Ibid.*

sizes the purposive or goal-oriented aspect of the term in viewing policy as an attempt to overcome and/or utilize environmental obstacles and/or opportunities in order to achieve a given goal or objective.[6] Each of these definitions, of course, contains important elements that are critical to the term "policy." Necessarily, no one definition can be said to be absolutely operative in all analyses since each definition is rooted in a specific context or a particular framework. For the purposes of this study, policy will be defined as:

> . . . a definite course or method of action selected (as by a government, institution, group or individual) from among alternatives and in the light of given conditions to guide and usually determine present and future decisions.[7]

Current definition

Conceptually, at least, policy differs fundamentally from administration. Where policy implies a process of formulation involving values or principles oriented to future action, administration usually implies the implementation or execution of previously charted programs within the context of a rational system of management. Operationally, however, policy and administration cannot be realistically separated. The character of a policy plays a vital role in shaping the methods by which that policy is executed in the public sphere. Similarly, the resources available to the administrator (funds, manpower, time) very often determine to a significant degree the extent to which a given policy can be carried out, or—perhaps more critically—qualify or limit the possible range of policy options in the first place. For example, a small state government with limited budgetary and manpower resources would probably encounter grave difficulties if it adopted a sweeping policy of nationalization of primary resource-extractive industries.

Hypothetically, such a policy could be politically attractive and could elicit strongly positive voter response on an ideological level. However, if the state's organizational apparatus and resources were insufficient to allow implementation of the policy and if no development of the prerequisite capabilities was foreseen realistically in the future, then such a policy option would probably be unworkable. If, despite any demonstrated administrative inadequacies, the policy was nevertheless adopted, that policy could only hope to achieve very short-run benefits (e.g., temporary constituency support, negotiating leverage, symbolic concern) for its formulators and, conceivably, could prove costly in the long

---

[6] *Man and His Government* (New York: The McGraw-Hill Book Co., 1963), p. 79.

[7] *Webster's Third New International Dictionary,* unabridged (Springfield, Mass., 1961), p. 1754.

run (e.g., adverse public reaction and voter disenchantment resulting from disappointed expectations). In sum, any set of policy proposals—regardless of their popularity or rationality—is necessarily constrained by the finite resources of administration.

In analyzing policy, it is important to recognize the role of unanticipated consequences. Given the complexity of social and political life and the inability of even the most powerful state or organization to control, much less anticipate, all of the conditions impinging on a given policy, policy is inherently indeterminant to some extent. Computer simulation technology, of course, has reduced the degree of uncertainty, but the problem of man being unable to imagine more than a small proportion of future contingencies remains. In this sense, we must be content to achieve a higher level of rationality in policy determination while recognizing its inherent probability.

In classical "separation of powers" theory, the arenas of policy formulation and policy implementation remain distinct, allocated respectively to the legislative and administrative sectors. The administrative role is often defined as apolitical and essentially value-free in this light (although it is clear that any organization or institution necessarily embodies and perpetuates certain values at the expense of others). No such distinct separation is possible in the contemporary context. The size and complexity of governmental institutions in all but the most limited levels of public activity mitigate against purity in policy-formulating and policy-implementing roles.[8] Unquestionably, the most distinctive and critically important quality of modern big government concerns the intertwining of legislative and administrative roles, particularly regarding the delegation of decision-making responsibilities to various boards, commissions, agencies, and departments of the bureaucracy. A useful example appears in the context of "administrative regulation" where officials perform quasi-executive, legislative, and judicial functions. In effect, governmental decisions are made in the bureaucratic sector in response to demands that may or may not have an external, political component. Such decisions may constitute recognizable policies as defined earlier in this chapter. In other situations, individual bureaucratic decisions may stem from conscious bureaucratically conceived policies entirely removed from the legislative sphere. We will undertake a more detailed examination of these phenomena in following chapters.

[8] For a useful appraisal of the bureaucracy's role and strategy in policy-making, with special emphasis upon the "big three" of agriculture, business, and labor see Charles Jacob, *Policy and Bureaucracy* (New York: Van Nostrand Reinhold Co., 1966).

Approaches to the Study of Policy

Scholarly efforts aimed at the study of policy and the policy process have utilized a number of different approaches. In very general terms, these approaches can be characterized as follows: (1) the study of policy as a process "output" in a rational system, (2) the case study approach, (3) the strategy of "disjointed incrementalism," and (4) the study of policy as an independent variable in the policy process. In addition, other works have attempted to integrate several approaches, fusing various ideas in an attempt to arrive at a more generally applicable theory of policy formulation.

Policy as a Process "Output." A significant body of analysis, beginning most notably with scholars in engineering and the biological sciences, has sought to build a rational framework for the examination of policy processes in much the same spirit that motivated classical economists in their formulation of models of the market mechanism. These rationalist theories attempt to construct a linear and logical relationship among the demands that are made of a policy system, the stages of program formulation within the system, the resulting policy outputs, and the consequent patterns of feedback and support responses. The diagrammatic representation of systems analysis can be presented as follows.

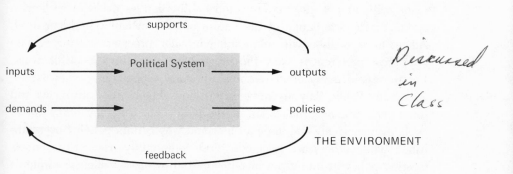

The basic implication for the study of policy of this model and of the various improvements and adaptations of its basic framework is the equation of policy with "output." Viewed as an output, policy can be considered to be the product of a determinable sequential process, as a totally *dependent* variable whose content, scope, and impact is shaped essentially by the demand inputs and process stages that precede it. One can understand or even predict the nature of a policy by quantifying and qualifying the inputs and the sequence of policy formulation of which the given policy is the logical end result.

The policy formulation sequence can be characterized in the following manner: (1) recognizing the existence of a policy problem or a demand for policy action, (2) determining the nature of the problem, (3) outlining the possible choices of action, (4) ranking choices of action according to priority, (5) anticipating the results or impact of each alternative, (6) choosing the most appropriate alternative employing the qualitative and quantitative values considered during the process, and (7) publicing and implementing the policy.[9] Although this conceptualization is quite formal, it does have heuristic utility.

Applying this sequence to the operational political sphere is initially attractive. One seeks to trace the development of a policy from the motivating interest group (including government) demand, through the political channels that cause the demand to be articulated in the public realm, through the decisional apparatus of the legislative and executive organs and the informational and technological channels of the bureaucracy to the final stage of policy implementation.

In many cases, however, policies do not appear to follow such a logical sequence. Increasingly, some policy decisions appear to result from or be sharply modified by stimuli generated from within the bureaucracy rather than from clearly expressed public demands. Many decisions are made without a logical examination of alternatives or even without a systematic determination of the nature of the particular problem itself. Again, as is well-known, unquestioned major processes or inarticulate normative preferences skew the process in many, imperceptible ways. For these and many other reasons, rationalist models are somewhat inadequate. While they are obviously useful as heuristic instruments and for a general conceptualization of the policy process, they often fail to explain conclusively and in detail how and why certain policies are established while others are rejected. Most importantly, rationalist models treating policy as an output or outcome fail to place sufficient emphasis on the policy *itself* and rarely make a concerted attempt to differentiate policy types. They accept the policy sequence as a given entity and the policy output as an explainable, dependent variable rather than determining whether or not the policy, in its own right, has any effect upon the decisional system that preceded it.

[9] A framework derived from writings of Harold D. Lasswell.

Case Study Approach. The case study approach involves the examination of individual policy problems (e.g., water resource management, civil rights, foreign policy decisions) in considerable detail in order to illustrate a particular example of policy formulation. Necessarily, this approach does not permit reliable generalizations concerning the policy process as a whole but only allows empirical observations in very specific contexts. Nevertheless, such studies are of considerable value to the study of policy because they facilitate detailed discoveries concerning particular behavioral and operational characteristics of policy-making and policy-makers. The conclusions from a variety of cases can be used to establish a general overview of the policy process even if, methodologically, they cannot be applied to explain or predict additional, specific examples of policy formulation with any degree of certainty. The well-known Inter-University Case Program encountered this problem. Despite the realism and didactic value of the cases, they simply failed to add up to the systematic generalizations which define a discipline.

Strategy of "Disjointed Incrementalism." The incrementalist approach to the study of policy has been popularized largely by Charles E. Lindblom.[10] According to his model, the policy process can be best described as a series of unrelated decisions each of which is taken as a result of an examination of alternate choices of action that differ incrementally rather than qualitatively from the *status quo*. In other words, each problem or issue confronting a decision-maker is resolved as if it were isolated from all other decisions and from any overarching policy. The individual issue is scrutinized and a response to that issue is designed through a consideration of options that do not differ in basic rationale from the existing method of handling that issue or some similar issue. Instead, the options that are evaluated are increments or extensions of existing orthodoxy.

To illustrate, consider a policy choice entrusted to an appropriate individual or agency concerning the continuation of an aid program to day-care centers in some community. Following the model of disjointed incrementalism, the person or collectivity responsible for such a policy would, in confronting the problem, consider only a certain set of possible solutions or modes of action of which the following options might be typical: (1) Continue the program with a 5 per cent increase in its bud-

[10] David Braybrooke and Charles E. Lindblom, A *Strategy of Decision* (London: Collier-Macmillan Ltd., 1963).

get. (2) Continue the program with a 5 per cent decrease in its budget. (3) Expand the program to include facilities for an additional 500 children. (4) Limit the program by reducing its size by 500 children. (5) Hire 6 more instructors. (6) Fire 6 instructors. (7) Retain the program essentially intact (and so on). *The policy-maker would not consider such qualitatively different options as:* (1) Change the program by integrating its services with other community agencies such as the local parks and recreation board, family-planning associations and the board of education. (2) Seek to establish broad relations with similar agencies in other communities. (3) Scrap the program and encourage local employers to provide appropriate child-care facilities for their employees. (4) Encourage the establishment of communal living centers where responsibility for day-care would rotate among the participants.

Generally, Lindblom would argue that policies are made only in the light of quantifiable technological and administrative variables as opposed to different value judgments and principles. Attention is focused parochially without regard to overarching problems and policies. Change is seen as a gradual evolutionary process rather than one of radical innovation. Lindblom describes two basic types of change: repetitive and non-repetitive. The first category involves social change that largely repeats frequent, previous changes, as in modifications of interest rates, tax rates, or school curricula.[11] Non-repetitive change encompasses permanent small alterations in policy in an indefinite sequence, as seen for example in the development of desegregation laws.[12] Both repetitive and non-repetitive change occur incrementally and usually without critical links with other policy areas.

The model of disjointed incrementalism seems to be highly instructive regarding several areas of policy-making, particularly in the bureaucratic sector. Given the frequent limitations in resources available to governmental agencies as well as the specialization and technocratic training of many officials, the likelihood of broad investigations involving critical evaluation and/or innovation into every policy problem is somewhat remote. By nature, the bureaucrat operates in a highly structured environment, acutely conscious of regulations and ranking. He plays "by the rules of the game" and, typically, is less concerned with the value judgments implicit in a given policy. He considers problems as they are presented to him and structures such problems, wherever possible, ac-

[11] *Ibid.,* p. 65.
[12] *Ibid.*

cording to a known set of variables and factors. It is surely true that the higher official's role is typically one of "putting out fires" which precludes the rational style of decision-making often attributable to him.

The incrementalist framework, however, is open to several important criticisms. The strategy sheds little light on cases where genuinely innovative policies are required (e.g., the introduction of universal medical insurance coverage, a guaranteed annual income program, foreign and defense policy crises) or where fundamentally different options are considered and policy reversals occur. The framework is also essentially conservative in that it accepts "the rules of the game" as given, and does not challenge the validity of those policies that are formulated incrementally in the light of limited, parochial considerations. It also tends to inhibit the development of computer-based systems of policy analysis by its emphasis upon commonsense, no-nonsense approaches.

In sum, the essential strength of this approach is its close approximation to reality in the present existential world of public policy and administration. Its essential weakness is that it often constitutes a council of despair, insofar as the development of a policy science is concerned. It is ahistorical and atheoretical in that it tends to assume that present limits of knowledge, prediction, and implementation are infinite. The propellor-driven aircraft will always be with us, according to this judgment, which is premature, to put it mildly.

Policy as an Independent Variable.   Quite recently in the study of policy, analysts have come to question the value of conceptual frameworks that treat policy simply as an output, as a dependent variable of the policy process. A group of observers, including Theodore Lowi, Lewis Froman, Robert Salisbury, and John Heinz, have sought a redefinition of policy analysis that will allow a more critical examination of the specific relationships between the nature of a given policy and the corresponding type of policy or political process.

> Rather than treating policy as an *outcome* of the political process, we are asking whether policy itself is a variable that may affect the political process.[13]

This approach criticizes other methods of studying policy and especially questions their emphasis upon the operational facets of the policy *process* at the expense of the characteristics of the policies themselves.

[13] Lewis A. Froman, Jr., "The Categorization of Policy Contents" in Austin Ranney, ed., *Political Science and Public Policy* (Chicago: Markham Publishing Co., 1968), p. 44, italics added.

When the goals of policies are not questioned because they are the values which must be kept separate from facts, the analyst becomes committed to the value context of these policies even if his political iedology would not support them if he looked more carefully at them.[14]

Salisbury and Heinz, developing a formulation by Lowi, demonstrate the relationships between selected characteristics of given policies and the types of policy processes that most often occur as a result of these characteristics.[15] Before presenting the formulation, it is useful to define several important terms; allocative and structural policies; distribution, redistribution, regulation, and self-regulation.[16] One should note, parenthetically, that it is not entirely clear whether these terms refer strictly to policy types, as the authors infer (and as Lowi probably intended originally), or whether they may in fact be applied more generally to policy process types and policy outcomes. In any case, the terms can be defined generally as follows. An allocative policy involves the conferring of *direct benefits*, material or symbolic, upon individuals or groups.[17] Allocations of the distributive type are characterized as short-term choices made without regard to limited resources through which the demands of many groups or individuals are indulged or deprived without coming into direct confrontation with each other.[18] In some respects, distribution parallels Lindblom's conception of incremental policy-making in that decisions of the distributive type are easily disaggregated and isolated and often resemble the dispensing of patronage or "pork-barrel" benefits. Certainly one is impressed by the extent to which interest groups tend to function in substantively discrete universes.

In contrast, a redistribution involves a direct choice between large, competing groups on a much broader social level regarding whom shall be indulged or deprived in the allocation of scarce resources. An example of a redistributive policy process is the implementation of a progressive income tax program designed to transfer social resources from the upper-income classes to less-privileged classes.[19]

Structural policies are those which establish authority systems or rules

[14] Lowi, *op. cit.*, p. 319.

[15] Robert Salisbury and John Heinz, "A Theory of Policy Analysis and Some Preliminary Application," in Ira Sharkansky, ed., *Policy Analysis in Political Science* (Chicago: Markham Publishing Co., 1970), pp. 39–60.

[16] *Ibid.*, p. 48.

[17] *Ibid.*, p. 43.

[18] Theodore Lowi, "Distribution, Regulation, Redistribution: The Functions of Government," in R. B. Ripley, ed., *Public Policies and their Politics* (New York: W. W. Norton, 1966), p. 27.

[19] *Ibid.*, p. 28.

to guide future allocations.[20] A regulatory policy process involves a direct choice between competing groups or interests but, typically, regulations cannot be disaggregated to the level of individual situations. Instead, regulations establish general rules by which later, specific decisions between competing interests can be taken. Policy procedures in the field of broadcast licensing, rules to guide the granting of air routes, and immigration quotas are examples of regulatory processes.[21] Self-regulatory policies are basically regulatory in nature but the decisional authority in cases of self-regulation is delegated to the group or interest most affected by or concerned with that policy. An obvious example of self-regulation is the process by which a professional group such as the American Medical Association or the American Bar Association is granted quasi-legal powers to supervise the professional training and conduct of its members.

The two motive factors used in the Salisbury–Heinz correlation are the nature of the demand pattern (integrated or fragmented) to which a given policy must respond and the costs of reaching a decision (high or low) involved in the resolution of the policy problem. "Costs," real or perceived, include the costs to a decision-maker of informing himself about the nature of the problem, the costs (or, inversely, benefits) to a decision-maker in political terms of choosing or refusing a particular policy option, and the costs (in terms of time, energy, and resources) of mobilizing sufficient support to insure the adoption of a particular policy. In effect, Salisbury and Heinz pose the following question: What kind of policy type (or policy process) will most often result, given a particular demand pattern (expressed in terms of integration vs. fragmentation) and a perceived level of costs of reaching a decision (expressed in terms of high vs. low)? Diagramatically, the inter-relation of these factors may be charted as shown on the top of page 24.[22]

Briefly stated, this formulation infers that allocative policies of either the distributive or redistributive type will be preferred when the costs of reaching a decision are assumed to be low. Conversely, policies of either the regulatory or self-regulatory type will be preferred when such costs are seen as high. An integrated demand pattern will most often precipitate a redistributive or self-regulatory policy process, while a fragmented demand pattern will typically bring about a distributive or regulatory policy process.

Obviously, complex problems occur in applying this framework and

[20] Salisbury and Heinz, *loc. cit.*
[21] Lowi, *loc. cit.*
[22] Salisbury and Heinz, *op. cit.*

Type of Policy Process

	Integrated	Redistribution	Self-regulation
Demand Pattern		(allocative)	(structural)
	Fragmented	Distribution	Regulation

Low   High

Costs of Reaching a Decision

its attending typology of policy processes to the real world of politics and administration. This is particularly so as it pertains to problem areas for which no single policy process is appropriate or adequate to satisfy demands and minimize the costs of decisions. Nevertheless, the approach does offer an example and a potentially useful tool for analyzing policy. If extended to relate the policy process categories more specifically to actual decision-making structures—both bureaucratic and legislative—it could provide an important counterbalance to other approaches that relegate the substance of policy issues to a secondary position.

POLICY OUTCOMES IN THE FIFTY STATES

An impressive example of work in the policy area is Thomas Dye's analysis of policy outcomes in the 50 states.[23] Using an empirical model designed for testing, he describes and explains policy choices in five salient areas: education, welfare, taxation, highways, and the regulation of public morality. Essentially, the research attempts to trace relationships between policy outcomes and the social, economic, and political conditions that determine them. The model (or representation of political life) he uses is useful as an indication of the thinking and procedures that characterize the policy sciences field. His great contribution is to *test* a set of theoretical propositions. Assuming that policy outcomes are the "result of *forces* brought to bear upon a *system* and causing it to make particular *responses*," [24] Figure 2–1 is designed to guide the research.

Although this model is largely self-explanatory, some of its char-

[23] *Politics, Economics, and the Public* (Chicago: Rand McNally & Co., 1966), pp. 1–4.

[24] *Ibid.*, p. 3.

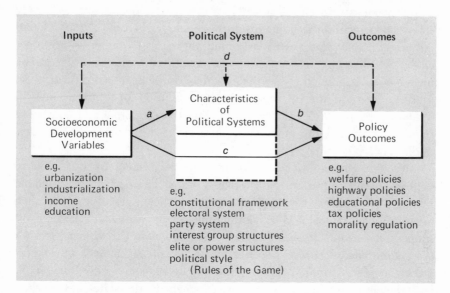

Fig. 2–1. Model for analyzing policy outcomes in American state politics. *Source:* Thomas Dye, *Politics, Economics, and the Public* (Chicago: Rand McNally Co., 1966), p. 4.

acteristics require mention since they illustrate contemporary policy formulations, including some of the difficulties involved. The basic language of policy science includes "inputs" and "outputs" which symbolize the values and demands brought to the political system (typically by interest groups), and the consequences resulting from their transformation into policy instruments. Socioeconomic variables such as urbanization, income, and regional traditions also provide inputs which influence the political sub-system. A presumably critical variable is the character of the political sub-system, i.e., its constitution, party system, interest group apparatus, etc. One of Dye's objectives is to determine empirically whether this sub-system has any independent effect upon policy outcomes or whether the latter are essentially the product of the socioeconomic factors just mentioned. Unlike some models, which are *normative* in that they prescribe what ought to be done, this model is an example of *empirical* political theory which attempts only to try to understand *why* state political regimes produce certain kinds of outcomes. The distance between this orientation and the current prescriptive mood in public administration is immense.

The model illustrates another intrinsic element in policy, or any other research: the extent to which the model is an *abstraction* of a much more complex reality. In effect, research is obliged to focus itself upon only a few salient variables, hoping that they include the critical ones. Computer technology, and particularly multiple regression analysis, are especially useful in greatly expanding the range of variables that can be included in a model. Nevertheless, this problem remains critical in social science and, indeed, there may be no solution for it, given practical limitations in research resources, including the discipline and continuity required to exploit the intensity of analysis made possible by the computer.

Although we can only summarize Dye's findings, he was able to explain around 50 per cent of the total variance caused by socioeconomic factors and political system variables on policy outcomes in the five areas in the 50 states.[25] His major finding is that *"economic development shapes both political systems and policy outcomes, and most of the association that occurs between system characteristics and policy outcomes can be attributed to the influence of economic development."* [26] Different levels of socioeconomic development in the states, rather than the character of their political or party systems, have the major impact upon policy choices. [27] To some extent, the political sub-system is an epiphenomenon of its social and economic milieu.

The several approaches to the study of policy outlined here are by no means definitive. Each approach shares strengths and weaknesses. None of them is absolutely correct, nor are any of them completely wrong. Instead, the value of each approach must be reckoned in terms of its utility and applicability in describing the making and carrying out of public policy in American society. Such an exercise is possible only through extensive and systematic testing and revision of each conceptual framework.

WHY POLICIES GO WRONG

Many barriers confront rational policy-making, including normative "political" ones. Such factors are evident in the following account of policy choices available to the United States government in attempting to control inflation:

25 *Ibid.,* pp. 286–87.
26 *Ibid.,* p. 293, italics added.
27 For research showing similarly that "hard" *properties,* such as interaction, political role, tenure, etc., are often more important than *dispositions* such as ideology in shaping the behavior of governmental elites, see Presthus, *Elites in the Policy Process* (New York: Cambridge University Press, 1974), Chap. 13.

A grim assessment of the economic outlook is being put forward by conservative economists, according to whom worldwide inflation has become such an overwhelming problem that draconian measures are needed to cope with it. A free translation of such measures would be a stern monetary and fiscal policy that would put the economy through a wringer in order to reverse the inflationary tide. For example, Paul W. Mc-Cracken, who headed President Nixon's first Council of Economic Advisers, says, "The only real solution to these problems is, of course, a more stable price level. Could this be achieved without a rise in unemployment? The answer is, of course, No. And one requirement of a well-rounded stabilization program would be reasonable provision for income maintenance."

A current CEA member, William J. Fellner, said last week that unless the United States and other Western nations quit excessive stimulation of demand, "the West will be on the road to thorough regimentation, to a loss of personal freedom and also to economic inefficiency." The dean of the "monetarist" school of economics, Milton Friedman, says "there is no other way" to stop inflation except by "a fairly protracted period of low economic growth and relatively high unemployment." Another such voice is that of Alan Greenspan, a business economist with good administration connections. He suggests that even the very mild stimulus planned by the administration is going too far. In the "trade-off" between unemployment and inflation [here is the normative, "political" element in economic policy], Messrs. McCracken, Fellner, Greenspan, and Friedman—all Republicans—worry more about the latter than the former. And while many prominent Democratic economists—usually more concerned with unemployment—are ready to accept a below-normal economic growth this year as inevitable, they are not ready to buy the more drastic solution offered by their Republican colleagues.

For example, Democratic economists Walter W. Heller, Arthur M. Okum, and George Perry all suggest the economy is already entering a recession which should be countered by additional fiscal and monetary stimulation. Mr. Okum concedes that inflation is a problem "but we should have learned from the 1970 experience that a recession doesn't end inflation or stop wage rates from climbing." He insists that the public would get more relief from inflation by a rollback of domestic oil prices than from a deliberately induced period of no growth that would cost 40 billion or 50 billion in lost production.[28]

From these comments, it is clear that there is "no one best way" of solving this critical domestic and international problem. Each of these two sets of economists, all of whom have access to similar kinds of data regarding the American economic system, seems equally convinced that the problem requires quite different solutions. Such discrepancies

[28] *International Herald Tribune*, March 1, 1974, p. 7.

will probably be narrowed somewhat by experience, as noted in the 1970 recession when the expectation of traditional economic theory that unemployment would be reflected in price and wage stabilization was not fulfilled. Nevertheless, it is clear that for some time recommendations for national economic policy will include significant amounts of essentially normative or "political" ingredients.

An equally vexing problem confronting policy-makers is that important policies have "side effects" that cannot be anticipated.

Unanticipated Consequences

Regardless of the approach used to study the policy process, no analyst or policy-maker can predict with certainty the impact and course that a given policy will have in resolving the problem for which it was designed. Policies are formulated in response to perceived needs, taking into account selected environmental factors, differing subjective preferences, and oriented in some way toward the future. At each stage, perceptions and value judgments of an incomplete or erroneous kind tend to occur, and, accordingly, the potential utility of the policy may be diminished. We mentioned elsewhere the impossibility of bringing into any decision calculus *all* (or even more than a few) of the critical variables that affect it, despite the major breakthrough achieved by the computer and simulation techniques.

Our perception of the existence of a demand for a given policy action may also be faulty in either qualitative or quantitative terms. Some demands are made more audible than others or are articulated with greater success in the political arena than others only because the group or interest behind a particular demand may have greater political resources. Claims on public resources do not have equal chances in the marketplace. Clearly, groups that possess greater political resources in terms of time, money, legitimacy, and access to policy-makers will exert more influence than those who have only limited resources. The demand promoted by the more resourceful interest need not necessarily be more rational or pressing than competing demands; it need only be made to *appear* more important and more worthy of resolution in the eyes of political elites in order that it be acted upon.

As a result, some policies are formulated in response to manipulated demands and may be implemented without the benefit of a thorough assessment of the problem to which they are directed. If the manipulated demand obscures other real social factors, including those that would otherwise have been considered in the formulation of the particular policy, the policy decision may be potentially hazardous. Almost axiomatically, small factors or considerations neglected prior to the formulation of a policy tend to become much larger and more difficult after its implementation. The policy-maker who often sincerely believes that the actions decided upon will be sufficient to satisfy what he had thought to be a clearly articulated demand is often, therefore, confronted 'with a set of unanticipated consequences that demand re-evaluation, further resolution, and the expenditure of additional resources.

Similarly, value judgments and predispositions built into a policy sometimes may prove to be misguided, creating eventual tension between anticipated and actual results. Objective conditions of the environment may change from the time of the initial articulation of a demand for policy action until by the time a consequent policy is implemented its rectitude and applicability may have become tenuous.

Southeast Asian Tragedy

In one way or another, almost all policies seem to produce unforeseen results, or, at least, to be somewhat less successful than anticipated. Occasionally, however, certain policies are so disastrous and appear in retrospect to be so misguided that they place in question the validity of an entire policy-making process. The most recent case in point may be American involvement in Southeast Asia in which several bench-mark assumptions proved to be wrong. The original decision to deploy American ground forces in Vietnam was predicated on the conviction that a conventional military victory was possible in Southeast Asia. This conviction was based largely upon quantitative assessments of the respective military capabilities of the two sides and qualitative assessments of the political and social climate of Vietnam (e.g., the willingness of the South Vietnamese people to oppose at all cost the political and military efforts of the North Vietnamese and the Viet Cong). As history has shown, however, American involvement proved to be incredibly costly. Military strategists had failed to anticipate the conviction and resiliance of the Communist forces, had erred in believing that conventional military units could adequately control or halt the activities of a mobile guerilla force, had failed to take into account the political instability of successive Saigon governments, and had not foreseen the disenchantment and political reaction that the war created within American society itself and in many countries around the world.

One can argue, of course, that it would not have been possible under any circumstances to anticipate these consequences prior to the actual decision to intervene massively in the Vietnamese conflict. However, the point remains that a policy, supposedly made with the best information available at the time and by the best tacticians, did produce a set of consequences drastically different from those originally intended. As these consequences grew more pronounced and became more distressing to the American people, the policy decision and the policy process that led to these consequences came to be criticized by an increasing number of observers. The right of the executive to conduct or enter a military conflict without congressional approval, the efficacy of Pentagon planning systems, the rationality of military decision-making, and many other facets of the policy process that led to the decision to enter Vietnam came under extensive examination. The likelihood that any similar decision will result again from the type of policy process that prevailed in the early and mid-1960's has been substantially reduced. New policy processes must respond now to new demands and a new environment and, in all probability, further unanticipated consequences will arise.

To repeat an earlier truism, the goal of policy analysis should be to facilitate the best possible formulation of public policy. Obviously, all consequences of a given action can never be anticipated nor can any evaluation of objective environmental conditions and policy demands be totally free from inconsistencies, errors, or incorrect value judgments. The policy analyst can only hope to minimize these difficulties and be prepared to meet further demands and consequences that arise during and after the formulation of a policy.

Throughout this chapter, definitions and descriptions of various policy approaches continually allude to decisional structures, decision-makers, and decision-making. Clearly, one can see that the new disciplines coming to be known as policy analysis and policy science are, in reality, concerned with many of the same problems and make use of many of the same analytical tools that characterized the efforts of earlier decision-making studies.[29]

Nevertheless, systems theory and computer technology have indeed made possible a more sophisticated science of policy determination. Perhaps with the development of these new areas, a clearer conception of the distinctions between traditional studies of decision-making and policy-making as defined here will emerge.

[29] As will be shown in Chapter 4, much the same can be said about the highly touted P.P.B.—programming, planning, budgeting system.

At various points in this chapter, reference has been made to the critical bureaucratic component in the policy process. We now turn to a more detailed examination of the role of the bureaucracy in policy determination.

3

Bureaucracy's Role in Policy-Making

Traditionally, the analysis of public administration has posited a constitutional and normative dichotomy between policy and administration. The former has been defined as the prerogative of the political or elected actors in government. Legally, they alone are responsible to the electorate. Moreover, in terms of democratic theory, only actors who are ultimately subject to control by ballots *should* determine the substance of public policy. In this view, civil servants are seen as mere instruments of their political masters. If democratic accountability is to be maintained, they as appointed officials must be restricted to a ministerial role of implementing policies hammered out in the political arena.

This rationale is immaculate from both legal and normative standpoints. It meets the crucial need for lodging ultimate control of government in the electorate. It prescribes the essential means of insuring democratic responsibility and accountability. The major problem is that it no longer fully meets the operational conditions of American government, except at the level of small local communities. The reasons for this hiatus between democratic theory and functional necessity are worth analyzing in some detail.

CONDITIONS UNDERLYING BUREAUCRACY'S ROLE IN POLICY-MAKING

Regarding bureaucracy's role in policy-making, it is important to emphasize that it is less one of initiative that one of buttressing, legiti-

32

mating, and carrying out policy determined mainly by elected political elites and their politically appointed aides at the secretary, undersecretary, and assistant secretary levels.[1] When the bureaucracy plays the major role in a given policy issue, it is probably because a vacuum exists in the area, a situation that is highly unlikely in major questions of foreign affairs or domestic economic policy. It seems better to regard the higher bureaucracy as a significant junior partner in the public policy process.

Perhaps the basic cause of bureaucratic policy influence is the exponential increase in the size and scope of government in the United States. One way to show the trend is through a table covering federal expenditures during this century.

As Table 3–1 shows, federal government expenditures as a proportion of G.N.P., which provides a reasonably accurate comparative base, increased from only 3 per cent in 1900 to about 20 per cent in 1975. When state and local governments are included, however, over one-third of G.N.P. is devoted to government. The dramatic upsurge in 1945, of course, represents the costs of World War II, while the percentage in recent years includes the vast costs of the Vietnam conflict.[2]

Modern war, of course, demands the synthesis of most elements of the economy, not only the military establishment and its needs, but the civilian production system which makes total war possible. Manpower, industrial procurement, the allocation of raw materials, agriculture, transportation, the apparatus of production and consumption control—

[1] Some observers would dissent, arguing that permanent officials play a more significant role. In a careful article, for example, Peter B. Natchez and Irvin Bupp maintain that "priority setting in the federal capital bureaucracy resembles nineteenth century capitalism. Priorities are established by aggressive entrepreneurs at the operating levels of government . . . because energetic division directors successfully build political support to withstand continuous attacks upon a program's resource base by competing claims. "Policy and Priority in the Budgetary Process," American Political Science Review, Vol. 68 (September, 1973), p. 963. It seems, however, that the substantive compartmentalization of programs in Washington, D. C. often means that "competing claims" do not usually exist. Although it may not be true of the majority of federal programs, it also appears that the major ones during the past decade—Vietnam, revenue-sharing, devolution of responsibilities to states and cities, and efforts to ease the negative balance of payments situation, etc.—originated and were pushed through by elected or appointed political figures at the highest levels.

[2] For example, from 1946–1968, the United States spent 94 billion dollars on military activities abroad and upon "military goods and services" to help other nations build their own military systems (Survey of Current Business, June, 1968, pp. 28–29; March, 1969, p. 32). That vast amounts of military spending afflict developing countries as well is clear—cf. International Institute for Strategic Studies, The Military Balance, 1973–74 (London, 1973).

TABLE 3–1. Federal Expenditures, Total and as a Proportion of Gross National Product (in billions)

	Civil Activities	Military Activities	Total Expenditures	G.N.P.	Expenditures as % of G.N.P.
1900	353	168	521	15,709	3.3
1910	452	242	694	28,783	2.4
1920	2,360	3,997	6,357	61,895	10.2
1930	2,366	734	3,100	91,105	3.4
1940	8,103	1,497	9,600	100,618	9.5
1945	10,615	84,569	95,184	213,100	44.7
1950	30,753	12,407	43,160	285,067	15.1
1955	40,626	65,570	65,570	390,860	16.8
1956	25,899	40,641	66,540	412,400	16.1
1957	26,170	45,433	71,603	440,300	16.3
1958	32,307	32,307	71,369	437,700	16.3
1959	36,769	43,573	80,342	482,700	16.6
1960	33,715	42,824	76,539	502,600	15.2
1961	36,839	44,676	81,515	518,200	15.7
1962	40,972	46,815	87,787	554,900	15.8
1963	42,669	49,973	92,642	572,400	16.2
1964	46,439	51,245	97,684	609,600	16.0
1965	49,105	47,402	96,507	648,700	14.9
1966	52,228	54,200	106,428	700,000	15.2
1967	54,547	58,300	112,847	737,000	15.3
1970	116,300	80,300	196,600	955,000	19.0
1972	153,600	78,300	231,900	1,093,100	19.0
1973	170,500	76,000	246,500	1,220,900	20.6
1974	194,100	80,600	274,700	1,340,000	20.1
1975 (est.)	216,700	87,700	304,400	1,455,000	20.3

all require central direction and planning. Government, the logical over-all director of this huge combined operation, reaches out into every sector of the community. Delegated legislative power expands to provide administration the means to quickly meet the emergency. For example, during World War II, the President was authorized to allocate, through the War Production Board, scarce materials and facilities as necessary "in the public interest and to promote the national defense." The Office of Price Administration was empowered to fix "fair and equitable prices," and other agencies received similar increases of power and discretion. Such agencies inevitably expanded. And once again, some of them survived when the war ended.

Total federal expenditures, which had amounted to only about 75 billion in 1960 had risen only 15 years later to about 300 billion, most of it for current defense and the costs associated with earlier wars, such as veterans' pensions, disability payments, etc.

Another measure of government's increasing role is provided by a similar review of secular trends in public employment. In the federal system, for example, the total number of employees in 1900 was only 375,000, which represented .5 per cent of the total U.S. population. Fifty years later, the number had risen to some 3½ million, amounting to just over 2 per cent of the total population. By 1972, civilian and military employees of the federal level included 3,000,000 men and women, about 3 per cent of the population. When one includes *all* levels of government, the total is more impressive; in 1972, one of every six Americans worked for governmental jurisdictions at the international, national, state, and local levels. Government was by far the largest employer and its property and possessions were valued at far more than even such private giants as General Motors which with some 800,000 employees (internationally) and a net worth of over $18,000,000,000 is small by comparison.

Mentioned in class

Dramatic increases in the proportion of employees for all governments symbolize the trend.[3] Among the states, during the decade 1960–1970, gains of from 29 per cent (Alaska, Alabama, and Rhode Island) to 79 and 89 per cent (Nevada and Arizona, respectively) occurred. Among cities, similar increases occurred: Washington, D.C. showed a 54 per cent increase to lead the nation, followed by Vallejo-Napa, California with 44 per cent. In 1973 fully 39 per cent of total national income was taken by taxes and other governmental receipts. The global rise in state and local government expenditures, which increased the most, was 170 per cent between 1960–1970. Federal expenditures, meanwhile, increased by 70 per cent. Such developments led in some cases to citizen demands for curbs on government spending, as well as studies by private research groups seeking ways of increasing productivity among government workers. As David T. Stanley of the Brookings Institution reported, "Government agencies can and should be put through an organizational wringer to squeeze out unproductive layers of supervision and proliferating staff units." [4]

The record, in effect, shows a secular upward trend, with war, depression, defense, technological innovation, and interest group demands

---

[3] U. S. Departments of Labor and Commerce, as reported in the *U. S. News & World Report,* June 19, 1972, pp. 78–80.

[4] *U. S. News and World Report, ibid.,* p. 78.

for increased services and subsidies providing the major thrust. As de Toqueville put it about 1840:

> The passage of time constantly opens to the central government new fields of action. . . . Society, which is in the full progress of development, constantly gives birth to new needs and each one of them is for the government a source of power; for it alone is in a position to satisfy them . . . the sphere of government is mobile and never ceases to grow with civilization itself.

The effect of such growth upon bureaucracy's role is immediate and unprecedented, mainly because of the integral role it necessarily assumes in designing and carrying out new and expanding programs. In a very real sense, the roles of both government and the bureaucracy became so complex, technical, and pervasive that it was virtually impossible to maintain the kind of democratic control and the nice dichotomy between policy and administration posited in an earlier and simpler era.

Delegated Legislation

An impressive example exists in the area of delegated legislation, a process greatly expanded by the demand for expertise and dispatch in modern government. This process often involves a conscious merging of executive, legislative, and judicial functions, in direct antithesis to the prescriptions of the founders of the country who, fearing powerful government, provided for a separation of powers among generally autonomous branches, each charged with major logically separable functions.[5] Delegated legislation usually takes the form of rules and orders, promulgated under the aegis of some basic organic statute. It is a necessary means of applying the general prescriptions of legislation to specific cases arising under such legislation. The Federal Communications Commission, for example, is empowered to regulate broadcasting policy in the United States, to issue and revoke the licenses of private and public organizations operating in TV and radio, to control the number and frequencies of broadcasting channels, etc. The organic statute (as amended) merely provides such virtually meaningless criteria as "the public interest, convenience, and necessity" to guide the Commission in discharging such functions. In order to provide the instruments required to perform its role, Congress necessarily delegates some of its own power

---

[5] Each branch does in fact exercise functions of the other branches, but these are usually peripheral to its single major responsibility. On the other hand, presidential leadership in *legislative* policy indicates the extent to which the historical trichotomy has been breached.

and authority to the Commission, which prescribes rules and orders covering both specific and general issues arising under the general statute. In effect, the Commission—an appointed, bureaucratic agency—exercises *legislative* functions, in addition to its major executive ones.

The Commission, moreover, also carries out a *judicial* function when it holds hearings in connection with the issuance or the (highly uncommon) revocation of broadcasting licenses. Such quasi-judicial hearings are often on an adversary basis, as contending parties petition for a single license. A special hearing examiner, representing the Commission, presides, playing a role something like that of a judge.[6] An entire independent field of administrative law, covering such requirements as notice and hearing, procedural and substantive due process, laws of evidence, rights of appeals, etc., has developed in this complex and significant area which will be mentioned only in passing.[7]

The point is that the pressure for action and expertise in decision-making in issues highly charged with technical matters necessitated the delegation of legislative and judicial powers to civil servants. The traditional court system could not handle the load. Nor could legislators be expected to have the knowledge or the time required to manage the details of regulatory administration. (Indeed, the regulatory agencies themselves labor under huge backlogs of cases.) In assuming a share of such functions, officials inevitably exercise *discretion,* which means they play a direct role in policy-making.[8] Their decisions, like those of the courts, become the precedent for future action.

Bureaucracy's Role in Initiating Policy

Even though major policy matters tend to originate elsewhere, bureaucracy sometimes plays a critical role in initiating policy, mainly because of its technical knowledge. Bureaucracy's close liaisons with major interest groups also enable it to play a role in recommending and carrying out public policies. Much of this influence arises because of bureaucracy's operational role in carrying out such policy; if changes are required in ongoing programs, they are among the first to know. Research

---

[6] See, for example, Winston Fisk, *Administrative Procedure in a Regulatory Agency* (Indianapolis: Bobbs-Merrill Co., 1965), pp. 13–69.

[7] Leading analyses include James Landis, *The Administrative Process* (New Haven, Conn.: Yale University Press, 1936); Kenneth C. Davis, *Administrative Law in Government* (St. Paul, Minn.: West Publishing Co., 1960).

[8] For an example of agency policy-shaping through rule-making, see R. F. Fuchs, "Agency Development of Policy through Rule-Making," *Northwestern University Law Review,* Vol. 59 (January–February, 1965), pp. 781–807.

indicates that bureaucratic-clientele interaction occurs mainly at the "frequently" level (twice a week or more), and that bureaucrats typically become aware of interest group needs through "constant contact." [9]

Another source of bureaucratic influence is among the permanent staffs of congressional and other committees. These officials are often the target of lobbyists, who work jointly with them in the preparation of legislation for ultimate legislative approval. The basis incentive in such interactions is often the shared expertise and mutual substantive interests of the staff members and group representatives.

The great departments at the federal level also maintain liaison men who work closely with such committees in the designing of legislation, the impetus for which often comes from the clientele interests of the department or bureau concerned. It is often said that about one-half of all bills are initiated by the bureaucracy, which as noted, has often developed them in consultation with relevant interest groups and committee staffs. As John Manley observes regarding executive-legislative interaction,

> The complexity of tax law presents a formidable problem to the Ways and Means Committee and helps explain the informal but firmly rooted practice of consultations between the Committee's tax experts, the staff of the Joint Committee on Internal Revenue Taxation, and the 'technicians' of the Treasury Department. The Joint Committee staff, which serves as an important link between the Senate and the Ways and Means Committee, also links the Committee with the Treasury Department. For many years Joint Committee staff experts, under Stans and continuing under Woodworth, have met with their counterparts in the Treasury Department and the Internal Revenue Service in what are known as staff "subcommittees.[10]

These subcommittees discuss various tax proposals and the technical problems involved in formulating the language necessary to put them into effect. Ideas generated by Treasury Department economists and others are discussed in these meetings. "What we do is kick ideas around, we brainstorm ideas," as one participant said. "Staff subcommittees," a Treasury official noted, "discuss the technical questions, the really hard kind. If it's a simple thing like rates the staff committee won't take it up." [11]

[9] Robert Presthus, *Elites in the Policy Process* (New York: Cambridge University Press, 1974), Chaps. 8 and 9.
[10] *The Politics of Finance: The House Committee on Ways and Means* (Boston: Little Brown & Co., 1970), p. 342.
[11] *Ibid.*

Bureaucracy's Internal Drive for Power, Security, and Loyalty

Another condition that partly explains the size and scope of contemporary bureaucratic influence is the incentive for power, security, and loyalty found within the bureaucracy, defined as an independent organism with its own momentum.[12] Departments and bureaus are highly imbued with a "service" motive, which is reinforced by the structure of government. As our "case studies" will indicate, most officials believe they *should* play a "representative" role for their constituent interests.[13] They endorse overwhelmingly the philosophy that it is legitimate that agencies should further such interests. There is thus a symbiotic bond between articulate private interests and the public agencies that share their functional interest. Security and growth are common objectives, and both prosper by the extension of programs and services in their respective sectors. To some extent, moreover, there is limited competition for such largesse, essentially because the government is structured in this fashion and, more important, perhaps, because governmental elites fully legitimate the ongoing system of interest group politics. As Arthur Bentley said, "Politics is trading." [14]

The ongoing system is well conceptualized as one of constant exchange among legislators, senior officials, and relevant interest groups. The currencies used in such exchanges often include, for legislators, campaign funds and related support, information, and various services. Higher bureaucrats receive budgetary support, information, and program continuity. Interest groups receive subsidies of countless variety, including the right to participate directly in the design and implementation of programs in their respective sectors.

Limitations on Bureaucratic Policy-Making. It seems important to emphasize that, despite the conditions just mentioned and the sophisticated technology at bureaucracy's command, it is often inaccurate to conceive of policy-making as a highly rational process, typically characterized by foresight and a nice consideration of most alternatives. Instead, much of the higher official's time is spent shifting from one contingency to another. He does not usually control his agenda in the

[12] The effects of organizational loyalty upon the capacity of agencies to carry out policy innovation are treated in Louis Gawthrop, *Bureaucratic Behavior in the Executive Branch* (New York: Free Press, 1969), Chap. 6.

[13] Presthus, *op. cit.*, p. 296.

[14] Or again, as one recent majority leader of the federal House put it, "Nothing for nothing."

way required for systematic planning and control. More often, he is concerned with *post hoc* reconcilations of unexpected events.

This highly contingent universe is well-characterized by George Kennan, one of our more introspective officials, who spent a quarter of a century in the State Department. Although his conclusions relate to foreign affairs, they seem equally germane to policy-making in any context:

> I have a largish farm in Pennsylvania. The reason you never see me around here on weekends (or rather, the reason you would never see me around if *you* were here weekends) is that I am up there to look after that farm. The farm includes two hundred thirty-five acres, and a number of buildings. On every one of those acres, I have discovered, things are constantly happening. Weeds are growing. Gullies are forming. Fences are falling down. Paint is fading. Wood is rotting. Insects are burrowing. Nothing seems to be standing still. The days of the weekend, in theory days of rest, pass in a . . . succession of alarms and excursions. Here a bridge is collapsing. No sooner do you start to repair it than a neighbor comes to complain about a hedgerow which you haven't kept up—a half-mile away on the other side of the farm. At the very moment your daughter arrives to tell you that someone left the gate to the hog pasture open and the hogs are out. On the way to the hog pasture you discover that the beagle hound liquidated one of the children's pet kittens. In burying the kitten you look up and notice that a whole section of the barn roof has been blown off, and needs instant repair. Somebody shouts pitifully from the bathroom window that the pump must have busted—there's no water in the house. At that moment a truck arrives with five tons of stone for the lane. And as you stand helplessly there, wondering which of these crises to attend to first, you notice the farmer's little boy standing silently before you with that maddening smile that is halfway a leer, and when you ask him what's up, he says triumphantly: "The bull's busted out and he's eating the strawberry bed."
>
> That's the only way I know to tell you what policy planning is like. The world is a big world. It has at least two hundred thirty-five big acres on it. On each of these something is incessantly happening. A nimble and astute person, working furiously against time, may indeed succeed in getting himself to a point where he thinks that with respect to one of those two hundred thirty-five acres he is some three or four months ahead of events. . . . But by the time he has gotten his ideas down on paper, the three or four months have mysteriously shrunk to that many weeks. By the time he has gotten those ideas accepted by others, they have become days. And by the time others have translated those ideas into action, it develops that the thing you were planning for took place day before yesterday, and everyone wants to know why in hell you did not foresee it a long time ago.[15]

15 *Memoirs: 1925–1950* (London: Hutchinson & Co., 1967), pp. 348–49.

CASE STUDIES OF BUREAUCRACY'S POLICY ROLE

The following case issues are reported *verbatim,* except for minor deletions and editing for ease of presentation and the addition of emphasis for certain statements that punctuate the agency's role in policy-making or the closeness of its relations with clientele groups. The extent to which public policy-making is a combined operation among senior officials, legislators, and interest groups will be clear from these examples which are part of a survey of bureaucratic-legislative-interest group interactions in Washington, D.C., and three states: Michigan, Washington, and Louisiana.[16]

Some State Issues

Each official was asked to describe in his own words a recent, salient case in which an interest group had made a demand upon his agency for some form of service. To preserve anonymity, we shall not mention specific names or the states involved. The first case illustrates bureaucracy's role in designing legislation, in collaboration with relevant interest groups.

> **Issue:** "The department of revenue notified me late in December that there had been a landmark case in Massachusetts involving taxation of national banks. Congress had removed a former shield preventing states from taxing national banks. As a *consequence of this* congressional directive, following the court decision, most state banks and related financial institutions were also then exempted in order that they might remain competitive. *The director of revenue said that there was much interest in this as a source of potential taxation and asked me to contact representative individuals or trade groups to discuss the possibility of this taxation affecting them, in advance of a special session of the legislature which was to commence in mid-January.*
>
> So I contacted the trade organizations and several of the larger institutions individually in both the credit union and savings and loan fields, and alerted them that the department of revenue was going to be holding hearings in order to air this and its implications for these businesses. So they came down to . . . [state capitol] and we all met in a large group at first, all of the financial institutions which were involved, and it became apparent that there would be different treatment appropriate to different ones, so separate hearings were set up for the

[16] Presthus, *op. cit.*

special institutions. Banking was in one area and they had their own dialogue with the department of revenue; and savings and loans and credit unions were another. After a request from the department of revenue, *we* gathered certain statistical data. By *we*, I mean the trade organizations as well as this division and attempted to influence their thinking in the drafting of the bill, namely, towards exemption or some kind of modification of levying the BNO tax on all of the income of these institutions. I worked with the directors of each of these trade organizations as well as individuals in the area. The bill was prepared, the exemption was not included, and we testified to the committee in the legislature asking for an exemption. Actual modifications were submitted by the trade organizations to the legislative subcommittee which considered it. *A very serious modification of the bill was accomplished as a result of this effort.* I testified personally at the open hearing and provided some background information to individual legislators. This is a very recent issue which involved quite extensive co-operation between the trade organization and the department.

Q. Is this the way you typically become aware of an interest group's concern with an issue?

A. As I mentioned earlier, this is frequently our most prominent cause *(sic)*, that is legislation. *Both of these trade organizations that I supervise have formal legislative committees.* In advance of the legislature (session), we meet with them and try to work out an accord on proposed legislation. Sometimes we see eye-to-eye and can mutually draft legislation and other times we don't, and a particular trade organization (this happened in the 1969 session), the credit union, will submit its own bill. I testified against portions of it, and those portions were thereafter altered by the legislature.

Q. Were these two trade organizations working for the same end and did they achieve their goals?

A. No, they didn't achieve their goals because each provision that I testified against was not accepted by the legislature as they proposed it. It was modified to an extent to which it was acceptable to me. They had to accept it because it meant half a loaf or none, and I suppose I did, too, because they're both quite influential and have good lobbying capacities.

Q. So your department got what it wanted?

A. No, it was a compromise for us, too. A compromise with which we could live, I felt. There were 12 suggestions in the bill and we were in accord with eight or nine, in fact, three or four were our suggestions, but three or four were controversial and those were modified.

Q. What were the major points at issue?

A. In this particular bill, revisions in loan limitations and various powers of managers of credit unions.

Q. What methods are generally used by both groups, the credit unions and the savings banks?

A. In dealing with the legislators, the credit unions have regional chapters around the state and they make it a point to become acquainted with those who are newly elected and those who are existing legislators, and very frequently they will hold dinners or chapter meetings at which they will invite the legislator to speak. The savings and loans aren't quite as well organized, simply because there aren't as many of them around the state on a regional basis, but during the legislative session they will put on a very extensive dinner. They also are called upon to buy tickets to various functions honoring each of the parties during the legislative session. I think that they are both very substantial buyers of tickets.

Q. At what point and time do they get involved?

A. On a specific bill they will usually have a sponsor. *Typically, the most substantial legislation is offered by them and usually in cooperation with this office, or hopefully in cooperation with us, and then submitted by someone who is known or has an interest in either a credit union or savings and loans. A number of legislators are credit-union members or directors of savings and loans.*

Q. At one point you mentioned that the main single tactic or method that both groups used in their relations with you would be in the meetings that are conducted before the sessions start.

A. Yes, particularly as regards legislation, we will meet with the legislative committees of the respective organizations and indicate whether or not we approve of the bill or attempt to modify the proposal if we feel it isn't a proper measure. We will work with them in drafting the bill.

Q. And both organizations have a person, full-time, whose business is to do this sort of thing?

A. Right. Apart from the legislature, if there are other matters of friction between individual credit unions or savings and loans and the division, and if the individual doesn't want to express them to us, I may get a phone call. I enjoy a close relationship with the directors of each of these leagues, so there are general matters in each of the industries that we keep each other aware of."

Here, the strength of functional relationships between the bureaucracy and its clientele is clearly apparent. Interaction is obviously sustained and coordination extends to the joint designing of bills and amendments.

As the dialogue indicates, the process is one of mutual accommodation, in which both elites must accept compromises.

The next case involves a Department of Water Resources, also in one of the states. Despite the agency's limited success, the example illustrates the initiative residing in the bureaucracy.

> **Issue:** "During the 1969 legislative session, *our department proposed changes* in certain of our laws that had been on the books for many, many years. Our basic law is from 1917. We felt that it was antiquated and some changes should be made that would only reflect changes of the times, related to our activities. We probably made one basic mistake in developing legislation internally, without too much contact with the so-called special interest groups. Through our assistant attorney-general, the bills were drafted and they were introduced into the legislature as *departmental request legislation*.[17]
>
> **Q.** Which interest groups were involved?
>
> **A.** We developed a conflict with the reclamation and irrigation district people, the associations themselves, and with the association of elected county officials, who were representing the county treasurers. There were actually two bills introduced which brought these matters to a head, one in which we proposed to change the manner in which water could be appropriated or could be withdrawn for certain purposes. To a degree it did affect the rights of irrigation districts. It affected the changing of procedures we had followed for many years.
>
> **Q.** How did you first become aware of these interest groups' concern?
>
> **A.** It was very embarrassing in that, as you are aware, bills are assigned to a legislative committee who hold hearings and take testimony. While we were waiting for our bill to be called, one morning a delegation of attorneys and directors of irrigation districts descended on our department here. They came in and said there was to be a hearing at 1:30 that same day. We hadn't even been notified of the hearings. We spent the morning telling these people why we had drafted the legislation, what its intent was, and we tried to convince them that it wasn't really adverse to their interests.
>
> **Q.** Is this the way you typically become aware of an interest group's concern with an issue?
>
> **A.** No. Normally we participate in *annual meetings* of the state reclamation association and the association of the state irrigation districts and discuss with them any proposed legislation. Our

[17] Note the extent to which bureaucratic participation in legislative policy is institutionalized.

problem in the 1969 session was that we developed our idea *after* the annual association meeting had taken place.

So the annual meeting is the major way we become aware of their concern, but we also get quite well associated with the officers of these irrigation district associations. This would be true also of county and city officials. We have contact throughout the year with representatives of all these groups.

Q. What was the final outcome?

A. They shot us down. Two bills went through. One involved the irrigation interests, it was locked up in committee and never got out. The other bill we had in would have placed a burden on the county treasurers so their association came into the hearing and made it known to the legislative committee of this burden. We modified the bill to make provision for reimbursing the county treasurers for their costs in complying with what we had been proposing. This was satisfactory to the treasury association. The legislation went through.

Q. What were the major points at issue?

A. Apprehension, distrust, a feeling that the department had moved too fast on a matter which involved the groups' interest.

Q. But the major reason you were putting together this legislation was to modify an existing law?

A. Yes, by modifying the law, we actually felt we could do a better job. That it would be in the best public interest.

Q. What were the major tactics used by the groups involved?

A. Legislative pressure. The chairman of the House Natural Resources Committee is from a farming area and so they went to the strongest people in his community and used those people for support. Of course, he was sympathetic to their views.

Q. Additional relevant details?

A. Their first approach was to come in and enter into discussions with their attorneys along the line that this bill should have been drafted in consultation with them. But we developed this idea so late, before the hearing, that the legislative committee chairman opposed our proposal and we never got to the arbitration stage for re-drafting a compromised bill.

Q. How effective do you think this interest group is?

A. They are very effective in their own area of interest.

Q. What is the main single tactic or method used by this group?

A. They developed a good liaison with key members of the legislature, who keep them informed of anything pertaining to their interest.

Q. How legitimate was this group's position on this particular issue?

A. Questionable.

Q. How significant a role do you feel interest groups generally play in helping you make policy?

A. Moderately significant.

Q. Which sanctions have you seen used against senior civil servants?

A. Infrequently, criticizing an official in the mass media, and it also happens that officials are fired. One other is by keeping the special interest group better informed than the department; in other words, putting the department at a disadvantage. The members of the legislature are the ones responsible for this, which has disturbed me the most. For example, during the legislature session, here we are, one block away from the capital and people who are 300 miles away are getting better information.

Q. In general, do you feel interest groups play a useful and necessary role?

A. Yes. They bring many situations to our attention, many general public feelings that we are not aware of. I think they should be listened to and their comments evaluated.

Q. Do you feel all or most of the relevant public groups make their interests known to the department?

A. No. We normally only seem to arouse those interests which are *opposed* to whatever we are proposing. It is very difficult to draw out those interests which are sympathetic. It seems that in any hearings we hold to make policy matters 99 per cent are against the proposals, but very few are in favor.

Q. Does your department have any provision for insuring that interests who are not organized will be heard?

A. Nothing other than the standard provision, what we call the administrative procedures act whereby public notice must be given of any regulations we are going to adopt, and if hearings are going to be held.

Q. Has your own or any other department to your knowledge ever created an interest group?

A. No."

This issue suggests the initiative that departments can exercise in proposing legislation, as well as the disruptive consequences of not consulting adequately with groups concerned. Here, also, we see how legislators and interest groups may at times work together against proposals of the bureaucracy. The pattern of functionally based interaction in policy-making is also indicated by the official's reference to limitations on the number of groups involved in the process.

The next issue also involves a state agency, this one in the vital area of health care. Among other things, it illustrates one of the most common avenues of agency-group interaction, i.e., the use of advisory councils made up jointly of officials and representatives of the interest concerned.

> **Issue:** "This issue arose in relation to physicians' fees in the medical program which started about two years ago. The problem was physician participation in the medical program and their dissatisfaction with the way the department runs the program in general. The program has instructed physicians to be primarily responsible for specifying drugs and hospital admissions to be paid for [by the program], in addition to fees and services. So the key to the whole program is the participation of physicians and their dissatisfaction with the way the department is administering the program.
>
> **Q.** What groups were involved?
> **A.** Only physicians. The problem started about two years ago with the meeting of the *state medical association.* At that meeting they agreed to finance, for a year's experimental run, a physicians' advisory group. We did look at the way a physician's services were authorized, denied, and paid for. We did include in the budget increased fees for them. This is one of the 5-state advisory committees.
> **Q.** How did you become aware of this group's concern with the issue?
> **A.** Through the joint meeting of the state medical association which resulted in setting up an advisory committee.
> **Q.** Is this the way you typically become aware of an interest group's concern?
> **A.** We usually try to channel our relationship with organized groups. The first indication we have of a problem is not usually contact with an organized group but rather individual complaints or letters. If we get a number of complaints, say, from foster parents, our response is usually to put them under some kind of umbrella group (i.e., an advisory group) and then relate to that group. *We couldn't possibly relate to individuals of all categories;* [18] there are too many of them.
> **Q.** What was the final outcome?
> **A.** After a two-year period we issued, with the committees and state associations' blessing, a questionnaire on fees. This went out about three weeks ago, and hopefully we can adjust fee schedules by the 1st of July.
> **Q.** What were the major points at issue?
> **A.** Dissatisfaction with the fee schedule. To improve communications with the medical program and make it less painful for phy-

---

[18] Here is one of the major functional contributions of interest groups to policy-making—the synthesizing of individual claims.

sians to participate. But the major issue was the fee schedule.

Q. What was the major tactics used?

A. State medical association meeting two years ago.

Q. How effective do you think this interest group is?

A. Effective.

Q. What is the main single tactic or method used by this group?

A. All of these go on simultaneously. We still receive correspondence from individuals and if it relates to a program issue or a broad problem we usually take them up with the committee. Of course, the association has relations on other levels. *For example, their fiscal arm manages medicare for the state.*[19] They have a full-time paid lobbyist in . . . who works with the legislature and all the state agencies. We also have a dialogue with him. So you have all these methods of communication going on simultaneously. We use the advisory committee to legitimize whatever action we finally take from all of these sources.

Q. How legitimate was this group's position on this issue?

A. Legitimate.

Q. How significant a role do you feel groups generally play in helping you make policy?

A. Moderately significant, because the department operates primarily under a framework of federal legislation which means that the major impact on operations is made by interest groups at the federal level, not at the state level.

Q. What, if any, sanctions have you seen used against senior civil servants?

A. Criticizing an official in the legislature, and criticizing an official in the mass media very gently.

Q. Any other sanction?

A. A special interest group is sometimes able to influence a program on which the civil servant is the expert. He has advocated a change or advocated the status quo and the special interest group does not go along with him, and prevails at the legislature. They don't attack the civil servant personally but his fate is handled through other means.

Q. In general, do you feel interest groups play a useful and necessary representative role?

A. Yes. Special interest groups give the public a mechanism they don't have individually to approach government departments, executive, and the legislature. Interest groups serve as a mechanism for contact with government.

Q. Do you feel that all or most of the relevant public groups make their interests known to the department?

A. No. Primarily, some interest groups are organized around an in-

---

[19] Here again, is a common functional attribute of interest group behavior.

terest. If they are not familiar with the system, whether it is legislative or bureaucratic, the time can rapidly pass when they can have effective input. They have to have effective leaders and be knowledgable themselves if their organization is going to have any real input. Many of them are too late. Something often happens before they find out.

Q. Does your department have any provision or method for insuring that interests who are not organized will be heard?

A. That is a very difficult question. We have our advisory committees of course. We have a mechanism for correspondence. We also have a mechanism for fair hearings, for recipients. Most of our top three levels in our local offices are involved in contacts with community groups, service clubs, church groups, etc. This formal presentation provides a method of feedback to them."

Here again, although the agency's initial role was less autonomous than in the previous example, its awareness of and liaison with the clientele group concerned is again clear. Some of the effects of federal structure are also suggested by the comment on the primarily federal focus of legislative determination and interest group influence in the state health field.

The common use of advisory councils, boards, and committees is also clear. This instrument provides an effective means of legitimating direct, "official" interest group participation in bureaucratic policy-making. In many programs, such joint committees are charged with administration, rate and/or fee determination, and enforcement. Grant McConnell has estimated that some 6,000 of such councils existed in the federal government by 1956.[20] An excellent example of their role is provided by the director of a state industrial insurance appeals board who, when asked whether his agency had ever created an interest group, replied:

Not really, because we have two interest groups *directly involved* in the work from a standpoint of the Association of Business having one representative on our Board and the state Labor Council also having a member on the Board. So that these two large groups, if they agree on legislation, then you could say that we have the two most powerful lobbying groups in the state backing any legislation. But we haven't created a group for the particular purpose of pushing a piece of legislation.

[20] *Private Power and American Democracy* (New York: Alfred A. Knopf, 1966), p. 268.

The extent to which the bureaucracy can play a positive, independent role in shaping policy and programs is well illustrated by the following issue, presented by a director of a state vocational education agency.

Issue: "About two years ago we made an approach to the executive director of the Food Dealers' Association.

Q. What was your objective?

A. It was to determine whether there was a need for an educational program for their employees, extending from the boxboy, supermarket cashier, to management.

Q. Was this Association the only group involved?

A. No. Out of that we organized an advisory committee and approached the educational director of the state labor group. We in turn recommended certain men from the state in terms of the food industry.

Q. How did you first become aware of this group's concern?

A. I am in the position of promoting and developing new programs in education and knowing the fact that businesses go into bankruptcy, and that the employees are important in terms of serving the public and that they should therefore have some educational training.

Q. Is this the way you typically become aware of an interest group's concern?

A. Yes. However, many years ago, the insurance association wanted to upgrade the requirements for its people and in order to do this they needed an educational program and so they came to us. So it works both ways.

Q. What was the final outcome?

A. In this food dealers' deal, there is a tremendous need for cashier checkers in supermarkets. So we asked the Food Dealers Association if they could donate a mobile trailer along with a tractor; we also worked out with a vocational-technical school the equipping of the mobile unit for services and it is on the road now. This is an open door for a two-year marketing program. Now we have an active advisory committee represented by the Food Dealers and labor to guide us in setting up a two-year program. The state board and our co-ordinating council got in touch with the community colleges. There were several bids.

Q. What was the major way you related to this group?

A. They have their directors and they meet to discuss some of the things in education, and then they involve all the food dealers in the state.

Q. How do they contact you?

A. By telephone, by mail, through this advisory committee, their state advisory committee, or the food dealers. I work with the schools and community colleges and they work with the food dealers. Labor is always involved.

Q. How is the advisory committee comprised?

A. We asked the head man in labor to submit the names of individuals, 3 to 5 from the state. I asked the same thing from the food dealers. So now we have an advisory committee of 7 members.

Q. Is there any additional information?

A. We are in the business of providing education. They are in the business of hiring the product that we produce. Now there may be, once in a while, legislation that they will be involved in, such as whether they can hire an 18- or 16-year-old. For instance, a checker had to be 18 years old if he was clerking in a beer store. *The Association changed this legislation,* so that there can be the involvement of students providing that at least one checker is 18-years old.

Q. How effective do you think this interest group is in dealing with your department?

A. This one has been very effective.

Q. What is the main single tactic or method used by this group?

A. The food dealers work with us. They have asked us to make a list of the things we think should go into a 2-year food marketing course. But they in turn will find out from their own top people what are the most important things that should go into the course.

Q. What is the most effective method of contact here?

A. We have periodic meetings of the advisory committee. They will also be on the lookout for men from their field who have the qualifications, the know-how, that we might certify as instructors.

Q. How legitimate is this group's position on the issue?

A. They are powerful and their ideas are good. Highly legitimate.

Q. How significant a role do you feel interest groups generally play?

A. In this case, it has been very good. But in general, I don't know how to determine this; sometimes they play a significant role, but then other times they don't have enough encouragement to see a program through.

Q. Which of these sanctions have you seen used against senior civil servants? [21]

A. I have seen an official transferred. I have seen an official criticized in the hearings, and also in the mass media. I have also seen an official fired.

Q. In general, do you feel interest groups play a useful and necessary representative role?

A. Yes. If they have a need for some kind of educational program and it isn't just to further themselves individually in a political deal, I think they really have something to contribute to the repre-

---

[21] This item was used, *inter alia,* to measure the effectiveness of interest groups.

sentation of individuals, and also to life by providing education in their area of concern.

Q. Do you feel that all or most of the relevant public groups make their interests known?

A. No, because it is a communication problem. They don't know that we exist and we don't know they exist.

Q. Does your department have any provision or method for insuring that interests who are not organized will be heard?

A. I suppose through newspapers and through publicizing our activities; within our state program we have employer–employee banquets and general publicity of our program.

Q. Has your own or any other department ever created an interest group?

A. We set up the advisory council for the purpose of promotion."

As the introductory comments show, this program was initiated by the agency staff which made an approach to the director of the Food Dealers Association. The conventional assumption is that interest group directors approach government elites to make their claims, but research suggests that the process is often a two-way one because interaction is so continuous that problems and policy initiatives emerge out of mutual awareness of conditions in a specific context.

Such evidence suggests the symbiotic relationships existing between agencies and their clientele groups, in contrast to the dramatic view that government–group interactions are characterized by "pressure" and conflict. Certainly, such conditions occur, but the generalization is that agency–group relations are likely to be normatively and substantively productive and affirmative. The system is essentially one of "representative bureaucracy." As seen elsewhere, the vast majority of senior civil servants endorse this "service" conception of their role.

Two Federal Issues

Two brief examples at the federal level are useful in illustrating bureaucracy's role in preparing the technical and informational substratum of public policy. The first concerns the role of a division in the U.S. Treasury Department, which worked closely with representatives from industry and congressional committees in preparing technical specifications and draft legislation which would provide for a federally subsidized program for a supersonic transport plane (SST). Ultimately, of course, the program was rejected, but the example remains instructive. It indicates the extent to which advancing technology expands the parameters of bureaucratic (and governmental) discretion. The huge expenditures and financial risks involved in developing a supersonic transport plane virtually dictate that government provide the major share of venture capital. This has been the pattern with earlier breakthroughs in jet aircraft for civilian use. Once it assumes financial responsibility, the government must become involved in technical questions of feasibility and design. Meanwhile, new regulatory problems arise, given the noise levels, extended runway requirements, and the load capabilities of the new planes. Here again, government's (i.e., the bureaucracy's) role is expanded to include the attending functions and responsibilities. In the process, the scope and indispensability of the bureaucracy as a quasi-autonomous branch of government grow, providing another fillip to its thrust for security and continuity.

One final example, which will not be presented *verbatim,* involves a State Department official dealing with an area division. This official, a seasoned foreign service officer, cited four groups, including the Department of Defense, as being the principal groups with whom his division interacted. Two foreign governments, as well as certain New York state interests, were involved in this case which consisted of attempts by a foreign government to ease the import of leather goods into the United States; these efforts were opposed by the relevant American leather-goods manufacturing company. Access into the bureaucracy occurred through the director of the interest's association, under the auspices of congressmen from the district concerned. Such was "the usual way" the official concerned became aware of an interest group's intervention in departmental policy issues.

Regarding the outcome, which was not yet final, the official predicted that some of the demands of the association and industry concerned would probably be met. The decision was complicated by the need to balance domestic industrial claims with foreign policy objectives, including the need of the country concerned to maintain a reasonable balance of payments. The interest group had worked at the very highest level, including attempts to compel Richard Milhaus Nixon to intervene in their behalf, which was "reasonable" given the foreign policy implications of the case. The interest group, the official noted, regarded the State Department as a lobbyist for the foreign government and its affected industry. The group, which he ranked as being "very effective"—i.e., the highest point on the scale—worked mainly through congressmen, was "highly significant" in departmental affairs, and its position and tactics in the issue were legitimate.

The case provides an example of the well-known symbiotic relationships between congressmen from relevant districts and interest groups representing an industry of some economic importance in such areas. Parenthetically, this is one group in the tariff area which, contrary to generalizations from a well-known case study, *did* know what its interests were, took decisive steps to defend them (including intercession with the former President), and possessed sizable political resources.[22]

The crucial role of interest groups in bureaucratic policy-making rests upon pervasive social influences. Advanced civilizations are characterized by an exquisite occupational specialization which provides the incentive for the creation of interest groups to represent each such sector. In medicine, for example, the fate of the general practitioner is germane; today medicine is increasingly organized into specialist categories of a bewildering variety. The motives are not entirely functional, but include occupational survival and prosperity. As Emile Durkheim concludes, interest groups expand as society becomes more functionally specialized, and the attending division of labor makes it possible for individuals and groups to survive occupationally since men prosper more when they differ more:

> In the same city, different occupations can co-exist without being obliged mutually to destroy each other, for they pursue different objects. The soldier seeks military glory, the priest moral authority, the statesman power, the businessman riches, the scholar scientific reknown. Each of them can attain his end without preventing the others from attaining theirs.[23]

Meanwhile, governments are also organized along functional lines, which enables them to play a representative role *vis-à-vis* the major institutional sectors in American society.

[22] R. A. Bauer, *et al., American Business and Public Policy* (Chicago: Aldine Publishing Co., 1963), pp. 317, 473, 477, 484, and 487.

[23] *The Division of Labor in Society,* translated with an introduction by George Simpson (New York: Free Press, 1964), p. 267.

4

Conditions of Bureaucratic Participation in Policy-Making

Certain normative and operational conditions shape bureaucratic participation in policy-making. Despite their essentially ministerial role in the "big" decisions, senior officials have some margin or latitude both in advising about policy and carrying it out. They can, in effect, elect to evaluate a given policy proposal as being highly desirable, merely feasible, or ill-considered. They can carry out an authorized policy wholeheartedly or halfheartedly or at some intermediate level of commitment. Insofar as political values influence such choices, the ideological preferences of senior offiicals are an important variable in policy-making. This facet of official behavior has been somewhat neglected, in part because of the legal-institutional approach to the field, manifest in the conclusion that officials are merely the instruments of their political masters, but also because research into the political values of higher officials has been difficult to carry out. Some such research has focused upon their socioeconomic backgrounds, which is useful because such "properties" seem to be highly correlated with normative "dispositions."

SOCIOECONOMIC BACKGROUNDS OF HIGHER
CIVIL SERVANTS

In this context, we will look at some recent research regarding both the social characteristics and political values of two samples of higher officials. The usual indexes of social class are education and occupation, often including both respondents and their fathers because class status is mainly a matter of heredity, so to speak. Including both kinds of data also enables one to generalize about social mobility among officials. Social mobility tends to shape political values, often in the direction of conservative preferences including the need for conformity.[1] This tendency is usually explained as the result of efforts to preserve hard-won achievements and is often visible in ethnic minorities who, in a real sense, have a great deal to lose by idiosyncratic social and political behavior. The historic role of intellectuals as servants of political power is a common manifestation of this mode of personal accommodation.[2]

Table 4–1 provides data on social class among a cross-national sample of senior officials in the United States and Canada. The Canadian data

TABLE 4–1. Social Class among American and Canadian Higher Civil Servants

Class Status *	Percentage in Each Category			
	Officials U.S./Can.		National † U.S./Can.	
Upper	49	74	3	7
Upper-middle	48	22	8	11
Middle	3	3	22	28
Lower-middle	.5	0	46	38
Lower	0	0	18	17
	(257)	(214)		

* Socioeconomic status is based upon occupation and education, with occupation weighted × 7 and education × 3. For details see A. B. Hollingshead and F. Redlich, *Social Class and Mental Illness* (New York: John Wiley and Sons, 1958).

† The "national" break-downs are from Joseph Kahl, *The American Class Structure* (New York: Holt, Rinehart & Co., 1957); and H. D. Woods and S. Ostry, *Labour Policy and Labour Economics in Canada* (Toronto: University of Toronto Press, 1962).

[1] See, for example, Kenneth H. Thompson, "Upward Social Mobility and Political Orientation: A Re-Evaluation of the Evidence," *American Sociological Review*, Vol. 36 (June, 1971), pp. 223–35; J. Lopreato, "Upward Social Mobility and Political Orientation," *American Sociological Review*, Vol. 32 (August, 1967), pp. 586–92.

[2] For an interesting historical analysis, see Lewis A. Coser, "The Alien as a Servant of Power: Court Jews and Christian Renegades," *American Sociological Review*, Vol. 37 (August, 1972), pp. 574–81.

are reported mainly to provide a foil against which the American findings can be compared.

The highly advantaged class status of higher officials is clearly apparent from a comparison of their rankings with the national scale. Much of their position is explained by their extremely high educational achievement. Regarding occupation, it is possible that our coding has inflated their class status somewhat, in that most of them were placed in the top Hollingshead category, i.e., "higher executives." While most observers would probably agree that this was proper with the federal samples, which comprised deputy-ministers and associate deputy-ministers in Canada and GS-18's in the United States, some of the state and provincial officials may have been ranked too high. Nevertheless, it is clear from the national comparison that this is an exceptional group.

Regarding mobility, other data indicate that just about 30 per cent of officials in both countries had fathers in the two upper strata. We conclude, therefore, that some two-thirds of them have experienced upward movement from the strata below upper-middle to their present status. The principal means has been through extended education, as well as long service in government (over 60 per cent are 50 or over, and have 25 years or more tenure).

Their educational achievement is remarkable, especially when one considers that most of them are middle-aged and would have been in university at a time when opportunity was less widespread than during the post-World War II period. Fully 70 per cent of American officials have university degrees, compared with about 20 per cent of their fellow citizens. Forty-five per cent have graduate degrees, with the largest proportions held by those in Washington, D.C., and Washington state. Among undergraduate majors, three fields—business, public administration, and economcis—account for just over 20 per cent of all majors. Among graduate degrees, the M.A. is most common; only 8 per cent have law degrees, while the Ph.D. is very common, especially in the federal system.

An interesting regional difference is the tendency for federal bureaucrats to rank higher on father's occupational status, compared with those in Michigan, Louisiana, and Washington state. Over all, 40 per cent of officials come from families where the father was a small businessman. For reasons which are hard to explain, Michigan officials come less frequently from families in which the father enjoyed executive status, comprising only 11 per cent of the sample, compared with fully 40 per cent in the federal bureaucracy, 32 in Louisiana, and 24 in Washington state.

In all, about two-thirds of this talented group of men are "self-made" through education and long service. Many of them have continued their education while in the public service. With the exception of certain elite segments, such as the Foreign Service, education by itself has been among the major factors in mobility in the American civil service. Unlike the British Administrative Class, where a degree from Oxford or Cambridge has often been a requirement for entry and ascendance,[3] American civil servants from many types of universities and regions have been able to compete successfully for advancement. The other differentiating characteristic is the extent to which they have risen through *specialist* rather than generalist roles. Obviously, once they have achieved the higher levels, their tasks become more administrative, but the road to such positions tends often to be one of specialist achievement and extended service in one or two agencies, contrasted with the British system of generalist orientations and rotation across functional lines.

THE POLITICAL VALUES OF HIGHER CIVIL SERVANTS

It is often assumed that a one-to-one correlation exists between an individual's political dispositions and his behavior. Thus it may be thought that individuals who work for government, with its subsidy and welfare orientation, would have strong "big government" values, perhaps attended by serious reservations about "free enterprise" and the capacity of private efforts and institutions to provide the social and economic security which the majority of citizens now seek. Recent research challenges this assumption. Some research indicates that "hard" properties such as occupational role, tenure, and interaction with other political actors are more important than ideological preferences in determining policy choices.[4] A careful analysis of policy outcomes in the 50 states found that environmental factors such as the level of economic development and educational achievement in a state were more important than its political structure and traditions in determining government policy.[5]

[3] See, for example, R. Kelsall, *et al.*, *Graduates: The Study of an Elite* (London: Methuen and Co., 1972), for the extent to which class factors continue to prevent working-class graduates of the elite universities from achieving the top levels in the civil service and other professions.

[4] See, for example, Robert Presthus, *Elites in the Policy Process* (New York: Cambridge University Press, 1974), Chap. 13; Ralf Dahrendorf, *Society and Democracy in Germany* (New York: Doubleday, 1967), pp. 278–79; Cutright Phillips, "Political Structure, Economic Development and National Social Security Programs," *American Journal of Sociology*, Vol. 70, pp. 537–50.

[5] Thomas Dye, *Politics, Economics, and the Public* (Chicago: Rand McNally Co., 1966), pp. 286–87, 293.

In this tentative context, let us turn to some evidence regarding the political dispositions of North American officials. Multiple regression analysis enables us to make some judgments about the relative weight of such variables, compared with hard property variables, in determining their behavior, which by definition is concerned with allocating public largesse to the great institutional sectors. Table 4–2 presents data regard-

TABLE 4–2.   Political Liberalism among Higher Civil Servants

| | Percentage of Political Liberalism * | | | | | | | |
| | High U.S./Can. | | Medium U.S./Can. | | Low U.S./Can. | | | |
Region/Elite								
D.C./Ottawa								
Legislators	20	33	37	33	44	34	(93)	(137)
Bureaucrats	21	26	40	43	39	32	(90)	(89)
Michigan/Ontario								
Legislators	13	27	37	35	50	39	(46)	(49)
Bureaucrats	23	22	43	43	34	35	(53)	(49)
Louisiana/Quebec								
Legislators	4	22	19	24	77	54	(52)	(41)
Bureaucrats	21	31	36	25	44	44	(53)	(32)
Washington/ British Columbia								
Legislators	12	41	38	28	49	31	(49)	(32)
Bureaucrats	29	17	44	50	27	33	(36)	(36)

* This index of political liberalism is based upon the following items: 'Democracy depends fundamentally upon free enterprise' (reverse scored); 'Everything considered, labor unions are doing a lot of good in this country'; 'An atheist or a Communist should have as much right to make a public speech as anybody else.' These are standard items for measuring this dimension.

ing the political values of higher officials. Once again, in order to provide a reference point against which to set the American bureaucratic sample, we include the Canadian data, for both legislators and civil servants.

Regional and Cross-National Variations

Several dramatic variations appear in this table. With the exception of those in Washington, D.C., senior officials tend to rank substantially higher on political liberalism (as defined here) than their legislative masters. Political liberalism generally rises with educational level, so it may be that the remarkably high educational achievement of bureaucrats explains this difference. It is also clear that sharp regional differences exist on this dimension. Louisiana officials (combining both the "high" and "low" positions) tend to rank lower than their counterparts elsewhere. However, differences among legislators are even greater, with Louisiana again ranking considerably lower than those in other regions.

Cross-national differences among officials are marked in some cases. The greatest variations exist between the Quebec and Louisiana samples, where the former rank somewhat higher, and between Washington state and British Columbia, where the difference is in the opposite direction. However, it should be noted that the British Columbia respondents tend to cluster in the "medium" range. On the whole, the American sample ranks rather "low" on this dimension, especially if one assumes that there is some logical association between working for the government and a "liberal" political .ideology.

More directly germane to the issue of ideology and policy preferences is the question of "economic liberalism," by which is meant a pro-"big government" disposition, which again would seem consistent for officials whose occupational life consists of carrying out precisely this version of government's role in society. Table 4–3 presents the cross-national evidence.

Looking at senior officials first, the American sample again differs substantially from its Canadian counterpart at several points. American federal bureaucrats rank substantially lower than those in Ottawa. Since the policy outputs in the two systems, with the exception of military spending, are remarkably similar, this variation is unexpected. Although each set of state officials ranks slightly higher than its provincial opposites, when compared with their distribution at the "low" end of the scale, it is clear that they rank strikingly low on this "big government" dimension. The divergence between the Michigan and Ontario samples is explained in part by our earlier finding that Michigan officials contained a larger proportion of individuals of less advantaged social origins which might explain their uniquely "high" ranking on this value. Meanwhile, Ontario officials rank quite low, which again may be partially explained by the long reign (a quarter century) of a very pro-business Conservative regime in that province. Quebec's and Louisiana's low rankings are partly explained by the item in the index regarding federal aid to education, which is suspect in both areas.

The position of legislators is similarly ironic in that they tend to rank quite low on this dimension yet their role is typically one of expanding government's role, with the possible exception of Washington state which retains a kind of frontier preference for limited government, compared

TABLE 4–3.   Economic Liberalism among the Political Elite

Region/Elite	High U.S./Can.		Medium U.S./Can.		Low U.S./Can.			
D.C./Ottawa								
Legislators	16	37	26	44	59	20	(90)	(122)
Bureaucrats	13	28	34	30	54	42	(86)	(88)
Michigan/Ontario								
Legislators	28	38	23	34	49	28	(47)	(47)
Bureaucrats	23	10	45	33	32	56	(53)	(48)
Louisiana/Quebec								
Legislators	22	40	33	43	45	18	(51)	(40)
Bureaucrats	15	12	29	30	56	58	(52)	(33)
Washington/ British Columbia								
Legislators	8	47	25	43	67	10	(46)	(30)
Bureaucrats	18	11	18	42	64	47	(55)	(36)

Header note: The three main column groups are labelled **Percentage of Economic Liberalism ***, with sub-columns **High U.S./Can.**, **Medium U.S./Can.**, **Low U.S./Can.**

* Economic liberalism is defined here by the following items: 'That government which governs least governs best' (reverse scored); 'Economic security for every man, woman, and child is worth striving for, even if it means socialism'; 'If unemployment is high, the government should spend money to create jobs'; 'A national medicare plan is necessary to insure that everyone receives adequate health care'; 'More fedreal aid to education is desirable if we are going to adequately meet present and future educational needs in this country.'

with such highly industrialized states as Michigan. It should be noted that differences between legislators and bureaucrats in the United States sample are statistically significant at the strong .001 level (t-test). Within regions, these two sets vary significantly in Michigan and Washington, D.C. A similar, but more pervasive variation exists in Canada, with officials in the three provinces ranking dramatically lower than legislators.

Cross-nationally, it is also clear that Canadian legislators rank dramatically higher on this dimension than their American peers. But here again, the difference does not seem to manifest itself in policy outputs. It is suggestive that the proportion of GNP spent for all government is about 40 per cent in Canada and very similar in the United States. The only major area in which policy outputs are substantially different is in military spending, where the Canadian total is a much smaller proportion of the public budget than in the United States. Otherwise, "big government" is manifest in both societies. From this, we conclude that the political-economic preferences of senior officials are either inapposite to their occupational role or they are irrelevant in the sense of having no operational effect on their role. It may be, as suggested earlier, that the high rates of mobility experienced by some two-thirds of these men have conditioned them toward the conservative drift revealed by these data. It is also well-known that socioeconomic status is negatively associated with economic liberalism and positively associated with political liberalism.[6] Thus the fact that American officials rank higher than legislators on political liberalism and lower on "big government" preferences seems entirely consistent.

THE INSTRUMENTAL BASIS OF BUREAUCRATIC POLICY-MAKING

Such findings suggest that other kinds of incentives provide more important motivations for bureaucratic participation in the expansive policies that characterize federal and state governments in American society. The explanation may lie in more instrumental kinds of relationships which form the basis of interaction or exchange theory. This theory will be outlined and tested in Chapter 8, but it must be mentioned briefly here as a basis for presenting some evidence regarding officials' perceptions of their role and the services they receive in return from articulate interest groups. Interaction theory holds that individuals maintain certain relationships because these are, on balance, beneficial in some way or another. Thus in a dyadic relationship one partner may receive affection, empathy, security, and so on from another.[7] In a work group, benefits of a more concrete type may be exchanged, as in a piecework system where each individual contributes some essential segment of a work process. Economically, interaction theory rests upon a cost–benefit equation, which directs that an individual will sustain only those associations that result in a net gain. Psychologically, the theory rests upon reinforcement—i.e., the well-documented fact that individuals tend to repeat experiences that are perceived as gratifying and to avoid those that are unpleasant.

In this context, we may suggest that senior officials, in their role of

[6] See, for example, Robert Presthus, *Men at the Top: A Study in Community Power* (New York: Oxford University Press, 1964), p. 317.

[7] Interaction theory has been developed in the U. S. mainly by George Homans in *The Human Group* (New York: Harcourt Brace Jovanovich, 1950); *Social Behavior: Its Elementary Forms* (New York: Harcourt Brace Jovanovich, 1961); see also R. Maris, "The Logical Adequacy of Homans' Social Theory," *American Sociological Review*, Vol. 35 (December, 1970), pp. 1069–81.

dispensing public largesse to interest groups, are motivated by certain reciprocal services or benefits.[8] Just as legislators receive information, ideological support, and electoral sustenance from interest groups, so higher officials may receive highly valued services. Table 4–4 presents the major services received from interest groups, as ranked by senior officials.

TABLE 4–4. Major Services Provided Civil Servants by Interest Groups

Services	Percentage Ranking Each Service			
	Wash.	Mich.	Louis.	Wash. D.C.
First Service				
Information about clientele reactions	33	37	24	48
Supporting departmental legislation	26	24	22	10
Participation in advisory bodies	19	15	24	15
Helping draft legislation	4	0	9	1
Identify appointees	0	2	0	1
Other	4	0	2	7
No response	14	7	20	19
Second Service				
Supporting departmental legislation	23	30	27	16
Information about clientele reactions	21	17	16	16
Participation in advisory bodies	21	17	13	28
Helping draft legislation	16	22	13	11
Identify appointees	2	0	4	2
Other	0	6	0	0
No response	18	9	27	26
	(N = 57)	(N = 54)	(N = 55)	(N = 92)

Fully half of the sample (N = 218) agree that "information about clientele reactions to their programs" is the major service provided by groups and their agents. Support for agency legislation was ranked next, by almost one-quarter. Virtually equal weight was given to participation in departmental advisory bodies and committees. Some state-federal variation exists, as federal officials are more likely to endorse "information about clientele reactions" compared with their state counterparts. Legislative support is more highly regarded by state officials. Only in Louisiana do over 10 per cent of civil servants believe that interest

[8] As Abraham Holtzman says, "Both sets of actors—the heads of the executive agencies and those representing the interest groups—need the other to accomplish their respective goals." *Interest Groups and Lobbying* (New York: The Macmillan Co., 1966), p. 112.

group help in drafting legislation is the primary group service. Nevertheless, the fairly high ranking this service receives at the second level of importance suggests how symbiotic is the interaction between "private" groups and governmental elites.

Regarding the second most important benefit, almost 30 per cent of the officials cited support for agency legislation first, followed closely by participation in departmental advisory bodies. Just over one-fifth mentioned clientele reactions to departmental programs. The emphasis upon this last service is in line with the case study issues cited earlier which suggest that senior officials are and want to be in close communication with their respective clientele groups. This "representative" orientation deserves some special consideration.

THE IDEOLOGY OF REPRESENTATION

Even though political and economic liberalism may not affect bureaucratic policy activities in the expected way, it does seem that American officials define their occupational role as one of group representation. Such an orientation is not unexpected, given the obvious fact that government structure is organized on a functional basis with the various departments and agencies patently assigned to substantive interests representing the great institutional sectors of society. On the other hand, there is the equally honorific thesis that government officials represent the "public interest," which might seem to require that they be mainly responsive to some collective interest above those of the special interests represented by agencies and departments. Some evidence on this issue is provided by a single item phrased as follows: "Government departments are usually organized to represent discrete interests in society (e.g., business, agriculture, labor). It is therefore reasonable that such departments should be mainly concerned with the social and economic interests of their special area." Precisely three-fourths of senior officials agree with this definition of their role. (In Canada, the proportion rises to 80 per cent).

This evidence indicates that a very large proportion of officials accept an operational reality defined essentially by the very structure of public administration. Given the scope and complexity of government operations, as well as the functional specialization of modern society, it is not surprising that this pragmatic definition of their role would tend to outweigh any opposing ideological preferences for some alternative set of decisional premises, to use Herbert Simon's phrase. Everywhere today, it seems, technology and organization determine that men and women work in similarly compartmentalized milieux. Perhaps especially for public officials, who are constrained to be politically neutral, the claims of occupational role and "representative bureaucracy" become especially compelling. Some evidence of the negative inducements encouraging such an accommodation is available in the extent to which officials experience group activity as sanctioning, or potentially so. Our research includes an item regarding the extent to which officials have observed the use of sanctions. Table 4–5 indicates the extent of such behavior.

TABLE 4–5.   Group Sanctions as Perceived by Senior Officials

Type of Sanction	Percentage Indicating "Yes"			
	Wash.	Mich.	Louis.	Wash. D.C.
Criticism in mass media	49	44	69	41
Legislative criticism	26	35	44	22
Censure by superior	14	22	44	7
Transferring official	12	17	40	11
Having official fired	16	11	24	8
	(N = 57)	(N = 54)	(N = 55)	(N = 92)

One caveat regarding these data must be made: fully three-fourths of federal officials failed to answer this item, compared with an average of only about 3 per cent in the three state samples. One can only speculate as to the reasons for the federal reaction. Perhaps they are more sensitive to the implications of any suggestion that sanctions are widely used. It may be that sanctions are actually more common at the federal level, given the large stakes at issue and the superior financial and administrative resources displaced by groups in Washington. On the other hand, there were no refusals among the Louisiana sample, among whom sanctions of every kind were more common. Insofar as the capacity to sanction civil servants is a reliable index of corruption in lobbying activities, the data may lend some weight to earlier judgments that lobbying is more corrupt at the state, compared with the federal, level.[9] Since a similar reluctance on sensitive items was exhibited by the Canadian federal sample, it seems that this judgment may be due to response bias

[9] See, for example, Lester Milbrath, *The Washington Lobbyists* (Chicago: Rand McNally, 1963), p. 350; L. A. Dexter, *How Organizations are Represented in Washington* (Indianapolis: Bobbs-Merrill, 1969), pp. 37–38; 134–35.

rather than any substantive difference. In any event, it is clear that senior officials receive both positive and negative sanctions which propel them toward a pragmatic definition of their role, in contrast to one based upon personal ideological preferences, except insofar as these are compatible with such a role.

GROUP CLAIMS UPON THE BUREAUCRACY

So far, we have said little about the kinds of substantive demands that groups and their agents make upon the bureaucracy. In general, of course, these are mainly "economic," but it is also useful to know more precisely the nature of such claims, as well as their relative frequency. Table 4–6 provides a scale, based again upon official responses.

TABLE 4–6. Specific Demands of Interest Groups

Demands	Percentage
Alteration or establishment of administrative standards	47
Amendment or creation of legislation	17
Economic support (subsidy)	12
Influencing external (foreign) policy	4
Increasing racial and/or social welfare and/or arts	4
Resolving jurisdictional conflict	2
Other	4
No response	10
	(N = 258)

Clearly, most groups are concerned with the area of administrative regulation, which reflects the discretion that officials enjoy in this area. Nevertheless, the extent to which civil servants have influence over legislation is apparent from the fact that this area ranks second among group claims. Economic assistance, usually involving a grant or subsidy of some kind, is the third ranking demand, followed not very closely by attempts to influence foreign policy and generalized social, ethnic, and welfare claims. The significance of the foreign affairs category probably reflects a certain amount of sample bias, in that the State Department includes a high proportion of GS-18's, and thus constitutes a relatively large part of our federal sample.

A related question is the extent to which interest groups are typically involved with preserving the status quo in their relations with government or, on the other hand, in trying to bring about change. It is sometimes maintained that major producer types of groups are generally satisfied to retain the advantages they presently enjoy, whereas so-called consumer and poverty groups are more likely to want to change the existing allocation of values. A corollary of this hypothesis is that preserving the *status quo* is relatively easy, compared with trying to introduce change in legislation or regulatory standards. Following such judgments, we coded hundreds of group case studies, with the hope that this dichotomy would enable us to differentiate kinds of issues, the types of groups that were involved in each, their characteristic methods, the degree of success achieved, etc. Over 80 per cent of the cases, however, proved to be innovative, in the sense that the groups concerned were trying to change an existing situation. Table 4–7, based upon the judgments of civil servants

TABLE 4–7.   Interest Group Goals: To Retain Status Quo or Effect Change

	Percentage Responding *			
	Wash.	Mich.	Louis.	Wash. D.C.
Effect change	80	96	94	49
Retain status quo	5	0	2	20
IG reacted to government	12	4	4	25
No defined purpose	2	0	0	7
	(N = 56)	(N = 46)	(N = 47)	(N = 77)

Chi-square:		x^2	df	
Comparing Washington, D.C. to Washington		13.8	4	p<.003
" " to Michigan		28.2	4	p<.000
" " to Louisiana		25.7	4	p<.000

* Percentages are based only on the number of civil servants who answered.

regarding the same question, provides an interesting check on the group case study evidence.

Here again, the consensus is that groups are typically occupied with attempts to bring about change. A marked variation, however, occurs between the states and Washington, D.C., significant at the strong .003 or higher level. In the federal milieu, officials are much more likely to state that interest groups either react to government's initiatives or seek to retain things as they are. This may mean that the federal bureaucracy has greater initiative *vis-à-vis* groups than its peers in the states. Only in Washington state is there any disposition to share the former belief, for reasons we are unable to explain.

ACCESS AND EFFECTIVENESS

Having looked at the claims typically made by groups, we turn next to some evidence concerning patterns of access and, most important, the extent to which groups and their agents appear to be successful in their attempts to influence the bureaucracy. It may be useful initially to determine at what point in the system groups and their agents enter, in the judgment of senior officials. This evidence is again based upon their case study experience. By a very narrow margin, most officials (32 per cent) believe that lobbyists or group directors enter at the top levels of the bureaucracy, i.e., among senior career officials. Access through a branch head ranks a close second (by 30 per cent), followed by access through a legislator, and a lower-level civil servant, respectively. One interesting difference appears regarding the utility of Cabinet members, which 14 per cent of federal respondents ranked first, compared with virtually none of their state peers. Chief executives are ranked next, but by only about 3 per cent of the sample.

More significant is the ease of access, as perceived by these high-level officials, over 50 per cent of whom have had 25 or more years of experience which should provide a firm basis for their generalizations. Table 4–8 provides the evidence, based upon a single item which asked how difficult it was for interest group agents to achieve access into the internal decision-making process in their agency.

Although the variations are statistically significant in only two cases, substantial differences occur at times, particularly between the federal and the state samples. Louisiana, which indicates a consistent anti-

TABLE 4–8.   Access into Agency Decision-making Process

Condition of Access	Percentage Responding			
	Wash.	Mich.	Louis.	Wash. D.C.
Access is quite easy	39	31	27	24
Access is fairly easy	30	43	17	40
Access is possible but not easy	22	20	44	22
Access is difficult	9	6	12	14
	(N = 54)	(N = 51)	(N = 52)	(N = 76)

Chi-square:	χ^2		df
Comparing Louisiana to Michigan	11.7	p<.01	3
Comparing Louisiana to Washington, D.C.	10.0	p<.01	3

interest group valence, ranks highest on the difficulty of group access. Washington state is at the other end of the spectrum, with about 40 per cent of its officials indicating that access is "quite easy." Federal bureaucrats rank lowest at the "quite easy" level, but show a marked increase at the second "fairly easy" level. On the other hand, they have the largest proportion (14 per cent) at the "difficult" level. On the whole, and not unexpectedly, given the traditional official-clientele relations in most bureaucracies, access seems generally easy, as an average of almost two-thirds of officials rank their agencies at the two highest levels. Here, as noted, access is eased by the common functional interests and the representational ethic that characterize bureaucratic-interest group interaction. A fair amount of occupational interchange occurs among them, but more important perhaps is the mutual sharing of common technical backgrounds of knowledge and experience. Their exchange of valued currencies further reinforces these bases of accommodation.

Access vs. Effectiveness

Access, however, must be distinguished from effectiveness. Democratic ideals in the United States honor free entry into the political system. Legislators, especially, emphasize their availability to constituents. As a result, organized groups and individuals as well can usually gain a hearing from governmental elites. Obviously, this generalization must be qualified in terms of unequal political resources, including education, interest, feelings of political efficacy, and the like, but ideally the principle holds. Nevertheless, the mere fact of access does not necessarily insure effectiveness. Examples are legion: the slow progress of civil rights legislation; the limited success of organized efforts to end the war in Vietnam; the difficulty of overcoming the seniority system in Congress; the demise of the urban renewal and poverty programs—all suggest the truth of this judgment. As Table 8–1 shows (page 143), local consumer and cooperative groups are very active, yet we have not found them to be very effective.

We turn next to evidence regarding the effectiveness that interest groups enjoy in their efforts to influence the bureaucracy. A useful index is provided by the responses of our official sample to an item which asked them to indicate how much and how frequently they had been influenced by lobbyists. Table 4–9 presents the distribution for only the highest level of experienced influence: *to the extent of coming to agree with the position advocated by the lobbyists.*

TABLE 4–9. Lobbyist Effectiveness vis-a-vis Senior Officials

Influenced to Extent of Agreement	Percentage Responding			
	Wash.	Mich.	Louis.	Wash. D.C.
Frequently	2	2	0	1
Occasionally	48	24	22	35
Hardly ever	28	36	51	41
Never	19	32	22	19
Don't know	4	6	4	4
	(N = 54)	(N = 50)	(N = 49)	(N = 85)

Not unexpectedly, very few respondents perceive themselves as being influenced "frequently," at this high level. At the next level, however, an average of just one-third indicate that they have been so influenced. Sharp variations exist, with Washington state and Washington, D.C., ranking substantially higher than their counterparts elsewhere.[10] It is suggestive that these rankings are related in some cases to those found regarding access. Louisiana, it will be recalled, ranked dramatically lower on access, and here is also lowest on effectiveness, although challenged by Michigan. Meanwhile, Washington state, which had ranked highest on access, also ranks highest on experienced influence at the nominally highest "occasionally" level. This evidence is nicely supportive of interaction theory, which posits a positive association between the frequency of contact and group influence."[11]

The data provide some evidence bearing upon another traditional hypothesis: that lobbyists are more influential at the state level, compared with the federal, mainly because of superior professionalization and the research facilities available to both officials and legislators at that point. If this were true, we would expect to find that federal officials were substantially less subject to lobbyist influence. Yet, the evidence indicates that they rank second to Washington state in experienced influence. The inconclusiveness of the traditional view is also supported by evidence, not shown here, that interest groups in the federal capital are considerably advantaged, compared with their state counterparts, in terms of such political resources as the size of their annual budgets, the salaries they

---

[10] Such cross-system variations, by the way, indicate that higher officials, in responding to sensitive questions, do not "all" confine their responses to stereotyped comments that serve protective or ego-reinforcing functions, as sometimes argued by "antiscience" students of public administration.

[11] For a test of this theory, see Robert Presthus, *Elites in the Policy Process, op. cit.*, Chap. 9.

are able to pay their directors, and the size of their memberships. If this is so, one must say that their *potential* for influence is greater, despite the professionalization that may make public officials less dependent upon the information and related services provided by interest groups. It is also true that the economic stakes are generally higher in Washington, which provides yet another incentive for greater influence.[12]

[12] *Ibid.*, Chap. 4.

5

Instruments of
Bureaucratic
Policy-Making

We have seen that officials play a direct and sustained role in shaping and carrying out public policies. This condition is mainly the result of their expertise, continuity, and representative role in the political system. The bureaucracy may, as some critics insist, have been overly responsive to selective constituencies, but there is little doubt that it has been actively responsive to articulate interests in virtually every articulate sector of society. In this chapter, we turn to some of the instruments used by the bureaucracy in influencing both the design and the implementation of public policy.[1]

COMPUTERS AND COMPUTER SIMULATIONS

The impact of computer technology, applied cybernetics, and policy sciences upon governmental policy increases steadily. Much of the time and manpower resources expended during policy formulation is involved

[1] Bureaucracy's role here may be defined as one of adaptation and innovation, i.e., the management of change. For analyses that treat the instruments available to the bureaucracy and the conditions required for this role, see Victor Thompson, *Bureaucracy and Innovation* (University: University of Alabama Press, 1969); and Ronald Corwin, "Strategies for Organizational Innovation," *American Sociological Review*, Vol. 37 (August, 1972), pp. 441–54.

—especially in the bureaucratic sector—in the collection and handling of information. Computers, in the most elementary sense, are machines for processing and storing information. They increase exponentially the quantity of information that can be handled, while augmenting to a remarkable extent the efficiency and speed at which data can be analyzed, stored, and retrieved. (Some idea of the computer's efficiency in data processing can be seen in the author's experience in the study of political elites reported elsewhere, in which only about 10 hours of computer time were required to analyze data encompassing some 12,000 IBM cards, using various techniques and analytical frameworks.) Given the scope and complexity of demands upon modern bureaucracy, and the value imputed to managerial techniques and the rationality of means in public affairs, the continuing growth of the use of computer technology in most jurisdictions would seem to be quite natural and generally desirable.

An obvious (if somewhat painful) example of the utility of computer applications in the bureaucratic sector concerns the operations of the Internal Revenue Service. In fiscal year 1973, the I.R.S. collected $237.7 billion in gross taxes, processed 116.9 million tax returns, issued 55.9 million refunds valued at $19.0 billion, and acted on 932,331 delinquent accounts owing some $523.1 million.[2] Manually, such a task would be staggering, if not impossible. Employing extensive computer facilities, however, the problem of processing revenue inflows and outflows is made more manageable and material costs are reduced significantly. Computers tend to improve the identification of potential and delinquent taxpayers, help prevent duplicate refunding, facilitate rapid verification of tax computations, and provide concise and readily available statistical information for government use.[3]

The scope for the direct use of computer technology in policy-making is somewhat more restricted in other fields, where subjective factors and fewer information-handling services are involved. This is really not a result of any inadequacies on the part of computers, but rather reflects the ideological and cultural biases that policy-makers *bring to* the computer, in the form of selective and slanted information, much of it

[2] *1973 Annual Report: The Commissioner of Internal Revenue* (Washington, D. C., 1973), p. v.

[3] Norman J. Ream, "The Computer and its Impact on Public Organization," *Public Administration Review*, Vol. 28 (November/December, 1968), p. 500; Alan Westin (Ed.), *Information Technology in a Democracy* (Cambridge, Mass.: Harvard University Press, 1971); see also the report of a symposium on electronic data processing, Geoffrey Y. Cornog, *et al.* (Eds.), *EDP Systems in Public Management* (Chicago: Rand McNally and Co., 1968).

unconscious. Although public policy can be viewed increasingly as an outcome of technological evaluations which are often highly rational, ideological and political influences continue to play a major role in determining many (if not most) policy actions. Insofar as it gives the impression that such factors can be displaced by pure reason, the field of "policy sciences" is somewhat misleading. Ideological and political imputs to the policy process are not usually reducible to precise formulae which can be systematically "plugged into" the decisional scheme. Computers, in effect, cannot overcome (assuming they should) the problems of subjective judgment and selectivity which reflect the inevitable "situational determinism" of all human thought and cognition. One suspects also that the inability to foresee all the eventual outcomes of policy decisions is more critical in explaining policy failures than any failure to include all potentially-relevant factors and alternatives at the planning stage of a policy issue. Among the major reasons is the impossibility of including in the decisional calculus more than a few of the important variables, given the present state of data analysis and collection.

Despite such limitations, computers are obviously of great value to the policy-maker in many respects. The efficient computation and comparison of information allows him to examine more precisely and in vastly greater depth more of the factors that seem to affect a given policy choice. Available resources can be evaluated and cost–benefit ratios can be reliably calculated. Computer simulations of several policy alternatives can be used to answer the question, What would happen if . . . ? [4] Simulations cannot predict policy outcomes with total accuracy, of course, because all relevant factors that might eventually affect the outcome are not and cannot be known. Even in the most systematic behavioral research, only a very few of the potentially relevant variables can be controlled, which means, as Hubert Blalock says, that we can never really "prove" conclusively any hypothesis[5] Progress, however, always occurs incrementally, and the computer has clearly made possible great strides in the systematic handling of vast amounts of information. This enables the decision-maker to seek more effectively the best *possible* paths of action by enabling him to act more rationally than before.

For example, a policy-maker concerned with housing problems could, hypothetically, employ a computer program positing the interrelatedness of a number of salient factors affecting the availability of housing (e.g., mortgage rates, construction costs, land costs, availability of services,

---

[4] L. T. Wilkins, "Computer Impact on Public Decision Making," in *ibid.*, p. 507.
[5] *Causal Inferences in Nonexperimental Research* (Chapel Hill: University of North Carolina Press, 1960), p. 3.

population densities, etc.) to predict the probable effect that a change in any one factor would have on other related variables. If a policy-maker were to consider raising the prime lending rate on mortgages by 10 per cent, he could insert this change into the simulation program and discern the effects that the change would likely have on the number of housing starts, the total amount of capital available for mortgages, and the degree of public indebtedness. Such information might cause him to reconsider his proposed action in quantitative or qualitative terms or, on the other hand, it might reinforce his conviction regarding the feasibility of the proposal. Similarly, if an actual environmental change occurs (e.g., a per cent increase in the cost of building materials), the policy-maker could simulate the probable effects that such a change would have on other factors, allowing him to design more effectively a workable policy response (e.g., increase the funds available for mortgage subsidies, decrease the prime lending rate). Simulations, therefore, reduce the number of unanticipated consequences that a given policy generates by increasing the policy-maker's ability to chart and predict the interdependency of policy variables. There is, at the same time, little indication that even the most versatile use of computer tactics, as seen for example in DOD's programs under McNamara, has much effect on economy in terms of controlling total expenditures. Questionable strategic decisions, such as the policy of preparing a military establishment which could fight simultaneously on two continents or to produce certain types of aircraft that prove operationally abortive, continue to occur. Perhaps the major contribution of computers is in the area of internal, managerial, highly routinized types of decisions, where by definition the components are subject to fairly precise definition and quantification.

Planning-Programming-Budgeting Systems

On August 25, 1965, President Johnson announced

> . . . a very new and very revolutionary system of planning and programming and budgeting throughout the vast federal government—so that through the tools of modern management the full promise of a finer life can be brought to every American at the lowest possible cost.[6]

The new system of management praised so highly by the President, known as Planning-Programming and Budgeting (Systems), was not really as much a "revolutionary" development in policy management as

[6] Cited in Murray L. Weidenbaum, "Program Budgeting—Applying Economic Analysis to Government Expenditure Decisions," in I. Sharkansky, ed., *Policy Analysis in Political Science* (Chicago: Markham Publishing Co., 1970), p. 385.

it was a logical step in the ongoing search for rationality in policy determination and government budgeting. The origins of PPB (or PPBS) can be generally traced to earlier utilization of performance budgeting systems and benefit/cost, cost/effectiveness or cost/utility analyses in various government departments, most notably the Department of Defense. The basic impetus behind these earlier developments had been a desire to link the budgetary processes to broader evaluations of the character and relative importance of government projects and activities,[7] employing rational, scientific criteria and orienting the total process to a more general assessment of national objectives.

As budget Director Charles J. Schultze concluded, shortly after Johnson's 1965 announcement, PPB was a natural improvement of these already existing processes rather than a radical departure from present practices:

> . . . [I do] not want to leave anybody with the idea that what we are doing is some revolutionary change. It really is an improvement in what we are doing now, a systemization and routinization, if you will.[8]

In many respects, PPB can be viewed most basically as an instrument for effective and responsive budgeting. Most budgeting systems are composed of three different aspects or functions: planning, management, and control. The planning function involves the linking of long-term goals and objectives to available resources and expenditure capabilities. The management aspect seeks to determine the most efficient method for the achievement of prescribed goals or tasks. The control function aims to supervise expenditures so that spending ceilings are observed and resources are allocated in the prescribed manner at the appropriate time.[9] While all budgeting systems contain characteristics derived from each of these three functions, most budgetary mechanisms are oriented primarily to only one aspect and subordinate, to a degree, the other two functions. Thus at different points in the evolution of governmental budget facilities, various orientations toward the budget process may prevail.

In the American case, early budgeting systems played essentially a control function. A relatively small number of budget officials supervised the distribution of money resulting from executive or legislative-initiated appropriations. With the advent of the New Deal and the consequent

---

[7] *Ibid.*, p. 388.

[8] Cited in *ibid.*, p. 396; see also *The Politics and Economics of Public Spending* (Washington, D.C.: Brookings Institution, 1968).

[9] Allen Schick, "The Road to P.P.B.: The Stages of Budget. Reform," *Public Administration Review*, Vol. 26 (December, 1966), p. 245.

expansion of government activities and growth in the size of government services, budgeting took on a management orientation. The predominant task became one of discovering the best instruments for applying public resources to specified projects and sectors. More recently, the orientation of budgeting systems has swung to the planning function. PPB is one of the more sophisticated manifestations of this new shift in budgeting emphasis [10] and reflects the growing importance of bureaucratic and technical values in policy processes. PPB is "predicated on the planning function yet it strives for a multi-purpose budget system that gives adequate attention to control and management aspects." [11]

PPB in the Defense Department

In 1961, Robert McNamara, then Secretary of Defense in the Kennedy administration, commissioned Charles J. Hitch to analyze systematically defense management procedures and future American defense requirements in the light of national priorities and objectives in order to formulate a five-year, program-oriented defense budget.[12] Hitch, aided by Alain Enthoven and other prominent DOD analysts, and using certain ideas from an earlier landmark study,[13] produced a significant report, the contents of which are less important to this chapter than the actual approach employed. Basically, the sequence of policy formulation involved in the new PPB approach, as it was first utilized in the DOD, can be characterized as follows: (1) establish the criteria of national interest in defense programs, (2) consider the military needs required to fulfill the national objectives in relation to costs, (3) determine alternate methods of achieving national defense goals, (4) examine and compare analytically these alternatives, (5) formulate an overall plan combining determined military force requirements and costs and project this plan into the future to assess foreseeable implications, (6) open the process to analysis by all interested parties, and (7) resolve and implement.[14]

The success enjoyed by the original DOD study prompted the Bureau of the Budget to require other federal agencies and departments to implement PPB systems. In the wide context of governmental policy formulation, the PPB approach can be summarized as follows: (1) identify na-

[10] *Ibid.*

[11] *Ibid.*, p. 246.

[12] Alain C. Enthoven and K. Wayne Smith, *How Much is Enough?: Shaping the Defense Program, 1961–1969* (New York: Harper and Row, Inc., 1971), p. 33.

[13] Charles J. Hitch and Roland N. McKean, *The Economics of Defense in the Nuclear Age* (Cambridge, Mass.: Harvard University Press, 1959).

[14] *Ibid.*, pp. 33–45.

tional goals and priorities, (2) relate these goals to specific programs (usually sub-divided into programs, sub-programs, and program elements as shown below), (3) relate the specific programs to resource requirements, and (4) relate the resource requirements to budget dollars.[15]

PPB, Levels of Policy Analysis

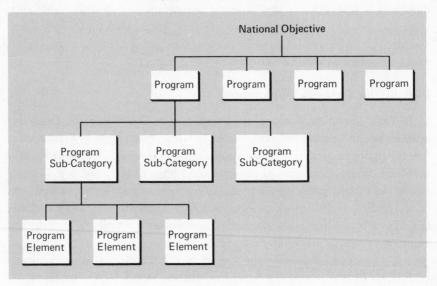

S. M. Greenhouse has described the PPB sequence in more elaborate terms. Basing his characterization on the assumption that the public policy process resembles the classic economic model of demand and supply (i.e., the main objective of government is to satisfy a demand for goods or services originating in the public, political sphere in the most efficient manner), while retaining popular technocratic criteria of policy evaluation, he describes PPB terminology and methodology in this way:

> The base is accountability in the citizen market. Therefore, the objectives must be product supply and distribution. Accordingly, programs are conceived and executed as production/distribution entities. Consequently, program alternatives are different production/distribution entities which might offer better benefit-cost ratios than existing ones. End products become the only items construed as outputs. And, progress is viewed and measured in terms of output/distribution timing and effectiveness vs. planned timing and effectiveness. Hence, the inputs are "whatever resources it takes to get the production-distribution job done."

As a result, alternative input-mixes become important comparison bases within any given program. Finally, systems analysis contributes diagnosis and appraisal to the whole.[16]

There is little doubt that this explanation of PPB is open to valid criticisms on several levels. Policies are not simply consumable products nor do all policies necessarily satisfy demands originating in the citizen market. However, the tone and terminology of the explanation are useful for a general understanding of the motives underlying PPB.

PPB: A Hypothetical Policy

To illustrate in more concrete terms the general application of PPB to policy-making, a simple and hypothetical policy problem concerning national defense stature will be considered. From collective national attitudes and the expert calculations of DOD and national security analysts, it is determined that a major policy goal of the United States should be to secure an effective second-strike nuclear capability that would deter any other nuclear power from launching an all-out attack on the continental United States. Having established this goal, various appropriate programs are considered: building an additional system of land-based ICBM's, producing an increased long-range bomber capacity, or launching a force of missile-carrying nuclear submarines. Each program alternative is examined in terms of the required expenditures and resources as well as its effectiveness in achieving the prescribed national goal. Accordingly, it is found that a land-based ICBM system, requiring an expenditure of $100 billion over seven years, would give the U.S. the second-strike capability of destroying 70 per cent of the attacking nation's industrial base and 55 per cent of its population. At a similar level of spending, the proposal for increased long-range bomber forces could only achieve potential destruction of 58 per cent of the enemy's industrial base and 40 per cent of its population. However, if the same resources were applied to the construction of a new fleet of nuclear submarines carrying atomic weapons, potential destruction levels could be expected to reach 78 per cent of the attacking nation's industrial base and 64 per cent of its population. If the value imputed to high levels of potential second-strike destruction capabilities outweighed other considerations in the minds of policy-makers, the third alternative would be preferred. The chosen program is then related in detail to budgetary guidelines, and

[16] "The Planning-Programming-Budgeting System: Rationale, Language and Idea-Relationships," *Public Administration Review*, Vol. 26 (December, 1966), pp. 272–77.

appropriate sub-programs and projects are considered. Ultimately a comprehensive policy proposal designed to accomplish the prescribed national objective in the most effective manner possible and within projected budgetary limitations is completed and submitted to the proper government officials or bodies for final approval and implementation.

Turning to a non-military example, PPBS analysis can be shown to be valuable in the organization of an agency such as the federal Post Office. The national objective of the postal department, to provide an efficient mail collection and delivery service, can be related to several program areas in the following way:

National Objective

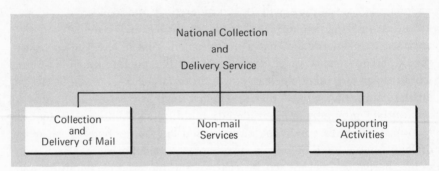

In turn, each program category can be further sub-divided into several sub-categories, shown on the opposite page.[17]

At each program sub-category level (and at any further levels of subdivision), alternative methods of achieving the prescribed goal or function are examined and compared using various analytical criteria such as cost/benefit or cost/effectiveness evaluations. Findings are related to budgetary limitations and available resources, and decisions are made concerning the most appropriate procedures to follow in the light of these analyses. In the process, a comprehensive structural-budgetary system geared to the prescribed national objective is erected.

Perhaps the most lucid evaluation of the impact of PPB on the public policy process is presented by Enthoven and Smith. Referring to its effects on defense policy formulation (but equally applicable to the role of PPB in other policy areas), they conclude:

[17] H. N. Hinrichs and G. M. Yaylor, *Program Budgeting and Benefit-Cost Analysis* (Pacific Palisades, Calif.: Goodyear Publishing Co., 1969).

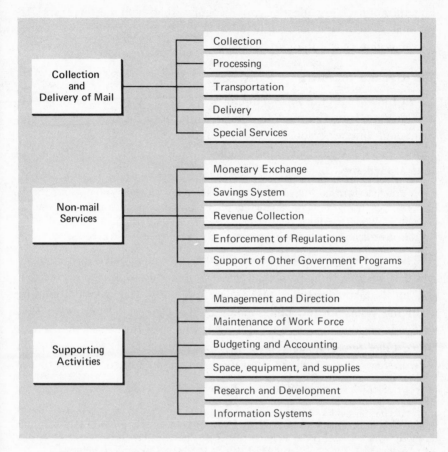

P.P.B. never became a closed, rigid, or perfected management system. Indeed, in its broadest sense, it was less a management system than a philosophy of management—a philosophy that, we believe, helped to channel the initiative, imagination, dedication, hard work, and judgement of the military and civilian leaders in D.O.D. along more rational and objective lines than previously.[18]

It is advisable to look critically at such evidence, most of it from advocates of the "system approach." Among the major criticisms is the tendency to assume that "human and organizational distortions can be eliminated by rationalized systems."[19] There is a certain abstractness about the entire approach, which tends to ignore or wish away 'natural laws' involving human behavior. One need not be an advocate of the radical

[18] Enthoven and Smith, *op. cit.*, p. 47.
[19] *Cf.* Jean A. Millar, "Selective Adaption," *Policy Sciences,* Vol. 3 (July, 1972), pp. 125–35.

humanization of organizations to recognize that such personal and 'irrational' ingredients must be included in the designing of policy. Critics also maintain that criteria of economy and efficiency were not met.[20]

The Decline of PPBS

On June 21, 1971, a memorandum was sent to all federal departments and agencies from George P. S. Shultz, Director of the Office of Management and Budget prior to the annual budgetary cycle. In restrained terms, the OMB memorandum announced the demise of PPB in the federal civil service:

> Agencies are no longer required to submit with their submissions the multi-year program and financing plans, program memoranda and special analytical studies . . . or schedules . . . that reconcile information classified according to their program and appropriation structures.[21]

The reasons for the failure of PPB at the federal level are complex but it is possible to make several general observations on the events that led to its abandonment.[22] As a new analytical framework attending changing priorities and philosophies in the Defense Department, PPB enjoyed considerable success. However, when the Bureau of the Budget urged other departments and agencies to emulate DOD by adopting its PPB system almost without alteration, problems ensued. Although the

[20] Cf. S. Melman, *Permanent War Economy* (New York: Simon and Schuster, 1974).

[21] As cited in Schick, "A Death in the Bureaucracy: The Demise of Federal PPB," *Public Administration Review,* Vol. 33 (March/April 1973), p. 146. PPB's decline is nicely symbolized by the difference in tone between this article and an earlier one by the same author, "The Road to PPB: the Stages of Budget Reform," *op. cit.*

[22] Some government officials, it should be said, maintain that PPB has not been abandoned. Note, for example, the testimony of Caspar Weinberger (then Deputy Director of the Office of Management and Budget) before the Senate Joint Committee on Congressional Operations:

Chairman Brooks: OMB spokesmen have stated recently, as I understand, that formal elements of the Program Planning Budget System instituted some years ago have been abandoned. Does OMB now have a new systems concept to substitute? . . .

Mr. Weinberger: No, sir. I don't believe it's accurate to say the Program Planning Budget System has been abandoned. As I understand the Program Budgeting System, it is a system which, rather than relying upon individual line items, attempts to present to the Congress the request of the President for the total costs of administering various programs . . .

Viewed in this way, the Program Budget System is still very much alive, and in use. We are making refinements and improvements to it, but we have not abandoned it. There have been changes in some of the very specific kinds of forms that previously were requested of various agencies. I don't think it would be accurate to say that the system has been abandoned or a new system substituted for it. (*Hearings,* March 1, 1972, p. 27).

terminology and procedures suited to DOD experience were not necessarily appropriate to the operations of other departments, little attempt was made (by BOB especially) to assess the different requirements of the other agencies and adjust the Defense Department's PPB system according to these needs. As a result, many departmental budget officials were confronted with a foreign analytical framework that they were required to superimpose upon the established budgetary processes and activities of their department. Resentment apparently ran high and enthusiasm for budget reform was restrained. Although most departments eventually did conform to PPB procedures, their commitment to PPB was apparently often merely perfunctory.

Perhaps the most basic problem that led to PPB's demise was the clash of its essentially analytical nature with the entrenched, anti-analytical assumptions of existing budgetary procedures.

> Budgeting is the routinization of public choice by means of standardized procedures, timetables, classifications, and rules. PPB failed because it did not penetrate the vital routines of putting together and justifying a budget. Always separate but never equal, the analyst had little influence over the form or content of the budget.[23]

> PPB failed to penetrate because the budgeters didn't let it in and the PPB'ers didn't know how to break down the resistance.[24]

To be sure, PPB did pose certain threats to incrementalists in the budgetary process. A thoroughgoing implementation of rationalist planning, programming, and budgeting systems would inevitably lead to the termination of some "low-yield" projects and would bring decision-makers and bureaucrats into conflict with each other over the definition of program objectives and purposes.[25] PPB would provide government critics with a new tool for assessing the costs and benefits of federal programs while expanding the range of program alternatives that must be considered by a budget official. In an environment such as a bureaucracy (especially a budget bureaucracy) where conflict situations are avoided whenever possible and where most analytical exercises are geared toward justifying existing programs and continuing existing expenditure patterns, the inquisitive and analytical nature of PPB may easily be perceived to be a threat.

[23] Schick, *ibid.*, p. 147.
[24] *Ibid.*, p. 149.
[25] *Ibid.*

PPB At the State and Local Level

By 1968, some 28 states and 60 local government agencies had indicated they were moving toward PPB systems. A brief review of some of their experiences follows.[26] Apparently, PPB at the state level has been only partially successful. As Allen Schick concludes (1971) "PPB, in most states has not advanced beyond 'first steps' and as states acquire more experience with PPB, they do not necessarily get better results."[27] Again, "New York was the first state to adopt PPB and the first to discard it."[28] After a favorable initial status, PPB specialists were gradually shunted off from the operating budget agencies. Several causes exist. Pre-planning for PPB was apparently minimal or non-existent; the objectives of the system were not made clear to other units; bureaucratic rivalries, particularly between PPB and the Office for Regional Development and the state Budget Division; the continued separation of program and financial decisions; and tensions between the values and assumptions of PPB advocates and the traditional agencies were among them.[29]

At the local level, experience with PPB has been similarly mixed. In 1968, a survey indicated that some 73 local governments had decided *not* to install the system, mainly because of lack of resources or authority.[30] One example of a pioneering effort to use PPB is Fairfax County.[31] After some unsuccessful experience with performance budgeting, the County turned to PPB. Problems of the ongoing performance budgeting system included the inability of departments to quantify units of work; the fact that the data submitted by operating agencies were usually only rough estimates of the work units needed for performance budgeting; and finally, the lack of cooperation from department heads who remained unconvinced of the program's utility.[32] In 1967, a program budget was introduced, consisting of all the activities performed by the county government and, following the federal model, describing the goals, measure-

[26] State–Local Finances Survey. "Implementing PPB in State, City, and County: A Report on the 5-5-5 Project" (Washington, D. C.: George Washington University, 1969), p. 140.
[27] *Budget Innovation in the States* (Washington, D. C.: Brookings Institution, 1971), p. 117.
[28] *Ibid.*
[29] *Ibid.*
[30] *Ibid.,* p. 140.
[31] Robert A. Luther, "PPBS in Fairfax County" in Fremont J. Lyden and E. G. Miller, eds., *Planning-Programming-Budgeting: A Systems Approach to Management* (Chicago: Markham Publishing Co., 1972), pp. 345–57.
[32] *Ibid.,* pp. 347–48.

ment indexes, and trends in each program sector. Some 100 such programs were defined and the cost estimates of each were determined.

Despite the general acceptance of the introductory step, PPB encountered several problems. Not only was there considerable uncertainty about the exact nature of the system, but there was no existing model in a county government which could provide guidelines. Plans were made to introduce the system, nevertheless, gradually and in orderly, planned sequences. Special attention was given to the three problems mentioned with performance budgeting, particularly regarding the need to convince those involved that departments must work together on a single program. Despite these efforts, "some department heads . . . demonstrated a general apathy or possible fear of the approaching program." [33] Inability to understand the very concept of PPB was apparent in the submissions of "administration" or personnel needs as "programs." Related problems involved paring down and synthesizing programs submitted by individual departments, the tracing of cost requirements, including the partial assignment of personnel costs to agencies collaborating in several programs; and the quantification of such intangible objectives as public confidence in, for example, the judicial system and of such variables as the time required between filing of a case and its ultimate reconciliation.

Such problems, many of which are cited by all levels of government, suggest why some of the initial high expectations of PPB advocates have been modified considerably by experience. An essential problem is the difficulty of quantifying intrinsically subjective program objectives and a certain naivete which seems to characterize even hard-headed managerial types. The mystique of systems theory and computer technology often aggravated such tendencies.

PPB in Two Cities

The experience of cities with PPB reveals a mixture of enthusiasm and disenchantment similar to that existing at other levels of government. In New Haven, for example, as early as September 1968, the Director of Administration indicated to the George Washington survey that the system was being abandoned, or more precisely that "nothing beyond preliminary planning was ever achieved." [34] Difficulties in retaining neces-

---

[33] *Ibid.*, p. 351.
[34] State–Local Finances Project, *PPB Pilot Project Reports* (Washington, D. C.: George Washington University, 1969), p. 141.

sary personnel, opposition of the city council, and racial conflicts in New Haven were among the problems cited.[35]

Detroit, on the other hand, expressed a restrained optimism about the progress of their program by 1968. As in Fairfax County, a major problem was the lack of a tested model of effective cost-benefit and program analyses in other cities. The kinds of data required for the system were not always available, especially regarding the benefits accruing to citizens from governmental programs.[36] Another comment which appears in other evaluations of PPB is that it is useful to view the system less as a completely new approach than as the conscious use of a variety of techniques to analyze the basis of a program, from every standpoint.

Moreover, while "the acceptance of the PPBs philosophy intellectually is a simple matter, to apply its concepts to every-day operations is vastly complex." [37] In Detroit, as in some other jurisdictions, training programs were set up, often involving local universities and federal and foundation grants. A pilot study was undertaken, consisting of a neighborhood center recreation program. Attempts were made to isolate and weigh the payoff from the program in terms of its favorable impact upon "ghetto dwellers." Some 30 meetings were held between a consultant and the relevant budget and operating officials. Important constraints soon developed, essentially regarding the need to provide immediate recreational services which abrogated the time schedule worked out for introducing the system. An "overwhelming" constraint proved to be the unexpected complexity of the problem, which required that its component parts be divided into many subprograms, with new time schedules.[38] Although the report concludes that "some progress was made," on the whole, the evaluation is quite restrained, as suggested by its weak concluding recommendation, "PPB is not a panacea, but no jurisdiction should fail to explore its concepts." [39]

In part, the advent of the Nixon administration seemed to have heralded a return to more traditional management emphases in the budgetary process as opposed to the analytical planning and programming emphasis of PPB. In 1970 the Bureau of the Budget was transformed into the Office of Management and Budget, responsible for the coordination of federal programs. The programming function was separated en-

---

[35] *Ibid.*, pp. 141–42.
[36] *Ibid.*, p. 130.
[37] *Ibid.*, p. 133
[38] *Ibid.*, p. 134.
[39] *Ibid.*, p. 138.

tirely from the budgetary mechanism and placed largely under the auspices of a new Domestic Council. Effectively, therefore, organizational authority over the processes of program management and budgeting was divided and the rationalist, integrationist approach of PPB was discarded.

The Uses of Social Indicators

A related instrument of policy-making involves a focus upon the *social* objectives of government, including the assignment of weights to such objectives in a self-conscious attempt to achieve more precise and rational planning. Largely as a result of consumer and conservationist pressures, administration's concern is rapidly trancending the traditional limits of quantitative economic considerations. Although per capita income, employment levels, and GNP statistics remain central questions, policy-makers are now concerned with less defined, qualitative aspects of social development. Here again, the urban crisis and Vietnam, as well as the contemporary world energy crisis, have brought a new questioning of established national priorities such as economic growth and increased consumer indulgence. Policy-makers, as a result, are increasingly challenged by questions of social alienation, civil rights, health care, preservation of the environment, and related issues for which traditional economic criteria are inadequate or inappropriate:

> This imbalance in the supply of information on public problems is due in large part to the fact that the normal routines of government demand a considerable amount of information on how much a government spends for each purpose, on what types of resources it uses, and on the activities it undertakes, whereas there is no routine requirement for information on national problems or achievements. . . . Governments thus produce information about their own activities as a by-product of everyday operations, but there is no such automatic provision of information about society's problems, or about whether we are making any progress in dealing with them.[40]

Or, in words of Raymond Bauer, "For many of the important topics on which social critics blithely pass judgement, and on which policies are made, there are no yard-sticks by which to know if things are getting better or worse."[41]

[40] Mancur Olson, "New Problems for Social Policy: The Rationale of Social Indicators and Social Reporting," *International Institute for Labour Studies Bulletin*, Vol. 7 (June, 1970), p. 26.
[41] Raymond A. Bauer, *Social Indicators* (Cambridge, Mass.: M.I.T. Press, 1967), p. 20.

In response to this apparent dearth of social information, a movement has emerged in academic circles and among some policy-makers in government to develop more valid and comprehensive "social indicators" or social intelligence variables to provide data relevant to current and future social problems. In effect, the movement seeks to quantify *qualitative* social considerations and develop more sophisticated and detailed methods of evaluating various societal characteristics so that more effective policies can be formulated to meet the demands for change among articulate sectors of the public.

The data requirements to which the "social indicators" approach is geared include demands for: (1) a closer specification of the objectives of public policy, (2) concepts and methods related to data on perceptions and attitudes, (3) data covering a wider range of human concerns, (4) more comprehensive models which take into account social interrelationships, and (5) more complete local, regional, and national demographic statistics. Typically, such data may take the form of quantitative social indices, measurements of subjective preferences, survey analyses, statistical breakdowns, or trend measurements.

To illustrate some of the types of variables upon which considerable emphasis is now being placed, the following partial list of "livability" indicators (i.e., variables outlining the degree to which an individual can realize his goals as a human being in the environment in which he lives) are presented:

Environmental Factors

   Possible Indicators
      air pollution index
      respiratory disease rates
      noise decibel readings
      water pollution index
      hours of sunshine
      single-owner housing

Security Factors

   Possible Indicators
      crime rates
      divorce rates
      accidental death rate
      fire insurance rates
      suicide rates
      percentage of population in mental hospitals
      unemployment rates

Self-Realization Factors

Possible Indicators
percentage enrolled in educational institutions
incidence of parks usage
percentage with "feeling of belonging"
car ownership per capita
telephones per capita
average time devoted to recreation per capita

Participation Factors

Possible Indicators
percentage of citizens on voters' list
percentage of citizens voting in civic elections
juvenile delinquency rates
percentage in community organizations
group membership rates

Basic Living Standard Factors

Possible Indicators
infant morality rates
life expectancy rates
per capita income
cost of housing index
cost of living index
welfare rate

The extent to which such factors can be specified and compared across time is apparent in *Social Indicators, 1973,* produced by the federal government's Office of Management and Budget. In such data, we find for example, that between 1940 and 1972 college-educated people increased from 5.8 to 19 per cent of those in the 25 to 29 age group; that the gap between earnings for males and females did not narrow between 1956–1971; that fully 87 per cent of the people drove to work in 1970, despite efforts to improve urban mass transit systems; that the proportions of households owning television swelled from only 9 per cent in 1950 to 96 per cent in 1972; and that life expectancy for the typical American is now 71 years, almost 22 years higher than at the beginning of the century, but non-whites are likely to die ten years earlier than whites.

Many of these facts are not new but their use and expansion as a part of contemporary policy-making is a new phenomenon. Analysts seek to determine the interrelations among indicators, their relative weights and significance with a view toward building data banks and models of social change. Such data must of course be evaluated with care to minimize errors derived from such problems as inaccuracy, conflict, and excessive subjectivity.[42]

In the face of growing reliance on statistical data for the definition and resolution of policy problems, such limitations should be kept in mind. Information, as such, can only be an analytical tool, rather than an end in itself. The search for more accurate and sophisticated social data is (or should be) open-ended and self-perpetuating. Accordingly, unless the policy-maker is fully committed to inaction, he must at some point decide that he has enough information to resolve a given policy issue. In many cases, of course, the pressure of events will force him into such a decision. He must realize that the value and validity of information is not absolute, and that other kinds of premises must also enter the deciding process. In effect,

> Analytical sophistication . . . [does] not provide all the necessary materials for charting the course of change. . . . The answers to informational questions rarely can be better than the sense of the questions or the reliability of the source of information.[43]

On the other hand, adequate policy-making obviously cannot occur without accurate and comprehensive information.

A related problem, mentioned elsewhere but worth repeating here, is that most officials do not control their agenda or the policy issues that arise. More often, they are confronted by discrete, unrelated issues that sometimes arise unexpectedly and demand solution without adequate time to consider several alternatives or to bring together enough information to make an optimal decision. A current example is the extent to which political leaders of the Western countries are unable to control inflationary rises in food prices because such are due to world conditions beyond the control of any given political system. The problem faced by such countries regarding oil from the Middle East is a similar example. As Herbert Simon put it, administrators "satisfice" rather than maximize. Almost without exception, they complain of the lack of time for systematic analysis and preparation for handling long-run issues. Too often, they are concerned with "putting out fires."

[42] Bauer, op. cit., p. 80.
[43] E. D. Sheldon and W. E. Moore (eds.), Indicators of Social Change (New York: Russell Sage Foundation, 1968), p. 23.

Technological Forecasting

Another related instrument of some utility for policy determination is technological forecasting which seems somewhat less concerned with the social consequences of change than with predicting the scope and direction of technological innovation.

> Technological forecasting is the probabilistic assessment, on a relatively high confidence level, of future technology transfer. Exploratory technological forecasting starts from today's assured base of knowledge and is oriented towards the future, while normative technological forecasting first assesses future goals, needs, desires, missions, etc. and works backwards to the present. The subject of both types is a dynamic picture of a technology transfer process. Technological forecasting may be aided by anticipation and may "harden" to prediction.[44]

Erich Jantsch's definition and description of technological forecasting, while no doubt accurate, appears somewhat pedantic and not altogether useful to the student of policy-making. The term "technological forecasting" would seem to be one of the many manufactured phrases of technocratic thinking intended to describe a concept that is not necessarily complicated nor fraught with deep technical hazards in the first place. At least in its most basic sense, technological forecasting simply involves efforts to predict the nature and probable impact of the growth in technology on given social phenomena. Various methods of technological forecasting and related evaluations of the impact of technical innovation have become increasingly necessary, especially in the worlds of business and government, so that policy-makers or planners may judge the future ramifications of scientific and technical change upon existing policies, production methods, organizational structures, etc., and perhaps of greater importance, allow policy-makers to design suitable approaches and concepts for future policy implementation.

As an example, consider a situation where a business manager is presented by his research staff with an attractive idea for an entirely new product. Before committing the company's resources to the production of that commodity, the manager must pose a series of questions:

> How long will it take to have the product ready for the market? How big is the market now, and, more importantly, in the future? What is the product's expected life before it has to be replaced or substantially

[44] Erich Jantsch, *Technological Forecasting in Perspective* (Paris: Organization for Economic Co-operation and Development, 1967), p. 15.

modified? Can it be improved to increase its potential? Will other profitable developments spin off it? How soon will other firms take up the idea? Will they leap-frog over it to the next development stage? What are the labor and capital requirements and how will they arise, slowly or suddenly, fairly soon or two years or ten years hence? [45]

All of these questions and their answers form the technological forecast for the proposed product.

Transposing these issues into the public sector of policy-making, one is confronted with similar questions: Given a proposed policy that has been made practicable by a technological innovation, how long will it take for the policy to produce the desired results following implementation in the public sector? For what period of time will the policy be effective and when will a subsequent policy attuned to future problems need to be formulated? What will be the side benefits or consequences of the policy and how many people will be affected, positively or adversely, by the various programs stemming from the policy? What are the resource requirements, both at present and in the foreseeable future, for effective implementation of the policy? These and other problems are the concerns of technological forecasters in government policy-making. [46]

In effect, both of the preceding examples belong to the realm of exploratory technological forecasting. The exercise of predicting the impact and success that a product or a policy may have in advance of its introduction into the "real world" assumes a definable past and present and an uncertain future. The forecaster seeks to foresee future developments by projecting analytically determined past and present trends forward in time, considering a sufficient number of variables so as to minimize the possibility of unanticipated consequences. Interestingly the technological forecaster can also *reverse* the process. By positing a future social condition or state of development, he can outline the steps, policies, or initiatives required to insure the achievement of the desired condition in the prescribed period of time. For example, President Kennedy's declaration in the early 1960's that America *should* adopt as an important national goal the landing of American astronauts on the moon before 1970 set in motion an intense process of technological innovation. At the time of the announcement, much of the engineering ability and scientific knowledge necessary for the achievement of such a feat did not

---

[45] Earl Victor, "Technological Forecasting," *The Economist* (London, 1968), p. 2.

[46] What impresses one here is the extent to which administrators necessarily live in a contingent universe. This requires in turn a fairly high tolerance for ambiguity, a characteristic that is not usually thought to be highly developed among individuals who are drawn into bureaucratic work mileaux.

exist. NASA planners were required to produce a detailed program of development and experimentation that would make Kennedy's objective feasible both in theoretical and practical terms within the given period of time. The resulting Mercury, Gemini, and Apollo space programs were essentially stepping-stones toward the prescribed goal. In crude terms, the present was engineered to fit the future. This type of exercise belongs to the category of normative technological forecasting.

In simplest terms, the methods of exploratory and normative technological forecasting can be diagramatically represented as follows:

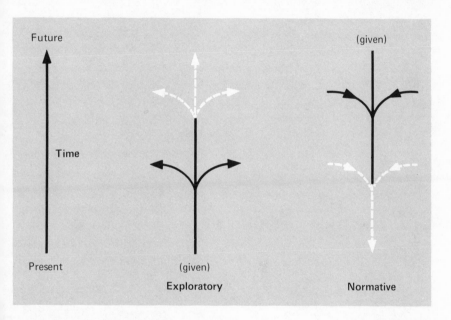

Objections are occasionally raised concerning certain implications of normative technological forecasts. Some observers feel that the normative approach limits future freedom of choice by setting the course of development in advance. In extreme cases the spectre of social engineering à la Brave New World is raised by those critics who claim that man is becoming a slave of his analytical tools rather than their master. Whatever the case may be, it is clear that orderly social development and especially the control of the environment require rational planning of some sort. The methods of technological forecasting—exploratory or normative—provide one facet of such planning.

II

COMMUNITY PARTICIPATION AND ORGANIZATIONAL THEORY

6

Community Participation and Citizen Organization

Few issues in public administration—or, for that matter, in the whole field of political inquiry—have generated as much recent interest and speculation as community organization and citizen participation. Social scientists have identified several developments in social organization that may be broadly characterized as a pervasive initiative toward local control and involvement in public policy-making. On many levels, the general public is becoming more aware of pressing social problems and is increasingly critical of governmental agencies, particularly those dealing with urban-oriented problems. The need for greater sensitivity to citizens' requests for consultation and participation is a central theme. Early rhetoric of "power to the people" has come to be expressed in terms of citizen action, neighborhood organization, and community development.

This chapter outlines several of the ideas and structures involved in theories of community organization and participation in the light of their saliency for contemporary public administration. In a somewhat more abstract context we will assess the significance of the thrust toward local control and involvement as it relates to the exercise of power, while questioning whether such a trend exists today on any but a purely symbolic level.

ALTERNATIVE STRATEGIES FOR MODIFYING BUREAUCRACY

It may be useful, despite the risk of oversimplification, to begin with a rough typology of strategies suggested by those who have challenged bureaucracy's role *vis-à-vis* the public.[1] The context in which such alternatives have been advanced includes the fact that bureaucracies consist mainly of middle-class individuals, who usually enjoy considerably more education, expertise, and security than the clientele with whom they deal. There are of course many exceptions to this generalization, but if one thinks in terms of sheer numbers, as contrasted with the highly advantaged members of producer and professional groups, it is clear that the vast majority of clients are disadvantaged when compared with their official servants. It is also noteworthy that, as a group, bureaucrats tend to share the dominant conservative values of American society, insofar as attitudes toward political liberties and the role of government are concerned. Bureaucrats are even more conservative along those lines than their political masters in the legislatures.[2] Thus it is probably correct to say that—ideologically and in terms of political resources—officials and most of their clients are at least potential enemies.

In this context, the following modifications of existing bureaucratic structure have been suggested as a means of making governmental systems more responsive.

The End of Bureaucracy: Utopia, Inc.

Beginning at the extreme end of the spectrum, there have been some arguments that bureaucracy as a system must be abolished in favor of open arrangements whereby individuals would carry out their tasks in a milieu where hierarchy, specialization, control, close supervision, recruitment by universalistic, skill-oriented criteria, quasi-permanent career identification, and the like would disappear.[3] This somewhat romantic

[1] For cross-national evidence regarding the rise of consumer and protest types of groups, see Robert Presthus (ed.), "Interest Groups in International Perspective," *Annals of American Academy of Political and Social Science,* Vol. 413, 1974; for a valuable survey of official–client relationships, from which much of this section is drawn, see Elihu Katz and B. Danet, *Bureaucracy and the Public* (New York: Basic Books, Inc., 1973).

[2] For evidence see Robert Presthus, *Elites in the Policy Process* (New York: Cambridge University Press, 1974), Chaps. 11 and 12, which indicate that bureaucrats tend to rank low on both political and economic liberalism, as measured by widely used indexes.

[3] For a representative interpretation, see Warren Bennis and Philip Slater, *The Temporary Society* (New York: Harper Colophon Books, 1968). For a similarly utopian thesis, see Frank Marini (ed.), *Toward a New Public Administration* (Scranton, Pa.: Chandler Publishing Co., 1971).

view tends, however, to neglect the hard fact that large-scale operations require many of the attributes now seen in many bureaucratic structures. In sociological terms, such characteristics are *functionally necessary* if organizations and society are to achieve their goals. No one doubts that such imperatives are sometimes distorted, that bureaucratic values are displaced to serve the personal ends of officials and their clientele groups,[4] but in operational terms of getting the job done, many of them are essential. As Dwight Waldo says, "I deeply suspect some of the projections of our organizations in the dawning post-industrial world: one gets up in the morning and decides whether he will work, what organization, if any, he will work in, and whether he will play the role of engineer, agronomist, budgeteer, oculist, or whatever, what project he will work on, with whom and to what end. . . . in sober fact I hope I never have to fly with an airline, have surgery in a hospital, or even stay in a hotel, run in the new 'ideal' style pictured in some of the literature." [5]

Understandably, much of the criticism of bureaucracy and government tends to include a utopian component which feeds nicely upon the frustrations that many citizens feel in dealing with bureaucracy in government. One example which has generated considerable heat is the role of the Interstate Commerce Commission in regulating the movers of household effects. The Commission has no jurisdiction over delay, for example, and clients who appeal for redress on this ground are doubly disenchanted to receive letters such as the following, "This Commission has no jurisdiction over claims for delay, however, and if you are unable to reach a satisfactory agreement with the carrier your recourse is to an appropriate civil court . . ." [6] Another letter punctuates what is surely a common appreciation, "Dear Senator Magnuson, A year has now passed since my experience with interstate movers . . . I have concluded that: Government is decidedly pro-industry and contra-citizenry. . . .   The ICC in my case was useless, but they write lovely letters." [7]

Despite such experiences, it is doubtful that regulation and service would be better *without* the Commission. This is hardly high praise, but it is difficult to conceive a situation in which bureaucratic structure and values would not be *required* when certain conditions of size, complexity,

---

[4] Some social activists, for example, argue that the very concept of "citizen participation" has been co-opted and used by the bureaucracy as a weapon against elected members of the political elites—cf. Daniel Moynihan, *Maximum Feasible Misunderstanding* (New York: Free Press, 1970).

[5] *Public Administration in A Time of Turbulence* (Scranton, Pa.: Chandler Publishing Co., 1971), pp. 281–82.

[6] Cited in Robert Fellmuth, "Home Moving," in *The Interstate Commerce Commission* (New York: Grossman Publishing Co., 1970).

[7] *Ibid.*

and the need for some continuity exist. In this sense, the "end of bureaucracy" alternative may properly be called utopian, a reflection of a long tradition of philosophic rejection of the complexities of modern industrial life.

Counter-organization

In an imperfect world, this strategy has much to commend it, and indeed, it can be argued that it is precisely the failure to organize that results in the disadvantaged position of consumer, welfare, and poor groups. Political elites, for very good functional as well as political reasons, tend to respond only to *collective* representations. Functionally, as one hears again and again,[8] they declare, "We cannot handle multitudes of uncoordinated claims." Indeed, perhaps the foremost value they attach to organized groups is the "labor-saving" role whereby groups reconcile and articulate the varied and sometimes opposing claims of their constituents and present a firm policy position to legislators and officials. Politically, of course, the voice of organized groups is loudest because of their potential electoral power. These characteristics of the present system of interest group politics are obvious but nonetheless critical.

The success of labor unions and professional associations in securing highly advantaged conditions of work is often less a function of their intrinsic social value than of the monopoly which they are able to exercise over their occupational sector. As Max Weber shows, the primary motivation of such associations is to achieve a monopoly of control over the conditions of participation in their respective spheres.[9] Other ends are also sought, but this truism underscores the efficacy of counter-organization. As shown elsewhere, the creation of organizations has provided welfare recipients the resources required for judicial tests of bureaucratic and legislative actions which unorganized individuals in their circumstances could rarely achieve.[10]

The major problem with the strategy of counter-organization is that

[8] That is, in personal interviews with some 500 American and Canadian legislators (1968–72); see Presthus, *Elites in the Policy Process, op. cit.*, p. 56.

[9] *Economy and Society,* edited by G. Roth and C. Wittich (New York: Bedminster Press, 1968) Vol. 1, p. 342.

[10] See, among others, Joseph Helfgot, "Professional Reform Organizations: Symbolic Representation of the Poor," *American Sociological Review,* Vol. 39 (August, 1974), pp. 475–91; Arthur Matthews, Jr., and Jonathan Weiss, "What Can Be Done: A Neighborhood Lawyer's Credo," *Boston University Law Review,* Vol. 4 (1967), pp. 231–43.

individuals remain unorganized for very precise, pervasive, and often irremedial reasons, the essence of which is their lack of political resources which prevents them from participating actively in the political system. Participation requires considerable amounts of time, interest, money, education, and political sophistication. Indeed, it is instructive that even these attributes are a necessary but not a sufficient cause of participation. Regarding money, for example, Philip Shrag shows that legal costs mean that it may take $1,000 for each side to push through litigation over a $50 case.[11] Scott Fitzgerald once noted that "the rich are different from you and me." But it is often forgotten that the poor are equally different. As Michael Harrington says, "There is, in a sense, a personality of poverty . . . the other Americans feel differently than the rest of the nation. They tend to be hopeless and passive, yet prone to bursts of violence; they are lonely and isolated, often rigid and hostile." [12] Here again is a condition that exhortations to restructure society and dismember bureaucracies can have little effect upon. It can be changed only at great cost and time by those who suffer from it.

Nor are officials always constrained to help. As Sjoberg, Brymer, and Farris found,

> Client-centered bureaucracies often find it advantageous to avoid lower-class clients who are likely to handicap the organization in the attainment of its goals. . . . The Federal Job Corps program has been viewed as one means for alleviating the unemployment problem among youths especially those in the lower class. This program has sought to train disadvantaged youth in various occupational skills. The success of the Job Corps is apparently to be evaluated according to the number of trainees who enter the industrial labor force. Consequently, the organization has sought to select those youths who have internalized some of the middle-class norms of upward mobility and who are likely to succeed in the occupational system.[13]

Regulation as a Strategy

Some observers have advocated the introduction of new forms of independent regulatory agents to intercede between bureaucracies and their clients. The most widely known of such innovations, of course, is the Ombudsman, an official whose role is to adjudicate and ease disruptions between individual citizens and government agencies. Since this

[11] "Consumer Rights," *Columbia Forum*, Vol. 13 (Summer, 1970), p. 7.
[12] *The Other America* (New York: The Macmillan Co., 1970).
[13] "Bureaucracy and the Lower Class," *Sociology and Social Research*, Vol. 50 (1966).

role is discussed elsewhere, we shall pass along to other, more traditional
forms of regulation, including the independent regulatory commissions.
Their record is not generally inspiring insofar as achieving the ends
sought by contemporary critics of bureaucracy. With many exceptions,
they tend to become captives of the highly organized groups whose
activities they putatively govern. Although they were initially created to
relieve the courts of the burden of handling great numbers of cases in
areas involving considerable technical complexity and expertise, they
have generally failed to provide the required dispatch. Beyond this,
they have often been used politically, as a reward for deserving supporters of the president; the commissioners who are charged with the
ultimate responsibility for their operations are only infrequently selected
on the basis of intimate knowledge of the economic sector involved.[14]
Insofar as their staffs are concerned, they sometimes become training
grounds for industry, especially for young lawyers in the income tax and
securities areas.[15] Although some observers argue that the Commissions
should reflect the regulatory preferences of the president, others indicate that they have been too much subject to the chief executive's will.
Some iconoclasts have called for their abolition, but here again, it is
doubtful that no regulation would be any better than the imperfect
system which now exists. Certainly, in an area like the stock market,
the consumer now receives considerably more protection than he did
in the period before the Securities and Exchange Commission came upon
the scene. No doubt, better regulation could be achieved if the Commissions were given more adequate budgets and more positive support
by Congress and the president, but the record indicates that Congress
is not among the most committed supporters of regulation and, indeed,
that its members often bring pressure upon the commissions to provide
special dispensations for their clients.[16]

Such conditions reflect certain underlying values and assumptions that
directly affect regulatory policy. One is that American political elites do
not believe in regulation by government, except as a minimal, essentially
post hoc activity. *Self-regulation* by industry and other institutional sectors is a more honorific norm in our political economy. As a result, the
regulatory commissions have no strong normative or philosophic legitimation to undergird their activities. The nation has achieved its exceptional

---

14 For documentation, see the previous edition of this book, Chaps. 25, 26, and 27.
15 See, for example, Frank V. Fowlkes, "Congress Prods SEC to get Firmer Grip
on Nation's Securities Industry," *National Journal*, Vol. 3 (February 20, 1971), pp.
387–88.
16 *Ibid.*, pp. 376–77.

productivity and generally high standards of living by a mixture of free enterprise and government assistance which has encouraged considerable personal initiative. The costs obviously have been high, but political elites, who are among the primary beneficiaries of the system, are generally unlikely to advocate measures that seem contrary to this benchmark norm.

As noted later, judicial review may be defined as a means of regulating administrative performance, but here again certain hard facts dampen its efficacy. As L. Fuller says, the relatively small volume of judicial review cases in federal courts suggests that *willingness* and *financial ability* do not often coincide.[17] Moreover, given the huge financial stakes involved, licensees of several kinds—television stations, for example—are reluctant to run the risks of challenging administrative decisions. One scholar concludes that "a kind of administrative blackmail extorts away the will to use the courts."[18] Perhaps the best-known student of administrative law, Kenneth Culp Davis, has shown that the Immigration and Naturalization Service in handling some 700,000 cases *annually* relies upon dubiously valid "technical operations" when exercising its powers.[19] This system, he says, is "unjust, illegal, and inexcusable."[20] As Walter Gellhorn concludes, "When all the advantages of judicial review have been taken into proper account, however, realists will still recognize that the possessors of legal rights cannot or will not always defend them."[21] Strain, time, knowledge, and money are the major barriers. It seems we must look elsewhere for pragmatic solutions.

Strategies for Improving Bureaucratic Responsiveness

The most practicable alternative seems to be one that attempts through the resocialization and restructuring of both bureaucrats and clients to achieve a more responsive and representative bureaucracy. Insofar as disadvantaged clients are concerned, this is essentially a matter of education and, ultimately, organization. Individuals can be instructed in their rights *vis-à-vis* government, both as consumers and citizens. The creation of neighborhood groups probably falls in this category, although it is also

---

[17] *The Morality of Law* (New Haven, Conn.: Yale University Press, 1969), p. 81, italics added. Cited in Walter Gellhorn, *When Americans Complain: Governmental Grievances Procedures* (Cambridge, Mass.: Harvard University Press, 1966).

[18] D. H. Nelson, "Administrative Blackmail: The Remission of Penalties," *Western Political Quarterly*, Vol. 4 (1951), p. 610.

[19] *Administrative Law Treatise*, Supplement, 1965, 4.16, pp. 102–12.

[20] *Ibid.*

[21] Gellhorn, *op. cit.*, p. 13.

an example of counter-organization. Specific attempts to bring clients into the administrative process can also be effective, although experience in the poverty program has not been entirely reassuring. More practical is the wider provision of legal services to disadvantaged members of society and the setting up of consumers organizations that can take collective action when this is required. Here, the provision of "store-front" legal aid and the willingness of many young lawyers to protect the weak against the strong, rather than *vice versa,* have been important developments. "Class action" suits are a related tactic which provide exploited consumers some redress. Ralph Nader's Center for the Study of Responsive Law in Washington, D.C., is yet another example of organizational restructuring that provides a voice for previously speechless minority groups. In England, Citizens' Advisory Groups have been created, staffed mainly by volunteers and easily accessible to the public.[22]

Essentially, the resocialization process involves instilling new attitudes of efficacy and participation in citizens, regarding both government and other social institutions. However, the process can be enhanced by inputs from the official side too. Officials tend to become isolated from the public, for a variety of reasons. There is undoubtedly some tendency for them to develop a proprietary interest in the functional areas with which they deal and the bureaucratic norm of impartiality may encourage this posture. Less happily, given their own social advantages, they may tend to treat clients in terms of their perceived, often lower social status.[23] Given the ubiquity of hierarchy in social life, there is probably a deep-seated tendency to honor the resulting "pecking order" in human interaction. Perhaps, too, those in political bureaucracies come to have an inordinate sensitivity toward and respect for power. Certainly, in the federal capital, it is clear that the consciousness of power differentials among individuals exerts a pervasive conditioning influence upon behavior. Indeed, power is probably a major currency of exchange and evaluation in most bureaucratic arenas.

Another source of bureaucratic isolation is class and related differences between most officials and their clients, and especially in those sectors where tension has been greatest in recent years. Perhaps, in addition, any anxiety of officials regarding their own personal security and mobility impels some of them to view their relationships with the

[22] A. J. Kahn, "The British Citizens' Advice Bureaus: An Overview," in *Neighborhood Information Centers: A Study and Some Proposals* (New York: Columbia University School of Social Work, 1966), pp. 16–36.

[23] Ironically, this is a violation of classical bureaucratic norms, which prescribe *impartiality.*

public as a zero-sum game where any concessions granted to outsiders culminate in a net reduction of their own potential benefits. There may also be a tendency to define existing problems as essentially the result of the inability or refusal of lower-class individuals to accept the necessity of existing bureaucratic structures.[24] Residues of the Protestant Ethic—which equates economic and occupational success with personal virtue and worth—probably remain strong, especially among the self-made segment of officials who have often achieved their middle-class statuses through hard work and extended education.[25]

Such values, which probably serve important rationalizing functions among officials, are deeply imbedded and it would be fatuous to believe that they can be easily changed. Bureaucrats are human, as someone observed, and they exhibit the same tendency as other humans to defer to those who already possess the most resources. One must also include in his appraisal of bureaucracy, the fact that it is a *vocation* in which personal gratifications and career motivations provide powerful incentives. Obviously, this condition can and does co-exist alongside the service motive, but it would be a one-eyed perspective that failed to recognize that bureaucrats, as politicians, serve more than one master.

The long tenure characteristic of higher bureaucrats may also affect their perspective of public claims and their treatment of individual citizens.[26] It is probably true that experience brings with it some lessening of idealism and attending redefinitions of the "public interest." Agencies, of course, are structured on a representative basis, and both position and functional knowledge probably tend to push officials toward a rationale that equates the community interest with the interest of their major clientele groups, and especially when such are articulate and well-organized and have the political punch to bring pressure to bear through legislators and elected executives. This suggests that one useful structural innovation might be to temper present appointment criteria of experience and expertise with youth and elasticity.

The crystallization of norms and loyalties that encourage parochial definitions of bureaucratic roles might be eased in this way. Precedents exist in the New Deal experience where Franklin Roosevelt systemat-

[24] Sjoberg, Brymer, and Farris, *op. cit.*

[25] One interpretation, widely criticized as being such, is the "Moynihan Report," issued by the Department of Labor, in which matriarchal family structure is cited as an important contribution to the inability of poor Negroes to adapt to bureaucratic systems in the schools, government, and industry, *The Case for National Action* (Washington, D. C.: U. S. Government Printing Office, 1965).

[26] The majority of higher officials have served 25 years or more, Presthus, *Elites in the Policy Process, op. cit.*

ically created new agencies and divided the same function among two or more of them in a deliberate effort to foster innovation and create intra-bureaucratic competition.

Whatever the difficulties, it seems that the modification of existing structures is the most feasible of the several alternative strategies. In this context, we turn next to some discussion of decentralization and participation, including some examples of efforts to put them into effect.

DECENTRALIZATION AND PARTICIPATION

Discussion of the phenomena of community organization and local control can be usefully reduced to two primary concepts: decentralization and participation. In simple terms, decentralization involves the allocation of authority more widely within a given unit of rule so that an increased number of individuals or groups may have easier access to and more influence on the processes of policy formulation and implementation. Trends toward decentralization frequently reflect popular sentiments that "big government" is almost by definition irresponsible and unable to fulfill individual human needs. Conversely, such trends also mirror the widely held conviction that a devolution of control will lead to greater probity, sensitivity, and effectiveness in governmental affairs. The new dispensation,[27] in effect, has both normative and operational components.

The concept of participation is seen essentially as a corollary of decentralization. Given reduced centralization of the organs of public power, a citizen may expect to have greater impact on the operations of government through his own actions. At the very least, the individual's margin of access to government is broadened proportionately with any increase in his proximity, in both physical and psychological terms, to the policy process. Participation, however, implies more than greater access to government; it also imputes considerable value to personal political activism. In effect, assessments of the validity or legitimacy of a government are directly related to the number of citizens *actively* involved in the practice of government. The measure of an individual's citizenship becomes his willingness to become personally in-

---

[27] The use of the term "new" here is somewhat poetic. Writing in 1895, Gaetano Mosca speaks of "extensive and organic" decentralization as the "surest" remedy for the evils of parliamentarianism. This would imply "transferring many of the functions now exercised by bureaucracies and elective bodies to the class of public-spirited citizens." *The Ruling Class* (New York: McGraw-Hill Book Co., 1939), p. 265 (paperback edition).

volved in public life, not marginally as a voter, but rather as a direct participant in policy determination and in the processes of judgment and choice involved in the allocation of scarce resources.

It should be added that contemporary demands for greater participation really mean participation by *different* groups than those who have usually monopolized access. There has always been constant participation by articulate (usually producer) groups in American government. What contemporary advocates of "participation" desire is the broader sharing of access to include groups that possess fewer political resources. Allied with this claim is the preference for a more humanistic style of administration that will ease interaction between bureaucrats who typically possess many such resources and clients who are often disadvantaged in this respect.[28]

Clearly, the concepts of decentralization and participation are not merely the product of certain recent social developments in the American policy. The very essence of political life, as epitomized by early Athenian democracy and the *polis,* centers about the value of citizen participation in a community of manageable and sensitive size. At various points throughout history, men have argued that individual and collective fulfilment is only possible when the citizen-activist participates in the exercise of self-governing or perceives that his interests are being effectively served by those of authority. A significant political history, therefore, involves the struggle between, on one hand, proponents of decentralization and/or citizen participation and, on the other, proponents of centralization and/or a more restricted view of democratic processes.

Some Correlates of Current Decentralization

The impetus toward decentralization and participation that surfaced in the 1960's is the product of a complex set of developments in American society over the last thirty or forty years. The social programs of the New Deal era brought a period of increasing centralization in American governmental activity. As the federal government initiated a growing number of high-cost, resource-intensive welfare measures, technical and managerial expertise and facilities necessarily came to be concentrated at the national level. Such conditions persisted after World War II. Government bureaucracies expanded geometrically and the

---

[28] See, for example, Louis Gawthrop, *Administrative Politics and Social Change* (New York: St. Martins Press, 1971).

complexity of the processes of policy determination and implementation increased dramatically as government assumed new and technically complex functions, such as the production and control of atomic energy. The states had neither the skilled scientists, the huge financial resources, nor the constitutional authority to assume leadership in such fields.

In the mid-1960's the dictates of the Vietnam war augmented this trend toward government centralization and strengthened the value imputed to technical expertise and managerial rationality. The individual citizen, lacking informational or technical resources, often came to feel removed from the exercise of power. "Size," as the primary characteristic of government, the military, and industry—and inertia as well—militated against grass-roots participation in policy-making and encouraged low perceptions of personal political efficacy among many ordinary citizens. As Table 6–1 shows, levels of political efficacy among a sample of American adults

TABLE 6–1. Comparative Levels of Political Efficacy, United States and Canada

	Percentage Agreeing	
	United States *	Canadian †
'Voting is the only way people like me can have a say about how the government runs things.'	68	76
'Sometimes politics and government seem so complicated that a person like me can't really understand what is going on.'	69	69
'People like me don't have any say about what the government does.'	34	49
'I don't think public officials care much about what people like me think.'	34	46
	(1,571)	(2,721)

* American data from 1966 Election Study, Survey Research Center University of Michigan.
† Canadian data from John Meisel's national election survey of 1965. The last item was phrased slightly differently in his survey, i.e. 'I don't think the government cares what people like me think.'

were sometimes marginal. Some indication that this condition affected Canadians even more strongly is provided by comparative data shown in the table.

Such data suggest that many citizens restrict their political role to voting. As students of politics and administration, we have to guard against assuming that politics is a central concern of most Americans. For many good reasons involving the lack of time, interest, information, and related civic resources, the majority of citizens tend instead to delegate policy-making to political elites, reserving to themselves the right to elect periodically a new set of elites.

Centralization increased even more as government programs most typically came to involve bureaucratic management and technological decision-making. Continuing rapid urbanization and industrialization brought more people together in crowded cities without providing adequate channels for the expression of citizen desires or the relief of individual alienation. Incidents of racial strife occurred with greater frequency as impoverished and disenchanted minority groups grew more vocal and critical of the direction and quality of their part in American society, and the priorities of governments. To many, the huge costs of the Vietnam war seemed incongruous, given the problems of urban communities.

The catalytic event that transformed the undercurrents of distrust and disenchantment into highly visible and audible demands for decentralization of power and citizen action was the wave of urban riots during the mid-1960's. Violent disturbances in black neighborhoods and among the urban poor of all races were not simply the result of a breakdown of law and order in the cities. More essentially, they reflected a struggle between established structures of city power and a rising movement to self-rule among the ghetto poor.[29] Municipal reformers, particularly black activists and militants, demanded changes in the structure of authority that would place more power over crucial urban issues in the hands of those most immediately affected:

> The absolute rule of Negro communities by outside forces has reached the highest degree possible without precipitating rebellion. At the point when practically all decisions affecting public life are made on the outside, a politically confident and conscious people, aspiring to be free, must insist upon a share in local rule.[30]

Certain measures had been taken earlier by government to involve more people in public policy-making. In the 1950's citizens were invited to participate as advisors in various federal undertakings related to urban problems, most notably the Urban Renewal program, the Workable Program for Community Improvement, and the various Juvenile Delinquency

---

[29] Joseph F. Zimmerman, "Neighborhoods and Citizen Involvement," *Public Administration Review*, Vol. 33 (May/June, 1972), p. 202.

[30] Milton Kotler, as quoted in *ibid.* See also Alan A. Altschuler, *Community Control: The Black Demand for Participation in Large American Cities* (Indianapolis: Bobbs-Merrill Co., 1970).

Demonstration Projects.[31] Normally, however, those involved in these programs were businessmen, civic leaders, or interest group representatives, rather than the ordinary resident of the target areas. One measure of their success in orienting governmental activities to the needs of the urban poor was the violence that followed and culminated in such racial explosions as those in Newark, Watts, Detroit, and Harlem.

Federal Programs

In the face of deteriorating situations in many American cities, the Johnson administration took the first major steps to involve the city poor, minority groups, and neighborhood organizations in policy-making. Under the general auspices of the "War on Poverty" and through such federal agencies as the offices of Juvenile Delinquency and Youth Development, Economic Opportunity, and Manpower and Training the federal government sought to attack urban problems in a comprehensive yet partially decentralized fashion. Through federal enabling legislation (e.g., Manpower Development and Training Act, Housing and Urban Development Act, Economic Opportunity Act), new quasi-public agencies oriented to urban problems of housing, education, health, welfare, crime control, employment, and delinquency were given federal funds, in addition to private funding from benevolent organizations.[32] Each agency, while responsible ultimately to a federal department, recruited most of its staff locally and endeavored to include wherever possible citizens from the affected areas and groups on their advisory boards, planning committees or evaluation bodies. The activities of such quasi-public agencies were to be integrated with other local undertakings through the organs of municipal government and their planning bodies and were to be coordinated with other state or federal programs through various interdepartmental and intergovernmental committees.

The success of many quasi-public agencies created during the Johnson administration was limited, although some, notably the Action for Appalachian Youth in West Virginia, the Mobilization for Youth, and Haryou-Act in New York, ABCD in Boston, and UPI in Washington,[33] had some success and survived for a number of years. The most important developments vis-à-vis community organization during the John-

[31] Carl W. Steinberg, "Citizens and the Administrative State: From Participation to Power," *Public Administration Review*, Vol. 32 (May/June, 1972), p. 191.

[32] Charles F. Grosser, *New Directions in Community Organization* (New York: Frederick A. Praeger, Inc., 1973), p. 22.

[33] *Ibid.*

son years, however, centered about two groups of innovative urban programs: the Community Action Programs (C.A.P.) and the Model Cities Program.

The Community Action Programs, established originally under the Economic Opportunity Act of 1964, were designed as urban initiatives, "developed, conducted and administered with the maximum feasible participation of the residents of the area and members of the groups served." [34] The content of these programs is less important to this discussion than the philosophy of their motivation and implementation:

> Above all [C.A.P.] includes the poor people of the community whose first opportunity must be the opportunity to help themselves. . . . The local agency applying for a community action program grant must satisfy only one basic criterion: it must be broadly representative of the interests of the community . . . above all it must provide a means whereby the residents of the program areas will have a voice in planning and a role in action. The initiation for community programs must be distilled from the community itself; there can be no substitute.[35]

This statement includes the basic tenets of community organization and citizen participation; programs must relate to the community both in their inspiration and execution and they must involve the "maximum feasible participation" of those people most directly affected.

A similar approach was taken by the newly created Department of Housing and Urban Development in 1967 with the introduction of the Model Cities Program. Under this scheme, particularly depressed neighborhoods of certain cities were chosen as subjects for intensive redevelopment and aid projects. In each model neighborhood, the city government, using HUD grants and local revenues, created a City Development Agency (CDA) to coordinate the full range of federally and municipally funded neighborhood projects. The CDA was also authorized to assist in the organization and financing of indigenous, non-profit corporations and resident groups involved in neighborhood development schemes.[36] At the governing level of each CDA organization, citizens from different sectors of the model area were involved and the professional staff of each CDA was effectively responsible to their citizen-governors.

A typical CDA would participate in a great variety of local programs

[34] S2642 Title II, Section 202 (3) *The War on Poverty: The Economic Opportunity Act of 1964*, pp. 52–53.
[35] *Ibid.*
[36] Robert Perlman and Arnold Gurin, *Community Organization and Social Planning* (New York: John Wiley Inc., 1972), pp. 250–55.

including education task forces, prepayment medical-care schemes, informational and referral services, counselling facilities, employment and retraining agencies, crime control, cultural and recreational services, business grants or loans, and so on.[37] Some programs would be planned and administered directly by the CDA while others were contracted out to different agencies and to neighborhood corporations.[38] Whatever the case, each program would remain intrinsically linked to the people of the community by limiting centralized direction and control to the greatest extent possible.

Failure in Philadelphia

The case of the Philadelphia Model Cities Program is useful as an illustration of the difficulties that arise in the establishment of such community organization and citizen participation projects. Established in 1967, the program immediately encountered conceptual problems concerning the meaning and application of the term "citizen participation." The Department of Housing and Urban Development had avoided setting down precise guidelines delineating the characteristics of citizen involvement in Model Cities Programs, preferring instead to leave the resolution of this problem to officials at the local level. In Philadelphia, City Hall espoused a rather jejune conception of citizen participation; residents of the model neighborhoods were to act as advisors to program administrators and aid in project implementation. However, the regional HUD office supported the position of the residents' association, the Area Wide Council (AWC), and sought city funds to permit the training of professional staff who would, in turn, organize and train area residents to assume some decision-making and administrative responsibility in the projects.[39]

In addition to the early strains between City Hall and the residents' association, several internal problems created tension within the AWC itself. Its 96-member citizen board soon proved to be largely impotent as the AWC staff, increasingly sympathetic to the more militant demands of Black and Puerto Rican minorities, resisted decentralization and delegation of active responsibility to other groups in the community.[40] In

[37] Ibid.
[38] Ibid., p. 255.
[39] Erasmus Kloman, "Citizen Participation in the Philadelphia Model Cities Program: Retrospect & Prospect," Public Administration Review, Vol. 32 (September, 1972), p. 403.
[40] Ibid., p. 404.

contrast to more moderate calls for cooperation and consultation, some AWC staffers advocated a more fundamental redistribution of power between the local government and the community and sought to restructure or reorganize local institutions which had failed to serve the needs of neighborhood residents.[41]

In response to the growing radicalization of the AWC and the support it had won among many residents of the poor, non-white neighborhoods of the North City, the mayor of Philadelphia grew less compliant and more intransigent in his relationships with citizen organizers. He and other city officials held up the funding of some community projects, cancelled others, and appointed loyal administrators to local programs without consulting neighborhood residents. The general effect was greater polarization between the AWC and City Hall, an increase in tension that was dramatized by an AWC staff member's participation in November 1967 in a protest against city authorities.[42]

By the time the new Republican administration took power in Washington in 1969, there seemed little chance that the internal problems of the Philadelphia Model Cities Program could be resolved. With new HUD guidelines limiting the latitude and extent of citizen participation in Model Cities projects, the mayor's position appeared to be strengthened significantly. He acted quickly to reject a proposal that would allow AWC-controlled corporations to channel federal funds directly into neighborhood projects, thus effectively ending the citizens' contract with AWC. In their place, he hoped to install a system of neighborhood advisory councils that would blunt the radicalism of more militant community groups.[43]

From 1969 to February 1972, a complex legal battle ensued as AWC brought a successful suit against the city and HUD in Washington for failing to provide adequate instruments for citizen participation in the Model Cities Program. The final victory of AWC in the circuit court of appeals, however, was somewhat hollow, for the spirit and organization of many of the citizens' organizations in the city had failed and a number of the Model Cities projects had ceased to function.

Assessing the Philadelphia experience, Kloman writes:

> . . . the chance for a very worthwhile experiment in citizen participation was abandoned, partly because of the basic insecurity and the tendency to temporize within City Hall and partly because the leadership

[41] *Ibid.*
[42] *Ibid.*, p. 405.
[43] *Ibid.*

of the citizens organization was unwilling to continue to work within the system.[14]

. . .

Whatever chance the program had to succeed, it depended on creating a basis for hope among the residents of the model neighborhoods that through citizen participation they would become an effective part of the process by which the quality of life in the inner cities was to be improved. Equivocation and backtracking on the part of HUD and the Administration in Washington have done little to nourish hope among the men, women and children whom the program was designed to help.[45]

Failure in New Haven

A similar fate has overtaken the country's first comprehensive poverty program, begun in New Haven in 1962 and including such novel programs as Head Start, the Neighborhood Youth Corps, legal aid, manpower training, etc. According to state and federal officials, after months of investigation, the program has "deteriorated into fiscal and administrative chaos and has become little more than a political pork barrel dominated by the city's powerful Democratic Party machine." [46] Although the program at one time had been called "the model agency" by federal officials, by the end of 1974, State Department of Community Affairs officials were calling it a "sick shambles" . . . in which "the irregularities and incompetence are amazing. . . ." Apparently, a variety of problems brought the program to grief. Tension between the state Republican administration and the City's Democratic leadership was cited by one Board member; "City Hall politics" was blamed by a State official; and Rev. Edwin Edmonds, one of the founders of the program, blamed the loss of the original goals that inspired it. "The whole program has been raped and nobody cares about the poor anymore." As a result, both state and federal agencies, such as the Office of Economic Opportunity and the Department of Community Affairs have withdrawn or sharply reduced their funding, and the future of the program is cloudy.

Having surveyed the trend toward and some of the consequences of decentralization and citizen participation in the community action programs during the Johnson administration in the mid- and late-1960's, it seems useful to examine critically some of the main assumptions of community organization and citizen participation.

[44] *Ibid.*, p. 407.
[45] *Ibid.*, p. 408.
[46] *New York Times*, November 18, 1974, pp. 1, 27.

Critique: Participation, Cooperation, or Cooptation?

It seems clear that a great part of the philosophy of community control is somewhat uncritically normative. The propositions that authority *should* be developed to local or neighborhood levels and. that citizens *should* be encouraged to participate directly and more effectively in the policy process differ to a very great degree from any conviction or demonstration that authority *can* be decentralized or that ordinary individuals *can* involve themselves more actively in community government. In realistic terms, many barriers prevent the achievement of large-scale decentralization and opening-up of the political system, while a great number of factors, both structural and psychological, tend to reinforce centralization and exclusivity in the exercise of power through government.[47]

The crucial prerequisite of civic participation and power is *political resources*. In order to exercise influence in the political arena, whether at the most basic level of interpersonal relationships or the most complex level of national government, one must have access to the political resources (e.g., constituency support, associations, information, conceptual skills, political efficacy, prestige) that will enable one's will to obtain or, at least, insure that his opinions will be heard. To attempt to exercise power through government without political resources is often a chimerical exercise. Government is not only a game of symbols, but rather an activity dealing with substantive power and influence.

These thoughts lead one directly to an unavoidable issue: Given current structures of power in American society and the corresponding weakness—in terms of political resources—of the urban poor and those who most vocally demand community control and citizen action, can the residents of a community effectively exercise sufficient power to make self-government practicable? Are concessions to advocates of citizen participation the product of a recognition of actual citizen power

[47] For research in several contexts indicating that "democratic elitism" is pervasive in community politics, essentially because of the unequal distribution of such critical political resources as time, interest, education, efficacy, and money, see Robert Presthus, *Men at the Top: A Study in Community Power* (New York: Oxford University Press, 1964); Robert Agger, Dan Goldrich, and Bert Swanson, *The Rulers and The Ruled* (New York: John Wiley Inc., 1964); Arthur Vidich and Joseph Bensman, *Small Town in Mass Society* (Garden City, N.Y.: Doubleday, 1958); and Floyd Hunter, *Community Power Structure* (Chapel Hill: University of North Carolina Press, 1953). The latter work of course is distinguished as the first study in the field, which inspired much of the subsequent research in the area of community politics.

or are they merely symbolic gestures to appease neighborhood dissent and legitimate the *status quo?*

By admitting citizens to the processes of policy-making, are those who presently monopolize political resources demonstrating their belief that a significant transfer of power has occurred or are they consciously seeking to co-opt citizen activists and neutralize a perceived threat to existing structures of authority?

Such questions are not intended to inspire a polemical or ideological discussion; rather, they seek to isolate a basic dilemma of community control—its assumptions that the instruments of power can be exercised without the prerequisite power-base, and that existing political elites are prepared to share the power often acquired through years of disciplined effort. As James Riedel concludes:

> My reading of the current upsurge in participation interest is that many are not talking about representative participation at all. They are asking for a direct transfer or reallocation of political (governmental) power and without having to achieve it through the tedious requirements of the existing political system. This is the pursuit of a phantom. Insofar as any redistribution of power is likely to occur, and it will, it will be because such individuals and groups who succeed will have, whether wittingly or unwittingly, played the age-old political game and won.[48]

Philip Selznick punctuates this dilemma in his early analysis of co-optation:

> Formal co-optation ostensibly shares authority, but in doing so is involved in a dilemma. The real point is the sharing of the public symbols or administrative burdens or authority and consequently public responsibility without the transfer of substantive powers; it therefore becomes necessary to insure that the co-opted elements do not get out of hand, do not take advantage of their formal position to encroach upon the actual arena of decision. Consequently, formal co-option requires informal control over the co-opted elements lest the unity of command and decision be imperilled. . . . The leadership, by the very nature of its position, is committed to two conflicting goals; if it ignores the need for participation, the goal of co-optation may be jeopardized; if participation is allowed to go too far, the continuity of leadership and policy may be threatened.[49]

48 "Citizen Participation: Myths and Realities," *Public Administration Review,* Vol. 32 (May/June, 1972), p. 218.

49 *T.V.A. and the Grass Roots* (Berkeley, 1949), quoted in *Public Administration Review,* Vol. 32 (January/February, 1972), p. 36.

Some Costs of Participation

We turn next to several problems concerning the costs and difficulties of making community participation and control more than a laudable aspiration. Strategies of citizen participation assume, above all else, that *Class* citizens are motivated to become involved in public affairs; yet even this basic assumption is questionable in that most individuals tend to avoid involvement or commitment even under the best of conditions.[50] In a political system that rewards *group* action and the mobilization of *group* coalitions, many individuals tend to resist collective action and are inspired to act, more often than not, only by isolated (non-coalition) issues.[51] Moreover, as the seriousness and tension of an issue increase, the reluctance of citizens to participate often increases correspondingly. Many people do not want to become involved in public issues unless they are themselves so seriously affected that participation becomes almost inevitable and clearly less costly than non-participation.

Moreover, decentralization and citizen participation pose significant administrative problems. Adam Herbert, in a recent article, presents some of these difficulties. In his opinion, administrative decentralization and neighborhood control:

> May slow down decision-making processes and complicate the implementation process.
>
> May create confusion regarding the chain of command within public agencies.
>
> May lead to major conflicts between professionals and citizens over program direction and implementation.
>
> May result in internal divisiveness as employees line up in groups which are either in favor of or opposed to working with citizens in quest for more responsive government.
>
> May make it difficult to convince top-level administrators to adopt a hands-off policy toward governmental operations at field or neighborhood level.[52]

In addition, important organizational issues must be confronted: What is the ideal size of a community-controlled government and how are its boundaries to be determined? What legislative, administrative, and judicial powers should such an organization have and how are its programs

---

[50] Cf. James N. Rosenau, *Citizenship Between Elections* (New York: Free Press, 1974.

[51] Riedel, *op. cit.*, p. 212, who estimates that those who are politically active between elections constitute about 2 per cent of the electorate. See also Sidney Verba and N. H. Nie, *Participation in America* (New York: Harper and Row, 1972).

[52] "Management Under Conditions of Decentralization and Citizen Participation," *Public Administration Review*, Vol. 32 (October, 1972), pp. 627–29.

to be financed? How do the notions of accountability and representative-
ness apply to a neighborhood polity? [53]

These difficulties and others are, of course, at least partially balanced
by certain benefits of decentralization and citizen participation in governmental activities. In a positive sense, decentralization and citizen
participation:

May encourage more citizen-committed persons to seek public employment.

May stimulate among employees greater appreciation of human needs
to which government is or *should* be responding.

May lead to new methods of evaluating services which more fully
incorporate both management objectives and clientele perceptions
and desires.

May lead to some cost savings because citizens can assist by pointing
out needless programs, wasteful projects, and more feasible options
given specific community characteristics.[54]

Whatever the difficulties and benefits of greater governmental decentralization and citizen participation may be, certain developments since
the end of the Johnson administration suggest that the federal government has seriously curtailed its earlier support of community action and
local development programs. Table 6–2, for example, outlines federal
budgetary outlays for community development and housing from 1965 to
1973 and compares these outlays to the total federal budget, including
national defense and space research and technology for the same years.

TABLE 6–2. Comparative Federal Expenditures, 1965–1973

Year	Total Outlay ($ millions)	Community Development and Housing	Space Research and Technology	National Defense
1965	118,430	288	5,091	49,578
1966	134,652	2,644	5,933	56,785
1967	158,254	2,616	5,423	70,081
1968	178,833	4,076	4,721	80,517
1969	184,548	1,961	4,247	81,232
1970	196,588	2,965	3,749	80,295
1971	211,425	3,357	3,381	77,661
1972	236,610	4,039	3,180	78,030
1973	246,257	4,844	3,191	78,210

Source: *Budget of the U.S. Government: Fiscal Year 1973.* Washington, D.C., 1972, pp.
546–50.

[53] See Henry Schmandt, "Municipal Decentralization: An Overview," *Public Administration Review*, Vol. 32 (October, 1972), pp. 571–88.
[54] *Ibid.*

Clearly, the advent of the Nixon administration brought a de-emphasis of community development programs at the federal level, despite the Republican Party's advocacy of greater governmental decentralization. From 1968 to 1969, budgetary outlays for all housing and community development projects dropped by approximately 52 per cent and only re-attained the high levels of the Johnson years in 1973, *despite a total budgetary increase of almost 38 per cent in the intervening years.* Urban renewal, Model Cities, rehabilitation loans, neighborhood facilities grants, and open space grants programs, established during the Johnson regime, were gradually abandoned by the Nixon administration in favor of limited revenue-sharing schemes. In addition, the C.A.P. projects operating through the Office of Economic Opportunity were discarded in compliance with the Administration's expressed desire to "remove almost all operating programs from O.E.O. and allow it to devote full attention to research and development." [55] The massive structure of the War on Poverty has thus been largely dismantled and the scope of community self-help programs significantly curtailed. Here, perhaps, is yet another example of the tendency for political ideology to be "routinized" by bureaucracy and traditional priorities in Congress and elsewhere. As Max Weber argued, social evolution seems to be characterized by a relentless "routinization of charisma," whereby innovative individuals and structures tend to be brought under the restraining influence of traditional bureaucratic norms.

Despite these reversals, residues of the "community control" movement remain and continue to influence public administration. As shown in our concluding chapters, welfare recipients and women in the military have launched successful suits against administrative decisions at all levels, resulting in permanent policy changes. Local and consumer types of groups have become better organized and more active in pressuring local officials. Indeed, in 1972 they ranked second only to business groups in a scale of interest group "activism," as perceived by senior civil servants in Washington, D.C., and three states. [56]

Community control and participation are best viewed as normative aspects of organizational and political theory. To some extent, they tend to center in the "ought" category of public administration. Another vital dimension of the field is organizational theory that seeks mainly to analyze administrative systems and to find regularities among them. We turn to some recent examples of this type of research in the following chapter.

---

[55] *Ibid.,* p. 129.
[56] Presthus, *Elites in the Policy Process, op. cit.,* p. 221.

7

New Developments in Organizational Theory

At almost all levels of his social experience, man pursues his material and spiritual goals within organizational structures. Most of his activities are guided in terms of organizational norms and values, and typically he defines himself and his position relative to society by referring to organizational membership. This condition is so pervasive that we tend to overlook its significance. We are speaking here not only of man's membership in voluntary associations—where most Americans belong to only one such organization—but more importantly to his membership in occupational and educational bureaucracies. The ubiquity and importance of such structures has created a sub-field in social science, which may be called organizational theory or organizational behavior. Some of this work has been inspired by very pragmatic efforts to improve the productivity of industrial organizations,[1] while other observers have been mainly interested in learning more about an emerging sector of human behavior.

For most of the latter group, the task of organizational theory is to outline the nature and personal consequences of the organizations through which most of us express and achieve our personal and collective goals.

[1] A provocative critique of this approach to organizational theory is Loren Baritz, *The Servants of Power* (Middlebury, Conn.: Weslyan University Press, 1960).

Organizational theorists analyze the internal structure, functional roles, and authority relationships of organizations, trying to discover the complex patterns of technical and human dependency that link all organizations to their larger social environment. One useful way of characterizing such organizations is as "miniature societies" which seem to inculcate and reinforce the norms and values of the larger social structure.[2] In working toward such understandings, one is inevitably led to a crucial and perhaps unresolvable issue: the problem of individual autonomy as it relates to the demands and constraints of huge, supra-individual organizations.[3]

The purpose of this chapter is to outline several of the new developments and approaches that have recently emerged in the literature on organizational theory and to relate them to some of the more traditional concepts of the nature of organizational structures. Necessarily, the discussions will not be comprehensive and will almost certainly neglect many new ideas in a rapidly expanding field. However, it is hoped that this chapter will serve to suggest the key problems that are confronting students of organizational theory, while providing a general basis for more thorough examination of these problems and allied issues.

Beyond Bureaucracy

The classic Weberian model of a complex social organization or bureaucracy was predicated on the belief that chaos and inefficiency in social affairs could be minimized by introducing rationality and predictability into societal relations. In his definitive work, Max Weber theorized that the ideal bureaucratic organization—that is, the organization that most effectively achieved a prescribed goal while eliminating arbitrariness and discord in interpersonal and inter-group relationships— would contain the following elements:

1. A division of labor based on functional specialization
2. A well-defined hierarchy of authority
3. A system of rules defining the rights and duties of members or employees or participants
4. A system of procedures for dealing with work situations
5. Impersonality in interpersonal relations.

---

[2] See Robert Presthus, *The Organizational Society* (New York: Vintage Books, 1965). For a statistical replication of a theory advanced in this book, see H. C. Pruden, "The Upward-Mobile, Indifferent, and Ambivalent Typology of Managers," *Journal of the Academy of Management*, Vol. 16 (September, 1973), pp. 454–64.

[3] This issue, of course, is central to the contemporary search of many people for "participation" and "citizen control," in both public and private bureaucracies.

Within such an organization, the individual would not be subject to the whims of his superiors or to doubts about his duties and responsibilities. Instead, patterns of authority and expectations of achievement are embodied within the structural framework of the organization and are administered impersonally through the dictates of rank and regulation.

The key concepts in the early models of organizational structures were order and predictability. In effect, an organization was an instrument for ordering interpersonal relations toward the achievement of a prescribed objective. Responsibility and authority flowed along an orderly hierarchical system and goods and services were produced in an orderly fashion corresponding to a linear demand-supply pattern. However, even though he regarded bureaucracy as the most efficient instrument yet designed to achieve large-scale ends, largely in response to the needs of capitalism, Weber foresaw the potential problems that would attend its over-emphasis on this concept of orderliness.

> This passion for bureaucracy . . . is enough to drive one to despair. It is as if . . . we were deliberately to become men who need "order" and nothing but order, who become nervous and cowardly if for one moment this order wavers, and helpless if they are torn away from their total incorporation in it. That the world should know no men but these; it is such an evolution that we are already caught up in, and the great question is not how we can promote and hasten it, but what we can oppose to this machinery in order to keep a portion of mankind free from this parcelling-out of the soul from this supreme mastery of the bureaucratic way of life.[4]

One solution to this tendency of bureaucracy was the possibility that certain charismatic leaders, typically political elites, could by force of personality galvanize the administrative machine into new innovative activity. On the other hand, Weber's major emphasis seems to have been upon the rational and legal aspects of bureaucracy, upon what he called the "routinization of bureaucracy." The ideal official was one who performed his role *"sine ira ac studio."*

Many critiques of the ideal models of complex organizations are centered about the issue of the depersonalization of the individual within the orderly and economically deterministic setting of bureaucratic institutions. The extension of bureaucratic values and organization into all facets of life is decried and observers seek to temper the dispassionate rationality of bureaucratic organizations by focusing more attention on

---

[4] Cited in J. P. Mayer, Max Weber and German Politics (London: Faber and Faber, 1943), p. 127; also, on Weber's conceptions of bureaucracy, Henry Jacoby, *The Bureaucratization of the World* (Berkeley: University of California Press, 1973), Chap. 9.

the need to conciliate individual desires and organizational goals. The economic utility of bureaucracy itself is seldom questioned. Given the value imputed to economic efficiency and productivity plus the obvious success that many bureaucratic structures in the private sector achieved in terms of efficiency and productivity, it is felt that such organizations will inevitably continue to play a prominent social role. That certain reforms are needed is almost universally recognized by academic observers. However, the basic structural assumptions of bureaucratic organization are rarely challenged with the thought in mind of initiating sweeping, fundamental changes.

Quite recently, some organizational theorists have begun to question the effectiveness of bureaucratic structures in responding to new social problems and changes. The pace of technological and scientific innovation and attending shifts in the social environment have caused increasing emphasis to be placed upon the criterion of *adaptability*. How responsive to the demands of change have traditional bureaucratic structures been? To be sure, rationality, predictability, and efficiency remain fundamentally important elements in the assessment of bureaucratic organizations but the capacity to adjust to social change has often become the *sine qua non* in the determination of an organization's viability.

The classic elements of Weber's ideal model of bureaucracy are not altogether suited to modern demands for adaptability. Indeed, the Weberian model, in its emphasis upon hierarchy, functional specialization, order, and well-defined procedures, generally mitigated against organizational and personal accommodation of environmental change. Roles and tasks are precisely assigned and premium value is placed upon structural integrity and stability. In effect, adaptability is sacrificed for efficiency and rationality and the organization (i.e., those who man it) typically becomes a conservative rather than an innovative institution.

Criticisms of this kind are especially relevant to modern analysts who are concerned with problems of social development. They assert that, at the very least, Weberian concerns about complex organizations are in need of refinement and extension in order to permit consideration of such pressing social problems as poverty, overpopulation, underemployment, or universal access to medical care.[5] A new type of normative bureaucratic organization geared specifically to these developmental issues is now required. Such a "development bureaucracy" must involve the following elements: (1) the capacity to manage change or to direct efforts

[5] Berton H. Kaplan, "Notes on a Non-Weberian Model of Bureaucracy: The Case of Development Bureaucracy," *Administrative Science Quarterly*, Vol. 13 (June–December, 1968), pp. 471–74.

to alter basic patterns of a way of life, (2) the capacity to design structures to plan social change, and (3) the capacity to focus attention on an entire way of life as opposed to more parochial concerns so as to increase on a broad social scale the adaptability of individuals and groups.[6]

More specifically, an organization designed to confront issues of social development must be able to shift priorities and strategies as the environment dictates. Flexibility and commitment are the keys. While structural differentiation and specialization continue to be required, no structure may become so specialized or so functionally specific that it cannot be changed to accommodate a new task or a new social demand. At all times, moreover, the development bureaucracy must remain client-centered; its existence must be a function of external priorities rather than of internal, institutional concerns. In many cases, the organization must pursue experimental alternatives and provide channels for innovative techniques and approaches.[7] Such classical bureaucratic imperatives as specialized training and professionalization must give way to subjective orientations.

Such prescriptions, of course, raise more questions than they answer. What type of organizational structure embodies these qualities of adaptability and flexibility so that developmental issues may be resolved most effectively? How is bureaucracy to be reformed to meet the demands of rapid social and technological change? How can we overcome the inherent tendencies of any structure toward survival, regardless of changing social needs? How do we find an equilibrium between the need for change and the demands for stability and the retention of values and structures that have met the test of social utility? Clearly, few easy solutions to such problems exist in theory or in practice. Bureaucratic structures are so deeply entrenched in almost all areas of our society that it is practically impossible to conceive of a society with radically different structures. The forces of socialization, both formal and informal, that lead the individual to accept social institutions in their present form are not easily broken or transformed. Indeed, it is difficult enough to convince people of the need for structural change without asking them to suffer the physical and psychological dislocations that inevitably attend the implementation of actual change.

There is also some question whether bureaucratic structures are as resistant to change as their critics maintain. Although its successes may

[6] Ibid., p. 472.
[7] Ibid., pp. 479–551.

possibly have been achieved *despite* its structure, NASA's truly unprecedented breakthroughs in the exploration of space were planned and developed using traditional bureaucratic structures, plus unlimited infusions
of resources. It is also possible that the centralization and hierarchical
components of bureaucratic structure actually permit change to be ef-
fected more expeditiously than through a system based upon full-scale
participation with its vast potential for veto power. It is suggestive in
this context that one observer concludes that "effective local planning
requires *less,* not more citizen participation." [8]

Teacher disagrees / He Thinks it was Project management ← ?

One of the more interesting attempts to outline the nature of social
organizations in the "post-bureaucratic" era involves the idea of "organic-
adaptive" structures.[9]

> In today's world [bureaucracy] is a prosthetic device, no longer use-
> ful. For we now require organic-adaptive systems as structures of free-
> dom to permit the expression of play and imagination and to exploit
> the new pleasure of work.[10]

Warren Bennis describes such "organic-adaptive" structures in the following way:

Class

> The key word will be ("temporary"; there will be adaptive, rapidly
> changing *temporary* systems. These will be organized around *problems-
> to-be-solved.*)The problems will be solved by groups of relative *strang-
> ers* who represent a set of diverse professional skills. The groups will
> be conducted on *organic* rather than mechanical models; they will evolve
> in response to the problem rather than programmed role expectations.
> The function of the "executive" thus becomes *coordinator,* or "linking
> pin" between various project groups. . . . *People will be differentiated
> not vertically according to rank and role but flexibly according to skill
> and professional training.*[11]

Bennis claims that the growth of organic-adaptive structures as re-
placements for more traditional bureaucratic organizations coincides with
the inevitable convergence and realization of three basic "idenes" or
motive ideas: freedom, collaboration, and science.[12] Given lowered expense and greater ease of transportation, increased scope and access to
educational facilities and the general trend toward the democratization

[8] James Q. Wilson, "The War on Cities," *The Public Interest,* Vol. 3 (1966), p. 29.
[9] Warren Bennis, *Changing Organizations* (New York: McGraw-Hill Book Co.,
Inc., 1966).
[10] *Ibid.,* p. 14. See also Bennis and Slater, *The Temporary Society* (New York:
Harper & Row, 1968).
[11] *Ibid.,* p. 12, italics in original.
[12] *Ibid.,* p. 1.

of many social institutions, the individual will demand more relevancy, involvement, and autonomy in his work.[13] He will move from job to job with greater frequency and will have less need of orderliness and continuity in the delineation of his rank and responsibilities.

The envisioned society of organic-adaptive organizations places great emphasis upon individual maturity and self-sufficiency. It probably also assumes a higher level of critical expectation for self-realization in work than is characteristic of any but a relatively small, highly educated segment of society. The assumption that most jobs can be pleasurable and will demand more intellectual commitment of the individual obviously applies to certain vocational sectors, but it seems reasonable to expect that many tasks will remain routine and non-inspired (unless, of course, one claims that technology will eventually eliminate all such tasks).

The prospect of increased organizational adaptability, however, is by no means entirely visionary or idealistic. In the development of project management, product management and program management systems, one can see concrete attempts to optimize adaptability through task organization on fluid work-team bases.[14] The fields of defense and industrial research and development are particularly well-suited to more flexible organizational structures. Teams of experts can be applied to various problem areas as time and priorities dictate. However, application of organic-adaptive structures to other areas, particularly government civil service, may prove more difficult. As long as individuals identify with specific departments and disciplines or patterns of authority for raises, promotions, and other superior–subordinate relations,[15] the independence and fluidity of organizational work-teams will be less than complete. Administrators or coordinators will be compelled to spend a certain amount of time conciliating the demands of various departments, thus effectively retaining hierarchical imperatives within the organizational structure.

Theories of organic-adaptive structures, development bureaucracies, post- or non-Weberian models of complex organizations, and other conceptions of the nature of organizational society beyond bureaucracy are clearly instructive and valuable. In some respects, however, they lack substance and tend to belong to the realm of utopian speculation rather

---

[13] *Ibid.*, p. 11.
[14] F. J. Lyden, "Project Management: Beyond Bureaucracy," *Public Administration Review*, Vol. 30 (July/August, 1970), pp. 435–36.
[15] *Ibid.*

than that of empirical evaluation. Accordingly, we turn now to a discussion of several more substantive developments in the field of organizational analysis.

Bureaucratic Structure and Personality: A Dissenting View

The main bearing of bureaucratic analysis has been upon the impact of the typical bureaucratic structure on the attitudes and behavior of its members. And the major conclusion has been that such structures tend to produce conformity, rule-tropism, anxiety, and a generalized preference toward continuity and routinization. Certainly there is considerable evidence to support such generalizations. However, a recent carefully done study, using more advanced and sophisticated instruments of analysis, raises several questions about this traditional image of officials.[16] Using a sample of 3,101 men, in all types of occupations (i.e., private and governmental) except the military, and basing his definition of bureaucracy on the hierarchical organization of authority, Kohn differentiated his sample according to their scores on several typical bureaucratic values. These included conformity, flexibility, "social orientation," which refers to resistance to change, tolerance of non-conformity, and attitudes toward change. The indexes were designed using factor analysis. Bureaucrats and non-bureaucrats were differentiated empirically by the level of supervision existing in each respondent's organization. About two-thirds of the sample worked in profit-making organizations.

Although the correlations are not high (from .05 to .17), "there is a small but consistent tendency" to contradict traditional assumptions. "Men who work in bureaucratic firms or organizations tend to value self-direction, not conformity. They are more open-minded, have more personally responsible standards of morality, and are more receptive to change than are men who work in non-bureaucratic organizations." [17] Such men are also more flexible and tend to spend their leisure time in more intellectually demanding activities. Entrepreneurs, moreover, are remarkably similar along such dimensions to bureaucrats, which again directly contradicts many existing assumptions. Regarding the effects of private vs. public work milieux, governmental bureaucrats tend to rank somewhat higher on the several dimensions found for both bureaucratic sets. It also appears that "any explanation of the social psychological im-

[16] Melvin L. Kohn, "Bureaucratic Man: A Portrait and an Interpretation," *American Sociological Review*, Vol. 36 (June, 1971), pp. 461–74.
[17] *Ibid.*, p. 465.

pact of bureaucratization . . . [applies] to the entire work force, not just to the white-collar portion." [18]

Certain demographic differences are found among the two sub-samples. Bureaucrats are born and live in big cities where large firms and organizations tend to be located—i.e., disproportionately in the Northeast, along the Great Lakes and in the far West. Their parents tend to come from Northern or Western Europe rather than from Southern or Eastern Europe. Few are black; few are Jewish. They are disproportionately Catholic. But most important, and consistent with earlier findings, they are more highly educated than non-bureaucrats. Of the above variations, *"only education seems to matter for explaining why bureaucrats differ from nonbureaucrats in values, orientation, and intellectual functioning.*[19] However, another significant factor is that bureaucracies somehow recruit people who have more of the isolated characteristics. Only with regard to closeness of supervision and "much greater" job protection do they differ from people with equal amounts of education who work in non-bureaucratic milieux.

Nevertheless when education is controlled and multiple regression is used to determine the weight of various occupational factors, it seems that job protection (a typical bureaucratic condition) contributes "notably" to bureaucracy's relationship to social orientation and to the overall measure of intellectual flexibility. *"It thus appears that men who are protected from some of the dangers that change might bring are less fearful of the new and the different, are better able to accept personal responsibility for their acts, and are even able to make fuller use of their intellectual flexibility.*[20] Here, parenthetically, we have a classical explanation of the virtues of academic tenure!

On the other hand, the study indicates that bureaucratization does make for some differences in the "conditions of occupational life": its members do more complex jobs than others of the same educational level; they are more closely supervised; work under externally imposed deadlines; enjoy more job protection; and they earn more than others of similar educational backgrounds.

In interpreting these data, the author notes that it may be that it is not bureaucratic structure that explains his findings but the kind of highly educated people recruited into bureaucracy. Also, he notes that the correlations are consistently quite small, which may be related to the fact

18 *Ibid.*, p. 468.
19 *Ibid.*, p. 468, italics added.
20 *Ibid.*, p. 470, italics added.

that only one dimension of bureaucracy was used in the study. He asks whether the findings reflect bureaucratization or only size. Finally, perhaps the use of several typical characteristics of bureaucracy rather than just the structure of authority relations might be producing misleading results. But even if the limitations are at work, the research is so careful and the findings are so contrary to established judgment that they stimulate rethinking and merit further analysis. Experienced officials have often noted that bureaucratic men are often highly intelligent and that they perform highly complex tasks, but they often conclude that such men are not typically marked by the need for self-direction or self-assertion. They tend to submerge themselves nicely into the collective mode of decision-making and responsibility that defines bureaucratic structures.

Turning to another level of analysis, there is considerable interest in the extent of cultural influences upon bureaucratic structure. Insofar as bureaucratic systems are "miniature societies" that tend to act as instruments of socialization in inculcating such values, this focus seems quite useful in understanding bureaucracy and in determining the extent to which its "ideal typical" norms are beyond time and space. Some evidence suggests that this kind of inquiry is worthwhile.

Cultural Influences and Organizational Structures

Organizational analysts readily admit that the structural characteristics of an organization are determined largely by environmental values, demands, responses, and limitations. They seek to determine the channels through which external social inputs are evaluated and acted upon within an organization and frequently stress, with considerable normative zeal, the need for greater organizational sensitivity to noninstitutional social variables.

Ironically, much less attention has been paid to the most pervasive of all environmental factors—culture. Few comprehensive comparative studies are available that define the patterns of dependency which link particular organizational structures to particular cultural environments. In simple terms, the question to be posed is "Do the structural characteristics and methods of dealing with issues of a given organization reflect, to any significant degree, the cultural traits of the society in which that organization operates?" The obvious corollary to such a question is, "If so, is it possible to deduce a typology of organizational structures relative to their various cultural settings?"

Crozier, in an impressive study of bureaucratic institutions in France, appears to answer these questions in the affirmative.[21] His examination involves several observations of persistent French cultural traits: He notes that the French continue to view authority negatively in universalistic and absolutist terms, and are suspicious and apprehensive of its application. However, they recognize that some form of authority is indispensable if cooperative undertakings are to succeed.[22] The French dislike and distrust disorder, conflict, and any personal, face-to-face, dependence relationships, and they are often intolerant of ambiguous situations.[23] They frequently find it difficult to cooperate in collective efforts [24] and are unwilling to defer to the whims of other men [25] or to any blatant application of personal, non-institutional coercion.

The accuracy of Crozier's assessment of French cultural traits is, of course, less important to this discussion than his attempts to relate these traits to French bureaucratic structures. The most striking characteristics of organizational activity in France, according to his study, are: (1) the extent of the development of impersonal rules, (2) the centralization of decisions, (3) strata isolation, and (4) the development of parallel power relationships in areas of uncertainty.[26] In general, then, the typical French organization has a highly developed system of ranking and regulation with little decentralization of decision-making authority. There is little informal communication between different levels of bureaucracy and few patterns of cooperation, especially along the vertical dimension.

In several respects, the French cultural traits that Crozier describes on the one hand and the organizational characteristics that he presents on the other are quite compatible and mutually self-reinforcing. Where individuals distrust the interpersonal exercise of authority, it logically follows that, in order to minimize internal tensions, authority patterns must be psychologically removed or depersonalized by embodying them within impersonal, non-political structural forms. While the individual may be hesitant to defer to authority in a direct face-to-face encounter, he is less inclined to react negatively toward a structural exercise of authority that, at least theoretically, applies to all individuals equally. The further removed in personal or psychological terms that authority is, the more

[21] Michel Crozier, *The Bureaucratic Phenomenon* (Chicago: University of Chicago Press, 1964).
[22] *Ibid.*, p. 222.
[23] *Ibid.*, p. 226.
[24] *Ibid.*, p. 216.
[25] *Ibid.*, p. 223.
[26] *Ibid.*, p. 187.

likely it will be that the individual perceives the costs of submitting to authority to be reduced and, therefore, acceptable. Thus, a highly centralized organizational system with highly developed impersonal rules and rigid definition of rank and responsibility (i.e., a system where authority and conflict are effectively removed from personal encounters) is best suited to the French temperament *vis-à-vis* authority and conflict.

In those situations where impersonal rules and ranking do not obtain, organizational activity will revert to a more personal, political, and, consequently, less stable state. Individual personality and access to political resources will tend to determine authoritative organizational relationships and, as a result, the rationality of decision-making will often suffer. Crozier claims that, wherever possible, the French will avoid such situations and will, instead, seek to re-establish a centralized, well-defined bureaucratic structure in which the occurrence of personal conflict is minimized.

In order to determine whether a direct relationship exists between organizational characteristics and distinctive cultural traits, as Crozier finds in the French example, it would be useful to undertake an extensive comparative analysis of similar phenomena in other societies. Crozier's attempt to extend his conceptual framework to other countries, although lacking in detail and not entirely convincing, does point the way toward the required comparative study. His discussion of the American case is generally instructive and does tend to validate the central claim that organizational structures relate closely to the cultural environment in which they operate: the individualism of Americans, their greater tendency toward cooperation (these two traits are not necessarily in conflict), and their emphasis upon democratic values and due process [27] are strongly reflected in the organizations they build. Like French organizations, authority in American bureaucracies is depersonalized by the development of a comprehensive system of impersonal organizational rules, but, unlike the French case, authority is frequently divided and decentralized to a greater extent in response to general social demands for democratization. Decision-making is often a collective effort rather than a product of purely hierarchical considerations. (Note that such observations are only made in relative terms—no one would claim that authority in the American system is completely decentralized nor is it valid to claim that all French organizations are totally centralized.) Individuals in American associations seem less inclined to remain isolated and tend to establish

[27] *Ibid.*, pp. 232–34.

patterns of cooperation, both across and within rank differentiations, with greater ease.

Crozier's attempt to assess the influence of culture on organizational structures and his tentative steps in the direction of a typology of organizations as they relate to cultural factors represent an important departure in an area of organizational theory for which considerable research and investigation are required, particularly in the case of developing, non-Western societies.

Before considering other new developments in the study of organizations, it is interesting to note very briefly a model of bureaucratic organization that Crozier derives from his consideration of French bureaucracies. He postulates that bureaucratic organizations are composed essentially of a system of "vicious circles." Bureaucracies are typically unable to correct their own errors and many of these organizational dysfunctions tend to be internally reincorporated, thus effectively reinforcing the imperfection of the organization.[28] Several examples are cited:

> [The organization's] struggle against centralization is not directed toward helping the organization to adapt better to the challenge of the environment, but rather toward safeguarding and developing the kind of rigidity that is protecting them (from the challenge of the environment). . . . [The] proliferation of impersonal bureaucratic rules reduces the tensions created by too close supervision, while, at the same time, the frustrations and the poor performances that develop in an impersonal bureaucratic world reinforce the need for close supervision.[29]

And, further:

> . . . the rigidity of task definition, task arrangements, and the human relations network results in a lack of communication with the environment and a lack of communication among the groups. The resulting difficulties, instead of imposing a readjustment of the model, are utilized by individuals and groups for improving their position in the power struggle within the organization. Thus a new pressure is generated for impersonality and centralization, the only solution to the problem of personal privileges.[30]

Thus bureaucracies, at least in the French case, do not always have the capacity to remedy their own organizational problems internally. Individuals become caught up in the "vicious circles" and the scope for innovation and effective confrontation of environmental problems is greatly decreased.

28 Crozier, op. cit., French edition, p. 255.
29 The Bureaucratic Phenomenon, op. cit., pp. 193–94.
30 Ibid., p. 194.

IS BUREAUCRACY NECESSARY?

This catalogue of bureaucratic dysfunctions raises the question, Is bureaucracy really necessary? Some recent critics have answered 'no,' while others have asked for sharp modifications in the classical norms and forms of bureaucratic structure and behavior.[31] Perhaps history is useful in considering the answer to this question. From its inception thousands of years ago in ancient civilizations of China and Egypt, bureaucracy has been a product of the size and scope of operations. Although the exact number is moot, whenever more than a few individuals attempt to collaborate in carrying out collective goals, organization, specialization, and hierarchy tend to appear. The King's Household in Britain expanded from reliance upon a few trusted friends (patrimonial system) to the need for skilled, quasi-permanent officials. A critical incentive, in addition to expertise, was the opportunity presented to avoid the delegation of too much influence to counselors by replacing them with individuals who had no claim, by birth or friendship, upon the King's largesse.

As Weber shows, the rise of modern bureaucracy is largely a result of capitalism and its highly rationalized, far-flung economic dominance in world markets. Yet, socialist regimes have proved to be even more dependent upon bureaucratic apparatuses. Centralization has often provided the basis for the scale of operation that characterizes bureaucratic structures in every context. As de Toqueville observed, the scope of government increases steadily with the advance of civilization and the assertion of new popular demands. Perhaps it is significant that such dramatic innovations in policy as the federal poverty and job training programs during the 1960's were launched under the usual bureaucratic forms.[32] The eminent French sociologist, Emile Durkheim, noted the

[31] See, for example, Richard Cloward and Frances Piven, "A Strategy to End Poverty," *Nation*, Vol. 202 (May, 1966), pp. 510–17.

[32] Doubts about this generalization may be eased by the following memo from the Office of Equal Opportunity:

August 20, 1971
Reply to Attn. of: OPD/D
Subject: Reallocation of Furniture

To: Jim Duffy: It has come to my attention that Susan Hager of the Education and Youth Branch will be leaving OPD in early September, thus vacating her office, M-612. With the new freeze on Federal employment, I doubt she will be replaced in the near future. As a result, the furniture now occupying M-612 should be reallocated. Even if Miss Hager is replaced, there are several items with which a

pervasive rise of occupational specialization and its functional consequences for society by limiting competition.[33] Insofar as specialization is
a cause and effect of bureaucracy, we have here another incentive for
bureaucracy.

Such observations suggest that it is perhaps romantic to assume that
bureaucratic structure and norms are either dispensable or subject to
sharp modification. As other institutions, bureaucracy is a mixed blessing
and it may be that its very advantages cannot sustain the attempts to
radically alter its structure or its style. Its classical virtues include rationality of means (not necessarily of ends), order, predictability, some
measure of political accountability, personal security, and specialization.
There is at least some evidence, too, that bureaucracy is highly adaptable
to different types of substantive programs, among which NASA is a recent
dramatic example. Counter-culture values of spontaneity, free choice,
anti-professionalism, non-competition, full participation—all are often
either inapposite to or destructive of bureaucracy's *operational* virtues.
These counter values are appealing, but they are not necessarily germane
when great tasks have to be done. As the principle of seniority (and
progressive taxation), bureaucracy is far from ideal, but it raises the least
protest among the most individuals.

Certainly, one would prefer to see bureaucracy function more quickly,
reward its members in terms of differences in productivity, reduce its
tendency toward waste, curb its inclination toward empire-building without substance, bring its poorer, less politically advantaged clients into
the act (others take care of themselves quite well), but one would also
like to see *other* American institutions—including universities—reduce the
distance between their ideals of rationality and free intellectual enquiry,
and their tendency to defer to government-defined policies and research,
as well as their use of particularistic bases of faculty recruitment.[34]

Such judgments, of course, are hardly satisfactory to those who want
dramatic and rapid change in society and its major institutions, but as
noted elsewhere, societies find it very hard to break away from time-

---

GS-9 is not usually equipped already in the office, namely a bookcase and a conference table.

As a result, I am requesting a reallocation of the bookcase to room M-821-I and
the conference table to room M-821-A. I would suggest we move on this one now
since I have observed that often furniture from offices to be vacated is "absorbed"
into other non-vacated rooms.

Thanks for your cooperation.

James R. Tanck, Special Assistant to the Director, Office of Program Development

[33] *The Division of Labour in Society* (New York: Free Press, 1964).

[34] See Caplow and McGee, *The Academic Marketplace* (New York: Basic Books,
1958).

honored cultural norms and forms. Change that is not in line with the essentially conservative preferences of most Americans is especially difficult to carry through. Recent efforts at innovation in the areas of community control, the alleviation of poverty, and urban development have hardly been successful and they are now receding in the public consciousness, as well as among political elites who were always ambivalent about them. As Katz and Danet conclude, "the romantic halo surrounding the mystique of 'the power of the poor' and of 'citizen participation' has sadly worn thin in the past five years." [35] Ideology is a poor substitute for political resources.

[35] *Bureaucracy and the Public, op. cit.,* p. 397.

8

The Bureaucratic
Policy Process:
An Empirical Test

Most governmental policy-making occurs through a process of inter-action or accommodation among "the political elite," which may be said to include legislators, high-level civil servants, and the directors and agents of articulate interest groups, typically representing the great institutional sectors of American society, including agriculture, business, and labor.[1] Policy may be regarded as the outcome of sustained and generally cooperative negotiation and bargaining among these elites, who play direct and authoritative roles in the political process. Although the substantive range of such policy-making is virtually infinite, ranging across the entire spectrum of human activity, the *process* by which it occurs tends to be highly standardized. In this chapter, we shall be concerned with this process, which may be called one of "elite accommo-dation." At the same time, the research reported here may be regarded as an example of work in "organizational behavior."

Much of the incentive for governmental policies comes from interest groups. To some extent, as the German sociologist Ralf Dahrendorf has

[1] For detailed analyses of the structure and policy role of this elite, see Robert Presthus, *Elite Accommodation in Canadian Politics* (New York and London: Cambridge University Press, 1973); and *Elites in the Policy Process* (New York and London: Cambridge University Press, 1974).

said, "Governments of Western societies are often mere switchboards of authority; decisions are made not by them but through them." [2]

An understanding of this reality and the attending policy process can be gained without necessarily including the substantive issues involved in it. For this reason, we turn here to an empirical study of policy-making as it occurs between senior bureaucrats and interest groups and their agents.

PATTERNS OF AGENCY–GROUP INTERACTION

Research indicates that, although legislators and legislative committees are the major target of groups, the bureaucracy is also a major target.[3] Despite the initiative enjoyed by the presidency in our separation of powers system, and the critical role of congressional committees, senior officials indicate a high level of contact with directors and lobbyists, most of it focusing, as we saw earlier, upon the establishment and modification of regulatory standards, but a substantial portion also relating to legislation. High-level bureaucrats, in effect, interact intensively with "lobbyists" [4] and it is upon their behavior that the analysis will focus. Before presenting the data, however, it is useful to discuss briefly the underlying theoretical structure of interaction theory, which is used to order our data. Quite simply, interaction theory assumes that individual and group behavior is highly determined by the exchange of valued benefits.[5] Individuals sustain relationships that prove gratifying, from which, in economic terms, they "make a profit." Such "profits" are of many kinds— which, parenthetically, adds to the utility of interaction theory—and include status, income, affection, security, empathy, and moral support. In effect, they range from "hard" types of currencies such as money and power to subjective incentives including friendship and love. Such a process may be conceptualized by the syndrome I-L-I, in which *Interac-*

---

[2] *Class and Class Conflict in Industrial Society* (Stanford, Calif.: Stanford University Press, 1959), p. 306.

[3] Presthus, *Elites in the Policy Process, op. cit.,* especially Chap. 9.

[4] The term "lobbyists" is defined broadly here to include virtually anyone who attempts to influence governmental policy-making, including for example, the prestigious members of their groups whom interest group directors often employ in contacting governmental elites (i.e., legislators and senior bureaucrats), as well as rank-and-file members of groups when they write or visit such elites in an attempt to press their claims.

[5] See George Homans, *The Human Group* (New York: Harcourt Brace Jovanovich, 1950); *Social Behavior: Its Elementary Forms* (New York: Harcourt Brace Jovanovich, 1961).

tion tends to result in shared sentiments and the imputation of *Legitimacy* to those with whom one interacts, culminating in *Influence* or the capacity to achieve one's will. The major hypothesis in the present research is that there is a positive association between these three variables in which, as interaction increases, legitimacy will increase, and so will the potential influence of interest groups. Putting this theory into the present context, the data presented here will test the proposition that senior officials who interact most with interest group agents will tend, all else being equal, to trust them more and to be more subject to their influence, compared with those who interact less frequently.

It must be emphasized that the data also indicate the extent of agency–group interaction, the impact which interest groups have upon policy through resulting influence, and the legitimacy that is ascribed to them by senior officials. We get, in sum, a picture of the policy-making *process.* In order to supply the substantive component, we shall present first several random "case issues" presented by group directors and senior officials. It should be noted that these cases are *verbatim* transcripts of interviews; minor editing of the tapes has been done to ease the exposition, but their essential character remains unchanged. The first issue concerns an American rural-housing, welfare type of group, recently formed, with only 300 individual members, financed mainly by the Ford Foundation and the Office of Economic Opportunity. Among its major resources, as the following exchange suggests, is the political sophistication and tenacity of the director, an economist by profession.

> *Issue:* We set out to get permanent legislation for the self-help housing program, a program for housing some of the poor, in 1967. The self-help housing program is one in which poor people can build good homes for themselves by doing the work under expert supervision. It cuts 25 to 40 per cent off the total cost of the house. This program, which had been used successfully in Nova Scotia and Puerto Rico, had been funded on a small scale here. OEO had provided the administrative funds and the Farmers Home Administration (FHA) had provided the mortgage credit. OEO had no more funds for this purpose because the war on poverty was already shifting to the war against Vietnam, and the projects were having trouble because OEO had one set of rules and FHA had another set and most of the needy people fell between the rules. Moreover, FHA could lend money only in rural areas and towns of 5,500 population or below. The idea was to get the whole program set up in Housing and Urban Development with a uniform set of rules on eligibility, rule out the rural/urban barrier and get more

money. The idea for the change originated on the West Coast with the Acting Director of the biggest of the self-help programs. He wrote the bill and got it introduced by Congressman Hagan, and later by Congressman Sisk.

Q. Did you enlist the help of any other public officials?

A. Initially, Hagan, who was later defeated, and then Sisk. Up to that point nothing had happened, no hearings, etc. I found out that Sisk would not push the bill because of pressure against it by the lobbyist for the AFL–CIO building trades, so I took the problem to two old friends, the Staff Director of the House Banking and Currency Committee and to his boss, the Chairman of the Committee.

Q. Could you tell me all the various methods you used and rank them?

A. We couldn't have done it if we hadn't been close to some Farmers Home officials, particularly the Administrator, Howard Bertsch, who was friendly to the idea. Our membership is inconsequential in numbers; we don't have any compaign funds; we don't have a professional public relations man; we don't even have a lobbyist. The labor movement, particularly the building trades, were uneasy about anything that might reduce employment for their members.

So how do you go about it? You fall back on a Congressman here and there, an old friend, liberal and sympathetic to poor people. You fall back on a strategically placed friend who runs the staff and who as it turns out (with his Chairman's consent) shoved the amendments into the hands of another member of the committee one day saying 'the Chairman wants you to introduce these this morning . . .' and they were approved by the Committee. We had another Congressman, a Chicano, who was supposed to have introduced the language, but he didn't show up to do the job, so the Chairman had to get it done by someone else.

Sisk backed off because he needed labor support to hold his seat and wasn't prepared either to argue with labor or admit to the folks back home that he couldn't. I knew that had to be stopped somehow, so I talked to the labor lobbyist and he said he had his orders and only his boss could change them. Then I tried to reach his boss but he was either too busy or pretended he was, so I wrote him a long letter and sent him some pictures of the poor people building their houses, and I told him that he didn't have to help us but he could at least leave us alone in trying to get the bill. I also reminded him that the craft unions already had a bad name for racial discrimination in jobs and told him he couldn't afford to be on record as being opposed to letting Indians, blacks and Chicanos build their own houses. (Most of the people doing self-help were minority people.) I also asked an old high-school friend who was on the National Labour Relations Board to call the craft-union lobbyist and ask him to leave the bill alone. I don't know whether he called or not, but somebody called the dogs off.

So you manipulate a change of law really by no means other than an idea and personal friends . . . particularly if the law deals with the poor and your friends are that kind of people.

Q. What was the specific outcome of the issue?

A. After I got into the act, after Hagan was defeated, we abandoned the idea of putting the program into HUD because they didn't want it . . . and agencies have a lot of influence on the Hill. Weaver, the secretary, was opposed to self-help because he figured it was a way of making poor people work harder for what they got than other people . . . and besides he had had a bad experience with a self-help operator in Cleveland and the whole program left a bad taste in his mouth. So we pulled it back to where we had a friend in the agency (FHA) and could count on agency support, if a Congressman called for advice. When the Committee bill went through, the language in it went before the Rules Committee of the House, Congressman Sisk, a member of the Committee, congratulated the Chairman on the portion of the housing bill and said 'I'm so happy you brought *my* bill in.' And Wright Patman said, 'if I could, I would name the bill after you.' The bill with our amendment passed the House, was kept in conference and became law.

Q. To what extent did you achieve your objective?

A. The original objective was to consolidate everything over in HUD, but we had to back off from that and work on just the rural program because of Weaver's unfriendly attitude toward the program. We got HUD in a limited way later; Senator Mondale passed the original amendment which became Section 106(a), which had to go through two original enactments before HUD could even be forced to touch the program at all and then in only a very limited way. (They did spend a half million dollars studying the program . . . to no avail.)

Q. In this issue, then, you focused your main attention on the House?

A. Yes.

Q. After that you focused on HUD?

A. No. The House of Representatives. That law was enacted by one staff director and 2 congressmen in the House, and successfully retained in conference with the Senate, which is important because the slickest way in the world to kill something is to 'lose' it in conference.

Several points are punctuated here. This director's sophistication regarding the legislative process is quite clear. In general, access appears to have been quite easy. The 'reality-oriented' perceptions of the director toward legislators and agency heads, as well as the extent to which both governmental elites are involved in policy making, are equally salient.

The next example involves a state regulatory agency, concerned with the rather unusual problem of cattle-rustling, and operating under a department of agriculture. The responses again indicate the importance that bureaucrats attach to the groups with whom they interact.

Issue: The specific issue is a case involving the theft of 19 cattle. My men in the valley were contacted by the sheriff's department, saying they had a lead on cattle being held in the area.

Q. What groups were involved?

A. The State Cattlemen's Association is always concerned about cattle theft.

Q. Your representatives from the department are in various parts of the state.

A. Right. We are the police force of the whole Department of Agriculture. Our basic function is to inspect cattle for brands. Twenty-one people who do nothing but inspect cattle for branding work for me. They inspect at public livestock markets and slaughter houses, prior to going in or out of the state. When cattle do not belong to those who have them, they are returned to their rightful owner. In a year we actually pick up about 5,000 head which actually belong to someone else. This is our specific responsibility.

Q. To what degree does this involve you with interest groups?

A. The secretary of the Cattlemen's Association calls me at least one a week to tell me that there are lost cattle.

Q. So in terms of interest groups they contact you because it is your responsibility to carry out the law?

A. To keep cattle theft in the news.

Q. So, in terms of the groups involved, it is simply those whose cattle are stolen, lost, or gone astray?

A. That's right, except in the case where someone else might contact you to bring it to your attention. We take it from there and try to determine what has happened.

Q. Is this the way you typically become aware of a problem?

A. Right.

Q. What was the specific outcome of this case?

A. On Christmas day, the sheriff, his deputies and two of my men found two men just prepared to butcher 19 head of cattle. They were taken to jail, where one admitted his guilt; the other one went on trial and was found guilty.

Q. So your relationship with interest groups is generally that they recognize that you carry out the law and therefore they contact you to report that a law has been broken, and to get action?

A. That's right.

Q. How effective are these kinds of groups in dealing with your department?

A. Moderately effective.

Q. What is the main single method they use?

A. They attend our meetings and also keep day-to-day contact.

Q. How legitimate is these groups' position on such issues?

A. Legitimate.

Q. How significant a role do you feel interest groups generally play in making policy in your department?

A. Highly significant.

Q. What, if any, sanctions have you seen used against senior civil servants?

A. Sometimes, having him censured by his superiors; occasionally, criticizing an official in the mass media.

Q. In general, do you feel interest groups play a useful and necessary role in our government?

A. Definitely, they are the people, who, when they feel the law should be changed to cover modern methods, go to department heads and the legislature to request a change. They provide a means of getting changes made in our laws.

Q. Do you feel all or most of the relevant public groups make their interests known to the department?

A. Yes.

Q. Does your department have any provisions for insuring that interest groups who are not organized will be heard?

A. Yes. Hearings and meetings prior to bills in the legislature. Organized groups are informed of these procedures.

Q. Has your own or other departments ever created an interest group?

A. No.

Regarding cohesion between bureaucrats and relevant groups, it is noteworthy that this official, as his counterpart in the previous case, believed that the groups concerned played a 'highly significant' role in his agency's policy. It must be emphasized, however, that these cases are merely illustrative, offered to provide a foil against which our aggregate data can be presented more meaningfully.

The Intensity of Interaction

It is important to note that, unlike interaction between legislators and directors, that between agency and interest groups is usually substantively oriented. The term "clientele groups" is often used to symbolize this kind of symbiotic relationship between an agency and its "natural" allies in the social arena. Since governmental structures are designed functionally, this condition may be regarded as a built-in structural component of policy-making. The Milk Producers Association tends to interact mainly with certain commodity committees of the Department of Agriculture. Airline Associations deal with the CAB and the Department of Transportation. The fact that this is virtually self-evident does not weaken its significance, which rests in the fact that interaction not only tends to be sustained, but it occurs between individuals who share similar occupational backgrounds, technical knowledge, and understanding of a given social activity. Contrast this condition with that of many legislators who, despite the substantive bases of committees, tend to see individuals representing a wide spectrum of interests, some of which are familiar (if they involve significant interests in the legislator's district), but many of which are inevitably peripheral to his major concerns.

We turn to Table 8–1 for more systematic evidence regarding the intensity of contact between senior officials and the agents of interest groups. The four regions included in the study are separated for comparative purposes.

TABLE 8–1. **Comparative Rates of Bureaucratic Interaction with Interest Groups**

Intensity of Interaction	D.C.	Louisiana	Michigan	Washington	Sample
Business	30%	25%	32%	28%	29%
LC & C *	14	18	20	13	16
Prof.–Ed.	12	5	10	21	12
Labor	5	18	3	4	8
Municipal govt.	17	5	3	4	7
Welfare	0	10	12	4	7
Agriculture	14	0	0	2	4
Altruistic	1	0	3	0	1
Other	7	20	20	25	17
	(92)	(55)	(54)	(57)	

$\chi^2 =$ Washington, D.C., vs. states, significant at .001.
* Local cooperative–consumer groups.

Not unexpectedly, business groups dominate the intensity scale, with almost twice the rate found among the category ranked second in the United States. Local consumer and cooperative groups rank second, followed by professional–educational groups. A striking facet of the distribution is labor's salient position in Louisiana, compared with its relatively low ranking in other regions, especially in Michigan where organized labor in the automobile and related industries is often regarded as being very influential and articulate. Similarly, in Washington, D.C., the AFL–CIO is active across a broad spectrum of legislative and administrative issues, yet it ranks very low. The explanation probably includes at least three factors. One is that different types of groups focus on federal and state systems. Agriculture, for example, obviously turns directly to Washington, as do municipal governments. More important, in the case of labor, for example, is the tendency of mass-constituency type groups to focus upon legislatures where their electoral power and 'grass roots' structure may be brought to bear most effectively. Also, there is probably some sampling bias involved, since it is hard to believe that a completely random sample of 92 federal officials would not include at least one or two who had interacted with welfare groups.

Labor's highly organized lobbying system in Louisiana is clearly apparent in its high ranking there. The contemporary emphasis upon local cooperative and consumer action is similarly apparent in the fact that such groups equal the average intensity rates of great economic interests such as labor and agriculture. Municipal governments, too, reflect contemporary trends, as they focus upon the federal capital to cash in on the vast subsidies inspired by federal efforts to ease urban decay and disorder during the past decade. Altruistic groups obviously interact only infrequently with bureaucrats at either the federal or the state level.

The generalization is that the higher reaches of the intensity scale are dominated by groups that seek *economic benefits* from government. Such a conclusion meshes nicely with a ranking of interest group goals by directors, in which economic currencies provided the major incentive for about 40 per cent of the cross-national sample. Moreover, when officials are asked to rank the specific *demands* typically presented by interest groups, generalized economic incentives are ranked first and second by 47 and 17 per cent of the American sample, respectively. Direct economic support is so ranked by only 12 per cent, with the remaining one-quarter scattered among influencing foreign policy, resolving jurisdictional conflicts, seeking support for the arts, and easing racial tensions. In the bureaucracy's case, in sum, incentives are less likely to take the form of direct subsidies than of attempts to change regulations and establish new standards.

We turn next to more detailed analysis of interaction patterns. Before doing so, a brief methodological note is required. Chi-squares and gammas have been computed for all distributions in order to indicate the statistical weight and strength of the relationships. A chi-square of .05, for example, indicates that the relationship between the variables in the tables could have occurred by chance in the universe from which the sample is drawn only 5 times in one hundred. It must be emphasized however, that such a test does not indicate a *causal* connection but only a statistical one which suggests that the association is worth presenting as a tentative generalization. Gamma is a correlation measure showing the strength of the association between the test variables. Although there is no precise criterion for "strong" gammas, values of about .25 and above may be regarded as indicating a noteworthy relationship. Table 8–2 presents frequency of contact by region.

TABLE 8–2.   Interaction Between Bureaucrats and Interest Groups

	Frequency of Interaction *			
	High	Medium	Low	
Washington, D.C.	41%	32%	27%	(90)
Louisiana	36	26	38	(50)
Michigan	29	27	45	(49)
Washington	44	35	22	(55)

χ^2 = not significant at .05.

* "High" is defined as having direct, personal contact with group agents "frequently" (twice a week); "medium" as having such contact "occasionally" (twice a month); "low" as "seldom or rarely."

Even though the cross-regional variations are not statistically significant, they are substantial in some cases, particularly between Michigan and the other regions. Washington state ranks highest at the "high" level, which may provide support for the conventional belief that newer states, with less highly developed political systems, tend to be more penetrable by interest groups, compared with older Eastern states, such as Massachusetts or Michigan.[6] Another suggestive explanation, supported by our research, is that "liberally oriented" civil servants (and legislators) tend to resist interest group claims more than their less-liberal peers. One suspects that this may have something to do with their "public interest" ideology, which resists the ongoing system of interest group politics in which relatively few, highly articulate groups may be perceived as having too much influence, compared with weaker consumer groups

[6] For evidence supporting this belief, see H. Zeigler and M. Baer, *Lobbying* (San Francisco: Wadsworth, 1969), pp. 36–37, 155–57.

or the unorganized public. In any event, the data indicate that an average of about 38 per cent of senior officials interact frequently with group agents, by the criterion used here.

We turn next to the association between interaction and influence. The hypothesis, it will be recalled, is that these two variables are positively and significantly associated. Table 8–3 tests this proposition.

TABLE 8–3.   Association Between Interaction and Influence, Case Study

Influence [a]	Frequency of Interaction			
	High	Medium	Low	
High	30%	14%	20%	(51)
Medium	40	37	25	(80)
Low	30	49	55	(101)

χ^2 = significant at .001.
Gamma = .28.

[a] "Influence" is measured here by the case study experience of the officials. A scale of influence was designed in which those who said groups were an "integral part of the day-to-day activity of the agency" were ranked "high"; while those who declared that "the group's assumed reactions were usually taken in to account during our decisions" were ranked "medium," and those who said "they are only one among many factors impinging upon our decisions" or "they have little or no effect upon our decisions" were ranked "low."

It is clear that the interaction effects are generally in line with I-L-I theory, although the critical effect appears among those who rank low on interaction. The gamma is a fairly strong .28 and the chi-square is a very strong .001, meaning that the difference found in this random sample could have occurred by chance only 1 time in 1,000 in the universe from which it is drawn. On the other hand, among those who rank highest on interaction, equal (i.e., 30 per cent) proportions of respondents rank high and low on experienced influence. In effect, those interest group agents who see bureaucrats most frequently tend to experience a higher rate of success in convincing the latter of the validity of their claims, as measured by officials' judgments about the salience of group influence upon decisions in their agency.

It seems useful to test this association using a different measure of influence. Here (Table 8–4) we rely upon an item which asked officials how often and how much they had been influenced by lobbyists in their work role.

A dramatically strong supporting association appears, with a chi-square of .0005 and a gamma correlation of .32. It seems safe to conclude from

TABLE 8–4.   Association Between Interaction and Influence, General

Influence *	Frequency of Interaction			
	High	Medium	Low	
High	42%	43%	12%	(73)
Medium	36	37	50	(89)
Low	22	22	38	(57)

χ^2 = significant at .0005.
Gamma = .32.

* "Influence" is measured here by a single item which asked officials to indicate how frequently they had been influenced by lobbyists to the extent of (1) questioning their position in an issue, (2) coming to lean more toward the lobbyists' position, or (3) coming to agree with the lobbyists' position. Each official was asked to indicate whether such had occurred "frequently," "occasionally," or "seldom or rarely."

this evidence that officials who interact most frequently with interest group agents are most susceptible to their claims. It is interesting to note, in passing, that the Canadian sample (N-194) included in the cross-national study proved even more strongly associated on these dimensions, with a gamma of .55 and a very strong chi-square of .0007.[7] Cross-regional variations are substantial, with Louisiana exhibiting the highest proportion of officials (i.e., 37 per cent) at the *high* influence level and the other regions rank similarly and considerably lower. When officials are asked: "How significant a role do interest groups play in policy-making in your agency?," fully 46 per cent of those in Washington state rank at the high point, while Washington, D.C., ranks lowest. It must be said, however, that we have some reservations about the federal data, since there are indications, particularly regarding the existence of group sanctions, where federal officials tend to either refuse to answer or to present a suspiciously favorable situation.

A Test of Interaction Theory

As noted, interaction theory assumes that influence will be positively related to the legitimacy imputed to those with whom one associates. We also expect, following the assumptions of functional cohesion, that most officials will tend to impute a high level of legitimacy to the groups with whom they interact, often on a clientele basis. Table 8–5 provides the data.

[7]For details, see Presthus, *Elite Accommodation in Canadian Politics, op. cit.*, Chap. 9.

TABLE 8–5. Association Between Interaction and Legitimacy, Case Study

	Perceived Legitimacy			
Influence *	High	Medium	Low	
High	51%	44%	25%	(87)
Medium	30	36	29	(64)
Low	19	21	46	(45)

$\chi^2 =$ significant at .04.
Gamma $= .24$.

* "Influence" is based here upon the perceived success of the group concerned in the case study issue as judged by officials.

Here again, the assumptions of interaction theory are supported, as just over 50 per cent of those who rank high on imputed legitimacy also rank high on influence, compared with only 25 per cent who rank low. It may be that officials are misperceiving the effectiveness of the groups concerned, but it is important to remember, with I. W. Thomas, that "if men perceive situations as real, they are real in their consequences." If officials believe that groups are both legitimate and effective, we may assume that such perceptions will have a positive effect upon the operational efficacy of such groups. Indeed, there is some evidence from our data that *symbolic interaction* often occurs whereby direct interaction is not always required for group effectiveness, since officials have been, so to speak, socialized to believing that their claims should be met. Perhaps the close relationships between highly focused interests in certain producer areas are germane here.[8] On the other hand, protest groups whose tactics and objectives are not sympathetically regarded by governmental elites (e.g., protest and consumer groups) may find it difficult to achieve their ends, despite the intensity of their representations, which often result in elected and appointed elites "digging in their heels" on the grounds that they alone represent the "public." Having looked at the various partial relationships in the I-L-I syndrome, we can now turn to the association among the three critical variables. The assumption is that the shared activities among members of the political elite and the exchange of valued currencies between them result in sustained interaction with attending legitimating effects that culminate in increased influence for the groups who enjoy such trust and interact most frequently

---

[8] Certain federal and state regulatory commissions, notably in railroads and the gas and oil industry, have often been regarded as unduly sympathetic to such interests.

TABLE 8–6. Association Between Interaction and Influence among American Civil Servants, Controlling for Legitimacy

	Legitimacy [a]								
	High (113)			Medium (71)			Low (3)		
	Frequency of Interaction								
Influence [b]	High	Medium	Low	High	Medium	Low	High	Medium	Low
High	46%	56%	14%	37%	25%	6%	0%	0%	0%
Medium	39	28	63	41	50	4	100	50	0
Low	15	16	23	22	25	0	0	50	0
	(46)	(32)	(35)	(27)	(28)	(6)	(1)	(2)	(0)

American sample: χ^2 sig. at .006, K's tau b = .19, Gamma = .29

American sample: $\chi^2 = .14$, K's tau b = .25, Gamma = .38

American sample: Fisher's exact test .66, K's tau b = .50, Gamma = 1.00

(64)
(83)
(42)
(189)

a The legitimacy index used here is based upon the following items: 'How reasonable and appropriate were the methods used by the group in this [case study] issue?' and 'In your opinion, to what extent do the activities of interest groups contribute to the larger public interest, or are they usually focussed upon narrower interests?'

b "Influence" is based upon an item regarding the salience of the role played by interest groups in an agency's policy-making, as perceived by officials.

with governmental leaders. Multiple-item indices of legitimacy and influence will be used here to provide more reliable measures of such effects. We turn first to a test using indices of influence and legitimacy based upon two variables each. Table 8–6 presents the evidence.

As the distribution indicates, there is a significant association (except for the "medium" sector) among the three interaction variables in this sample. Looking across the high row, for example, we find a linear decline in experienced influence as legitimacy decreases. Forty-six per cent of those who are high on both legitimacy and interaction also rank high on influence, compared with 37 per cent in the medium sector, and 0 in the low sector. The very small number of N's in the latter category, of course, makes it impossible to generalize about this sub-set of only 3 officials. However, the fairly strong correlations among the test variables in all three sectors suggest that there is a positive association among them, as expected from interaction theory.

It should be added that the theoretical closure of the relationship is probably less important than the *operational* significance of the fact that interaction is so strongly related to influence, as shown in Table 8–4. This finding indicates that those groups who see officials most frequently tend generally to enjoy the greatest influence in official policy-making. Meanwhile, the frequency and the legitimacy of interaction between officials and interest group agents indicates the strength of bureaucratic participation in policy-making. Such policy often occurs within the framework of legislative measures, which must necessarily delegate considerable discretion to officials charged with carrying out such legislation. The latitude enjoyed by officials is probably most clearly apparent regarding the regulatory commissions, whose members operate under such broad prescriptions as the "public interest, convenience, and necessity." [9] Such subjective guidelines usually become meaningful only in terms of specific decisions, which over time provide the basis upon which regulatory policy is predicated.

Our research enables us to generalize (Table 8–7) about the comparative effectiveness of the kinds of groups representing the major institutional sectors of American society.

As the data suggest, business groups tend to exert the greatest influence upon public policy, using this measure. Fully 70 per cent of their di-

---

[9] For a useful analysis of the conflicting bases of regulatory policy and citations of various points of view regarding "proper" regulatory behavior, see Louis Jaffe, "The Illusion of Ideal Administration," *Harvard Law Review*, Vol. 86 (May, 1973), pp. 1183–99.

TABLE 8–7. Lobbying Effectiveness among Interest Groups

Effectiveness *	Percentage of Type of Group					
	Business	Prof-Ed.	Labor	Welfare	Altruistic †	
High	70	59	48	38	25	'(215)
Medium	20	24	30	35	25	(99)
Low	10	18	22	28	50	(86)
	(121)	(114)	(79)	(29)	(57)	(400)

χ^2 significant at .0001.

* Effectiveness is based upon the weighted index of lobbying influence for a combined legislative and bureaucratic sample, as experienced by directors.

† These are "cause" groups, including religious and ethnic types.

rectors rank themselves as "highly" influential in this context. Such groups also enjoy the greatest resources, in such terms as budget, salaries of directors, felt legitimacy, and intensity of interaction. As noted earlier, regarding participation, such resources are a necessary, although not sufficient, factor in political influence. That is, a director may possess impressive amounts of useful political resources, but if he fails to use them, or uses them unwisely, he will not be effective. Nevertheless, the data in Table 8–7 are suggestive in demonstrating that directors themselves perceive their effectiveness quite differently. Again following I. W. Thomas who believed that "if men perceive situations as real, they are real in their consequences," we may conclude that directors who perceive themselves as being effective in their relations with senior officials (and legislators too) are probably likely to operate more persuasively than their less confident peers. Success, as is well known, breeds success.

We need not rest our case upon this index, however, in indicating the effectiveness of business–industrial groups. Certain "psychopolitical" resources of directors may also be compared to place them (i.e., their groups) in a scale of political effectiveness. Such resources include feelings of legitimacy, perceived commitment of their members to the organization's goals, perceptions they have of legislators as being cooperative, neutral, or hostile toward their group's interests, etc. An analysis of such factors provides the scale shown in Table 8–8, in which business groups again rank highest.

As the data indicate, business directors rank highest on persuasiveness, legitimacy, and cooperative ethic. The margin over welfare groups is narrow, except for persuasiveness. Despite its vast resources in membership and budget size, labor tends to rank lower on several dimensions,

**TABLE 8–8.   Psychopolitical Resources of American and Canadian
Interest Group Directors**

	Business U.S./Can.	Labor U.S./Can.	Prof.—Ed. U.S./Can.	Welfare U.S./Can.	Altruistic U.S./Can.	Sample † U.S./Can.
			Percentage Ranking 'High' *			
Resource						
Legitimacy	61 44	32 24	52 44	58 43	44 47	49(280) 40(187)
Cooperative ethic	90 72	81 58	88 67	86 70	80 61	86(578) 66(612)
Commitment	48 43	39 22	49 38	46 52	41 47	45(294) 40(239)
Persuasive-ness	70 36	48 16	59 28	38 18	25 3	48(215) 20(102)

* 'High' refers to the following conditions: legitimacy, the proportion ranking 'always' re-garding perceptions of legislators' approval of their group; cooperative ethic, rejection of the proposition that legislators are 'competitors in a struggle to shape public policy;' commitment, proportion of members 'intensely' identified with the group's goals; persuasiveness, proportion ranking at the 'high' level on a weighted index designed according to the influence each director felt he had exerted over governmental elites through lobbying.

† The N's in this table are quite small because the analysis from which they are derived was controlled for both frequency of contact and type of organization, and multiple-item indices were used. When this is done, many cases are lost because respondents fail to answer one or more of the items required to make up such indices. Also, the table includes only the 'highs' in each resource category, which immediately excludes from one-half to two-thirds of the sample. The explanation for the large N in the 'cooperative ethic' row is that unlike the others, this was a simple 'yes' or 'no' type of response. Despite such problems, the relative position of the groups on each resource is probably accurate.

compared with other groups. Labor directors are especially marginal on legitimacy, defined as the extent to which they believe governmental elites regard labor's attempts to influence them as proper. A dramatic cross-national variation occurs here between American and Canadian labor directors, with the former exhibiting significantly higher rankings on every dimension of psychopolitical resources. Canadian labor's disadvantaged position is particularly great on the "persuasiveness" dimension which not only indicates that directors feel unable to convince political elites of the validity of their claims, but also that directors do not tend, as one might expect, to systematically exaggerate their political efficacy.

The explanations for this cross-national variation are several. Public opinion polls in Canada indicate that labor is only marginally legitimated by most members of Canadian society. For the past two decades, a sub-stantial majority have indicated that they do not believe that unions should take an active role in politics, and the proportion of union mem-bers who share this view is only 6 points lower than among men and women in other occupational roles. That Canada is more recently industrialized than the U.S. is also germane, as well as the attending fact that only one-third of the Canadian labor force is organized, compared with almost one-half in the United States. Perhaps because Canada has a labor party—The New Democratic Party—which despite its success in several provinces has had little national impact, this may also inhibit Canadian labor's popular legitimacy, tending to set it apart from the political and social mainstream. It should be noted in Table 8–8 that labor directors are quite aware of their precarious legitimacy, as indicated by their low comparative ranking on the "legitimacy" dimension.

It seems clear that governmental elites in both societies are aware of the relative legitimacy and influence of interest groups, and that such impressions have operational influences upon the extent to which they feel obligated to entertain their claims. Legislators are experts in the estimation of power and influence, and its attending survival implications, in political terms. The data also suggest certain aspects of the political milieu in which senior officials play out their essentially political roles.

Summary

What do these findings tell us about the bureaucratic policy-making process? Based as they are upon random samples of federal and state officials and group directors, they provide some useful generalizations about the structure of the policy-making process. Interaction between the two sets of elites is typically "frequent" and tends to occur upon a functional and representational basis. Ascriptions of legitimacy to interest groups by officials are high and positive. An overwhelming majority of officials, moreover, tend to define their role as one of "service" to groups in their own substantive or functional area. Most of them interact with group agents "frequently" and there are no significant variations on this score between federal and state officials. While it is often said that lobbyists are more active (and influential) at the state, compared with the federal level, there are no significant differences between them here. Washington state does rank highest in frequency of interaction, but Washington, D.C., is second and by a substantial margin over Michigan and Louisiana. The data suggest that different types of groups displace varying amounts of influence over public policy, with larger proportions of business, welfare, and professional directors enjoying greater influence than their peers in altruistic and labor organizations.

The evidence suggests, in effect, that it is useful to conceptualize the policy-making process as one of "elite accommodation," in which major groups representing the great institutional sectors of American society bargain and negotiate with governmental elites in a generally cooperative and symbiotic context. Such groups are viewed by most members of the governmental elite as a highly legitimate and functionally essential part of the political system. Bureaucracy is a full-time partner in the attending process, but one suspects that it is essentially a junior partner, insofar as the major decisions are concerned. Such decisions tend to originate outside the formal political structure,[10] while within it their resolution is mainly in the hands of high-level, politically appointed or elected members of the political elite.

[10] The U. S. policy of containment following World War II, for example, was apparently designed by a rather small group of men, very few of whom held *elected* office, although several held high appointive positions. Cf. John C. Donovan, *The Cold Warriors: A Policy-Making Elite* (Lexington, Mass.: D. C. Heath, 1974). For an analysis which uses similar facts and language ("concentric rings of policy making," p. 118; "closed politics," p. 119) but arrives at a more traditional, pluralistic definition of policy-making in foreign affairs and defense, see Roger Hilsman, *The Politics of Policy Making in Defense and Foreign Policy* (New York: Harper and Row, 1971).

III

PERSONNEL: POLICIES AND PROGRAMS

9

The Role of Personnel Management

We saw earlier that organizational theory now emphasizes the individual in the organization–individual equation. Contemporary attitudes toward work and the demand for participation in many contexts symbolize this general orientation, which provides a new challenge to personnel management. Organizations are faced with the obligation to find some reasonable balance between the needs of the organization for rationality, continuity, and productivity and those of the individual for self-realization, diversity, and growth in his work and workplace. In the past, personal ambition and economic necessity tended to push people into rather stable occupational roles. But today it seems that many individuals bring an entirely different set of expectations to the job role. Among the results is a new emphasis upon positive, developmental personnel policies.

THE DIVERSITY OF PUBLIC PERSONNEL SYSTEMS

Although some of the material in this section is quite descriptive, it seems essential to an understanding of the personnel field. Certain assumptions and procedures, developed over a long period of time, have become hallmarks of the field and it is necessary to know something about their origin and purpose if one is to understand current assumptions and practices, some of which have probably outlived their usefulness.

One cannot, unfortunately, speak of a standardized personnel system in American public administration. Instead, a substantial number of organizations have the authority to make decisions in personnel matters and to establish autonomous systems. In the federal system, for example, the Civil Service Commission is the central agency charged with general personnel functions, yet many agencies have their own systems(including the Atomic Energy Commission, the Tennessee Valley Authority, the FBI, and the Foreign Service.) We shall also see later that there is a category of high-level positions in which, for all practical purposes, appointments are made by the head of the agencies concerned. These are called Schedule A and B and non-career executive assignments. The so-called "super-grade" positions are those for which the usual scheme of entry by competitive examination is not thought suitable, often because of the "political" character or demands of the position, or perhaps because some highly unusual skills are required. Despite such variations, there is an area called personnel administration discussed generally in this chapter, followed in subsequent chapters by analysis of some of its major aspects.

FUNCTIONS OF PERSONNEL MANAGEMENT

Although the major activities covered by the term vary considerably, "personnel management" consists of a body of duties or tasks that must be performed by someone in every large-scale organization, including business, universities, and the military. Such tasks usually include the following:

1. *Job analysis and position classification:* the description of the work to be performed in a given job which provides the basis for effective recruitment.
2. *Recruitment and placement:* the process of matching individual skills and aptitudes with job or class specifications.
3. *Evaluation, promotion, and transfer:* the procedures used to recognize accomplishment and to use individual abilities to greatest advantage.
4. *Compensation scales:* plan for assuring equal pay for equal work, with salary gradations based on the skills required by the job.
5. *Training, counseling, and improvement of working conditions:* the most important of a variety of services designed to motivate employees.
6. *Relations with employee organizations and unions:* handling relationships with these groups.

7. *Disciplinary action:* the supervision of individual suspension and dismissal cases.

8. *Personnel records:* maintaining such employee records as rosters, time cards, sick- and vacation-leave records, eligible lists, payrolls, and employee folders.

These activities, and the conditions that inspired them, have evolved over a long time, but they are always being changed in the light of new social and technological developments, including the new insights provided by behavioral research and on-the-job experience. Nevertheless, both norms and institutions change rather slowly and one of the best ways to understand them is through an historical perspective. For this reason, we begin with a brief review of several historical and cultural influences that have shaped modern personnel management in government.

THE CULTURAL CONTEXT OF PERSONNEL SYSTEMS

Public personnel management in the United States has always suffered from somewhat negative popular attitudes and from manipulation for political purposes. To some extent, these perceptions are related, although popular ambivalence about civil service work also stems from a generalized "anti-government" bias which had its origins in the fear of oppressive government apparent in the men who drafted the American Constitution. One institutional manifestation is our separation of powers system, designed to weaken government and thereby diminish the probability that it would exceed its powers.

Insofar as patronage is concerned, government jobs have sometimes been held by individuals not qualified for work in the private sector of society. Alternatively, they have been given to people who might be reasonably competent but who were also from the ruling political party. During the early years of the Republic, it was quite common for job-seekers to appeal for preference on the grounds of family and connections.[1]

This practice was in part an English legacy, for in the eighteenth and nineteenth century, the children of advantaged families (other than the eldest son) were often given government sinecures.[2] Class attitudes to-

[1] See for example, Leonard D. White, *The Jeffersonians* (New York: The Macmillan Co., 1951).

[2] J. Donald Kingsley, *Representative Bureaucracy* (Yellow Springs, Ohio: Antioch Press, 1944), especially Chaps. 2 and 3.

ward work severely limited occupational choice, and a career in Whitehall was quite acceptable socially. Even today, an appointment in the administrative class (the small group of some 5,000 officials who direct the huge British civil service) has considerable prestige. In the middle of the nineteenth century, laws formalized class privilege by making entrance to the higher service dependent upon an Oxford or Cambridge education which only upperclass children could secure. On the whole, the result was healthy because it gave the top-level British civil service a high degree of competence. The virtues of the "administrative class" have been extolled for decades by American observers. Today, partly because of democratic ideology and partly because the old preparation did not meet all the needs of a technological age, the elite is being democratized somewhat by provision of avenues of entrance other than the university honors course.[3] At the same time, questions are being raised about the effectiveness of civil servants trained in the classical tradition.[4]

The development of personnel administration in the United States has been subject to a different set of influences.[5] The equalitarian philosophy of the young republic fostered the concept that one man was as good as another, legally, if not by natural endowment. It was felt, moreover, that the work of government was so simple that any citizen was qualified to do it. Thus arose the famous spoils system so familiar to Americans. In brief, it consisted of passing out government jobs to the followers of those who won elections. This resulted in considerable turnover when a new party came to power. Government jobs were filled by party workers, their friends, and relatives. A public job was a reward for political service or a haven for those who had not found their niche in the private economy. As a result, competent people tended to avoid public employment.

During the last half of the nineteenth century, the abuses of the system inspired considerable protest.[6] After the assassination of President Garfield by a disenchanted office seeker, Congress passed the Pendleton Act of 1883, which has provided the basic civil service legislation up to now. Since that time, the civil service movement has made constant gains—

[3] For a careful study showing that recruitment practices have not changed significantly, see R. Kelsall, et al., Graduates: The Sociology of an Elite (London: Methuen and Co., 1972), pp. 98–99, and passim.

[4] See, Timothy Balough, "Apotheosis of the Dilettante," in Hugh Thomas, The Establishment (London: New English Library, 1962).

[5] For some historical trends in personnel administration, see Paul Van Riper, History of the U. S. Civil Service (New York: Harper & Row, 1958).

[6] The main sponsor of civil service reform was the National Civil Service League of New York City; see Frank M. Stewart, The National Civil Service Reform League (Austin: University of Texas Press, 1929).

particularly during the last quarter-century—until almost all federal employees are now under some form of civil service or merit system. All states have some kind of merit system for those social security programs partly financed from federal funds, and three-quarters of the states have civil service systems covering other positions. Furthermore, patronage has been substantially reduced in cities and counties. Nevertheless, huge areas in some states and in local government are still subject to patronage.[7] The battle against patronage continues on at least two fronts. The first entails pushing back the patronage boundaries through new merit system laws. The second requires the policing of civil service to insure that the merit system is not manipulated to permit patronage in day-to-day administration.

FROM CIVIL SERVICE TO MERIT SYSTEM

The terms "civil service" and "merit system" have so far been used interchangeably. They do mean essentially the same thing, but the growing use of "merit system" is to a considerable extent symbolic of a basic change in philosophy. The original civil service laws were written as a protest against the abuses of spoils and patronage, but the mere existence of these laws did not insure their observance. As a result, the first several decades of civil service administration were characterized by a negative attitude; civil service commissions were cast in the role of protecting the virtuous against the wolves of patronage. Personnel administration was lodged in a control agency usually called the "civil service commission." Politicians were not the only culprits to be fended off by the defenders of purity; operating departments were also suspect, sometimes justifiably, because they were headed by political appointees.[8]

Public personnel management has also been characterized by values which tend to separate it from the mainstream of program administration. This resulted mainly from the spirit of reform wherein "civil service" people distrusted line management which often seemed to represent the spoils system. But it was also manifested in a kind of dead-center me-

---

[7] See, for example, Ari Hoogenboom, *Outlawing the Spoils* (Urbana: University of Illinois Press, 1961); W. R. Gump, "Fuctions of Patronage in American Party Politics: an Empirical Reappraisal," *Midwest Journal of Political Science*, Vol. 15 (February, 1971), pp. 87–107; H. O. Waldby, *The Patronage System in Oklahoma* (Norman, Okla.: The Transcript Co., 1950); see also reports on patronage in Indiana and Pennsylvania in *Good Government* (September–October, 1957), Vol. 74, p. 45.

[8] A useful study at the national level is Paul Van Riper's, *History of the United States Civil Service, op. cit.*

diocrity springing from protectionism and legal tenure. City managers were among the first professional groups to feel uncomfortable under such restrictions, and they have continued to regard the public personnel fraternity skeptically. On the whole, personnel work has been restricted to housekeeping, rule making, and policing, and members of management have been among the objects of its sleuthing. This, of course, is too broad an indictment, yet it is essentially true that what is described here as "developmental personnel management" has not been generally characteristic of civil service philosophy.

Public personnel philosophy has now turned almost full cycle. Personnel management was once highly centralized. Appointments, promotions, dismissals, recruiting, and position classification were either performed directly by the civil service agency or had to be approved by it. Central personnel agencies were jealous of their prerogatives and suspicious of operating officials, a suspicion partly justified because of the empire building and protective mentality often characteristic of those who have entrenched authority. Personnel agencies rationalized that it was part of the inexorable order of nature that they should determine all personnel actions. No one else could be trusted to do so.

The evolution of public personnel management in the last century can be described in three broad phases. These followed each other quite naturally, although the rate of change varied among governmental jurisdictions. The first phase was one of civil service *reform*, which began around 1850 and is still going on in many regions. The second phase consisted of the introduction and widespread adoption of *technical improvements* in such areas as psychological testing, job analysis, the mechanization of procedures, and record keeping. The third phase, which is characterized by decentralization and a focus upon the *motivation and development* of civil servants is well underway and more and more public jurisdictions are accepting its assumptions.

It is now apparent that certain defects in the early approaches actually impeded the important goal of getting the job done with reasonable dispatch and effectiveness. Both citizens and politicians often concluded that workers protected by civil service did not work hard enough and put security and job protection ahead of creativeness and productivity. They were, it was alleged, more concerned with rights and prerequisites than with obligations. And it was widely thought that protective laws made it difficult to discipline governmental workers because it was almost impossible to dismiss them.

The net result has been disappointing. We have eliminated most party patronage by law, guaranteed equality of treatment, introduced the logic of scientific management, and established an elaborate system of protectionism, but all this has generally failed to produce a highly motivated working force. By and large, the man who pays the bill believes that civil servants are obsessed with security, grasping for ever greater rights and perquisites, and committed to a slower work pace than their counterparts in industry. Many higher administrators feel similarly, as evidenced by their frustration at their inability to motivate their subordinates. Regardless of the validity of this general indictment, the important thing is that many knowledgable people, including some administrators, tend to feel that public employees as a group are somewhat marginal in terms of competence, motivation, and achievement. Insofar as America is a business civilization, civil servants have also suffered from invidious comparisons with self-made entrepreneurs.

These attitudes have caused considerable soul searching among those who believe that a competent public service is an essential part of our democracy. The result has been a tendency toward wholesale condemnation of classic civil service reform. Indeed, some observers believe we have failed to achieve a first-class public service *because of* these reforms, including (1) civil service protectionism, (2) the emphasis on techniques, (3) the negative, policing attitude of civil service reformers, (4) the centralization of personnel actions, and (5) the failure to recognize as a human being the man who does the work. The remedy, they insist, lies in complete decentralization of personnel administration to the responsible heads of agencies. This change, moreover, should be accompanied by a philosophy directed toward the needs of line management instead of the prerogatives of central control and the fear of patronage. Emphasis should be placed upon developing leadership and motivation to insure that people perform up to their capabilities. Special efforts must be made to attract and retain talented young people.

NEW CONCEPTS OF PERSONNEL

The last decade has brought a profound need for change in the philosophy and practice of personnel management, especially at the federal level. This need has been triggered primarily by the dramatic change in the manpower needs of the nation, resulting from the growing complexity of science and technology, particularly in space and military development. Fully three-fourths of the nation's physical scientists and engineers now work in these two fields.[9] This condition makes a productive work climate in government for biological and physical scientists especially significant, both to augment their own productivity and to attract others. We saw earlier too that young people now bring more demanding expectations to the workplace.

Such conditions are bringing about changes in traditional attitudes and practices in personnel administration. Discontent, in fact, has been in the air since the 1930's. Starting with the Commission of Inquiry of Public Service Personnel in 1935, continuing with the Brownlow Report in 1937 and the two Hoover Commission reports in 1948 and 1955, a crescendo of criticism appeared, culminating in the Municipal Manpower Commission Report of 1962.[10] Then came the Brookings Institution's series of research studies on the City of New York and the federal service. The latter were conducted by behavioral scientists, and their often critical conclusions were based on empirical data. Currently, such developments as the Watergate affair have added another fillip to ambivalence among youth about government as a career. The net result is that the old civil service protectionism is being modified in the light of the needs of the new "meritocracy" in which government must compete with industry and the universities for the most competent and committed graduates.

The nation's need for high-level manpower reflects a number of developments. Our social system has become increasingly bureaucratic and technical. The men needed to run this kind of society need managerial and technical expertise, which, in turn, calls for higher levels of education. Job content is becoming ever more intellectual, even in the manual crafts. Furthermore, job requirements are constantly changing because scientific and technical discoveries are appearing so rapidly. One result is that vocational education and training are becoming continuous; adult schooling is becoming a way of life. It is of course true that the present challenging of traditional occupational values includes a rejection of professionalization and its guild orientation. Nevertheless, it is hard to believe that there will be any long-run deviation from the path of scientific and technological development now apparent in the Western world. In this milieu, very highly trained and educated individuals will remain at a premium. For government, the question is how to attract and retain

[9] National Education Association, *Research Report, 1965-R4* (April, 1965).
[10] *Governmental Manpower for Tomorrow's Cities: A Report of the Municipal Manpower Commission* (New York: McGraw-Hill Book Co., Inc., 1962).

them in an era when such individuals have become more selective regarding work and careers.

The Developmental Mood

Developmental personnel management is an emerging concept which may be defined as a more positive attitude toward the whole personnel function and the potential capacity of individuals to acquire new skills and to assume new responsibilities. One of its major thrusts is toward overcoming traditional civil service negativism. The point to be emphasized here is that the developmental mood is real, and that the forces behind it will require public personnel people to recognize and adopt it.

Changing occupational values of high-level manpower are now forcing organizations not only to bid against each other for recruits but also to provide organizational devices which will keep them satisfied. In other words, organizational *climate* is receiving increasing attention as a phase of personnel. There are signs that the forces of change are now at work in government. If one were required to point to harbingers of change, he could refer to the various Annual Reports of the U.S. Civil Service Commission. While earlier reports gave hints of what was taking place, the 1964 issue was marked by its emphasis on such items as projecting manpower requirements, effect of automation on employees, meeting the problems of scientific and engineering manpower, and the search for quality in staffing, career development, and motivation. Subsequent Reports have a similar positive tone. In 1971, for example, in what the Commission calls "a pace-setting year," the Intergovernmental Personnel Act was passed, strongly supported if not inspired by the Commission, which received new authority to help state and local governments improve their personnel management through training programs, the coordination of federal–state–local recruitment, the temporary assignment of federal officials to state–local agencies, and vice versa, and the establishment of the inevitable Presidential Advisory Council on the general subject. It is clear that the Commission is making some progress in overcoming the negative image that legislators, political appointees, some career administrators, and some academic observers have had of "civil servants" and civil service's protective mechanisms. Whether it is operationally possible to create a pervasively progressive milieu in large-scale bureaucracies remains moot. Even so great an admirer as Max Weber came to believe that they could be galvanized into new directions only by charismatic political leaders—i.e., by external forces.

The challenge confronting public personnel is further highlighted by the fact that political considerations have had to be joined with questions of competence in recruiting high-level personnel. Presidents Eisenhower and Johnson, for example, found it advisable to bring the chairmen of their civil service commissions into the White House circle. A similar movement is taking place in the cities; Mayor Daley of Chicago brought in Professor O. W. Wilson as police chief, and in New York Mayor Lindsay brought in a whole bureau of personal assistants. Such political appointments are beginning to be more influenced by considerations of professional and technical competence. Despite such traumas as Watergate, a greater measure of professionalism may be characterizing the appointment process. Complex modern government cannot be run by political hacks. There is developing a set of practices in the governmental subculture wherein a marriage of competence and politics is taking place. This does not mean that party loyalty is no longer a prime consideration but, rather, that it is increasingly freighted with competence.[11]

MANPOWER POLICY

The results have included an emphasis on the need for a national manpower policy based upon the utilization of the entire working force. Such a policy is gradually emerging in piecemeal fashion; for example, its components include the Poverty Program, which attempts to upgrade the vocational skills of the poor. This puts public personnel departments at the heart of social policy, because public objectives are necessarily

[11] Problems remain, however, if only because "political" appointments remain most common at the most important, higher-level *policy* positions. Regarding federal attorneys-general, for example, Ramsey Clark concludes, "Political appointment of the United States Attorneys inhibits the development of a career service. . . ." He is referring to the fact that such appointments are actually made by the Senators and Mayors in the states concerned. Clark adds, "The power of a district attorney is immense—the public has intrusted many of its cherished rights to his discretion. While his role in the system of criminal justice is crucial, his office generally reflects the neglect characteristic of the entire judicial system. The salaries of assistants are poor and the turnover is high. The typical D.A.'s office is staffed by young lawyers seeking a brief trial experience, a few people with political ambitions, some who have found no other job, and often a handful of older lawyers who could not or did not succeed in private practice. With rare exception, there is little chance for career development. . . . In a survey in 1965 it was found that only 18 per cent of the more than six hundred Assistant United States Attorneys in the nation had practiced law for five years. The average salary was 15 per cent lower than that of federal lawyers in Washington with the same length of practice. A career program with good salaries, opportunity for promotion and transfer, and continuing training and legal education will be necessary to develop high progressional standards in these offices." *Crime in America* (London: Cassell and Co., 1970), pp. 190, 191.

involved in efforts to improve the skills of all citizens. Indeed, the overall major social problems of personnel administration are (1) to upgrade the skills of people to meet the needs of the new technology and (2) to place them in appropriate jobs. A challenge to public personnel management is how to deal with the "make work" jobs provided under this new orientation. Such jobs, created for the poor, including high-school dropouts, evoke some anxiety on the part of employee groups who fear that they will not be confined to work that would otherwise not be done but will infringe upon the jobs of those already employed. This "welfare" phase of public personnel administration does not dovetail easily with the traditional civil service system, yet it is not new, because the issue appeared before during the New Deal projects of the 1930's.

The general manpower situation in the nation today includes considerable unemployment for those without special skills and at the same time, a surfeit of trained people. This situation has rarely existed before. It is partly the result of cyclical economic movements, including the inflation and imbalance in payments brought about in good part by vast expenditures in maintaining military bases abroad and unprecedented public budgets at home. It arises from the increasingly specialized nature of our technical and productive apparatus, as well as the difficulty of keeping educational outputs synchronized with manpower needs in the various institutional sectors of American society. It is perhaps trite to say that space science triggered an intellectual as well as a technical revolution, but certainly informed opinion has changed from one of playing down intellectual achievement to one in which it has become respectable.

In a word, we are still living in an age which places great value on professional and technical proficiency and attainment, the term "meritocracy" having been coined to characterize it.[12] In our judgment the contemporary disenchantment of young men and women with highly trained technical and professional occupations is a temporary phenomenon and indeed there are reports from university administrators of a pervasive current switch in student interest away from "soft" normative courses involving black studies, revolution, developing societies, etc., toward "hard" fields of law, medicine, business education, etc. Government's competitive position is affected because public employment suffers from negative prestige. Not only does government have to compete

[12] Michael Young, *The Rise of Meritocracy* (New York: Random House, Inc., 1959). Despite the changes in occupational values mentioned earlier, in the long run professional-technical values will probably remain dominant among most people.

against other employers, but it suffers from the additional handicap that the most competent individuals do not regard government employment as highly as other fields of work.

This situation may not mean the end of the spoilsman, but the politician will probably be under increasing pressure from those who demand effective administration. The unskilled unemployed will continue to make patronage demands,[13] but the counterpressures for technical expertise will tend to modify them. Although there is something to be said for those who contend that the watchdog function of "civil service" administration is not entirely passé, it is possible that government's current efforts to abolish poverty and create jobs will result in a national policy upgrading the placement of *all* workers rather than, or in addition to, the competitive hiring of those possessing scarce skills. We seem to be evolving a policy of governmental guarantees of subsistence to those who have lost out in the competitive job milieu, and public agencies will be increasingly charged with using these people. Here, it seems, legislators, senior officials, and articulate interest groups are influenced by the vast costs of welfare programs and the attending appeal of the alternative of such public employment programs.

Another factor has entered the manpower picture—namely, the rapid obsolescence of skills, not only in the manual occupations but also in scientific and professional areas.[14] The educational level of entry to occupations is constantly rising, as evidenced by a recent requirement in California that apprentices in the building trades take junior-college or related courses in connection with their training. The technology of jobs and occupations, as well as the drive of marginal occupations toward professionalization, is changing so rapidly that constant retraining seems to be the order of the day.

THE PROBLEM OF PRECARIOUS PRESTIGE

This emerging picture brings a new significance to the old problem of prestige in the public service. Most competent and successful Americans do not hold public employment in as high regard as private occupations. This attitude is of considerable interest to students of comparative ad-

---

[13] Here, of course, the impetus is not political patronage, but the patronage of social class and ethnicity.

[14] Note that Ramsey Clark has advocated retraining for young attorneys-general, most of whom have been out of law school for only 5 to 10 years. This "open-ended" orientation is one of the great strengths of American professional and business life.

ministration, because the opposite view has usually prevailed in Britain and continental Europe, where a career in the higher civil service has attracted socially advantaged people, as well as those who have demonstrated extraordinary intellectual attainment. Indeed, until recently, the cult of the gentlemen confined members of the aristocracy and upper-middle classes to such occupations as the clergy, the military, and the civil service. In the United States, on the other hand, greater mobility has always existed, reflecting our equalitarian philosophy and the absence of a feudal past, as well as vastly greater equality of educational opportunity, especially at the university level. During the Federalist era, the administrative staff was fully manned by the well-born, but since then, mobility has been more a matter of individual skill and educational achievement, with the exception of political appointments where ascriptive criteria may often be seen.

In the 1920's Leonard D. White probed American attitudes toward public employment. While he did not use sampling techniques, he secured questionnaire responses from several thousand people in a variety of occupations and social categories. Their attitudes were markedly averse to public employment of all kinds. Federal employment was regarded most favorably, while state and municipal vocations were ranked lower. Among all respondents, almost two-thirds favored industrial over public employment. Indeed, private employees were held to be four times as courteous, three times as efficient, and twice as honest! No doubt, the halcyon economic conditions of the 1920's inspired some of these uncritical attitudes. Women regarded city employment more favorably than men did, while younger people tended to have a higher regard for municipal service than did older ones. Highly educated persons looked unfavorably on governmental work, and the foreign-born thought more highly of public employment than natives did, probably owing to the higher prestige attached to public service in the Old World.[15]

PRESTIGE IN THE 1960'S

Some forty years later, the Brookings Institution sponsored a study of attitudes toward the federal public service, utilizing rigorous methodological procedures. It dealt with the federal service, and was generally

[15] Leonard D. White, *The Prestige Value of Public Employment in Chicago* (Chicago: University of Chicago Press, 1929); see also, John A. Armstrong, *The European Administrative Elite* (Princeton, N.J.: Princeton University Press, 1973).

concerned with professional and higher-status jobs in Washington.[16] This study comprised a thorough tapping of attitudes of various categories of American opinion, using accepted psychometric procedures and carefully selected samples. While the results were less markedly negative than White's, they were generally similar. Americans still regard federal employment less highly than work in the private sector. Moreover, the more education people have, the higher their occupational status, and, the greater their social and economic attainments, the lower they rank federal employment. In effect, the people the federal service needs most are those who find it least attractive. People in general view job security and fringe benefits as the most favorable characteristics of federal careers, but "the evidence strongly suggests that it [security] has no great utility as a recruiting appeal for the highly qualified, even though it does have substantial value in retaining such people in the government, especially after ten years or so of service." [17]   Federal jobs appeal more to women than to men, and more to younger than to older people. The man on the street has a very strong, if somewhat blurred, conception of the federal service as comprised dominantly of clerical jobs, with paperwork as the controlling activity.

PRESTIGE IN THE 1970'S

Little research has been done on the problem of prestige in the recent past. Since the cultural forces that have given public employment a precarious status in the United States change very slowly, it seems probable that the conclusions of White and Kilpatrick remain generally valid. We know that the bases of occupational prestige are remarkably similar internationally.[18] Essentially, public evaluations of job prestige rest upon two factors: the length of training and education required to perform a given role, and the income that one derives from it. Judging by these two criteria, it would seem that the higher bureaucracy would rank quite well, since its members are very impressive in terms of educational achievement. Comparative data show that judicial figures tend to rank either at the top or very close in prestige. However, such roles are not

16 Franklin P. Kilpatrick, Milton C. Cummings, Jr., and M. Kent Jennings, *The Image of the Federal Service* (Washington, D. C.: The Brookings Institution, 1964); David T. Stanley *et al., Professional Personnel for the City of New York* (Washington, D. C.: The Brookings Institution, 1963).

17 Kilpatrick, *et al., op. cit.,* p. 245.

18 A. Inkeles and P. Rossi, "National Comparison of Occupational Prestige," *American Journal of Sociology,* Vol. 61 (1956), pp. 32–39.

usually defined, one suspects, as public employment. It may be that the evaluation rests upon more *specific* types of educational requirements, such as those possessed by a physicist or medical doctor. Insofar as his role is one of generalist administration, it may be that the higher bureaucrat will have difficulty meeting this definition or condition of occupational prestige.

Regarding income, historically, of course, government servants have not been highly compensated in hard currency. Security and service have been more prominent elements than economic gain. Even though this condition is changing as pay in the public service becomes equal or better than that of its private counterparts,[19] the differences between the higher bureaucracy and similar private occupations remains great. Turnover among young lawyers in the Department of Justice, the Internal Revenue Service, or the Securities and Exchange Commission attests to this condition.

It is important here to note that prestige varies in the eye of the beholder. Salaries of $25,000 to $35,000 now available to those in the higher reaches of the career service are quite likely to be viewed as generous if not princely by the average American whose family income in 1973 was about $8,000. However, among major executives and independent professionals, such incomes are less happily perceived. More important, American business culture places a very high value upon large incomes earned in the private arena. Recruitment into the upper political strata of government, i.e., into the under-secretary and assistant secretary levels, is almost entirely from the ranks of business executives and major law firms. In this context, the prestige attached to public employment necessarily suffers, not only by the standard of income, which we have seen is critical, but also in terms of role and work place.

Certainly, for a time, when the Johnson and Nixon Administrations were sponsoring welfare and egalitarian types of programs, the prestige of government work must have risen, as idealistic young people found an opportunity to influence the priorities of American governments at every level. As shown earlier, however, these emphases were rather short-lived and by 1973, the *status quo* had returned. As Charles Schultze and his associates found, "Defense continues to be by far the largest single government program, absorbing 30 per cent of the national budget and directly employing 3.4 million people."[20] Nor did

---

[19] Charles Schultze, *et al., Setting National Priorities* (Washington, D.C.: Brookings Institution, 1972), p. 299, for incomes of public servants at the local level.

[20] *Ibid.,* p. 24.

their recommendations for new priorities include much hope for change.[21] The positive thrust emanating from the earlier concern with domestic problems of the cities, poverty, and the blacks has also been blunted by the Watergate Affair, which, despite its focus in the political executive branch, must also have had dysfunctional consequences for the prestige of the public service career.[22]

In this chapter, we have set down some of the broad environmental and cultural conditions that shape American public personnel administration. Their effects will be apparent in succeeding chapters as we turn to the major technical characteristics of the field.

---

[21] *Ibid.*, pp. 455–68.

[22] For some tentative evidence, see Robert D. Lee, Jr., "Watergate and the Image of the Federal Service Revisited," *Public Personnel Management*, Vol. 3 (March–April, 1974), pp. 111–14.

10

The Federal
Personnel System

The central personnel agency for the federal government is the Civil Service Commission, composed of three members appointed by the President and subject to Senate confirmation. They serve for overlapping terms of six years, one being appointed every two years, and one member must be from the minority political party. The President designates the chairman and a vice-chairman who serves as chairman in the former's absence. The chairman has administrative powers in his own right and acts as the executive head of the agency. Most state and local systems have similar agencies, to which many of the following generalizations apply.

ROLE OF THE COMMISSION

The Civil Service Commission is responsible for the administration of the major personnel functions, but in the recent past its role has changed considerably.[1] Prior to the early 1940's, the Commission recruited, *Change* examined, and classified on a centralized operating basis; that is, the Commission did the work itself. Since then, the actual operating activity has been performed on a decentralized basis by the line agencies them-

[1] On the historical development of federal personnel administration, see O. Glenn Stahl, *Public Personnel Administration*, 6th ed. (New York: Harper & Row, Inc., 1971).

selves and by components of the Commission in the field. These include 10 regional offices, 65 area offices, and hundreds of boards of examiners stationed in the line agencies. The examiners are agency officials who administer examinations under the supervision of the Commission.

The C.S.C. defines its own functions in the following way:

> As the central personnel agency of the Federal Government, the Commission gives leadership, on behalf of the President, to personnel management operations in the executive branch. It develops and makes policy and program recommendations to the President and to the Congress. It represents the President in Federal personnel management matters as they are being considered by the Congress.
>
> Also, we carry out specific statutory responsibilities directly assigned by the Congress including the laws relating to civil service position classification, pay, training, retirement, life insurance, health benefits, leave, incentive awards, performance ratings, political activities, veteran preference, voting rights, and intergovernmental personnel.[2]

In most cases, these personnel management activities are carried out at the agency level by agency officials. The C.S.C. itself generally serves as catalyst, mentor, and friendly counselor to the agencies which administer their own programs according to general guidelines set down by the Commission.

The devices used to ease such decentralization include central determination of broad policy, centralized setting of standards and goals, and feedback to the Commission regarding programs administered by the agencies. The functions of two of the Commission's bureaus illustrate its current role. The Bureau of Programs and Standards has a Program Planning Division which acts as a broker for ideas on the improvement of personnel administration. The term "broker" is used to emphasize the Bureau's role as a catalyst to stimulate progressive thinking throughout the service rather than pose as the sole source of ideas itself. In addition to its concern with improvement of personnel administration in general, the Bureau has the specific tasks of conducting research in test development and developing job standards to guide the agencies in their classification decisions.

Feedback is accomplished by sending out inspection teams from the Commission's regional offices, an activity carried on by its Bureau of Inspections and Classification Audits. Whereas inspectors once focused their attention upon classification and pay standards, they now devote

---

[2] U. S. Civil Service Commission, *A Pace Setting Year: Annual Report, 1971,* Washington, D. C., U. S. Government Printing Office, 1972, p. 2.

more time to the developmental aspects of personnel administration. The inspectors provide liaison between the Commission and the agencies, and one of their duties is to advise the agencies how to improve their operations.

The personnel management goals of the Civil Service Commission have been outlined as follows:

> *Responsiveness* . . . not alone to the mission needs of Government programs, but also to rapidly changing social and economic needs. An apt synonym for "responsiveness" here is "flexibility."
>
> *Balance* . . . between responsibility to employees and responsibilities to the public.
>
> *Comparability* . . . the system must remain competitive with private enterprise with respect to employee pay and fringe benefits.
>
> *Merit and fitness* . . . they must continue to be the prime factors in filling Federal jobs.[3]

Federal Entrance Examinations

Since the mid-1930's the federal government has been interested in recruiting college graduates. For several years prior to 1955, recruitment was carried on through a series of special examinations given once a year. The principal vehicle for securing future administrators was the Junior Management Assistant (JMA) Test, which covered the subject matter of administration and resulted in a high casualty rate. Competition with industrial recruiting, particularly with government's poorer competitive position in salary, prestige, and fringe benefits and the decrease in available applicants due to the declining birth rate of the 1930's; the impact of the loyalty-security programs; and the Eisenhower Administration's lukewarm attitude toward the civil service—all led to a drop in applicants for the JMA Test. This challenge was met by the inauguration of the Federal Service Entrance Examination (FSEE) in 1955 and the Professional and Administrative Career Examination (PACE) in 1974.[4]

The FSEE changed the basis of recruiting and examining from one of a series of rather specialized tests to a single test of general knowledge which a college graduate could be assumed to have acquired. In effect, the emphasis on specialized knowledge gave way to a somewhat greater stress upon a general liberal arts background. Students interested in

---

[3] *Ibid.*, p. 1.

[4] Aimed at encouraging college graduates to enter the federal system, and following generally the design of its predecessor, PACE went into service in October, 1974. See, among others, Bill Andronicos, "FSEE Yields to a Better PACE," *Federal Times*, Vol. 10 (July 3, 1974).

becoming administrators could indicate a desire to become management interns, the idea being that administrative skills would be developed on the job, rather than through preservice college instruction. The new method simplified the examining process by substituting a single examination for the dozen or more then being given. Selective certification for specialized backgrounds was retained, however. The FSEE had several immediate advantages. It opened up federal service to thousands of graduates who had theretofore been neither attracted nor eligible. Another useful feature was continuous recruitment, since the tests were given throughout the year.[5] Its successor, PACE, has not been in effect long enough to permit a similar evaluation.

Federal Liaison with State and Local Governments

Although the federal government has long had indirect relations with state and local personnel systems, many of them associated with grant-in-aid programs in which federal surveillance has come along with the grants, these have often been by-products of other objectives. During the 1930's, for example, state personnel systems were required to meet federal standards in order to qualify for federal funds. In some cases, federal grants were suspended as a result of maladministration at the state level.

A more positive program was initiated in 1971 by the Nixon Administration in the form of new legislation. As with the Revenue-Sharing Act of the same year, this program represented an effort on the Administration's part to decentralize government's tasks.

On January 5, 1971, the President signed a bill authorizing a program extending federal aid and expertise in the training and management of personnel to state and local government. Consistent with Nixon's philosophy of diversifying government and placing greater emphasis on programs at the state and local levels (the "New Federalism"), the Intergovernmental Personnel Act sought to provide the instruments through which the quality of governmental personnel systems in the jurisdictions below the federal level could be raised and the various experiences in personnel management coordinated.

Among the provisions of the Act were the following:

1. The Civil Service Commission was authorized to make grants to state and local governments to help meet the costs of improving and strengthening their personnel management capabilities.

[5] Philip Young, "The Federal Service Entrance Examination," *Public Administration Review*, Vol. 16 (Winter, 1956), pp. 1–5.

2. The C.S.C. was mandated to help the states and localities develop new employee training programs.
3. In addition to technical assistance, the C.S.C. was authorized to award Government Service Fellowships to support graduate-level studies for employees selected by state and local governments.
4. The Act provided for temporary assignment of personnel between Federal agencies and state and local governments or institutions of higher learning.
5. State and local employees were permitted to enter federal training courses conducted by the C.S.C. and other federal agencies.
6. Recruitment and examination procedures among the various levels of government were to be coordinated.
7. A Presidential Advisory Council on Intergovernmental Personnel Policy was established.[6]

The success of these measures cannot be determined with any certainty as of yet. The philosophy of the Act appears to be sound; but, given the entrenched interests of various bureaucracies and the proved difficulties in other intergovernmental projects, prospects for great improvement throughout the personnel systems of state and local governments resulting directly from this Act would appear to be somewhat limited.[7]

THE FEDERAL EXECUTIVE ELITE

Although the federal service has a total of almost 3,000,000 employees, the most interesting, prestigious, and rewarding roles are those of the 11,000 or so executives who occupy the highest positions in the system, defined here as GS-16 and above.[8] Many of these officials play an essentially political role, including a direct part in policy-making under the direction of political leaders, both elected and appointed at the Secretary, Assistant, and Undersecretary levels. These are also the kinds of positions to which most university graduates aspire. For such reasons, this elite corps will be considered here in some detail.

[6] U. S. Civil Service Commission Annual Report, 1971, Washington, D. C., 1972, p. 52. See also Joseph M. Robertson, "Impact of IPA on Public Personnel Administration," Public Personnel Review, Vol. 33 (April, 1972), pp. 133–34.

[7] For details of the administration of the IPA program, see IPA Grant Administration Handbook, U. S. Civil Service Commission, Washington, D. C., U. S. Government Printing Office, September, 1971. Also of interest is the Message From The President Urging Passage of the Manpower Revenue Sharing Act, February 7, 1972, House of Representatives, document no. 92-246.

[8] The term "rewarding" is used in both the psychological and economic sense: salaries for Level I to V positions range from $36,000 to $60,000, while those in GS extend from $29,678 for grade 16 to $36,000 for grade 18.

The Structure of Executive Positions

According to a Civil Service Commission survey, the typical executive is a career appointee who is male (only 1.1 per cent of the entire group is female), 53 years old, and has 26 years of service. He entered the Federal service at grade 5 and received his first supergrade appointment at age 45. He holds a Bachelor's degree which he obtained prior to entry into the service and has acquired some further education during his employment. He has worked in one or possibly two agencies but has made no move (i.e., from one agency to another) since reaching grade 13. Finally, he will be eligible for retirement in 4 years.[9]

Such officials may be divided into "political" and "career" categories, although the division insofar as functions are concerned is often formal. As our survey and case study evidence indicated earlier, higher executives are highly political in the sense that they interact and accommodate with legislators and interest group directors, as well as with their peers in what may be defined as essentially political contexts. The dichotomy is really between those who are appointed 'politically' and those who are usually appointed as permanent, career officials. U.S. Civil Service Commission defines an executive as "any full-time employee of the executive branch whose salary equals or exceeds the beginning salary ($29,678) of the General Schedule grade 16, regardless of the personnel or pay system involved."[10] Such a definition illustrates the need for arbitrary determinations in job classification, since one can think of equally salient criteria for defining such positions, including number of people supervised, significance of the work done, and years and kind of experience required to qualify for an 'executive' role. Obviously, the chosen criterion is quantitative and exclusive. Table 10–1 shows the breakdown of categories in the executive class.[11]

As the breakdowns show, only 595 of the total group occupy politically appointed positions (i.e., levels I to V), including departmental secretaries, undersecretaries, directors of bureaus and of services or administrations, and chairmen and members of commissions. The turnover rate among such appointees is quite high, compared with that among their "career-oriented" peers.[12]

[9] U. S. Civil Service Commission, "Executive Manpower in the Federal Service" (January, 1972), p. 8.
[10] Adapted from "Executive Manpower in the Federal Service," op. cit., p. 1.
[11] Ibid.
[12] Dean E. Mann, "The Selection of Federal Political Executives," American Political Science Review, Vol. 48 (March, 1964), pp. 81–99.

TABLE 10–1.   Executive Categories in the Federal Civil Service, 1972

Personnel System	Number	Percentage
Executive Schedule (Levels I–V)	595	5
General Schedule (GS 16–18)	5,804 *	53
Public Law (P.L. 313 Type)	1,244	11
Other Salary Systems	3,400	31
Foreign Service	(1,924)	(17)
AEC	(428)	(4)
TVA	(39)	(1)
DMS (VA)	(215)	(2)
Other	(794)	(7)
Total	11,043	100

* This number includes 251 executives in the legislative and judicial branches whose positions are classified in grades 16–18 of the General Schedule.

The breakdowns confirm another important characteristic of the federal system, the existence of several independent personnel and salary systems, of which the Foreign Service is obviously the largest, followed by the Atomic Energy Commission. Some provision is made for including specialists within this charmed circle, under so-called Public Law positions, which cover scientific and professional jobs. A similar provision exists in the British civil service where a 'dual hierarchy' permits technical experts to rise as high as their generalist brethren.

The distribution among the various occupational categories attests, however, to the fact that administrative generalists still dominate the executive category, comprising twice as high a proportion as the second-ranking occupation. Table 10–2 presents the evidence.[13]

TABLE 10–2.   Executive Class, by Occupational Role

Occupation	Proportion of Total	Occupation	Proportion of Total
Administration	23	Social science	4
Law	13	Biological science	3
Physical sciences	13	Health and medicine	3
Engineering	11	All others	26
Fiscal	4		100%

[13] "Executive Manpower . . . ," *op. cit.*, p. 6. The Commission notes that the figure of 23 per cent for 'administration' is "misleading in one sense," namely that many of those included are *also* professional or other occupational members. One assumes, however, that they are all presently occupying *administrative* positions.

Some of the new departures discussed earlier in the context of community control are apparent in the Executive Manpower Report's emphasis upon the extent to which some executives are involved in controversial public issues. After 1967, by Executive Order, the Schedule C provisions for appointing executives to "positions of a confidential or policy-determining character" were replaced by a system for Noncareer Executive Assignments.[14] Although the distinction is somewhat tenuous, since most senior executives influence policy, men appointed under N.E.A. are directly involved in such controversial programs as poverty, job training, drug control and rehabilitation. The Manpower Report indicates that just over 40 per cent of all senior executives are involved in such "advocacy" programs.[15] The significance of this issue lies mainly in its patent symbolization of change in government's role from one mainly concerned with the problems of articulate, highly legitimated producer and professional groups in American society to a greater involvement with previously "invisible" ethnic and minority groups. However, as noted earlier, such programs have been sharply cut back under the Nixon Administration, and it now seems that the French aphorism is again appropriate: "The more things change, the more they remain the same." Certainly, the generally conservative political values of federal legislators and bureaucrats, only 17 per cent of whom, for example, rank 'high' on an "economic liberalism" (a liberal, 'big government' valence) index, compared with 40 and 30 per cent, respectively, of Canadian respondants, suggest that American political elites are probably less comfortable with such welfare programs than with traditional producer-oriented policies.[16]

Executive Motivations and Mobility

Two salient aspects of governmental personnel administration are the motivations and career mobility patterns of this leadership elite, which undoubtedly serves as a model for many of their subordinates. Interesting data on this question are presented in Table 10–3 from the *Manpower Report*.[17]

Age seems to be a significant variable, as seen in the much larger proportion of those under 50 whose primary incentive was a challenging

[14] *Ibid.*, p. 7.
[15] *Ibid.*
[16] Robert Presthus, *Elites in the Policy Process* (New York: Cambridge University Press, 1974), Table 11–7.
[17] Adapted from *ibid.*, p. 15.

TABLE 10–3. Main Reasons for Entering Federal Service, by Age

Incentive	Over 50	Under 50	Total
Challenging assignment	26%	35%	29%
Chosen occupation	26	24	25
Best offer received	16	8	14
Public service	11	13	12
Other	21	20	20

assignment. However, the responses may reflect the career disenchantments that accompany age, as much as the "objective reality" of career motivations. Older executives are also much more likely to elect the somewhat uninspired "best offer received" category.

The marginal ranking of the "public service" incentive is not unexpected, especially since most of these executives would have come in following World War II when, in contrast to the élan of the New Deal era, the federal service was probably less appealing to those with idealistic motivations. On the other hand, when the data are presented occupationally, non-scientists prove to be some five times more likely than scientists to rank the "public service" incentive highest. A substantial, although less dramatic, variation also appears between career and non-career executives, with the latter considerably more likely to rank this value highest. Since executives brought in under Schedule A and B categories (i.e., "political appointments" for which competitive exams are not deemed practical), typically from private industry, must often accept considerably lower salaries, the public service rationale may loom large in their minds. Unfortunately, the survey does not include any analysis of personal political values and class backgrounds which would have provided explanatory data for career incentives and, more interesting, patterns of mobility.

Three Role Typologies

Nevertheless, the *Report* includes some interesting descriptive data on career patterns which increase our knowledge of federal personnel structure and behavior. Three typologies are suggested: full career, in-and-outers, and high-level entrants.[18] As the terms suggest, full careerists are those who have worked only in the government. They constitute fully three-fifths of the sample. They are the "true bureaucrats," whose

18 *Ibid.*, pp. 19–21.

knowledge of the labyrinthine channels of federal organization must be formidable indeed. In-and-outers, who comprise some one-fifth of the sample, are those who have moved back and forth between government, business, and education one or more times. The remaining one-fifth are the high-level entrants who came in at the senior level (GS–13 or above) and remained in the service permanently.

Several interesting personal and institutional characteristics differentiate these typologies. Full career people, on an average, have lower educational levels, limited to the bachelor's degree. They engage in the least professional and publications activity, change jobs least, and on the average tend to be found in Agriculture, Justice, Labor, General Services Administration, Post Office, Treasury, and the regulatory agencies. As noted, they tend to be complete bureaucrats, often serving in old-line, highly traditional departments or agencies.

In-and-outers also have some salient characteristics. Educationally, they usually have a Masters' degree, in addition to the B.A. By definition, they have less commitment to a given agency; fully half have served in two or more agencies after achieving their super-grade status. They tend to be found in such departments as Labor, State, and Interior.

High-level entrants differ sharply from the entire career group. They rank highest among all groups on professional activities and publications and their educational achievement is also highest. Three-quarters have worked for only one agency. They tend to appear in such agencies as the Atomic Energy Commission and the departments of Health, Education and Welfare, Defense, and the Veterans Administration. On the whole, however almost 80 per cent of the entire executive corps have remained in the same agency in which they attained their GS–13 status. Only about 15 per cent have held high-level jobs in three or more federal agencies. This evidence bears upon our earlier comments regarding the dominant specialist ethos in the American higher service, contrasted with that of the British or Canada in which a systematic policy of rotation is encouraged in line with generalist conceptions of the administrative role. The latter, in turn, is a direct reflection of traditional orientations in the system of higher education in the two societies.[19]

Regarding the recruitment of the executive elite, it is instructive that

[19] Some dysfunctions of the generalist orientation are traced in Timothy Balough, "The Apotheosis of the Dilettante," in H. Thomas, *The Establishment* (London: New English Library, 1962); Brian Chapman, *British Government Observed* (London: Allen and Unwin, 1962); and R. Wilkinson, *Gentlemanly Power: British Leadership and the Public Schools* (New York: Oxford University Press, 1964).

fully 78 per cent are appointed from within the agency concerned.[20] Sixteen per cent came from outside government, while only 6 per cent came from other agencies. The vast majority of these involve career appointments, as contrasted with such patently "political" appointments as those at the I to V level, which require the advice and consent of the Senate. Such career appointments are usually made from within the department or agency concerned. A total of about 800 appointments to such positions occurred between 1933–1961.[21] As the *Report* states, "It is logical to assume that if a program manager were looking for a highly qualified man to run a part of his operation, he would look first within his organization. . . ." [22] Here again, valuable information is provided regarding the agencies that are most likely to subscribe to this policy. Virtually 90 per cent or more of all positions are filled from *within* in the following agencies: Supply, Administrative officer, Fiscal, Engineering, Biological science, Health and Medicine, and Personnel.[23]

Certainly, the policy of internal appointment has something to recommend it, mainly on grounds of subjective benefits such as the attending fillip to morale and intimate knowledge of the candidate's personal and occupational character. On the other hand, the policy can lend itself to practices which challenge the philosophy that initially inspired the merit system and its institutionalization in the civil service commission. Indeed, recruitment on the broadest possible basis is often looked upon as an essential element in the professionalization of most occupations. Thus in the academic profession, the ideal that faculty recruitment be at least national and even international in scope is widely espoused.

"In-breeding" is sometimes held to insure the "unanimity of the graveyard"; and nepotism is proscribed by explicit rule. In-house appointment, in sociological terms, raises the possibility that "particularistic" criteria including friendship, dependency, loyalty, seniority, and so on may come to share equal weight with "universalistic" criteria of education, technical competence, and professional achievement in the filling of super-grade positions. One suspects that some highly talented individuals will be reluctant to dedicate their careers to a system which depends so heavily upon internal-agency sources for upgrading. As David Stanley says,

---

[20] "Executive Manpower . . . ," *op. cit.*, p. 25; as determined by a survey covering the period January 1, 1970–June, 1971.

[21] For a careful study of appointments at the "political" level, see Dean E. Mann, with Jameson W. Doig, *The Assistant Secretaries: Problems and Processes of Appointment* (Washington, D. C.: Brookings Institution, 1965), p. 25.

[22] *Ibid.*

[23] *Ibid.*, p. 27.

judiciously citing existing "disadvantages," "there are assumptions, not entirely valid, that . . . most higher positions should be filled from within the agency." [24] And again, "Federal executives have not done a bad selection job—at least as far as the present higher civil service is concerned. GS-15 and the 'super-grade' jobs are filled mainly by promotion. Only 11 per cent of the group studied have entered the service at or above GS-15. Selection reflects personal observation and acquaintance-ship." [25] He emphasizes the difficulty of encouraging agencies to use a service-wide Career Executive Roster, from which "only a handful of appointments were made." [26]

To a much lesser extent, a similar comment can be made about appointments at the political level, among the under- and assistant secretaries, most of whom are recruited from within the government service. As Dean Mann concludes regarding difficulties of recruitment at this level, there is really no shortage of talent in the country. Instead, "it is rather, a shortage of willing individuals who can somehow pass through the screen of varied, vague, and often conflicting eligibility requirements established by the numerous groups who often exercise veto power over appointments to such positions." [27]

To some extent, although the earlier concern with patronage appointments is no longer a salient consideration at the federal level, what has been called "the triumph of techniques over purpose" remains a problem. The exquisite paraphernalia of personnel management sometimes complicates the recruitment process, not only at the level of political appointments, but also for permanent positions. Among other things, this condition illustrates the weight of tradition in human affairs, reflecting as it does the early concern of personnel management with protection against patronage.

[24] *The Higher Civil Service* (Washington, D. C.: Brookings Institution, 1964), p. 82.
[25] *Ibid.*, p. 95.
[26] *Ibid.*
[27] Mann, *The Assistant Secretaries, op. cit.*, p. 5.

11

Positions, People, and Pay

All organizations are made up of two basic elements—people and their functional roles. Bureaucratic organizations make systematic efforts to define and order such roles, and to match their technical and "personal" requirements with the individuals recruited to fill them. The range and complexity of what is usually called "position classification" is apparent in the fact that, by 1974, over 13 million civil servants in the United States were filling governmental jobs covering literally thousands of discrete occupational roles.[1] Whether one is designated an executive, an administrator, or a manager is obviously to some extent an arbitrary decision, but if one is to establish standards for recruitment, evaluation, promotion, and pay in large-scale organizations, it is obviously necessary to define such positions precisely. In the process, a certain amount of mythology is inevitable.

MYTHS OF PERSONNEL CLASSIFICATION

An organization chart is a visual presentation of the roles performed in an agency. Broken down into detail, it includes a place for every individual role in the organization. Each of these roles is referred to as a "job" or "position," which denotes the duties performed by a single incumbent during his tour of duty at a particular place.

[1] *Statistical Abstract of the United States*, 1974.

The Separation of Positions from Persons

Every area of social science—and personnel administration is applied social science—has its fictions and myths. The social scientist, however, uses such terms, not in the popular sense to indicate something of doubtful validity, but to explain a rule of action thought to be desirable, yet often difficult to achieve. Perhaps the leading myth of personnel administration is that position classification and evaluation should be carried on without consideration of the individual who is occupying the job at the moment. His personal characteristics, desires, ambitions, and skills should not influence the position classifier to whom a position is merely a combination of duties and tasks performed by someone having special qualifications. The analyst must ignore such data as the fact that a job may be virtually the private domain of Karl Marx, who has occupied it for twenty years and who does almost as he pleases. To the analyst the job could just as well be filled by any person who meets its formal specifications.

Now this is not as bad as it may seem to those who deplore the depersonalization of the individual. As a matter of fact, analysts do pay attention to the individual and sentiment when studying jobs; they cannot avoid doing so. The pressure for the reclassification of positions upward is so great that there is little danger that they will ignore human values. From an overall organizational standpoint, the hazard probably lies in the other direction, namely, that they will be unable to resist these pressures and will be less than objective about their recommendations. Thus the belief that the job analyst studies positions instead of people is a useful fiction, which in operational terms enables the organization to adhere somewhat more closely to "universalistic" criteria, i.e., to reasonably objective standards of skill and achievement.

Impact of the Man on the Job. The influx of scientific and professional people into the federal service during the 1960's put considerable strain on traditional classification procedures, and particularly on the concept that the job was to be studied separately from the personal characteristics of its incumbent. Administrators of new scientific operations found that classification dogmas created problems in recruiting and retaining high-status professionals. Competition with industry and the universities for such men necessitated a more flexible attitude toward job grading. Although such an approach was resisted by some devotees of orthodoxy, the U.S. Civil Service Commission took the view that traditional theory could accommodate flexibility and a campaign devoted to the "Impact of the Man on the Job" was inaugurated which resulted in considerably less rigidity. Here again is an example of how personnel management can respond to changes in the marketplace.

Separation of Position from Pay. Every organization has both a job hierarchy and a pay hierarchy. In public administration, the former is referred to as the classification plan and the latter as the compensation plan. Here again one encounters a myth, namely, that position classification is carried on separately from the determination of pay. There are several reasons for this, perhaps the most persuasive being that the classification plan is used for many purposes other than setting pay. Indeed, the formal job hierarchy provides the basis for almost all personnel activities. People are recruited as carpenters, stenographers, and engineers. The same applies to placement, training, layoff, promotion, and job accounting. As a matter of fact, most organizational decisions hinge upon job analysis—who does what, when, and how.

The separation of classification from pay sometimes generates considerable tension between budgeting and personnel authorities. If the budget agency has strong leadership, it will probably conduct the salary surveys and studies and make the pay recommendations. Many personnel administrators, however, feel that this is a personnel function and that the budget bureau should not recommend pay rates for individual classes. It is generally conceded that classification is a personnel activity, with the result that budget officials often make pay recommendations on the basis of a classification scheme designed by the personnel staff. The proper approach is to regard personnel and budget staff work as phases of an integrated management process.

Designing the Hierarchy of Positions. There are several ways of analyzing and grading jobs so they will fit into a systematic hierarchy. Most civil service establishments use a position-classification scheme. In the past industrial systems differed in that they used statistical methods. Positions were graded just as in public agencies but attempts were made to be more precise—to measure—whereas traditional classification had proceeded largely through subjective judgments and verbal standards. More recently, however, public personnel management has begun to use industrial practices.

Personnel administration and especially classification in the federal system have often been a torrent of words, with job descriptions occurring at three levels: (1) each employee writes a job description of his own work, (2) this is then fitted into departmental job specifications, which in turn must conform to (3) detailed standards issued by the Civil Service Commission. Today, many of such older procedures are being eliminated by the use of industrial types of job evaluation, following standards and techniques set down in the Job Evaluation Policy Act (1970).[2]

Public personnel officials have often assumed that position classification systems are more suitable for government because of the greater variety of jobs.[3] In the light of several developments, however, students of personnel management should become familiar with industrial systems. As early as 1965, about 20 per cent of state and local governments were using some form of point evaluation system.[4] Moreover, when management consulting firms carry out job evaluations and related tasks for government, they tend to use industrial practices, with which they are most familiar. Finally, government activities of an industrial nature—shipbuilding, for example—naturally tend to use industrial methods.

A salient argument for the point and factor-comparison approaches is that they insure the participation of line supervisors and operating personnel in the evaluation process. A committee of such persons actually makes the evaluation, which generally results in greater line acceptance, easing the tensions regarding classification that often exist between supervisors and classifiers. On the other hand, experimental studies measuring the effectiveness of the two techniques conclude that non-quantitative classification and job ranking achieve substantially the same results as the quantitative factor and point systems, with about the same cost. Even if one breaks down jobs in statistical detail, the final evaluation necessarily reflects the experienced analyst's judgment of the whole job.

Traditional Position Classification. Governmental job-evaluation procedure, referred to as "position classification," was essentially qualitative in the past until it became tied in with pay, when simple statistical devices such as averages and quartiles were used. Like much of personnel management, position classification developed as part of the reform movement to combat inequities resulting from political favoritism. It was not uncommon, for example, to find a clerk or secretary in one part

[2] Public Law 91–216, March 17, 1970.

[3] Glenn Stahl, for example, gives point and factor systems only four pages in a brief chapter on job evaluation, *Public Personnel Administration*, 6th ed. (New York: Harper and Row, 1971), pp. 196–200.

[4] One symposium involving public personnel directors, however, questions the possibility of achieving objectivity through such methods—*cf. Public Personnel Review*, Vol. 26 (July, 1965), pp. 180–85.

of the Capitol receiving $4,500, while another on the next floor got $2,100. Thus "equal pay for equal work," was sought by establishing a "classified service," whose positions were graded into classes based on similarity in duties, responsibilities, and qualifications. Each class had a single pay rate which was uniform throughout the entire service. By and large, this objective has now been achieved in the federal service and in state and local jurisdictions having mature personnel systems. However, new problems confronting government continue to require new methods of position classification that will remain in step with rapid social change.

Here again, innovation presents problems. As one expert maintains:

> If we are honest with ourselves, we know that position classification has concentrated on wage and budget administration. We have given only lip service to its use in personnel programs or in assisting the executive to solve his management problems. . . . Today's executive struggles to conceptualize objectives and programs and to provide entirely new services and approaches to those programs in the midst of onrushing changes in social need, governmental objectives, and technological change. Those of us responsible for position classification . . . [must] take steps to make position classification truly a sub-system of the total management system.[5]

The General Survey. Traditional classification has two phases: the general survey of all positions and continuous maintenance. The survey usually takes place when a jurisdiction initiates systematic job evaluation, often when a new civil service law appears. It may occur when a new department or bureau is launched. Sometimes private consulting firms are engaged to do the classification survey, which has been fairly well standardized and corresponds roughly to the steps taken in an organizational study. Obviously, the basic component of all organization is jobs. The job analyst and organization analyst both study jobs, although for different purposes. Ideally, the organization staff should do its work before the classification staff appears. The former should decide the overall organizational pattern, whereas the latter should classify jobs on the basis of management's objectives. The position classifier is not a designer of organizations. If a new job is involved, he takes management's job description and indicates into what class it should go. If the job already exists, he does not accept management's judgment entirely but decides for himself what duties are being performed. The classifier must constantly resist pressure to classify positions upward. His business

[5] Merrill J. Collett, "Re-Thinking Position Classification and Management," *Public Personnel Review*, Vol. 32 (July, 1971), p. 172.

is to "call the shots" objectively. He is out of context, however, when he tells management how to organize.[6]

The Duties Questionnaire. The basic instrument in a classification survey is the duties questionnaire in which each employee describes his job. The form usually allows the supervisor to comment upon the job without altering the employee's version. The questionnaires are then sorted into broad general categories. When the job data are insufficient, ambiguous, or inconsistent, the analysts go into the organization and interview and observe those concerned. Since it is too expensive to observe every job and interview all incumbents, they sometimes conduct "desk audits," as they are called, on a random basis. Additional face-to-face contact between incumbent and analyst takes place in maintenance work after the survey recommendations have been carried out. Having the employee describe his own job not only gives him a feeling of participation but his own statement may serve as evidence if he should later appeal his classification.

The classification staff divides the completed questionnaire into rough categories in terms of an overall classification scheme, mainly on the basis of preponderance of duties, their difficulty, and complexity. Numerous refinements follow. When the scheme has been crystallized and the positions allocated, it is time to write the class specifications, which become the official record for the class. The "specs," as they are called, contain the official class title, the writeup of duties, responsibilities, and job relationships, a list of typical tasks, qualifications for them, and the usual avenues of promotion. A class specification need not and often does not contain the amount of pay, except when used as a recruiting bulletin.

Factor-comparison procedure involves three broad steps. The first one determines the factors to be used in defining a position. These commonly include "mental requirements," "skill requirements," "physical requirements," and "working conditions." Experience and experiment indicate that increasing the number of factors beyond three to five will not refine results very much. The second step consists of the selection of "key" or "benchmark" jobs. These are representative jobs thought to have some characteristics which make them comparable to other jobs. For instance, "stenographer" is first related to the clerical and steno-

---

[6] Classification surveys, of course, often produce solid information for general organizational reform and redesign. See, for example, Elmer V. Williams, "Administrative By-Products of Classification Surveys," *Public Personnel Review*, Vol. 32 (October, 1971), pp. 235–37.

graphic hierarchy. The third step occurs when an evaluation committee fits these jobs into the pay scale by defining each factor in terms of pay. When the key jobs have been evaluated, the other jobs are fitted into the appropriate relationship. In brief, each factor for each job has a money value which adds up to the total pay for the job. For example, a key job might be evaluated as follows:

Mental requirements	$ 68
Skill requirements	108
Physical requirements	68
Responsibility requirements	100
Working conditions	44
	$388

The main difference between the factor-comparison and point-evaluation systems is that the latter provides numerical points instead of dollars and cents. The points can be, and usually are, converted into money. In those jurisdictions where the personnel agency does not recommend compensation rates, the point system is naturally to be preferred. Thus a comparison between a junior clerk and a laborer might run as follows:

	Junior Clerk	*Laborer*
Mental requirements	3	1
Skill requirements	2	1
Physical requirements	2	5
Responsibility requirements	2	1
Working conditions	2	2
	11	10

Problems in Classification. American public administration tends toward what has been termed "pigeonhole" classification, which springs in part from the same source as jurisdictional disputes in industry. As administrators, workers often try to inflate their jobs, to make them seem unique and important. They emphasize experience and seniority, even for simple jobs. As a result, there are relatively few "common labor" jobs; everyone is at least "semiskilled," even though he is a neophyte. This condition is partially due to mechanization, functional specialization, and the production control which goes with them. But also present is individual ego and the desire to secure social as well as monetary recognition for one's specialty. One result is that most classification plans tend to have a large and increasing number of classes. Some look upon this with dismay, mainly on the ground that it restricts flexibility in job assignment. Observers have compared American pigeonhole classification unfavorably with the broad and general categories used in Britain. American personnel experts, however, reply that this is an unfair comparison because it usually excludes the great mass of British craftsmen, technicians, and laborers, among whom job classes are much the same as ours.

Another problem is to determine who should have the power to approve the classification scheme and the allocation of positions to the classes set up in it. In the U.S., this is a combined operation. Congress now establishes a broad general classification scheme, the Civil Service Commission breaks it down into class standards, and the operating agencies set up their own classification schemes within this framework. But federal departments are now so large that overcentralization still exists, and relations between the classifiers and supervisors can become the focus of considerable tension. Pressure upon supervisors for the upgrading of positions can be powerful; furthermore, a given supervisor may have his own official status improved if those under him are upgraded. There is a feeling among congressmen, many taxpayers, and management consultants that the common organizational tendency toward empire building is exaggerated in government where the competitive pressures for economy are largely absent.

Federal practice delegates the power to classify to the heads of executive agencies, and usually this means further delegation to their subordinates. Personnel specialists, of course, are advisors to line executives who make the actual decisions. Some observers, however, maintain that decisions should be made by the classifiers themselves, independent of the line of command. They claim that operating personnel, in doing their own classifying, will allow subjective considerations to enter into a procedure which "should" be objective. In most state and local jurisdictions, the power to classify still resides with the Civil Service Commission. There has been comparatively little delegation to operating personnel.

A PROBLEM OF ORGANIZING

Classification activity in traditional personnel administration is related to the study of jobs and their interrelationship, which, in essence, is the process of organizing. Yet orthodox classification theory has insisted on emphasizing *tasks*, and only to a minor extent has concerned itself with *people*. As noted earlier, the assumption has been that positions should be considered without reference to their incumbents. Indeed, more often than not, a defensive attitude has been assumed toward people who are constantly seeking higher classifications. Classification, or job grading, is said to account for the great preponderance of grievances arising under collective-bargaining contracts. The result is that the classifier has learned to, or at least tried to, rely on technical job factors in which the personal attributes of incumbents are not included.

This stance on the part of classifier is another manifestation of influences which have often isolated personnel work from the mainstream of management. Although there is considerable logic supporting such independence, the current job revolution is forcing a re-examination. The emphasis on tasks will probably remain an essential part of job analysis but the view that individual and personal considerations do not modify tasks is being undercut. This development reflects the need for flexibility in dealing with what one study of New York City's personnel setup called "professional, technical, and managerial manpower." [7] Federal practice has also been influenced by the difficulty of recruiting and retaining high-level personnel in these categories. Its slow and inflexible recruitment methods caused it to lose talented men who turned instead to local or state government or to the universities, which could move more expeditiously and provide the conditions necessary to meet individual differences. A similar difference exists between state and private universities, with the former generally unable to make appointments as swiftly and simply as the private schools. The protective ethos means that more clearances must be sought at more levels. The resulting disadvantages have become apparent in governmental personnel work, and attempts are being made to overcome them.

One result is the linking of the classification process with management analysis. David Stanley, for example, found a marked underutilization of special skills in New York City and attributed it in part to rigid pigeon-hole classification, coupled with a structure which divided classification between budget and personnel people. He suggested a greater synthesis between management and analysis and classification, combined with broader general classes to permit greater flexibility in transfering and placing individuals. [8] Recent federal experience has also modified rigid class categories and given more recognition to the "impact of the man on the job." Classification experts insist that they have always recognized that their decisions may legitimately be influenced by the discrete

[7] David T. Stanley, *Professional Personnel in the City of New York* (Washington, D.C., Brookings Institution, 1963).
[8] *Ibid.*

skills and attributes of people. Nevertheless, it was necessary in the 1950's to take special measures in the federal service to alter the rigid viewpoints of some classifiers. There seems little question that a significant change is occurring in both thought and practice, even though it is taking place within the traditional framework. Personnel control practices are moving in the direction of more flexibility without losing their essential function.

This trend was confirmed by O. Glenn Stahl, who formerly directed classification job standards for the U.S. Civil Service Commission.[9] Although Stahl was occasionally defensive with those who took a sharply critical attitude toward public personnel administration,[10] he said that the "time has come to slough off the preoccupation with exclusive decision-making by specialists in classification. In the federal service, to the dismay of only a few diehards, we are openly encouraging supervisory participation in job evaluation. In scientific research positions, panels of senior specialists and officials take part in evaluative judgments." [11] He goes on to remark how infectious responsibility is and how responsible and sound such decisions really are. Such reappraisals of the time-honored independence of the third-party classifier are bringing about several gains: more assumption of classification responsibility by operating management, less tendency to berate the personnel system as some external threat, and possibly even better job evaluation, with less temptation to "beat the system."

Position Management in the Defense Department

The Department of Defense has had a program which joins organization analysis with classification under the heading "position management." The motivation for the program undoubtedly lies in the eternal struggle to control grade "escalation" under the classification system. An effort is made to regulate the average grade factor by attention to positions GS-13 and above. The interesting point is the linking of classification study and action with the organizing process. Instead of studying only individual positions, the *interrelationship* of one position to another is of primary concern.

This development, however, is related less to questions of techniques than to spirit and underlying philosophy. Before World War II every

---

[9] "Job Classification: Instrument or Strait Jacket?" (paper presented to the Public Personnel Association, Los Angeles, October 5, 1964).

[10] See his "The CED Report on Federal Executives," *Good Government*, Vol. 81 (Winter, 1964), p. 70.

[11] *Ibid.*, p. 14.

federal classification action had to be pre-audited and approved by the Civil Service Commission. War needs forced the decentralization of these decisions to the agencies, despite misgivings on the part of classifiers. Eventually, the Navy set up a system of area wage officers who had final classification authority. This caused much dissatisfaction among line officials, especially at research installations which had to hire scarce scientific and technical personnel. The Navy soon relaxed this arrangement and in the 1950's gave classification authority to the line commanders, subject to post-audit by the area wage officer. This system seems to be working quite well as the classifiers accept integration of their operations with line management as a practical alternative.[12]

This example relates nicely to the problem of developmental personnel management in recognizing it as a component of overall management, as part of a coordinated system, the phases of which include mission needs, economy and effectiveness, proper utilization of skills, attraction and retention of skilled people, employee motivation, and employee development.

The Organizing–Evaluating–Coaching Syndrome. We have occasionally used the expression "mainstream of management," referring, of course, to the decision-makers of the line. A new concept of "staff" seems to be emerging in which this demarcation has become less distinct. This practice, which has been going on for some time, is due not only to behavioral-science research, as pointed out by such writers as Dalton, but also to the maturation of administrative thought.[13] Perhaps the main factor has been the growing awareness that good managers do not just happen, but that conscious effort and planning must go into their development. The competition for high-level skills emerging in today's "meritocracy" has also compelled organizations to do something about executive development, which is now characterized by what can be called an "organizing–evaluating–coaching syndrome."

These three activities fit together because they center on superior–subordinate relationships. They involve acceptance of the propositions that the line manager is the key figure in personnel decisions and that third-party control which ignores him cannot possibly result in a highly motivated organization. Nevertheless, some unresolved questions persist regarding behavior in the superior–subordinate matrix, which, as in many human contexts, finds theory far in advance of practice. One revolves

[12] U.S. Department of Defense, *Position Management System*, January, 1965 (mimeo).

[13] Melville Dalton, *Men Who Manage* (New York: John Wiley, Inc., 1959), pp. 71 *ff.*

around whether the paranoia sometimes seen in executive behavior can be brought under better control.[14] Industrial organizations seem to be evolving a pattern of executive behavior quite at variance with the bull-in-the-china-shop stereotype.[15] One of its features is to have superior and subordinate discuss the aspects of the latter's job in a relaxed atmosphere. They talk about the job rather than the person, in order to avoid the punitive aspects of personal criticism. This policy brings the line manager directly into the process of job analysis.[16]

RECENT DEVELOPMENTS IN POSITION CLASSIFICATION

As mentioned earlier in this chapter, quantitative industrial systems of job evaluation are being used with greater frequency today in the public sphere. In 1970, a task force created by the Job Evaluation Policy Act was mandated to "prepare a comprehensive plan for the establishment of a coordinated system of job evaluation and ranking for civilian positions in the executive branch."[17] The results of the efforts of the Task Force, encapsulated and reported as a Coordinated Job Evaluation Plan,[18] clearly demonstrate the trend toward applying industrial experience to the public personnel system.

The Plan recommends the incorporation of all existing position classification schemes in six new evaluation systems (with attendant pay structures):

> EES—Executive Evaluation System
> APTES—Administrative, Professional, Technological Evaluation System
> SOES—Special Occupations Evaluation System
> SAMES—Supervisor and Manager Evaluation System
> COMOT—Clerical, Office Machine Operation, Technical Evaluation System
> CFWS—Coordinated Federal Wage System [19]

[14] Harry Levinson, *Emotional Health in the Field of Work* (New York: Harper & Row, Inc., 1964), p. 243.

[15] D. Ronald Daniel, "Team at the Top," *Harvard Business Review*, Vol. 43 (March–April, 1965), pp. 74–82.

[16] The new emphasis upon counseling is stressed in E. D. Leonard's "Counseling and Employee Development," *Personnel Administration*, Vol. 28 (September–October, 1965), pp. 32–35; see also J. M. Michael, "Problem Situations in Performance Counseling," *Personnel*, Vol. 42 (September–October, 1965), pp. 16–22.

[17] *Job Evaluation Policy Act*, Section 301 (PL91-216, March 17, 1970).

[18] Reported in *Proceedings of the U.S. House of Representatives' Committee on Post Office Civil Service* (Washington, D. C.: U. S. Government Printing Office, 1971).

[19] *Ibid.*, p. 4.

Each evaluation system is classified in relation to a set of master factors:

Job Requirements
   1. Knowledge
   2. Specialized training
   3. Skills
Difficulty of Work
   1. Complexity
   2. Mental demands
Responsibility
   1. Impact
   2. Scope
   3. Job controls
   4. Supervision exercised
Personal Relationships
   1. Internal
   2. External
Physical Effort and Work Environment
   1. Environment
   2. Hazard
   3. Physical effort
   4. Intensity of effort
   5. Security requirements [20]

These variables are weighted to determine the emphasis given to each factor in arriving at a total judgment for a given job. For example, typical positions under EES and COMOT are described by the following breakdown:

EES
Job requirements	35%
Difficulty of work	25
Responsibility	25
Personal relationships	15

COMOT
Job requirements	40%
Responsibility	40
Personal relationships	15
Physical effort and work environment	5 [21]

These breakdowns and weightings of master factors are correlated with comprehensive listings of benchmarks (i.e., listings of all the most

[20] *Ibid.*, p. 11.
[21] *Ibid.*, pp. 5–6.

important duties and responsibilities of a given position) and guide charts (i.e., guidelines that identify the relative value expressed in points for each factor of a job which is ranked against the bench-mark descriptions) [22] in order to produce a detailed classification of positions ranked comparatively by points. Consequently, merit classifications and pay assessments are made for all positions such that the hierarchy of these values corresponds to the hierarchy of position classifications.

The Compensation Plan

The salaries and wages paid to public servants are set in a variety of ways, among which the following are the most important:

1. By legislatures, as spelled out in detail in the law. This method applies mainly in those states and local jurisdictions which do not have mature personnel systems.
2. By legislatures according to a broad schematic outline, but with the detail left to administrative or executive determination. This applies to the federal classified service.
3. By collective bargaining, as in the U.S. Government Printing Office, Tennessee Valley Authority, and in a growing number of other federal agencies.
4. By local or area wage determinations based upon periodic study of prevailing rates, as with "non-graded" federal employees.
5. By haphazard or unplanned determination, also characteristic of immature personnel setups.

Pay Determination.   It has long been common to compare governmental pay unfavorably with private compensation, except at the blue-collar and clerical levels, but this is no longer so patently true. Recent federal pay raises have tended to make the compensation of grades GS 13 to 15 compare quite favorably with those in industry. These are the positions, of course, occupied by the great majority of career executives. Although comparisons with business executives at the corporate level are still unfavorable,[23] given such incentives as stock-options, pension benefits, consultant arrangements upon retirement, plus salaries often in six figures, the fact remains that federal pay levels approach those of

[22] *Ibid.*, p. 4.
[23] See, *Improving Executive Management in the Federal Government* (New York: Committee for Economic Development, 1964), p. 67.

the vast majority of privately employed executives.[24] By 1971, for example, pay had reached quite satisfactory levels, as shown in Table 11–1.

TABLE 11–1.   General Schedule in the Federal Civil Service, Pay Rates (effective December 22, 1971)

Grade	Range of Pay	Grade	Range of Pay
GS–1	$ 4,564– 5,932	GS–10	$12,151–15,796
GS–2	5,166– 6,714	GS–11	13,309–17,305
GS–3	5,828– 7,574	GS–12	15,866–20,627
GS–4	6,544– 8,506	GS–13	18,737–24,362
GS–5	7,319– 9,515	GS–14	21,960–28,548
GS–6	8,153–10,601	GS–15	25,583–33,260
GS–7	9,053–11,771	GS–16	29,678–37,590 *
GS–8	10,013–13,019	GS–17	34,335–38,915 *
GS–9	11,046–14,358	GS–18	39,693 *

* The rates of basic pay for employees at these levels is limited by section 5308 of title 5 of the United States Code to the rate of Level V of the Executive Schedule (as of the effective date of this salary adjustment, $36,000).

Source: U.S. Civil Service Commission, *Minority Group Employment in the Federal Government,* Washington, D.C., U.S. Government Printing Office, 1972, p. 138.

Several features of this distribution are noteworthy. One is the broad spread between initial salaries and those in the higher reaches of the scale. This avoids a common problem, seen for example in academia, where the distance between beginning and senior salaries is often only about 100 per cent. Here, we find a much greater dispersion which increases the career attractiveness of the federal system. It is also apparent that the spread *within* a given grade increases steadily as one ascends the scale pay, which accommodates the fact that upward mobility grows more difficult as one rises, by providing greater income incentives. No salary is ever high enough, of course, but given the security, fringe benefits, and generous pension rights of the federal service, the situation seems equitable.

The distribution of full-time federal employees under the General Schedule and the aggregate expenditures for civil service salaries (June 30, 1971) is presented in Table 11–2.

[24] Here again is an aspect of public administration worth considerable discussion, in some such terms as how critical monetary incentives *should* be in the public service; the extent to which conditions of commitment, personal responsibility, and measured productivity are comparable in the government milieu, and thus *should* provide the basis for comparisons with higher incomes received in private industry. Some observers argue that systematic reductions in staff, with the resultant savings being reallocated among fewer executive positions, but at higher incomes rates, may be one possible answer.

TABLE 11–2.   Distribution of Full-Time Employees under General Schedule Pay Rate (June 30, 1971)

Level	Number of Employees	Per Cent of Employees	Average Salary	Aggregate Salary
GS–1	3,008	0.2	$ 4,401	$ 13,239,552
GS–2	22,115	1.7	5,097	112,938,665
GS–3	107,711	8.3	6,046	651,292,565
GS–4	179,392	13.8	7,023	1,259,918,711
GS–5	163,888	12.6	7,954	1,303,598,070
GS–6	82,057	6.3	8,954	734,766,782
GS–7	114,149	8.8	9,742	1,112,081,318
GS–8	25,929	2.0	10,916	238,042,415
GS–9	139,575	10.8	11,810	1,648,406,021
GS–10	19,356	1.5	13,139	254,292,668
GS–11	144,790	11.2	14,238	2,061,638,688
GS–12	126,636	9.8	16,832	2,131,561,869
GS–13	96,987	7.5	19,861	1,926,301,234
GS–14	44,772	3.4	23,313	1,043,776,041
GS–15	23,042	1.8	27,553	634,896,480
GS–16	3,450	0.3	32,062	110,614,856
GS–17	1,020	0.1	35,244	35,949,354
GS–18	385	0.05	36,000	13,860,000
Total	1,298,302	100.0	$11,809	$15,332,175,289

Source: A Pace-Setting Year: US Civil Service Commission Annual Report, 1971.

The system presently utilized by the federal government for adjusting white-collar salaries under the General Schedule was established by the Federal Pay Comparability Act of 1970. Under its provisions, final responsibility for considering annual pay adjustments and increments is vested with the President, in conformity with policies approved by Congress and based on national income surveys of private employment conducted by the Bureau of Labor and Statistics. The President receives two sets of recommendations concerning federal wage policies every year; one submitted by the Director of the Office of Management and Budget and the Chairman of the Civil Service Commission, and the other provided by an Advisory Committee on Federal Pay. The former contains an analysis of the BLS survey results and conclusions concerning pay adjustments derived from consultations with the Federal Employees Pay Council, a body representing governmental employee organizations. The latter represents the observations of a panel of three impartial experts drawn from outside the government.

Armed with these two sets of recommendations, the President adjusts the pay schedules and reports his completed action to Congress before

October 1. At this point, both houses of Congress have thirty days to ratify or reject his recommendations. In the case of congressional disapproval, pay schedules are re-examined subject to final executive determination and the requirements of regular comparability adjustments.

Local Wage Surveys. The practice of setting governmental pay rates through wage surveys has been gaining acceptance at all levels of government. The wage-analysis specialists who do this work are confronted with two statistical problems: how to secure a representative sample of jobs and employers and how to establish norms of central tendency or averages. If a general salary survey covering all classes in a governmental jurisdiction is sought, the task is naturally more complex than if only blue-collar jobs are involved. The area wage boards that study non-graded federal jobs cover only skilled trades and related vocations such as those of machinists and apprentices. When the survey must cover the entire hierarchy, it is customary to select certain representative or bench-mark jobs such as those of "typist," "general clerk," "structural engineer," and "janitor." The information on these classes of jobs is then projected by both mathematical formula and expert judgment to set rates for related classes.

Brief job descriptions are prepared next, short enough so that employers are willing to read them! The analyst then calls upon the sample of employers furnishing information, which often requires a selling job to secure their cooperation. The pay schedules of public employees are a matter of public record, which anyone has the right to see, whereas private organizations tend to be secretive about their pay schemes, since revealing them might put their organization at a competitive disadvantage, as well as cause various degrees of heartburn among disenchanted employees. Private employers must therefore be assured by the analyst that such data will be treated confidentially. Sometimes the analyst may refuse to divulge the names of cooperating firms. Here, of course, he can get into trouble with the unions and other groups of public employees who may object to such secrecy, on the ground that low paid, non-union firms have been over-sampled, compared with unionized work places. Indeed, many unions are suspicious of this whole approach to wage setting, ostensibly because they question its fairness, but perhaps more basically because they believe that their own role as a bargaining agent will be undercut. As a result, unions have sometimes gone to the courts to force personnel agencies to reveal the sources of their wage data. Here again, in the context of policy-making, is a good example of the complexity of an issue which seems fairly straightforward, yet as one goes into it, raises both substantive and ideological issues.

In the recent past, such procedures have generally resulted in public pay levels that are equal to and in many cases above those of private employees doing the same types of work. This favorable position seems to be especially notable at the municipal levels, despite a generalized decline in the quality of many services. [25] On the other hand, federal employees have also received fairly generous pay increases during the 1970's. At present, it seems that pay scales in the federal and state–local systems are quite equitable. Perhaps the greatest disparities exist near the very top of the GS hierarchy where, in terms of employees surpervised and the amounts of money involved in programs, high-level bureaucrats are disadvantaged compared with their counterparts in the private occupational arena. Perhaps security and the chance to contribute to the larger community welfare provide adequate compensation.

Responsibility for Pay Determination. Who should make ultimate pay decisions? Should it be the legislature, some administrative body or the executive? It is obvious that Congress cannot set individual salaries for millions of federal positions or for the ten thousand classes for which the Civil Service Commission has issued standards. The Classification Act of 1923 established the principal that individual salaries should be set administratively, in line with broad guides established by Congress. With certain exceptions, this policy is followed today. In local government, the council usually approves the pay for each class, sometimes in a salary ordinance enacted annually at budget time. In some cities, this power is scattered among several independent agencies. The following procedures seem to be the most desirable for states and cities:

1. The central personnel agency classifies positions.
2. The personnel agency or the budget bureau conducts the community salary studies and recommends the pay scale for each class.
3. The final pay schedule for each class is determined administratively, by either the Civil Service Commission or some other designated single central body.
4. The elected governing body determines how much is available for salary purposes in each department.

[25] See, for example, Charles Schultze et al., *Setting Federal Priorities* (Washington, D. C.: Brookings Institute, 1973), p. 299.

5. The departments adjust their payroll totals to fit the limitations placed upon them by the appropriation ordinance.
6. If money is not available to pay going rates for all positions in the budget, the number of positions should be reduced accordingly.

The preceding plan would be as objective as possible in an imperfect world. Specialists study the wage structure of employers in the community. They advise a centralized administrative body regarding their findings. That body, in turn, determines the prevailing rate in the community for each class in the job hierarchy. The mayor or city manager, through his annual budget, informs the council of the total amount needed for each department or program. The council then passes the appropriation ordinance, setting limits on total amounts to be spent by departments or programs. Finally, the mayor or manager approves the departmental programs or budgets, which pay personnel at the prevailing community rate. Departments would have to trim their personnel budgets to the amounts allotted. In this way, legislators retain ultimate democratic control of expenditures and programs without making decisions that are essentially administrative.

Recent Developments in Federal Wage Policy

The Federal government has undertaken a program since 1969 to eliminate special pay schedules in the federal civil service and bring all white-collar employees into the General Schedule system. Special schedules consisting of higher rates of pay than those normally provided for by GS ratings were frequently used throughout the 1960's to attract well-qualified persons into the civil service. With recent improvements in regular government pay rates and a gradually developing surplus of applicants, it was felt that special schedules were no longer required. Accordingly, by the end of fiscal 1971, almost half of the 80,000 employees working under Special Schedules were integrated into the GS, mainly at the GS-11 and 12 levels.[26]

Twenty-six schedules providing for higher rates are still retained, for the most part covering medical and paraprofessional hospital positions administered by the federal government (e.g., laboratory workers, X-ray technicians, and physical therapists). The ultimate goal of personnel managers in the government, however, would seem to be to eventually eliminate *all* special schedules and bring all employees under a common, pay mechanism. Here, perhaps, is an example of the bureaucratic thrust

[26] U. S. *Civil Service Commission Annual Report, 1971,* Washington, D. C.

for order and standardization. In practical terms, the probability of ending all extraordinary manpower requirements (and, therefore, eliminating all attendant extraordinary pay and other inducement) seems somewhat remote. Problems will continue to arise which require the expertise of individuals outside the public sphere and special incentives will be necessary to attract them.

Attempts are also being made to standardize pay rates in the field of blue-collar governmental employment. The coordinated Federal Wage System, established by executive order in 1968, seeks equitable wage rates within geographical areas for trade, craft, and labor services. According to this system, blue-collar pay rates are to be maintained at levels prevailing in private industry within a given region by setting one pay rate within each public service pay grade at the same level as that which commonly exists outside the public sphere.[27] If the employee is fulfilling his job requirements, he will be advanced to this pay rate (or to a yet higher level) and will, therefore, be effectively guaranteed a wage competitive with private rates in his occupation and locality. The new system replaces the many separate wage boards maintained previously by individual departments and agencies to govern trade, craft, and laboring occupations within their own jurisdictions.[28]

One further development in federal wage policy should be mentioned: on June 1, 1971, the government announced an automatic 4.5 per cent cost-of-living annuity increase to apply to most federal civil servants. This step parallels the trend apparent in many private industries as a response to employee discontent over the rapid escalation of living costs. The question of whether the government's action will become a precedent governing future pay policies or whether the move was merely an isolated response to the increase inflationary pressures of the period can, of course, only be resolved over time.

Participation Bonuses and Incentive Systems

Increasingly, private industries in the United States are investigating and, in a significant number of cases, adopting profit-sharing, savings-sharing, or production-sharing schemes to counter problems of low em-

[27] For a discussion of this and related issues involving the links between classification plans and compensation plans in the public sector, see, among others, David L. Norrgard, "The Public Pay Plan: Some New Approaches," *Public Personnel Review*, Vol. 32 (April, 1971), pp. 91–95.

[28] See William J. Lange, "The Federal Wage Board System of the United States Government," *Public Personnel Review*, Vol. 32 (October, 1971), pp. 238–45.

ployee motivation. The obvious theory behind such programs is that productivity and efficiency in an industrial operation will be increased if employees perceive it to be in their interest to work more rapidly, more carefully, or more efficiently. Work achievement that results in increased output, reduced waste of material and time, or better quality products, can be rewarded by returning a share of the greater savings or profits to the workers. Accordingly, they can relate more directly to the production goals of the firms and, in theory, they will feel less alienated from the products of their own labor.

Incentive programs related to commodity production are, of course, inapplicable to most governmental operations. Governments deal by and large with service to particular constituencies and these services are not easily related to production/cost ratios or to the performance of individual servants. As a result, any incentive program in government must necessarily be related to aggregate group accomplishments in a department or agency or a bureau. Such accomplishments, in turn, can only relate to efficiency quotients or to resource-savings variables rather than to a commodity or a production goal. This type of incentive system oriented to group achievement in service organizations is often referred to as a participation bonus or a systems incentive.

In more definite terms, participation bonuses are:

> . . . programs of financial reward under which all regular employees of a given department or agency, meeting certain eligibility requirements, are compensated in addition to their regular pay through sharing, according to a predetermined formula, in the labor and supply savings the organization is able to generate.[29]

Increased efficiency in a government system or subsystem, of course, can also mean greater benefits to the taxpayer although these benefits are usually less direct and less pronounced than those which accrue to the civil servants immediately affected.

Although no significant program of participation bonuses yet exists in the federal government, one can speculate that a number of benefits could result from the implementation of such a system:

1. Higher pay to employees at lower costs to the public because salary increases would be a function of greater efficiency rather than greater costs
2. More qualified employees would be attracted by potentially higher salaries

---

[29] J. J. Jehring, "Participation Bonuses," *Public Administration Review*, Vol. 32 (September/October, 1972), p. 539.

3. Improved employee relations would likely result as premium is placed upon group cooperation and efficiency
4. Less supervision might be needed as many workers tend to supervise more closely their own work under conditions of higher motivation.[30]

At present, a federal employees' incentive program does exist but awards under this system are distributed to individuals for superior performance or valuable suggestions rather than to groups for agency savings. In 1971, 96,879 employee suggestions were adopted and recompensed in the amount of over $5 million, while 105,937 superior performance awards were distributed at an aggregate value of some $22.9 million. Civil Service Commission estimates that the suggestions and achievements that merited these cash awards saved the federal government almost $350 million in measurable operating costs, in addition to the other non-measurable benefits that accrue from innovation and greater employee motivation. The employee suggestion esteemed most commendable during this period was an idea for less costly carrying of practice bombs on military training flights. This suggestion was estimated to have saved the military $6.4 million in 1971 and, consequently, its author was awarded a $7,455 prize.[31] The greatest number of incentive awards at the federal level were given to Defense Department employees for suggestions involving military activities.

Such incentives are probably most significant as an index of the Commission's awareness of the need for developing indexes of *measured productivity* which can be used to design pay schedules flexible enough to reward differential performance. Obviously, the heart of the problem is the design of truly effective instruments of evaluating performance as a basis for equitable differences in income. Unless government service is different from other types of institutional structures, with dramatic attending differences in individual productivity, the wholesale raising of executive salaries across-the-board, as by automatic cost-of-living increases, will only tend to crystallize existing disparities.

[30] *Ibid.*, p. 540.
[31] *A Pace-Setting Year: U. S. Civil Service Commission Annual Report, 1971*, pp. 72–73.

12

Recruiting, Examining, Evaluating, and Promoting

The efficient operation of a complex organization obviously requires an adequate supply of trained personnel. Specific procedures must be established to govern the mechanics of employee recruitment and examination and, subsequently, patterns for continuing evaluation and promotion (or demotion) must be maintained so that the requirements of the organization and the individual aspirations of the employee are conciliated. In the classical Weberian model these processes are seen as functions of orderly decision-making based on such rational, "non-particularistic" criteria as skill, knowledge, and education.

We turn now to a discussion of the processes of recruiting, examining, evaluating, and promoting as they are typically found in the federal personnel system. Closely bound up with recruitment is an old issue regarding the best type of preparation and qualities required for administrative effectiveness,[1] often posed as a dichotomy between "generalists" and "specialists."[2]

[1] Here again is an aspect of public administration that merits continuing debate among students of the field.
[2] Robert Presthus, "Decline of the Generalist Myth," *Public Administration Review*, Vol. 24 (December, 1965), pp. 11–16. The definitive work on the generalist Administrative Class remains R. K. Kelsall, *Higher Civil Servants in Britain*

ADMINISTRATIVE GENERALISTS

The term "generalist" has various connotations, both positive and negative, in the lexicon of social science. Typically, "generalists" are contrasted with "specialists" and the dichotomy is vital, since different approaches to fundamental requirements of successful administration underlie each construct. In the British and Canadian systems, for example, the generalist rationale is dominant and based essentially upon the assumption that the well-educated amateur is capable of handling most of the problems of modern administration. Members of the British administrative class have often been educated at Oxbridge in classics and literature. Their foremost qualities are literary and verbal facility, self-confidence, and the capacity to keep their ministers out of trouble. Their role is usually described as one of shaping policy, drafting and rationalizing the legislation required to carry it through, and providing the continuity required to overcome the dislocations brought by periodic elections and the rather frequent rotation of ministers (and themselves) from one department to another.

A more specific and perhaps critical appraisal of the role of British higher civil servants is implicit in the following quotations from two of its younger members.[3] The first, only 27 (1966), is a secretary to a junior Minister in Transport. He has also had jobs in the London Highways Division. As he says,

> I've never worked so hard in my life and I've never been more happy. Before becoming a private secretary (to a Minister) there were a lot of frustrations. One was never allowed to do anything important, and any document one wrote was automatically re-drafted higher up, and it was impossible to feel one was making a personal contribution of any sort. But that was the training period, and in this job I feel I really am doing something worthwhile. I've come to admire the Civil Service system of

(London: Routledge and Kegan Paul, 1955). More recent data are available in the "Fulton Report," see especially Vol. 3 (1) and 3 (2) *The Civil Service* (London: Her Majesty's Stationery Office, 1968–1969). As the old saw goes, this *Report,* comprising several volumes, tells one more than anyone wants to know about the British civil service. Its main drift, however, is a fairly rigorous criticism of the existing system along several lines, including recruitment, which has changed little over the recent past. Although the proportion of English university students graduating from Oxbridge declined from 22 per cent in 1938–1939 to 14 per cent in 1963–1964, the proportion of administrative class recruits remained virtually the same, about three-quarters, during these periods, see Vol. 3 (1), p. 402. Moreover, the proportion of natural and applied science recruits remained the same, despite a rise from 1939 to 1963 from 26 to 41 per cent of graduates in these disciplines.

[3] Jonathan Aitken, *The Young Meteors* (London: Secker and Warburg, 1967).

administration tremendously. Of course, to a certain extent the Civil Service is over-cautious and over-perfectionist, and we'd certainly have a higher degree of efficiency if we had a lower degree of perfection. A civil servant would invariably rather take six months and get a problem absolutely right, than take one month and make even a small mistake that could easily be corrected later on, but that's the standard of professional efficiency expected of one. I'm very happy with the responsibilities and the pay, but just a shade concerned with the life. I was rather upset the other day when I went to see my parents and my mother said to me, "You are getting more and more like a machine every day." . . . What are the attractions of the life? Well, mainly the work of course, but it is also good to know that one is finished with the rat race. There's very little jockeying for position, and none for publicity, so consequently the anonymity, the security and the lack of stress are great attractions. We operate below slogan levels, colour is deliberately damped down and we do not get emotionally committed to our work. This inevitably makes us appear like dessicated calculating machines, but you know if civil servants got emotionally involved like Michael Foot [a left-Labour MP], the country would grind to a halt in no time. I am content to be a professional administrator.

Another Foreign Office official says, "I suppose I enjoy it so much because it is a quasi-intellectual occupation, yet at the same time very practical. One is surrounded by very intelligent and highly agreeable people, and contrary to its public image, the Foreign Office isn't at all full of snobbish types. The salaries compare well with industry, and when overseas the tax-free living allowance can be a great help. One drawback is the continual pressure to conform, but I suppose that is inevitable in any government department."

Critiques of the Generalist Style

Judgments about the efficacy of the generalist-based systems vary. Critics such as Lord Balough and Brian Chapman have attacked the British system vigorously, stressing the inability of broadly educated men to handle the complexities of modern government. In the economic sphere, Balough's professional domain, he has used such examples as the drastic drain on British gold reserves following World War II, brought about by misguided efforts of the Economics Section of the Treasury (which included at that time no professionally trained economists) to peg the world price of the pound.[4] A similar drain on reserves, estimated

---

[4] Timothy Balough, "Apotheosis of the Dilettante," in H. Thomas, *The Establishment* (London: New English Library, 1962); Brian Chapman, *British Government Observed* (London: Allen and Unwin, 1962); I. Davidson and G. Weil, *The Gold War* (London: Secker and Warburg, 1970), p. 123.

to have cost $500 million, occurred in November, 1967, just before the devaluation of that year.[5] The Canadian higher service suffers to some extent from similar generalist assumptions, and perhaps especially in the limited regard for research-based policy. There is some tendency to rely rather more upon rhetoric and well-written exegeses of policy ventures. Certainly, in a world of exquisite occupational differentiation, which clearly adds effectiveness in many sectors, the generalist view seems mildly anachronistic. In government, however, where there are few if any standards for determining effectiveness, it is not always possible to determine precisely the costs of the system. What we do know is that occupational specialization brings increased skill and productivity in many contexts.

Contrasted with this philosophy is the American system with its essentially specialist assumptions. As its opposite, this system reflects in great part the differing assumptions of the educational systems of the two countries. On the other hand, it mirrors the belief that occupational skills and processes are different and that most people are incapable of becoming very knowledgeable in more than one or two fields. As a result, the American bureaucracy tends to be led by men who have come up through technical posts, with high administrative responsibility often being the result of demonstrated success in such posts. Alternatively, a substantial proportion come in from business and law. The top-level direction comes from officials with a specialist experience and orientation, quite unlike the British and Canadian systems.

For the purpose of this chapter, we shall refer to a generalist, or more particularly, an administrative generalist, as a person equipped with a certain flexibility of mind and an ability to think objectively, who is at home with a wide variety of problems in a number of different organizational contexts. He is skilled at dealing with people of diverse back-

---

[5] The Treasury's traditional ambivalence toward experts is apparent in Winston Churchill's remark, inspired by his dissatisfaction with the advice he received as Chancellor of the Exchequer during the late 1920's, as reported by his secretary P. J. Grigg: "He accused Treasury officials of not consulting enough with R. G. Hawtrey, who occupied the somewhat weak position of Director of Financial Enquiries. I remember his demanding from time to time that the learned man should be released from the dungeon in which we are said to have immured him, have his chains struck off and the straw brushed from his hair and clothes, and be admitted to the light and warmth of an argument in the Treasury Boardroom." Cited in Max Nicholson, *The System: The Misgovernment of Modern Britain* (London: Hodder and Stoughton, Ltd., 1967), pp. 215–16. According to Nicholson, Churchill's need for expert advice was great, since he was "perhaps the least interested and least gifted with economic understanding of all who have held that office in this century," *ibid.*, pp. 215–16; see also, pp. 413–88, *passim*.

grounds and, above all, has some knowledge about how to coordinate different groups and projects.

We are not using the term "administrative generalist" here in the narrow sense of an educational and social elite, usually associated with the British administrative class. In the American culture the generalist has often moved upward through specialist roles; he is much more management-oriented, and the lack of such orientation has often been mentioned in critical literature as a defect of the British system.[6]

[6] See, for example, Estimates Committee, Sixth Report: *Recruitment to the Civil Service* (London: Her Majesty's Stationery Office, 1965); see also, with special reference to the assumptions underlying the "dual hierarchy" between generalists and specialists, the critique of a management consultant group, *Fulton Report*, Vol. 2, pp. 58–59:

"(a) on the question of financial control, administrators did not have the technical competence properly to challenge the specialists except on obvious or relatively trivial points. This was for the most part also true when the administrators raised non-financial matters;

(b) delays and inefficiences result from dividing the responsibilities for making many decisions between specialists and administrators. Misunderstandings arise, papers are sent to and fro for clarification, time is occupied by explanations;

(c) under present circumstances there is a waste of specialists' time since administrators change jobs more frequently than specialists. Thus specialists find themselves having to explain the technical background to newly-arrived administrators;

(d) in industry, managers with specialist backgrounds are very often entrusted with the expenditure of funds without having their decisions under continuous scrutiny by laymen. There is no evidence that this leads to unwarranted expenditure. Indeed, cost control is an aspect of the training of architects, engineers and quantity surveyors;

(e) there is no evidence to suggest that specialists are unsuited to the role of policy-makers in their own specialist field. Indeed, as we have said earlier, accountants are very heavily involved in policy formulation in industry and engineers are also prominent in the policy areas of large companies. There is also no evidence to suggest that specialists could not quickly assimilate the necessary knowledge of the working of the government machine;

(f) the specialists strongly objected to the subordinate status that the relationship implied. In particular they were prevented from exercising the full range of responsibilities normally associated with their professions and exercised by their counterparts in industry. This is a deterrent to future recruitment of top class professionals;

(g) in a joint or parallel hierarchy, no single individual has clear management esponsibility.

In our view, therefore, there is no case for joint parallel hierarchies. Although in the blocks we examined there was a large volume of non-technical work—some of it routine, some of it requiring considerable expertise in, for example, drafting legislation and regulations and the financial procedures of government—nevertheless we consider the best organisational form to be a single integrated structure under a single head. Where the administrative content is preponderant, it may be that a non-specialist with the right background may be most suitable to head the group. However, in all the situations we examined, it would have been more appropriate had the head of the group spent most of his career as a specialist and been given the necessary training and experience in the administrative procedures of govern-

A different but interesting characterization of the "generalist" in American public administration is provided by Michael Cohen [7] who uses the term "mobility generalist," defined as those career employees who have moved between various government departments during the course of their service (rather than remaining in a single department or agency), as a methodological device for isolating a group of civil servants whose characteristics *qua* administrative generalists are then examined.

The Cohen sample is taken from the U.S. Civil Service Commission print-out of all super-grade positions (GS-16 through GS-18) in four departments and one agency directly related with social welfare programs and parallel fields for the month ending May 31, 1969. Of the 596 employees in these grades for whom adequate information was available, 270 were defined as generalists (i.e., they had been employed in two or more different departments) and 326 were classified as specialists (i.e., they had remained within one department throughout their career). Although questions may be raised as to the validity of this distinction, certain suggestive results are produced, as indicated in Table 12-1.[8]

In summary, generalists typically have M.A. degrees, have started their careers in business, industry, or the federal government service, have entered public employment between GS-1 and GS-10 levels, are primarily active in an administrative capacity directing or managing staff, have taken three or more in-service training programs, and have published no articles. In contrast, specialists are more likely to have earned a Ph.D. or M.D., to have begun their careers in a professional practice or in a college or university, to have entered public service between levels GS-15 and GS-18, to have been less occupied in administrative functions and more oriented toward operational programs, to have taken less than three training programs, and to have published eleven or more scholarly articles.

Administrative generalists, therefore

> . . . appear to be individuals with strongly administrative backgrounds, training and career. These transferable mobile public adminis-

---

ment. It is essential, in our view, that such posts as these, and higher ones, should be open to specialists with the appropriate qualifications and that personnel and management training procedures should be devised to assist and encourage them to fit themselves for top posts. At lower levels, we believe that there is scope for much closer integration of specialists and administrators both in teams and in unified hierarchies where the individual posts are filled by administrators or specialists according to the requirements of the task."

[7] "The Generalist and Organizational Mobility," *Public Administration Review*, Vol. 30 (September/October, 1970), pp. 544-52.

[8] *Ibid.*, p. 551.

TABLE 12–1.   Career Profiles of Higher Federal Executives

Characteristic	Departments Employed	
	Specialist	Generalist
Education		
M.A.		+
Ph.D., M.D.	+	
Place began career		
Business or industry		+
Professional practice	+	
College or university	+	
Federal government		
Executive Branch		+
GS level of entry		
1–10		+
15–18	+	
Present occupation		
Administrative		+
Job function		
Director, manager/ operational program	+	
Director, manager/ management support		+
Director staff		+
Training programs		
3+		+
Articles published		
None		+
11+	+	

+ indicates finding of a significant factor differentiating the two categories.

trators tend to be generalists in the specialty of administration itself, especially in planning, developing, and operating the management support and staff units.[9]

[9] *Ibid.* For precise distinctions between specialist and generalist roles in the British system, and the following conclusion regarding the present utility of administrative class generalists, see *The Fulton Report,* "Report of a Management Consultancy Group," Vol. 2: "We have been impressed by the scope, complexity and subtlety of the problems being faced by members of the Administrative Class. Many of these problems are new to government, new in scale and increasingly involve the development of close and intricate relationships with the community at large. All this places new demands on those who manage the government machine and assist in the formation of policy. Whilst the traditional skills of the Administrative Class in running the government machine will obviously remain important, these new demands call for new additional skills that must remain outside the scope of even the most able generalist. Increasingly the requirement will be for a new form of professional manager in public administration: appropriately qualified, appropriately trained, skilled in modern techniques, seasoned by experience and responsibility in a major function of a Department and able to develop and utilise the skills of his staff." p. 23.

Here, in effect, we have some useful empirical evidence indicating the existence of two discrete administrative roles whose occupants have different backgrounds, career experiences, and intellectual orientations. While the categories are not perfectly uni-dimensional, they provide a conceptual base for ordering the complex reality of governmental personnel structure.

Duties of Administrative Generalists

Staff Jobs. Administrative generalists often work for staff agencies, and many spend their careers in the budget and personnel fields. They will often be found doing administrative research and analysis in a budget bureau. Many go into personnel administration, where they become position classifiers, wage analysts, trainers, and—eventually—personnel directors. Others become assistants to department heads, administrators of auxiliary services, management consultants, superintendents of institutions, and managers of special programs. As they grow more mature and capable, they assume all types of responsibility, some in active program or line administration, others in staff jobs with duties essentially investigative.

Organization Work. The public administration graduate's skill is essentially that of an organizer and coordinator. The first few years will usually tell whether he is fitted to exercise these skills in one of two broad ways. If he is cut out for staff work, he will spend most of his career as an analyst, either in personnel or budget. Here he will be concerned with organizing and coordinating line operations; he will be essentially a consultant to those who make program decisions. As such, he will enjoy considerable status and be comparatively well paid. If he demonstrates exceptional abilities, he may become a budget director, a personnel director, or a chief of administrative services.

Assisting a Line Executive. On the other hand, if he becomes an administrative assistant to a program executive, his career pattern will probably be different. If he is able to establish good relationships with his chief, the latter will unload many duties on him. These include reviewing certain types of correspondence and composing replies, interviewing people whom the chief cannot see personally, and investigating problems and suggesting possible solutions. If he manifests considerable ability to get along with people, the chief will use him as a troubleshooter. He will also tend to become the chief's repository for facts, having at his fingertips a wide variety of data about production, condition of the budget, personnel quotas, and program planning. He will relieve his chief of a mass of detail, yet essentially he will not be a researcher but a coordinator of facts. With this kind of experience he may someday become a program chief.

Emerging Career Service

The main conclusion to be drawn from these observations concerning the characteristics and roles of administrative generalists in American public service is that, in the usual sense of the term, careers in "public administration" are now not only possible but are also vital to the functioning of American government. Despite the tendency in this study toward imputing prime value to scientific and technological expertise, and despite the current slow-down in civil service hiring, there continues to exist a need to recruit persons into the public service whose expertise is in administration itself. Indeed, the skillful handling of administrative and personnel problems is necessarily a vital part of the policy process in the United States, given government's size and complexity and the continuing need for revitalizing human relations in its structured context.

In the previous edition of this text, the following judgment was expressed: "The pioneer of the mid-twentieth century is living in a world of science and teeming urban crowds from which he cannot escape. America must have administrators who know how to manage large-scale hierarchies in a world increasingly dominated by the laboratory spirit— a world of atomic reactors, supersonic speed, and slide rules." [10] Although these words are peculiarly rooted in the ethos of the 1960's, the idea remains relevant in the 1970's. The types of problems administrators must now resolve may have changed somewhat and new structures may be evolving to meet them, but the need for competent public administration and personnel management has not diminished. Whether man can escape, in Weber's phrase, "the iron cage of history," the stifling effects of hyper-organization remains moot, but certainly no one can say that Americans are unaware of the problem.

We turn now to a specific discussion of the mechanisms of recruitment, examination, evaluation, and promotion as they pertain to the American public service. The material is often detailed but it provides the factual substratum upon which meaningful generalizations must be based.

[10] John M. Pfiffner and Robert Presthus, *Public Administration*, 5th ed. (New York: The Ronald Press Co., 1967), p. 283.

RECRUITING AND EXAMINING

Cultural attitudes have played an important role in shaping our civil service. An earlier edition of this book cited our equalitarian political philosophy as a bar to testing for educational achievement, popular demands for "practical" civil service tests, and the contrast between our system and the British program of general testing. In the post-war era, however, these views have undergone important modification. Today, college graduation or some equivalent is usually required in tests for any higher position. Aptitude tests or standardized commercial tests, depending on the type of public service position, are widely used. Recruiting in America, as in Britain, has tended increasingly to be geared to superior achievement in the nation's school systems and fairly well-defined patterns of career development have emerged.

Usually following federal models, state and local jurisdictions have developed aggressive recruitment systems designed especially for university graduates, with the hope of providing permanent career opportunities in a variety of occupational fields. In Michigan, for example, after declaring that the "constitutionally based civil service system of Michigan . . . is generally recognized as the best system in the nation," a brochure announces competitive examinations for trainee positions for college graduates in over 40 job classes.[11] The conditions of appointment and promotion are clearly enunciated and the general tone is highly affirmative.[12] Appointees need be neither U.S. citizens nor Michigan resi-

[11] Michigan Department of Civil Service, "College Graduates: Civil Service Career" (Lansing, 1970).

[12] That job specifications and their underlying rationale are not always equally positive is suggested by the following example. The author, Philip Schrag, first counsel of consumer rights in New York City, recounts his experience with the official in charge of writing job specifications for the City's civil service. Schrag had designed certain job descriptions to attract lawyers interested in consumer affairs to which the official objected:

"We can't have people like that working for the city. We want career people, who will stay 20, 25 years, not these kids on their way through. Ya know why?"

"Actually, I don't," I admitted.

"Because in just one or two years they don't build up any equity in the pension fund."

Now I was mystified. "So what?"

"We don't want people with no equity in the pension fund," he said. "We want people who build up 10, 15 years equity, a substantial amount of money due them from the pension fund."

"But what difference does that make?"

Schwartz answered slowly, beating his words out with one finger: "A man with 10 years' equity in the pension fund doesn't put his hand in the till, 'cause he can lose his pension rights."

dents. Opportunities are offered to have a committee of civil servants visit campuses to discuss careers in the state government. Some choice is offered regarding the location where the written test is to be taken. At the same time, the historical tension between egalitarianism and merit is symbolized by the provision that the maximum age for trainees is 50,[13] and preference points are granted to veterans.[14]

Descriptions of typical duties and requirements include the following:

Budget Analyst Trainee

Duties: Reviews fiscal requests for state agencies; analyzes materials received; may attend hearings with agency personnel; drafts narrative sections of the budget. Reviews legislative bills having fiscal implications. Reviews agency budget allotment schedules after appropriation bills are passed to determine that spending plans are as recommended. Maintains continuing review of fiscal operations through agency budgetary control reports. Conducts research and prepares reports.

Minimum requirements: Possession of a master's degree in the social sciences, preferably in political science, economics, public or business administration.
Location: Budget Division of the Executive Office in Lansing.

Clinical Psychologist Trainee

Duties: Selects, administers, scores and evaluates psychological tests. Gives achievement, intelligence, personality, interest and vocational tests. May administer projective tests. Records the behavior of patients during examination situations. Confers with psychiatrists and senior psychologists regarding significant reactions. Assists a senior psychologist in research studies related to pychological or behavioral modification techniques.
Minimum requirements: Possession of a master's degree in clinical psychology or equivalent graduate school credit toward a doctor's degree in clinical psychology from an accredited college.
Location: Department of Mental Health and Social Services at various institutions throughout the state.

Social Work Trainee

Duties: In a mental hospital or psychiatric clinic, provides casework and group work treatment for patients. Prepares socio-psychiatric case history information for use in pre-admission screening and diag-

---

"But these young lawyers aren't thieves!"
"Everyone near the till is a potential thief," said Schwartz. "That's why we have civil service. We lock 'em in; they have to stay with the city forever."
13 *Ibid.,* p. 5.
14 *Ibid.,* p. 11.

nosis. Interprets the social aspects of mental disturbances to relatives, interested persons, and community agencies. Determines the home and community circumstances prior to admission and preliminary to patient's release from hospital care. Takes part in the family care program by locating and evaluating homes for patients and placing patients in suitable homes and on jobs. In the Department of Social Services, in a county department or a child caring facility, investigates and makes recommendation concerning the licensing of boarding homes; locates homes to meet the needs of specific children; supervises children in their adjustment to boarding homes. Makes adoption studies, places children for adoption and supervises adoption placements. Makes investigations for the licensing of private institutions, agencies, and day care centers. Helps parents, relatives, and children in meeting problems arising from children's physical, mental, or emotional handicaps. Works with schools, child guidance clinics, health agencies, and other community programs in meeting needs of individual children.

Minimum requirements: Possession of a master's degree in social work from an accredited college of social work.

Location: Department of Mental Health and Social Services in various institutions throughout the state.

The problems of administering to the manpower requirements of the 600 or more occupations found in the federal civil service system are equally complex.[15] Position classifications and job responsibilities must be carefully outlined in order to determine the qualities—technical, clerical, administrative, and personal—required of potential employees. Attention must be paid to aspects of public policy that define in part the operations of the personnel system; for example, the widespread public demand and governmental commitment to the policy of equal employment opportunity, political criticisms of the size and costliness of governmental bureaucracies, and the problem of veterans' employment. In effect, the recruiting and examining processes must be integrated into the continually changing social environment of modern personnel management.

A dramatic example of such integration is seen in the long and honorable efforts of governments at every level to break down barriers of discrimination in employment, including those of race, religion, and sex. The following review outlines this complicated program, including some of the effects of the Equal Opportunity Act of 1967 and the vexing question of tension between such aspirations and the merit system.

[15] Richard F. Kanost, *Public Personnel Administration: The U. S. Federal System* (Lincoln: University of Nebraska, 1971), p. 41.

EQUAL EMPLOYMENT OPPORTUNITY

We are committed to the elimination of any vestige of discrimination, whether it is on the basis of sex, religion, national origin, color, or race.[16]
Robert E. Hampton,
Chairman, Civil Service Commission

Officially, the federal government has adopted a policy of ending all discrimination in employment practices. In the federal civil service, since the civil rights legislation of the Johnson administration, culminating in the Equal Employment Opportunity Act of 1967, concerted attempts have been made to insure openness throughout the personnel system to present and prospective employees, regardless of their sex, racial and national origin, or religion. To this point, these programs have met with mixed success.

As Table 12–2 indicates, total minority group employment reached 19.5 per cent of all pay systems and 28.6 per cent of all wage systems by May 31, 1971. Qualitatively, however, it seems that a great part of this total employment is confined to lower level civil service positions; maintenance and routinized staff jobs covered by wage-system agreements and the lower classifications of the General Schedule. Most notably, a close relationship is evident between General Schedule levels and minority group employment, such that there is a marked decrease in percentages of minority employment as one advances through the GS classifications (e.g., only 3.9 per cent of GS–14 thru 15 and 2.7 per cent of GS 16 thru 18). Effectively, therefore, opportunities for full upward mobility and career advancement for Americans who belong to minority racial groups would seem to be somewhat limited. These limitations may stem from persistent inequalities in the civil service [17] or may, more basically, reflect external social factors that impose ceilings on the career mobility of minority group members even before they become government employees (e.g., lower levels of educational opportunity).

Levels of minority group employment also vary considerably from department to department as illustrated by Table 12–3. In these same departments, levels of minority group employment under *wage systems* (predominantly maintenance and service staff) are often significantly higher; for example, 89.6 per cent in Labor, 58.2 per cent in Treasury,

[16] *The Civil Service and its Publics, Annual Report, 1970* (Washington, D. C.: U. S. Government Printing Office, 1971), p. 19.
[17] It will be apparent, for example, that the proportion of women among the some 11,000 officials at GS-16 and above is about one per cent; see Table 12–4.

TABLE 12–2. Minority Group Employment in the Federal Government
(as of May 31, 1971)

	Total Full-time Employees	Negro		Spanish-surnamed		American Indian		Oriental American		All Other Employees	
		Number	Per Cent	Number	Per Cent	Number	Per Cent	Number	Per Cent	Number	Per Cent
Total: All pay systems	2,578,124	388,577	15.1	75,539	2.9	18,868	.7	20,644	.8	2,074,516	80.5
Total: General Schedule or similar	1,307,082	146,459	11.2	26,008	2.0	11,752	.9	10,885	.8	1,111,978	85.1
GS-1 thru 4	300,466	65,113	21.7	9,394	3.1	6,186	2.1	1,906	.6	217,867	72.5
GS-5 thru 8	384,189	55,605	14.5	8,971	2.3	3,196	.8	3,094	.8	313,323	81.6
GS-9 thru 11	316,019	17,450	5.5	5,025	1.6	1,597	.3	3,239	1.0	288,708	91.4
GS-12 thru 13	225,348	6,616	2.9	2,045	.9	595	.3	1,968	.9	214,124	95.0
GS-14 thru 15	75,410	1,568	2.1	553	.7	171	.2	661	.9	72,457	96.1
GS-16 thru 18	5,650	107	1.9	20	.4	7	.1	17	.3	5,499	97.3
Total wage systems	517,083	106,468	20.6	30,346	5.9	5,704	1.1	5,301	1.0	369,264	71.4

Source: U.S. Civil Service Commission, Minority Group Employment in the Federal Government, Washington, D.C., U.S. Government Printing Office, 1972, p. 15.

TABLE 12–3.   **Percentage of Minority Group Employees under All Pay Systems, by Government Department**

Department	Negro	Spanish-surnamed	American Indian	Oriental American	Total Minority Employment
State	13.6	2.3	0.1	0.9	16.9
Treasury	14.6	1.8	0.1	0.6	17.1
Defense	11.4	4.2	0.3	1.0	16.9
Justice	9.6	2.6	0.1	0.4	12.7
Interior	4.6	2.1	15.4	0.6	22.7
Agriculture	6.2	1.8	0.4	0.5	8.5
Commerce	16.6	0.7	0.2	1.0	18.5
Labor	27.1	1.8	0.4	0.5	29.8
H.E.W.	22.4	1.5	3.2	0.7	27.8
H.U.D.	19.6	1.8	0.3	0.8	22.5
Transport	6.5	1.1	0.4	1.1	9.1

Source: U.S. Civil Service Commission, *Minority Group Employment in the Federal Government*, Washington, D.C., U.S. Government Printing Office, 1972, pp. 32–136.

76.2 per cent at H.U.D., 47.7 per cent at H.E.W. and 53.6 per cent at the State Department. Such hard data suggest some of the dilemmas of achieving equal opportunity in the face of unequal educational achievement, often resting in turn upon factors of social class. There is also the problem of the tension between merit and equal opportunity, to which we turn next.

Dilemmas of Equality

In assessing the success of the federal government in establishing equal employment opportunity for minority groups in the federal service, one is confronted with a difficult issue: Given the rationale of the "merit system" (i.e., the determination of position, promotion, pay, and other organizational qualities through universalistic criteria such as achievement, ability, skill, and knowledge), is it consistent to introduce particularistic criteria (e.g., race, ethnicity) into personnel recruitment and management in order to achieve racial equality or balance? In terms of organizational theory and bureaucratic rationality, one could respond negatively:

> The nub of the merit idea is that *a person's worth to the organization— the merit of his attributes and capacities—is the governing factor in his selection, assignment, pay, recognition, advancement and retention.* Other considerations—such as sex, race, religion, political affiliation,

economic status, age, and so forth—are irrelevant and have no proper place in implementing the merit objective.[18]

This argument belies the problem to some extent. In order that government agencies work effectively with minority groups or, perhaps more importantly, in order that they be perceived as legitimate by minority groups (or, for that matter, by society as a whole), it is essential that federal employment be open to these groups. Moreover, it is not sufficient that well-qualified minority group members be guaranteed entrance to and equality of career opportunities in the public service; less qualified persons from underprivileged and minority group backgrounds must also be trained for civil service positions. Earl J. Reeves emphasizes this point:

> Initial efforts to open up job opportunities for minority group members concentrated on attempts to hire well-qualified blacks, especially in a few conspicuous positions. But recently the Civil Service Commission has recognized that in order to make a significant breakthrough, they must develop programs to reach those who have previously been regarded as unemployable because of limited education and lack of experience. . . . It has become necessary, therefore, to develop methods for recruiting minority and other disadvantaged persons who are not presently qualified and provide the necessary training to make them employable.[19]

Clearly, then, extensive efforts will have to be made to improve and make more universally available the type of training programs that will permit minority group members to pursue careers in the civil service on an equal basis with other employees. Concomitantly, entrance examinations and evaluation systems may have to be altered to increase their relevance to the different cultural and social backgrounds of potential non-white employees.[20]

[18] O. Glenn Stahl, quoted in *Public Personnel Review*, Vol. 32 (July, 1971), p. 176 (italics in original).

[19] Earl J. Reeves, "Making Equality of Employment Opportunity a Reality in the Federal Service," *Public Administration Review*, Vol. 30 (January–February, 1970), p. 44.

[20] Reeves notes, for example, that there may exist a cultural bias in the Federal Service Entrance Examination. In 1967, a survey of 191 colleges and universities showed that 71.7 per cent of the students taking the FSEE successfully passed, while only 29.6 per cent of the applicants at predominantly black institutions were able to pass the same exam., *ibid.*, p. 45; see also Robert Sadacca, "The Validity and Discriminatory Impact of the Federal Service Entrance Examination," a paper published by The Urban Institute, Washington, D. C., 1971.

Are Quotas the Answer?

To some observers, the logical extension of equal opportunity employment policies involves the creation of quota systems in agencies and departments to insure that a certain proportion of employees are members of minority groups:

> A formal policy of non-discrimination, of employing people "regardless of race, color, or creed," however estimable, usually works out in practice to be a policy of employing whites only. Hence Negroes' demand for quotas represents a necessary tactic, an attempt to fix the responsibility for increasing employment of Negroes on those who do the hiring.[21]

One can question, however, whether the adoption of quota systems in the federal labor force truly represents an extension of attempts to democratize employment practices, or whether such a policy, by denying employment to one individual while granting it to another on criteria of skin pigmentation or racial origin, in fact represents an essentially anti-democratic development. Certainly, the point is debatable.[22]

In 1967, sex was added to the other prohibited forms of discrimination by virtue of President Johnson's Executive Order 11,375. At the same time, a Federal Women's Program was established with the expressed objective of "creating the legal, regulatory, and administrative framework for achieving equality of opportunity without regard to sex." [23] The Program sought to encourage qualified women to compete for federal employment and participate more widely in various in-service training programs that would facilitate career advancement. Through internal educational and advertising initiatives, the FWP aimed to eliminate the customs, attitudes, and habits of many civil service employees that had, in the past, constrained the career mobility of women and often prevented their entry into the majority of high-level positions.

The Federal Women's Program was integrated into the Equal Employment Opportunity Program by President Nixon in 1969. Consequently, several coordinated efforts were undertaken at the college and university level to recruit women into the federal service and, internally, more

---

[21] Charles Silberman, *Crisis in Black and White* (New York; Vintage Books, 1969), p. 241.

[22] Our hope is that students will devote some time to discussing such vital issues.

[23] Helene S. Markoff, "The Federal Women's Program," *Public Administration Review*, Vol. 32 (March–April, 1972), p. 144.

extensive training programs and better child-care facilities were provided for female employees. However, these initiatives have done little to resolve the basic disparities confronting women in the federal service. At the present time, levels of full-time, female white-collar employment in the federal system are about as shown in Table 12–4.

TABLE 12–4. Women in the Federal Civil Service

Grade	Total Employment	Number of Women	Per Cent of Women in Grade	Per Cent of All Women Employed
GS–1 thru 6	1,093,337	504,194	46.1	76.7
GS–7 thru 12	690,500	142,994	20.7	21.7
GS–13 and above	191,352	7,539	3.9	1.1
GS–16 and above	10,299	158	1.5	− 0.05
Ungraded	6,533	2,600	39.8	0.4
Totals	1,981,722	657,327	33.2	100.0

Source: Helene S. Markoff, "The Federal Women's Program," *Public Administration Review,* Vol. 32 (March–April, 1972), p. 144.

Clearly, the majority of the female labor force remains in the lower job classifications, filling clerical and secretarial positions rather than decision-making posts. There are, of course, notable exceptions. Beginning with the special appointment of Barbara H. Franklin in April, 1971 to the White House Staff to recruit women for policy-making positions, the Nixon administration had filled certain important posts with well-qualified women. Among these positions, the most noteworthy include the Chairman of the U. S. Tariff Commission, the Vice-chairman of the U. S. Civil Service Commission, a membership on the Equal Employment Opportunity Commission, and a commissioner's post on the Federal Communications Commission.[24] President Ford continued Nixon's policy of bringing in women at the political level; early in 1975, he appointed Carla A. Hills to be Secretary of Housing and Urban Development, and the first women appointed to the Ford Cabinet. The new Cabinet head's experience was largely in private legal practice in California.

[24] For a more complete listing of women appointed by President Nixon to high civil service positions, see the Citizens' Advisory Council on the status of women, *Women in 1971* (Washington, D. C., U. S. Government Printing Office, January, 1972). A somewhat inflated appraisal of the extent to which change in this area has occurred is Anne Armstrong, "Progress of Role of Women Is Steady and It Is Sure," *U. S. News and World Report* (May 14, 1973), pp. 66–69. Mrs. Armstrong was then Counselor to the President and a member of the Nixon Cabinet.

DIVERGENT CONCEPTIONS OF RECRUITMENT AND ROLE

It is clear from the foregoing comments that public personnel management is characterized by a basic incongruity. On the one hand, there is the desire to recruit the most competent young people and provide them with a career milieu in which universalistic criteria of achievement are the going basis for appointment and advancement. On the other hand, the system also employs subjective criteria in its efforts to achieve equal opportunity for minority groups and women. Unless one believes with Andrew Jackson that the tasks of government are so simple that virtually anyone can perform them, this dualism is bound to create problems. In this context we turn to the difficult problem of finding, developing, and keeping outstanding people in the public service. High rates of turnover (about 25 per cent annually throughout the federal service) and government's pervasive role in economic stabilization and international affairs have brought a fresh urgency to this need. Devotion and loyalty are no longer enough; the bureaucracy now requires exceptional competence and especially at the higher levels. In Western Europe, where political systems and the range of governmental services are roughly similar to ours, the public service is an honored craft that attracts the best talents in society. In the United States, however, the indifferent prestige of the public service and its restrictions on individual initiative have meant that outstanding men and women have often turned to other fields. Although the prestige of public employment compared with private has increased somewhat, recent findings still tend to reveal a negative perception of government work among such individuals. There are, of course, many exceptions to this generalization. During the Depression years, for example, highly skilled individuals flowed into government service, pushed by economic necessity and pulled by the social program of the New Deal. In the main, however, the difficulty of attracting and retaining talented people has been a persistent aspect of our public service. Here again, contemporary events are having an impact upon public administration. Popular disenchantment with government, the obvious failure of many programs to deliver as planned and promised, high-level federal scandals—all have inspired new demands for further and different education for public executives. As might be expected, there is little agreement on content.

There is no consensus, either within our universities or outside, regarding the proper training and education for public executives. On the one hand are those who believe that good managers are "born," that certain qualities of insight, judgment, and tact are required for executive success and that such qualities can only with great difficulty be inculcated by training and education. One problem with this rationale is that American hegemony in industrial development obviously rests in great part upon highly trained specialists being available in many substantive spheres of organization and management. As Servan-Schreiber concludes, it is widespread *educational opportunity* and its consequences which mainly explain American success in the area of multi-national corporate developments. Perhaps the effect is to raise the overall general level of competence and thus to provide an edge over Western European managers who do not typically believe in management training or the entreprenurial view that often accompanies it. The most telling indictment of the "good managers are born" thesis is probably apparent in the British experience where in the higher reaches of both government and industry, management is a relatively undeveloped skill.

Despite this, there are a bewildering variety of attitudes and opinions about the "proper" training and education for public executives. If one, for example, looks at a recent symposium on the subject in the *Public Administration Review* (although its major thrust was toward continuing education) the revealed philosophies of the various commentators apply equally to the more basic question of the most productive way of improving administrative performance through education.[25]

As noted, there is no consensus in our universities regarding the proper education and training of such individuals. Roughly, a division exists between those who advocate highly specialized vocational training and those who have been impressed by the apparent success of British liberal education in preparing individuals for their higher civil service. In order to provide a background for a brief consideration of these views, we must trace briefly civil service traditions and recruitment practices in Britain.

The British Administrative Class. It is customary in this country to view the British administrative class as an elite, open mainly to those who have graduated with highest honors at Oxford and Cambridge. That this is only part of the picture can be seen by the fact that, in the mid-1950's, about half its members had entered the class by promotion. Furthermore, the aristocratic character of the service is being eased by the fact that some Oxford graduates from less advantaged social classes

[25] Thomas W. Fletcher (Ed.), "Symposium on Continuing Education for Public Administration," *Public Administration Review,* Vol. 33 (November/December, 1973).

are now gaining entry; there is also some increase in recruitment from the provincial universities.[26] Finally, the new alternative methods of selection, of promotion from the executive class and from outside the universities based upon stress interviews are bringing in a limited number of persons from a wider social spectrum. On the whole, however the system has been remarkably resistant to change.[27]

What tasks are performed by the British administrative class? One is struck by the fact that most accounts of their duties center around intellectual and literary processes. Their work consists mainly of processing policy reports which often bear upon parliamentary discussion of ministerial policy. Almost from the beginning of their careers, they are involved in reading files and writing reports on whether Wiltshire should have a new town hall, how much revenue a one-penny tax on tobacco imports would raise, and in phrasing a reply from their minister to a disenchanted constituent. These officials, trained to be gentlemen and scholars, are quite adept at avoiding trouble for ministers. Some of them become permanent department heads under transitory political ministers. British administrative officials, in effect, are advisers on policy rather than managers, although, as hierarchical leaders, they must also devote some time to the servicing and control of their respective organizations in personnel, fiscal, and organizing matters.

It was pointed out above that the distinction between the administrative and executive classes in Britain is slowly breaking down. This is partly due to democratic trends, and has certainly been influenced by the political power of Labor. The administrative class has always been a social as well as an administrative institution, just as the House of Commons was once dubbed London's finest club. The aristocratic thrust of the high civil service, however, persisted for several decades after the democratization of the House of Commons. Leveling forces are at work, but recent data suggest that traditional values remain pervasive. In 1964, for example, over 90 per cent of new recruits in the Foreign Service and 80 per cent in the home civil service were "Oxbridge" graduates. Of fifty-one successful candidates, two-thirds had degrees in classics and history, and only a very few had a math background.[28]

[26] R. Kelsall, *et al.*, *Graduates: The Sociology of an Elite* (London: Metheun and Co., 1972).

[27] See, for example, Nicholson, *The System*, *op. cit.*

[28] *Sunday Times* (London), June 21, 1964, pp. 109–10. On the backgrounds of the highest administrative class officials, see John Sharp Harris and Thomas Garcia, "The Permanent Secretaries: Britain's Top Administrators," *Public Administration Review*, Vol. 26 (March, 1966), pp. 31–44.

The American View. The nature of a liberal education provokes considerable argument at home and abroad. There is no question that our higher civil servants should be broad-gauged and cultured persons. But this condition should not be equated exactly with European practice. Higher education in the rest of the world, whether European or Asian, has usually meant a rather formal study of classical literature, history of past civilizations, ancient and modern languages, literature, and philosophy. Even today, for example, Cambridge University has no formal political science program, although some rather traditional aspects of the discipline are taught. In the physical sciences, the thrust has been toward its pure and theoretical aspects. American higher education in the liberal arts has departed rather widely from this classical emphasis. Even the University of Chicago, with its emphasis on philosophical values, has been more interested in the contemporary world than in traditional classical subjects.

There remains in America, however, a gulf between those who advocate a broad liberal arts education and those who favor a vocational approach in preparing administrators. One, it is said, wants to educate for life, the other for making a living. On the one hand there is much deploring of vocational trends, coupled with appeals to return to philosophy, the humanities, and the classics. University schools of education are often criticized for emphasizing methodology at the expense of content. It is sometimes said that we are raising a generation of teachers who know how to teach but not what to teach. The attainments of American school children, and even college graduates, are compared unfavorably with those in equivalent European grades, particularly on the Continent. A French child in his early teens, it is generally agreed, is more advanced in mathematics, history, and languages than his American contemporary. A British graduate of Oxford or Cambridge is likely to be a better linguist, a more polished speaker, have more social poise, and know a great deal more about what happened in the world before 1900. On the other hand, it is doubtful that universities anywhere quite match the leading American graduate centers in their professional dedication and productivity.

Although we admire members of the British administrative class and wish that America could produce more officials with similar qualities, we do not believe that America could or should copy British practice. Pervasive cultural differences in educational philosophy, class and status, and social mobility make a similar development here impossible, assuming it were desirable. We feel, moreover, that the representative function of our higher civil services is eased by a broad base of recruitment, even though such a theory of representation is not entirely persuasive. There should be several avenues of entry into the higher bureaucracy, which needs highly diversified talents. Furthermore, it is inconsistent with the American interpretation of democracy to establish an elite closely bound up with educational achievement, often reflecting in turn class advantages as much as intellect, which challenge performance as a basis of recognition. Most important, however, is the fact that serious questions must be raised about the *capabilities* of the British higher civil service.

In terms of the diversity in the social origins of government employees, our civil service is hardly representative socially. Warner analyzed the family backgrounds of federal executives—both civilian and military—and compared the results with his own earlier findings regarding business executives.[29] In general, high-status federal executives tended to come from families in which the father's occupation was business executive, business owner, professional man, or white-collar worker. Very few are from lower-middle or working-class origins or are female. Percentages in the various categories do not differ very much between business and federal executives, except that in the former the father is somewhat more likely to have a business background.[30]

In the military areas, there is more continuity from father to son, and the father is more likely to have had an occupation with high social status. A similar generalization holds for the State Department. Nevertheless, "although foreign-service executives do come in greater than expected proportions from high prestige occupational groups, it is certainly not true that the "foreign service" is *exclusively* the domain of people of such origin." [31]

Warner and his associates conclude that American society "is not becoming more caste-like." The evidence shows "that our society, although much like it was in past generations, is more flexible than it was; more men and their families are in social motion." [32] The "sons of men from the wrong side of the tracks are finding their way increasingly to the places of power and prestige." While this is perhaps an unduly happy judgment, American equality of educational opportunity at the university level has clearly provided a major instrument of mobility, compared with Western Europe and Canada.[33]

[29] W. Lloyd Warner, Paul Van Riper, Norman Martin, and Orvis Collins, *The American Federal Executive* (New Haven, Conn.: Yale University Press, 1963).

[30] See comparative tables in *ibid.*, pp. 29 and 36.

[31] *Ibid.*, p. 14, italics added.

[32] *Ibid.*, p. 23.

[33] Robert Presthus, *Elite Accommodation in Canadian Politics* (New York: Cambridge University Press, 1973), Chaps. 2 and 10.

Recent Criticism of the Generalist Ethos. Some British observers have come to believe that their administrative class is an anachronism in a technological society.[34] While American academic opinion in the opening decades of this century tended to idealize the administrative class, more recent observations indicate that a re-evaluation is in process. One industrial inquiry (the Franks report) has recommended greater emphasis on the American pattern of technical–managerial education obtained at the Harvard Business School and the Massachusetts Institute of Technology. Meanwhile a comprehensive and critical parliamentary inquiry into recruitment and performance in the civil service has recently recommended many changes.[35]

Finally, five business schools were established at English universities during 1965. This spirit of national self-evaluation springs in part from the failure of British industrial productivity following World War II to keep pace with the growth rate of other western countries. Also pertinent is the growing involvement of the state in industrial production.

The American Higher Civil Service. C. Wright Mills insisted that the United States did not have a professional civil service. It is true that we do not possess a permanent top-level corps whose members are dominantly generalist as in Britain and on the European continent. The recommendations of the second Hoover Commission for a senior civil service aroused little enthusiasm either on the part of Congress or the professionals. Yet it seems significant that half of the appointments resulting from President Johnson's talent search were filled from the career service itself. Some observers believe that we are developing a *de facto* senior civil service without the alleged shortcomings of an elite, generalist corps. Warner and Van Riper found that their sample of high civil servants possessed a dedication and service motivation quite in conflict with the popular stereotype. Furthermore, the states and the cities are developing their own cadre of career professionals, with the states lagging somewhat behind but nevertheless beginning to develop career aspects. It is true these people tend to be agency-oriented, with the exception of the city managers, but critics of the British system point to the lack of such specialty interest among their career leaders. The important thing is that America is developing a career tradition.

---

[34] Among others, see Nicholson, *op. cit.;* the *Fulton Report, op. cit.*

[35] Oliver Franks, *British Business Schools* (London: British Institute of Management, 1963); House of Commons, "Recruitment to the Civil Service," Sixth Report of the Estimates Committee (London: Her Majesty's Stationery Office, 1965).

Education for the Higher Bureaucracy

College courses in public administration have been offered almost exclusively in departments of political science. This was quite natural because the interest was there—political scientists have always wanted to improve the administration of government and have often taken an active role in it. Paraphrasing Napoleon, one might almost say that every political science professor carries a Cabinet Minister's baton in his briefcase. It was equally natural that the first courses in social work should have originated in departments of sociology, just as business administration started in the economics curriculum. In the latter instances, however, the professional curricula have become largely divorced from the academic departments. Indeed, they are often separated by an ideological gulf which reflects considerable tension between them. Why did this occur, and has it happened to political science and public administration?

Liberal Arts vs. Specialization. Liberal arts or "academic" departments often have an antivocational point of view. Their faculties are primarily concerned with the theoretical, philosophical, and historical aspects of their subjects. With notable exceptions, they tend to avoid the vocational and operating phases of their disciplines. An economist, for example, is likely to be immersed in the theory of the incidence of taxation, whereas a tax specialist in the department of commerce normally directs his attention to accounting phases of current tax laws. Similarly, a sociologist will be inclined to study the general causes of poverty, while the social worker will probably be more interested in how to rehabilitate a particular family of indigents. A political scientist may focus upon the historical development of the separation of powers doctrine, the benefits of pluralism, and the wisdom of the Greeks, with less attention to pragmatic variations in the distribution of political resources and their implications for real participation in contemporary society.

Such issues have been widely discussed in both professional and lay circles in recent years. One side indicts vocationalism for producing narrow specialists when, in fact, society is said to need leaders with a broad general education. The other replies that we are living in a world where we can no longer afford to educate people merely to be gentlemen. The issue has been sharpened by some question of the operational efficacy of generalist qualities of poise, amateurism, and self-confidence in a complex scientific culture. It is also maintained that the objective need for specific knowledge is not inconsistent with producing a well-rounded personality with the basic understanding of human affairs required of a useful citizen in a democracy.

Political Science Departments vs. Schools of Public Affairs

A related issue concerns the placement of the public administration curriculum in the university. There is little argument that political science is the parent discipline, but many significant and successful institutional arrangements place the professional curriculum outside the political science department (e.g., Harvard, Pennsylvania, Syracuse, and University of Southern California). More recently, schools of public affairs have blossomed in several universities, with public administration covered in them rather than in political science departments. The evolutionary "jelling" of the core content in such schemes, moreover, embraces such other disciplines as economics, anthropology, sociology, and psychology.

Research and teaching place increasing emphasis on quantitative analysis, general systems approaches, computer technology, and policy sciences.[36] There is also some indication of a revival of the "case method" of instruction.[37] While political scientists are now using general systems approaches, behavioralism and system-based research emphasize an *interdisciplinary* approach to which separate programs in public administration have proved more sympathetic than the traditional political science department. It is clear, too, that separation provides greater independence and growth possibilities for public administration programs, which have close relations with off-campus client groups because of the practical utility of their programs. The fulsome relationships between them and various federal programs are illustrative. Indeed, some of them could not exist without such grants for essentially applied research and training programs, a condition which has some dysfunctions and may limit their capacity to attract staff with basic research interests.

Public administration, nevertheless, has a good deal to lose by the current move toward separatism. As noted earlier, political science is the root and parent discipline of the field. Public administration exists in an historical, political, and constitutional context, an understanding of which is necessary for an understanding of the field. Many of the valu-

---

[36] Emerging intellectual trends are often symbolized by the appearance of new journals; see *Policy Sciences and Public Policy*, works devoted to various aspects of policy determination in several contexts.

[37] See, for example, the varied cases in Robert Golembiewski and Michael White, *Cases in Public Management* (New York: Rand McNally Co., 1973); p. xvii outlines some advantages of the case method.

able new behavioral departures deal essentially with the internal, microscopic, operational aspects of administration which, however useful, can provide only a partial view of the complex sources of administrative behavior and policy-making. As our case studies have shown, bureaucracy functions as a representative of the dominant functional sectors in American society, which inevitably gives it a highly political character. Insofar as the splintering off of public administration brings a narrowed focus, the consequences may be marginal.

Beyond such substantive losses is the question of career avenues for doctoral graduates of such independent programs. The normal career for such graduates is usually in a political science department, yet such departments are sometimes reluctant to add men from professional schools of public administration. They apparently fear that such men may be too narrowly trained and lack serious research interests. No doubt, a certain amount of intellectual snobbery is also involved. On the other hand, the typical graduate of such programs is a terminal M.S., which has contributed a great deal to the upgrading of public administration at all levels of government.

As noted, the move for autonomy of public administration springs partly from empire building on the part of individuals who have been frustrated by their colleagues in political science departments. It has also been influenced by disenchanted alumni who protest that they were handicapped by not being taught certain professional courses. A great deal of the vocationalizing of curricula in every sphere results from pressures outside the university, including emerging semi-professional interests who seek legitimation through such affiliations, often aided by professors with special interests. Despite the splitting off of public administration, pressure of this kind will probably be brought upon some departments of political science to expand their administration curricula in at least two directions. One will be toward more courses of the practical management type; the other, toward teaching and research in the social aspects of organization. The former will lean toward industrial management, the latter toward the methodology and concepts of psychology, sociology, and anthropology. It also seems that internships, in both executive and legislative sites, will expand in an effort to improve education for the public service.[38]

Although the development of public administration curricula has not

---

[38] For a useful symposium on various kinds of internships, see Thomas P. Murphy (Ed.), *Government Management Internships and Executive Development* (Lexington, Mass.: D. C. Heath and Co., 1973).

yet reached the stage where an attempt at national standardization is desirable, practically everyone agrees that the undergraduate curriculum should not be vocationalized. This does not mean that it is improper to offer a few courses in the general aspects of public administration, but that specialization should probably be confined to the graduate level. Experimentation and variety should be encouraged at this stage. Perhaps some institutions should develop the scholars and idea men while others turn out the specialists. Perhaps there should be a few institutes in areas such as governmental accounting, logistics and supply, work-load analysis, training and motivation, and statistics. Certainly the administration of huge government agencies will suffer unless there is an adequate supply of such specialists.

The Examination Process

Closely related to such developmental issues is the process of recruitment and selection. The usual method of entering the federal civil service is through competitive examination. Examinations are publicized through an announcement prepared by the Civil Service Commission containing a statement of duties, minimum requirements of education and experience, and compensation. In addition, information and evaluation of an applicant can be obtained in some cases through the use of qualification investigations and/or personal interviews conducted by a panel of civil service examiners.[39]

Civil service examinations, for example, the Professional and Administrative Career Examination (PACE), usually consists of several parts, each of which is weighted. The written portion may have a weight of forty points; the oral, fifty points; training and experience, ten points. Those who fail the written test, which is given first, are usually not permitted to take the oral. Contemporary written tests are almost exclusively of the short-answer type, with multiple-choice questions preferred. Essay or free-answer questions are still used occasionally when the field of competition is small, the preparation of a short-answer test is uneconomical, or the subject matter does not lend itself to short answers.

Multiple-choice items are preferred for two reasons: They are less open to criticism, and research has shown that they have higher reliability. The two measures used in judging test effectiveness are validity and reliability. A test is valid when it measures what it purports to

[39] See, for example, U. S. Civil Service Commission, *Federal Personnel Manual*, supplement 337, Washington, D. C., U. S. Government Printing Office, February 24, 1971.

measure; it is reliable when it does so regularly during repeated use. Another advantage of the short-answer test is ease of scoring. Most civil service departments have a back-breaking load of examinations, and the test scoring machine has been most useful in this respect.

Tests can, in general, be divided into two categories—achievement tests and aptitude tests. The popular insistence, frequently written into law, that tests be "practical" has led to considerable emphasis upon achievement tests. This means testing for job knowledge, job content, and immediate ability to perform. Aptitude tests, on the other hand, attempt to discover innate abilities and potential capacity for development, including mechanical aptitude, verbal facility, vocational interests, and intelligence.

Many aptitude tests have been "standardized" and marketed commercially. "Standardized" means that they have been administered to persons thought to have the desired abilities and those who have not. For instance, a mechanical aptitude test would be standardized by trying it out on selected groups of skilled craftsmen. Until recently, civil service agencies hesitated to use commercial aptitude tests for two reasons: They could often be purchased and studied by candidates in advance, and there was a certain political hazard involved because such tests do not have "face" validity in the eyes of many laymen. Indeed, to those inclined to be critical, the items often seem unrelated to job knowledge and sometimes even nonsensical. Criticism is lessening, however, because the public is becoming more familiar with testing, as a result of growing experience with tests in the armed services and the school system. Nevertheless, civil service testing must still be prepared to defend itself upon pragmatic grounds. Here again is an example of how democratic values affect personnel management.

Construction and Validation of Tests. In the larger agencies, examining is a profession or career. Examiners specialize in particular functional areas such as engineering, law enforcement, skilled trades, and clerical work. Most civil service agencies prepare their own tests, built from card files containing thousands of test items so that, in preparing a test, one need not start entirely anew. Some agencies analyze the results of test items on the basis of difficulty. These data are entered on the cards containing the items, with the result that an examiner will have some indication of their difficulty when choosing items for a new test. Other agencies analyze a test item by item as a part of the scoring process, eliminating from the final score those items shown to be defective. Ideally, it would be desirable to validate all civil service tests in the same way commercial tests are standardized, that is, by administering them to groups of persons known to have the desired achievement or aptitude.

That civil service tests are not formally validated does not mean that they are invalid. As a matter of fact, testing is subject to constant practical scrutiny from a variety of sources. There is the pragmatic experience of the testers themselves, who, through experience, acquire a know-how worthy of respect. Many agencies also submit questions and answers to persons in the line departments after the test has been given but before it has been scored. (Experience has shown that it is usually inadvisable to submit it to the departments in advance.) Outside subject-matter experts are often brought in to help prepare and score tests in specialized fields. Finally, examinees are allowed to inspect their own corrected papers and are permitted to make formal protests. In New York City, for example, the answers are published after the test has been given, subjecting the examiners to widespread criticism.

Civil service testers are often called upon to defend themselves from political and legal attack. Examinations are sometimes taken into court on the ground that they are not "practical." In addition, newer types of testing sometimes use a statistical system of scoring not readily understood by laymen. Not long ago, the grading of oral examinations was challenged in a series of New York suits; consequently, many jurisdictions now record these tests *verbatim*. The end result of such litigation, however, has been to uphold the exercise of considerable discretion by testing agencies.

It seems that the time is at hand when the American public will both tolerate and finance a program of thoroughgoing test research such as that carried on by the military. This will require not only sympathetic legislative bodies but also the development of professional maturity among those in public personnel work. It seems a safe prediction that its leaders will look increasingly to research for the solutions to problems that have not been solved by experience alone. This is what happens in all budding professions. Ultimately, the basic testing research now conducted in the universities will find its way into the governmental arena.

THE PROBLEM OF PERSONALITY

Appointing officers tend to suspect civil service tests because they lack confidence in their ability to measure personal qualities. This is perhaps the primary reason for the "rule of three," long used in most jurisdictions, which permits the appointing officer to choose one of three candidates from the top of the list. Supervisors want to employ individuals who will satisfy at least two requisites of effective human relations: They must handle the public without creating antagonism toward the agency, and they must fit into a working team. Recent management research has shown the second to be especially important. Afraid that examining procedures will fail to give proper attention to such qualities, appointing officers often feel they could do a better job of selection using only the personal interview. There are at least two reasons why this cannot be allowed. The first relates to the protective tendency of civil service: Appointing officers may appoint brothers-in-law or personal favorites. In addition, psychological research has shown that the interview has questionable validity, even in the hands of an experienced executive. It tends to be superficial and desultory.

Testing Personal Qualities.   Pencil-and-paper tests measuring some aspects of personality are now available. Notable among these are the so-called temperament or personality inventories, consisting of questions that require the applicant to evaluate himself relative to certain aspects of psychiatry and abnormal psychology. Such tests evoke a great deal of controversy, however, and there is a school of experimental psychologists which condemns them, mainly on the ground that individuals will not give honest answers in a competitive test that asks them to reveal any abnormal and intimate behavior or beliefs. It is also maintained that the real value of these tests lies in their use as therapeutic or clinical aids rather than as vehicles for competition. Their usefulness seems to be confined to placement, counseling, and screenings for sensitive posts.[40]

The most common method of assessing personal qualities is the oral interview in which the candidate is questioned in ways designed to reveal his "personality." Usually, this interview is only incidentally related to subject matter or the skills required for the job concerned. The main idea is to obtain a look at the candidate and to detect positive or negative qualities. Candidates are usually graded competitively. The oral score is combined with the other parts of the test. Special rating forms are often used as a result of court decisions which have held that these ratings must be objective. Many jurisdictions also record the conversation mechanically to provide a record in case of appeal. Oral interviews are

---

[40] For the use of a personality test (thematic apperception) in personnel research, see W. Lloyd Warner, *et al.*, *The American Federal Executive, op. cit.*, pp. 191 *ff.*

usually conducted by personnel examiners assisted by outside specialists. Representatives of the employing departments may sit on an oral board, but this is frowned upon by those who believe that the procedure results in bias, especially in promotional tests.

One of the approaches used in testing is the group oral, in which half a dozen applicants are observed in a group situation. Examiners, who do not participate beyond giving initial instructions, observe their behavior, using every means to encourage participation. Whereas the individual oral is quite brief, group exams give the appointing people an hour and one-half to evaluate each candidate's performance. To counteract the possibility of one or two candidates monopolizing the discussion, the test may be divided into two sessions. In the first, individuals are called upon to make a statement on the assigned topic; in the second, discussion is *ad hoc*. Some observers believe that the group test is better at revealing personality traits than the individual interview, which is often quite subjective.[41]

The Rule of Three. As noted, personnel systems usually follow the "rule of three" which permits the appointing official to choose among the top three individuals certified to him. The purpose is, at least in theory, to overcome the objection that written tests cannot appraise personality factors adequately. A related objective has been to appease appointing officers by bringing them into the process to a greater extent. But perhaps the main reason for this rule is the often unexpressed but genuine belief that the examining process produces individuals who may qualify intellectually for a given post but have serious personal problems that will prove disruptive on the job. Despite these considerations, the Hoover Commission recommended that the rule of three be abandoned. Seeking more latitude for appointing officials in line with its "managerial preferences," the Commission recommended instead that applicants be

----

[41] The comments of a young English advertising executive may be germane: "There's no other business easier for the smooth confidence trickster to succeed than in advertising. If you're good at *interviews*, you don't have to be good at anything else at all, because agencies hire you entirely on how well you interview, and provided you're prepared to be a bit dishonest about your age and what you've done, and how much you're being paid by your present agency, you can easily change jobs every six months, and always at a better salary. . . . I've changed agencies five times in the last four years, always for a bigger salary, simply by conning a bit at interviews. In fact, changing jobs is very easy because so many of the creative people in London are so bad, although their badness bears no relation to the amount of money they're earning. Its the sharp ones who are making the money, and there are a lot of extremely good people who . . . didn't grasp the basic principle that what you have to do is cheat and lie a little and change jobs quickly. . . ." Aitken, *The Young Meteors, op. cit.,* pp. 174–75, italics added.

grouped into several categories, such as "outstanding," "well-qualified," and "unqualified," and that appointing officials select individuals from the higher categories, moving down as each list was exhausted. Once again, however, American public administration's inapposite goals were institutionalized as veterans would be placed at the top of each category to which they had been rated. In recent times, of course, the pressure upon government to encourage the hiring of blacks, women, the poor, and other minorities has aggravated this historical dilemma. Indeed, the ramifications extend quite beyond public administration into such fields as higher education where student enrollments and faculty appointments are subject to federal scrutiny and influence.[42]

The Impact of Watergate on Selection. Largely as a result of the Watergate scandal, there is an emerging concern in personnel administration with integrity. Problems of competence and personality remain central, but it seems safe to predict that appointing officers will be increasingly concerned with the extent to which candidates meet reasonable standards of probity and sensitivity to the public trust inherent in the civil service. Conflicts of interest, especially at the highest levels of the service where "political" and professional qualities tend to merge, have long been common but typically ignored. Today, new codes of ethics are being drafted in many jurisdictions in an attempt to specify more precisely the conditions of ethical conduct. Superficially, this seems to be a fairly simple problem, but its ramifications are virtually infinite. Is the common practice of young lawyers serving five or ten years in the Security and Exchange Commission or the Internal Revenue Service in order to prepare themselves (among other objectives) for lucrative positions in business and industry involving negotiations with these Agencies unethical? Agreement would be difficult to achieve on this example, yet federal laws now prescribe that former civil servants shall not deal directly for two years with private interests in areas in which they have special government knowledge and experience. Again, should representatives from interested institutional sectors sit on government advisory boards and commissions charged with making rules and regulations affecting their interests? This may seem somewhat questionable, yet it is common practice. Federal laws now provide that high-level appointees must divest themselves of stock-holdings in corporations whose affairs are related to the government positions involved. Yet it is almost impossible to enforce such a prescription, because stock-owner-

[42] This again is a provocative issue which merits special discussion among students.

ship can be temporarily vested in members of one's family or dummy corporations. Even these random examples suggest some of the problems involved in setting down and enforcing rules of ethical behavior in a business society.

Traumas such as Watergate are required to focus attention upon these aspects of public service. The extent to which attitudes on government's part are changing, as well as the extent to which traditional private values persist, is nicely demonstrated in the following example from the experience of New York City Mayor, Abraham Beame who, according to the *London Times*,[43] "has already lost two of the men he appointed to top level jobs in his administration . . . [who] are victims of post-Watergate insistence on clean records for high-ranking officials." The *Times* continues:

> Mr. Seymour Terry, who was to be the new Administration's troubleshooter with the title of Director of Special Programmes, and a salary of $39,500, has asked to be released from the appointment after intensive cross-questioning by the city's Board of Ethics. Mr. Terry who is in the insurance business, had unwisely sent letters to his clients, stating, "My new circumstances will no doubt enable you to get even greater benefits from your association with Terry Brokerage Co. than before." When accused of implying that he would use his political office for the benefit of his business, Mr. Terry pleaded that he had made a "minor mistake," and that it was all a question of semantics. "I am guilty of poor sentence structure," he said.

The other official was Mr. David Dinkins, who would have been the city's first black Deputy Mayor. He backed out after admitting that he had not filed income tax returns for four years. "I have not committed a crime," he said. "What I did was fail to comply with the law."

SCORING AND CERTIFICATION

The scoring of civil service tests and the ranking of candidates raise many problems. Early laws usually set a passing mark of 70 or 75, based upon the familiar grading system of the public school. This was in the day of the essay test and comparatively small numbers of candidates. The advent of short-answer tests, machine scoring, and a multitude of applicants has made the absolute passing mark virtually obsolete. Today, written tests may have several hundred items, divided into sections that can be separately scored and weighted. When a large number of success-

[43] December 31, 1973, p. 3.

ful candidates have to be marked on the basis of a percentage passing mark, it often becomes necessary to rank them to the hundredth or thousandth decimal point, for instance: 87.99, 87.98, 87.97, etc. Such precision is obviously meaningless, and accounts for the adverse view that some observers have of personnel management techniques.

Many test administrators prefer to establish a separate passing mark for each test, based upon the probable number of people to be employed. Instead of stigmatizing failures, the eligible list consists of those at the top of the list, with the cutoff based on the probable number needed in that class during the life of the list. The others are informed that their passing score was not high enough to qualify them for the list.

This practice has certain budgetary advantages in eliminating unneeded individuals before the more expensive oral test is administered. In times of high unemployment, many agencies are overwhelmed with candidates and are obliged to run large numbers of unneeded applicants through the examining machinery. High cutoffs, however, sometimes encounter opposition because of alleged violation of civil rights. The frontier concept that one man is as good as another still pervades our culture. The Jacksonian doctrine which held that any citizen could handle a government post adequately, is also strong enough politically to permit a charge of discrimination on intellectual or educational grounds. It is sometimes difficult to reconcile natural rights with civil service needs.

Establishing the Register.   Tests results are used to establish an eligible list or register, usually issued by the Civil Service Commission. Upon the request of an appointing officer, the personnel agency certifies the top three names on the eligible list. After interviewing all three, the officer makes a probationary appointment, the remaining two going back to their respective positions on the list to be certified again at the next request. An eligible list expires after a specified period, usually one or two years.

A favorite method of avoiding the merit system is to cut the appropriations of a personnel agency so that it cannot conduct enough examinations to keep its eligible lists up to date. If no list is available, the appointing officer may make a *temporary* appointment of someone who has not yet taken the examination.   Usually, the law limits such appointments to a specific period such as ninety days, but, formerly, such appointments could be continued indefinitely in the absence of an eligible list. It was not uncommon to find as many as half of the employees in some cities or states in a "permanent temporary status," meaning that they had served for years without being tested. Newer laws combat this practice by providing that no person can serve more than one temporary appointment in the same position and that no position shall be filled by two successive temporary appointees. A rough index of the quality of personnel work in an agency is its percentage of such appointments.

An emergency is often required to bring about reform in human institutions, and this was certainly true of personnel administration in World War II. Shortages of manpower, both among applicants and among the technicians needed to process them, forced the streamlining of many procedures. Eligible lists were frequently outdated before they were issued because applicants had obtained jobs elsewhere. The examining and appointing processes were too slow. One by-product of this experience is continuous testing for those classes that have a large turnover and are therefore always in short supply. These include clerical, stenographic, engineering, skilled-trade, and custodial occupations. Examinations are given on the spot, and those who pass are fitted into places on the eligible list. In the past, it was customary to give those low on a list a chance for appointment, but under continuous examining this is less likely be so.

PROBATION

Most jurisdictions provide that a new employee must serve a probation period for a limited time, usually six months. During this time, the supervisor is supposed to give him special attention in matters of instruction, indoctrination, and general adjustment to the job. Personnel theory views probation as the last phase of the testing process, for at this time the individual may be discharged without right of appeal and reinstatement. Ordinarily, however, there are very few dismissals during probation. Personnel people often become highly emotional about the failure of supervisors to live up to their obligation to conduct rigorous probationary appraisals. Although there has been little systematic research on probation, the consensus is that it is not realizing its possibilities as a testing mechanism. The truth is that no one likes to be judged, and few people have the fortitude to judge others when careers are at stake.

Various measures have been used to encourage supervisors to pass judgment on probationers. Perhaps the most common is to require frequent ratings, often three during the six months. Sometimes a special form is used, containing a question asking the supervisor whether he recommends retention of the employee. Supervisors, however, do not usually like to evaluate people; whenever possible they avoid unpleasant personal judgments.[44] Here again, the mixed objectives of government employment come into play as the "welfare" component sometimes makes vigorous evaluations fatuous. Some local jurisdictions are tackling this problem through the so-called field-review method. Here a personnel technician visits the supervisor just before the end of a particular employee's probation. Through informal conversation with the supervisor, the personnel man attempts to put him in a frame of mind that will permit an uninhibited response. Specific questions from the rating form are woven into the conversation in order to avoid the stereotyped and unduly telescoped responses that often result in filling out a form. The principal objection to this method seems to be the cost involved in the time of the personnel technician. It could be argued, however, that such expenditures may more than offset the cost of training, turnover, and reduced productivity by eliminating misfits at the beginning.

EMPLOYEE EVALUATION AND PROMOTION

The folklore of our competitive culture demands that employees be rated on the basis of their worth to the organization and that promotions be made in accord with these ratings. Most civil service laws require that workers be assigned efficiency ratings once or twice a year. Because of the reaction against the term, such procedures are now rarely referred to as "efficiency ratings;" instead, less offensive terms such as "merit rating" or "performance rating" are frequently employed.

As noted, however, supervisors or administrators hesitate to rank workers on the basis of performance. Ordinarily, employees resent not only low ratings but also ratings that are not commendatory. Equally, many supervisors resist assigning poor or average ratings to their employees, often due to personel involvement or their concern for the impact of negative worker assessments on evaluations of their own ability as superiors. The resulting tendency to place most employees in "good," "very good," or "excellent" categories often defeats the purpose of evaluation itself. It is important to note that such problems are characteristic of bureaucratic structures everywhere, not merely of government.

[44] John M. Pfiffner, and Marshall Fels, *The Supervision of Personnel,* 3d ed. (Englewood Cliffs, N. J.: Prentice-Hall, Inc., 1964).

Performance Rating

Throughout the public service in recent years, there has been a marked tendency to re-examine the philosophies and mechanics of superior–subordinate relations. Most notably, the punitive philosophy of motivation, characterized by punishment for failure to do one's part, has been modified to a significant extent. Today the role of the supervisor involves considerable teaching and counseling. Employee evaluation under this new philosophy is directed primarily at helping the employee adjust to the organization and to his role in it. Evaluation in this sense becomes an important phase of contemporary personnel administration which emphasizes placement, employee development, and face-to-face dealing with disciplinary problems. The milieu is one of counseling rather than a punitive one.

There is a certain inconsistency in the role prescribed for the supervisor under this new dispensation. On the one hand, he is supposed to be the trusted confidant of the employee and, on the other, he is the one who administers discipline and is responsible for productivity. This inconsistency may be more apparent than real, however, because the employee–supervisor relationship may range from complete *laissez-faire* to rigid, arbitrary authority. While supervisors occasionally have to take disciplinary action, this is not necessarily inconsistent with their more common role as counselors.

The basic federal law outlining the mechanics of the employee evaluation process was the Performance Rating Act (1950). Although this law has been revised, it is nevertheless useful to outline its basic provisions for they continue to guide the general implementation of evaluation systems in the federal government. Briefly, the act requires that the performance of all employees be assessed at least once a year by a line supervisor. The assessment is based upon a comparison of an employee's execution of his tasks with a mutually understood list (written or oral) of the duties and responsibilities of that particular position. On this basis, the employee is assigned one of three putatively objective ratings:

Unsatisfactory—The employee has failed to meet the minimum requirements of satisfactory performance in the position and should not be retained in such a capacity.

Satisfactory—The employee has met the standards of satisfactory performance for his position.

Outstanding—The employee has excelled in all significant respects in the performance of his duties and responsibilities and, accordingly, warrants special commendation.[45]

On being given an "unsatisfactory rating," an employee usually receives a 90-day warning period to upgrade his performance and is provided with a specific, written report outlining those areas of responsibility where his work has been found to be inadequate. If the employee fails to attain satisfactory performance by the end of this period, he is normally dismissed from his position and/or assigned to less responsible tasks, or is discharged from the civil service entirely.

A "satisfactory" rating normally qualifies an employee for standard incremental advancement in the General Schedule (or equivalent pay system) and keeps the door open for possible promotion. An "outstanding" rating normally leads to an employee's promotion and may even qualify him for a performance award of some sort.

Recently, as has been noted, the trend in evaluation has been toward greater supervisor–employee discussion rather than essentially formalistic rating procedures. Responsibility for performance rating has often been devolved to a more immediate supervisor and greater emphasis has been placed upon continuing evaluation and group assessment. In a later chapter, we note that employee motivation may soon be transformed from its traditionalistic individual orientation to concepts of collective performance. As a result, existing employee evaluation patterns may be supplanted by newer measurements of aggregate group efficiency including the use of participation bonuses or systems incentives. In the interim, individual performance ratings increasingly are being recorded only in the case of unsatisfactory or outstanding performances; if no rating form is prepared, an employee's achievement is judged to be satisfactory.[46]

Federal Merit Promotion Plan

Responsibility for developing specific promotion plans in the federal government is assigned to the various departments and agencies. The Civil Service Commission, as the coordinating and supervising body for personnel affairs, outlines the general policies and basic structural features of the promotion plan for the entire public service but its details and implementation are generally decentralized.

[45] Kanost, *Public Personnel Administration: The U. S. Federal System, op. cit.*, p. 95.
[46] *Ibid.*, p. 101.

In state and local jurisdictions, a competitive promotional examination is often required of employees. Its supporters maintain that the great advantage of open competitive promotion is the factor of motivation. People are put upon their mettle to study and prepare for more responsibility. Included in such studies are general administration, personnel, industrial psychology, and various allied fields. Thus individuals develop ideas for improving administration, as well as their own performance. Such a process, it is held, helps to combat the inertia and timeserving that too often characterize big institutions. It also helps government attract talented people who will not commit their careers to a system which does not reward them.

Most federal agencies, however, have displayed a certain aversion toward competitive promotion by examination. Instead, they employ the approach recommended and embodied in the Federal Merit Promotion Plan as outlined by The Civil Service Commission in the *Federal Personnel Manual*.[47] This plan specifies that:

> Agencies must develop, publish, and administer merit promotion plans which . . . establish the methods to be followed in selecting employees for promotion to positions grouped together for promotion purposes by certain common features which allow for like treatment. Each plan identifies the positions covered, minimum area of consideration, methods of locating candidates, qualification standards, evaluation procedures.

Further,

> Each promotion plan specifies the positions to which it applies. Positions may be grouped in a plan by job series, grade level, occupational field, organizational subdivision, geographic location, a combination of these factors or any other reasonable grouping.[48]

Each agency promotion plan is formulated cooperatively by line officials, employees, and employee organizations with a view toward achieving the following goals: (1) A sufficient number of highly qualified candidates (generally at least three) for promotion consideration, (2) Attractive career opportunities for employees and assurance that no competent employee is confined to a dead-end job, (3) the most effective use of employees and accounting for the present and future manpower

---

[47] The main source of information used in this section is the U. S. Civil Service Commission, Supplement 335 to the *Federal Personnel Manual*, Washington, D. C., U. S. Government Printing Office, March 9, 1971. See also C. S. C., *Federal Facts*, "On The Federal Merit Promotion Policy," Washington, D. C., U. S. Government Printing Office, September, 1971.

[48] *Ibid.*, p. 9.

needs of the agency, and (4) *limiting the scope of the search for potential candidates for promotion so that administrative efficiency be preserved.*[49]

The potential dysfunctions of the last prescription deserve comment, since they illustrate again the ambivalence of personnel management which, on the one hand, attempts to insure impartiality and rigor in its recruitment and promotion policies, yet, on the other, encourages policies that include subjective preferences. However often honored in the breach, a hallmark of professional occupational standards is broadly based, universalistic recruitment and promotion policies. Serious attempts are made to find the *best qualified* individual without regard to geography, sex, ethnicity, and even "personality," which opens the door to highly impressionistic bases of selection. Although present federal practice permits supervisors to appoint from outside the agency concerned, the Commission's policy is that:

> *It is essentially proper that positions be filled by promotion from within the organization as a general rule.* When an agency does an effective job of selecting and training employees, it should have a pool of employees with potential for career advancement to most positions. . . . An agency, however, has to guard against the dangers of inbreeding in positions above the entrance level where fresh viewpoints and new ideas are necessary.[50]

Certainly, as the survey cited earlier (see p. 178) indicates, within-agency promotions are the general rule. While they have several advantages, they also symbolize the conflicting norms and policies that characterize American personnel management. Its twin goals of merit and equal opportunity are sometimes hard to reconcile.

[49] *Ibid.,* p. 11.
[50] *Ibid.,* p. 11, italics added.

13

Labor-Management Relations in the Public Service

The motivation of people in huge government organizations is perhaps the major problem of personnel management. Students of human behavior and higher administrators are always trying to strike a nice balance between the needs of the organization for predictability and continuity and those of the individual for security and growth. Fortunately, these goals are not entirely incompatible. If an organization is going to operate effectively, its members must accept and work toward its collective mission. They must perceive it to be in their interest to modulate purely egotistical demands and to accept the structural and behavioral constraints of the organization. Obviously, this generalization varies according to type of organization, ranging from so-called "total" institutions like asylums and prisons to university research institutes where there is perhaps a maximum of individual autonomy. In practical terms, all this evolves to a bargaining situation in which the individual's occupational contract must be seen as beneficial, rather than as a "master–servant" relationship. Such expectations have been influenced recently by inflation, the vast growth of the public labor force (mainly at state and local levels), and the increasingly technological drift of public administration. These factors have brought great strains upon employee relations in the public sector. Civil servants have become much more militant about their rights as employees, and they have often taken collective action to guarantee them against higher management.

ADOPTING THE INDUSTRIAL BARGAINING MODEL

The extent of these developments is clear in the report of a Commission on labor management relations in the public service. According to this group, the "major upheaval" is especially apparent at the state–local level where: [1]

1. State and local employee roles are now nearly two and one-half times (9,358,000) what they were in 1947 and are expected to pass the 12,000,000 mark by 1975

2. Government unions of employees at all levels now constitute the fastest growing sector of organized labor and represent about one-tenth of total union membership (about 18,000,000), in contrast to the five per cent they represented only five years ago

3. Independent public employee associations have now passed the half-million mark while professional associations involving state–local employees now involve one and one-half million officials

4. Though no state sanctions strikes,[2] a seventeen-fold increase in work stoppages occurred between 1958–1968, passing the 250 mark during the latter years

5. Twenty states during 1958–1968 enacted or significantly amended comprehensive public employee–management labor relations laws.

As the Commission concludes, labor–management relations have become a top priority item on federalism's list of unresolved problems.

Although strikes have always characterized the public service, especially among municipal teachers' associations, the move toward the extension of the industrial model of collective bargaining into the public sector has obviously become more rapid in the recent past. Perhaps the very structure of public bureaucracies, including their pervasive formalism and hierarchies of authority and status, have inspired a special reaction among employees who are also aware of such larger political

---

[1] Advisory Commission on Intergovernmental Relations, *Labor–Management Policies for State and Local Government* (Washington, D. C., 1969), p. 1.

[2] Apparently, California is an exception; see *Los Angeles Metropolitan Transit Authority v. Brotherhood of Railroad Trainmen*, 54 Cal. 2d 684, where the state Supreme Court held that public employees of the Transit Authority did have the right to strike, according to the Transit Authority Act.

movements as citizen control and participation. Similar movements are occurring among white-collar people in private bureaucracies as well. Whatever the reasons, labor–management relations in public personnel management are becoming much like those in the industrial world.

Beginning with the traditional industrial model, it is easy to trace a fairly standardized procedure, the basic features of which are known as "collective bargaining":

1. An independent employee organization, officially recognized by management as having the power to speak for employees on certain matters.
2. The periodic settlement, through negotiation, of disputes over policy matters affecting the whole range of employer–employee relationships, formalized in a written agreement called the "contract."
3. The settlement of current disputes under the contract through a grievance system in which union officers deal directly with supervisors.
4. The establishment at the shop level of an area of freedom of speech and freedom of petition rather similar to civil liberties on the political level.
5. Official recognition by the employer that one of his own employees, the shop steward, will transact union business on company time.

This brief description of industrial collective bargaining precedes a discussion of governmental employee relations because similar issues exist in each area and similar bargaining procedures are being introduced. It has been assumed, at the same time, that the legal protection and security of civil service provide an adequate if not superior substitute for unionism. Is this necessarily so?

COLLECTIVE BARGAINING IN GOVERNMENT

Blue-Collar Unions

Although local variations exist, the organization of public employees conforms to a general pattern. In the first place, wherever skilled craftsmen—printers, carpenters, machinists, or plumbers—work for a governmental unit, they usually belong to their own traditional unions, which are often very conservative. Any given jurisdiction is likely to have locals of both or either of the craft and industrial unions set up by the American Federation of Labor and the Congress of Industrial Organizations for governmental employees. An "industrial" union covers all the employees of a given employer or industry regardless of their occupations or jobs. Thus a janitor, a laboratory assistant, and a clerk are all eligible for membership in the same industrial union.

So far, we have referred only to those unions "affiliated with the labor movement,"—that is, with the AFL–CIO. In many places, however, there are also independent organizations which are very similar to traditional unions. Historically, they were affiliated with the AFL–CIO, or often they were organized by persons who were once labor leaders. It is difficult to distinguish a union from other employee organizations, but the criteria relate to militancy, type of work, and occupational level of membership.

Traditional Attitudes Toward Bargaining

The "cultural set" in the United States has been based upon a galaxy of values which include little enthusiasm for negotiation between government as an employer and organized employees. Indeed, the very existence of organizations of governmental employees was long a matter of controversy. Not until the passage of the Lloyd–LaFollette Act in 1912, was the prohibition of lobbying by organizations of federal employees removed. Even labor's good friend, Franklin D. Roosevelt, in his oft-quoted letter to Luther C. Steward, stated that "the process of collective bargaining, as usually understood, cannot be transplanted into the public service. . . . The very nature and purposes of government make it impossible for administrative officials to represent or bind the employer in mutual discussions with government employee organizations." [3]

This cultural aversion toward unions in government was usually expressed both in the law and in emotional reactions against strikes. Legal opinion held that the sovereign could not enter into collective bargaining contracts with his employees. [4] This was the same principle which maintained until recently that the government was not liable for the torts of its employees, under the ancient precept that "the king can do no wrong." Only in our lifetime has this legal barrier to tort liability been broken down.

The other cultural factor affecting public attitudes toward public-employee unionism was an emotional reaction against strikes. While

[3] Cited in Van Riper, *History of the United States Civil Service* (New York: Harper & Row, Inc., 1955), pp. 350 *ff.*

[4] See Wilson R. Hart, *Collective Bargaining in the Federal Service* (New York: Harper & Row, Inc., 1961), pp. 38–54.

some segments of the public have always deplored strikes, even in industry, governmental employees have been regarded as being in a category distinct from those on private payrolls. Policemen and firemen, in particular, are so identified with the public safety that the thought of their going on strike outrages the citizens' sense of propriety. The result has been that government employees have been quite generally prohibited by law from going on strike, and collective bargaining agreements have often contained a clause wherein the union has agreed not to strike.

There is an opposing opinion that the prohibition of strikes should be based not upon the private–governmental distinction but on the degree to which the occupation affects the public health, welfare, and safety. For example, the delivery of milk may affect the public interest more than sweeping the streets or keeping the schools open.[5] At any rate, it is a truism that strikes by government employees arouse emotional public reactions which have sustained a cultural taboo against strikes.

CHANGE OF CLIMATE

This climate of opinion began changing dramatically in the late 1950's, as shown by three events. The first was the report of Mayor Richard Wagner's task force and the resulting executive order of 1958 which put collective bargaining in New York City on a firm basis and which also served as a model for President Kennedy's executive order of 1962. Philadelphia also adopted collective bargaining in 1958.[6] The second factor symbolizing the change was the militancy of schoolteachers in several parts of the country in the mid-1960's, resulting in strikes.[7] The third, and perhaps the most influential, event was President Kennedy's Executive Order 10,988, of January 17, 1962. It is important to understand that these three were not isolated events, but that steps toward the industrial pattern of collective bargaining were being taken on all levels of government and in several geographical areas.[8] While such movements have deep historical and cultural roots which make change a

[5] Leonard D. White, "Strikes in the Public Service, Public Personnel Review, Vol. 14 (January, 1949), pp. 3–10.

[6] Chester A. Newland, "Trends in Public Employee Unionization," The Journal of Politics, Vol. 26 (August, 1964), pp. 586–605.

[7] Wesley A. Wildman, "Collective Action by School Teachers," Industrial and Labor Relations Review, Vol. 18 (October, 1964), pp. 3–19.

[8] Kenneth O. Warner (ed.), Management Relations with Organized Public Employees (Chicago, Public Personnel Association, 1963).

gradual process, this development seemed to have gathered decisive momentum by the 1960's. There is reason to believe that personnel administrators were taken by surprise, because their dominant belief systems had resisted the introduction of industrial patterns of labor relations into government.[9] Indeed, their natural reaction was either to resist change or to channel it so as to retain as many of the old ways as possible.

On June 22, 1961, John F. Kennedy appointed a task force to study and report on employee–management cooperation.[10] It consisted of the Secretaries of Defense and Labor, the Postmaster General, the Director of the Budget, the Chairman of the Civil Service Commission, and the Special Counsel to the President, Theodore Sorenson. The Secretary of Labor, Arthur Goldberg, was made Chairman, and it seems that he dominated the proceedings, since the Task Force Report bears his stamp.[11] While the chairman of the Civil Service Commission was vice-chairman of the Task Force, the center of gravity, at least for the time being, had swung from that body to the Department of Labor. The concept that the industrial model of employee relations should be adopted for government employees was in the air, and those who so believed were to be decisive. A discerning observer gives much credit to Ida Klaus as the "working genius of the task force."[12] Acting as its consultant, she had previously served on Mayor Wagner's task force in New York City, and she was ideologically committed to collective bargaining.

The driving force, however, came from political elements in the Kennedy Administration, in the face of considerable ambivalence, if not opposition, on the part of career civil servants, whether staff personnel people or line administrators. Two considerations weighed heavily in the political process. The first was that the AFL–CIO had voted solidly for Kennedy and was thus a decisive factor in his razor-thin margin of

---

[9] Wilson R. Hart, "The U. S. Civil Service Tries To Live with Executive Order 10,998: An Inferior Appraisal," *Industrial and Labor Relations Review*, Vol. 17 (January, 1964), pp. 203–20.

[10] A comprehensive treatment of federal bargaining developments is William Vosloo's *Collective Bargaining in the United States Federal Civil Service* (Chicago: Public Personnel Association, 1965).

[11] *A Policy for Employee-Management Cooperation in the Federal Service; Report of the President's Task Force on Employee-Management Relations in the Federal Service* (Washington, D. C.: Government Printing Office, 1961), hereafter cited as Task Force Report. Executive Order No. 10,988 can be found in 27, *Federal Register* (January 17, 1962), pp. 551–56.

[12] Hart, "The U. S. Civil Service Tries To Live with Executive Order 10,988," p. 206.

victory. The second was that there had been pending for several years legislation, known as the "Rhodes-Johnson Union Recognition Bill," which was so disproportionately union-oriented that even some friends of labor in the Administration thought that it should be sidetracked. A third but unarticulated factor was the desire of organized labor to make some headway in organizing white-collar workers in the face of the dwindling proportion of blue-collar people in the labor force.[13]

It should be noted that collective bargaining of a rather traditional type is not entirely new to the federal service. The Tennessee Valley Authority has had a rather long record with the industrial variety of labor relations,[14] and the Department of the Interior has long been engaged in collective bargaining particularly at its power installations such as that at Bonneville. Although these agreements often covered white-collared workers, they were in the beginning based on traditional craft unions.

Following the recommendation of the Task Force, President Kennedy's Executive Order provided for three levels or types of recognition: informal, formal, and executive. Informal recognition, which was granted to any employee organization with members in the unit concerned, permitted the union to present its views to management but did not require negotiation. Formal recognition was extended to organizations having a majority of employees in the unit, and unions were given the right to enter into collective negotiations with management officials with the object of reaching an agreement with all the employees of a unit. Executive Order 10,988 also permitted advisory arbitration for employee grievances, contract interpretations, and bargaining unit determinations. However, the Order did not alter Congress's exclusive legal right to determine wages and fringe benefits.

The Nixon Executive Order

Under President Johnson, a Review Committee on Federal Employee–Management Relations was established to assess the impact of Executive Order 10,988 on federal departments and agencies. For the most part, the Committee urged extension of union organization and negotiating rights beyond those recommended and/or granted by earlier commissions and by the Kennedy Order. The Committee's basic proposal involved

[13] See *ibid.*, especially pp. 204–8.
[14] Harry L. Case, *Personnel Policy in a Public Agency: The TVA Experience* (New York: Harper & Row, Inc., 1955).

the establishment of a central decision-making authority for employee–management problems and provided for a defined set of third-party procedures for negotiations of disputed issues.[15] Because of continuing opposition from senior Defense Department officials, however, the Committee's Report was never formally conveyed to the President and its recommendations were not acted upon during the remaining period of the Johnson administration.

In 1969 much of the material gathered for this original Report and some of the proposals advanced by the commissioners reappeared in a report to President Nixon from a new committee under the direction of Civil Service Commission Chairman, Robert E. Hampton. This document formed the basis for Nixon's Executive Order 11,491 of 1969.

Briefly, the Nixon Order emphasized the need for exclusive representation ·of federal civil servants based on secret ballot elections and on third-party procedures for the resolution of labor–management disputes.[16] The Order created a Federal Labor Relations Council consisting of the Chairman of the Civil Service Commission, the Secretary of Labor, and the Director of the Office of Management and Budget. The Council was empowered to resolve many major policy issues but, in effect, did not have final arbitrary decision-making authority over labor–management disputes for which no negotiated settlements seemed possible. Instead, a Federal Service Impasse Panel was created to settle negotiation conflicts invoking binding arbitration if necessary.[17] Decisions relating to bargaining units, representation, and unfair labor practices were placed under the auspices of the Assistant Secretary of Labor for Labor–Management Relations.

Although the Nixon Order went further than any previous executive act to establish the third-party mechanism for bargaining sought by public employees' unions, it did not completely meet the demands of labor. Indeed, the unions had pressed for a decision-making authority for labor–management issues entirely independent of the executive branch of government. They had tried to obtain legal recognition of public service unions (i.e., through legislation rather than by executive order) so they could have recourse to the courts to challenge cases of

[15] Richard J. Murphy, "The Difference of A Decade: The Federal Government," *Public Administration Review*, Vol. 32 (March/April, 1972), p. 110.
[16] *A Pace-Setting Year for Personnel Management: U. S. Civil Service Commission Annual Report, 1971* (Washington, D. C., 1972), p. 17.
[17] Murphy, *op. cit.*, p. 110.

third-party arbitration that were percevied as unjust by labor. These demands were not met by Executive Order 11,491, which also contained the traditional clause prohibiting recognition of an organization that "asserts the right to strike against the Government of the United States or any agency thereof." [18] The unions protested this condition and successfully petitioned a Federal District Court to rule that the language of the clause violated employees' First Amendment right to association. Accordingly, the disputed clause was deleted from the Order, but, effectively, the prohibition against participating in a strike against the U.S. Government still existed by virtue of other pieces of federal legislation.

Almost immediately after the issuing of 11,491, federal public service labor policy was challenged by two costly strikes: the walk-out of approximately 200,000 postal workers and a strike by several thousand air traffic controllers of the Federal Aviation Administration. Although we shall not go into the details of these and other recent public service strikes at this point, it is important to note that the postal workers' and air traffic controllers' disputes were the first truly *national* strikes in federal government history. The controllers' walk-out was largely unsuccessful but the postal workers did succeed in obtaining the largest pay raise ever received in that department and also eventually forced the reorganization of the Post Office as a government corporation.[19] The success of the postal workers effectively insured their *de facto* right to negotiate wages and fringe benefits, thus rendering 11,491 ineffective and setting a precedent for other federal employees to follow.

In September 1971, Executive Order 11,616—designed to amend 11,491 —required negotiated grievance procedures in all future contracts with public employees at the federal level and broadened the scope of bargaining by union representatives. In many respects, the new Order only recognized a situation that already existed. Public service unions are not likely to return to their position of the mid-1960's but rather will, in all probability, continue to press for full union rights and representation. It is interesting to note, moreover, that many areas of the federal civil service still remain outside the jurisdiction of collective agreements. Excluding the Postal Service, only 31 per cent of all federal employees were working under collective agreements through 1972,[20]

---

[18] Cited in *Civil Service Commission Annual Report, 1971, op. cit.*, p. 18.
[19] Murphy, *loc. cit.*
[20] *Ibid.*, p. 111.

although a considerable number of additional groups would seem to have the right to enter into similar agreements and have not done so as of yet. One should also note that three agencies not previously covered by executive orders and recent labor policy pronouncements—the State Department, the Government Printing Office, and the District of Columbia—are now developing employee relations programs of their own.[21]

Some indication of the scope of organization in the federal service is provided in Table 13-1.

TABLE 13–1. Membership in the Largest Federal Public Service Unions Having Inclusive Recognition

Union	Membership
American Federation of Government Employees (AFL—CIO)	530,550
United Federation of Postal Clerks (AFL—CIO)	301,155
National Association of Letter Carriers (AFL—CIO)	203,928
National Federation of Federal Employees	77,099
National Association of Government Employees	68,615
Metal Trades Councils (AFL—CIO)	66,089
Post Office Mail Handlers (AFL—CIO)	44,494
National Association of Internal Revenue Employees	38,502
International Association of Machinists and Aerospace Workers (AFL—CIO)	32,350
Rural Letter Carriers Association	31,134
All Others	148,195

Source: *A Pace-Setting Year for Personnel Management: U.S. Civil Service Commission Annual Report, 1971,* Washington, D.C., U.S. Government Printing Office, 1972, p. 69.

GRIEVANCE PROCEDURES

A universal aspect of hierarchies is their tendency to stifle upward communication. Those in positions of leadership are often annoyed when they have to listen to the complaints of subordinates. Even those who loudly proclaim that they maintain an "open door," accessible at any time to all employees, become restive at expressions of discontent. Executives are human in that they do not like bad news. Employee complaints are especially disturbing because they imply a criticism of management. They seem to suggest that the boss is not the wisest, most humane, most beloved, and cleverest person in the organization. This naturally threatens his ego, for man made into a supervisor often sees

[21] *Ibid.*

himself as infallible. He wants others to confirm this picture of himself and becomes irritated when they fail to do so.

Industrial Precedent

The industrial grievance system has institutionalized upward communication by opening the channels and furnishing pushers in the form of union business agents and shop stewards. The shop steward, shop committeeman, or chapel chairman as he is known in the printing trade, is the lowest official in the union hierarchy—a sort of noncom. He differs from other officials in being a full-time employee, not of the union but of management. He is a fellow worker who has been elected by his colleagues to represent union interests at the shop or office level. Many contracts provide that he may devote a certain amount of company-paid time to union business, perhaps an hour a day. The supervisor is expected to deal with the steward on all grievances; indeed, an alert steward will often initiate grievance claims. Management sometimes complains that stewards go around manufacturing grievances on company time. Like other people, however, stewards vary a great deal in their militancy, and certain managements have even provided special training courses for them because of their failure to do enough on behalf of employees.

Applying Industrial Grievance Procedures to Government

Similarities between industry and government are detectable in many kinds of grievances. Here again the lessons of industry could be applied to public service. Industrial grievances are usually settled between the employee, the steward, and the immediate supervisor. When informal negotiations of this kind fail, the grievance is put in writing. The matter is then usually taken up with the next higher supervisor, and if not settled, goes on to a formally constituted tribunal where trial procedure prevails, with witnesses and recording of testimony. The head of the company is usually the final resort, but sometimes there is provision for arbitration. The majority of grievances deal with job evaluation and job rating of individual employees.

The Kennedy Executive Order included a grievance system based upon the industrial pattern, with the exception that it provided for advisory rather than binding arbitration. As the Order prescribes, "each employee in the competitive service shall have the right to appeal to the Civil Service Commission from an adverse decision of the administrative officer so acting." [22] The Commission was empowered both to establish the ground rules to be followed by government agencies in disciplining employees and handling grievances and to adjudicate employee appeals.[23]

More recently, following the Nixon Executive Orders, all government employees have been guaranteed certain rights in grievance proceedings. Any employee on active duty status must be given a reasonable amount of time during duty hours to ready his own case in preparation for a grievance hearing. Each hearing in an adverse action proceeding must be conducted by a qualified examiner who is not subordinate to the official having final decision-making authority over the outcome of the grievance. Any material used by an agency to substantiate or support that agency's charges against an employee must be made available to the employee sufficiently in advance of a hearing so that he or she may adequately review the evidence. Moreover, any material not provided to the employee in advance of a hearing is not admissible in that hearing. Further, verbatim transcripts of an adverse proceeding must be taken and made available to the employee in all cases.[24]

The same regulations permit a representative from a union holding exclusive recognition to be present as an observer during a hearing, unless the employee expresses a desire to the contrary, in which case the Commission's officer is empowered to decide whether or not the observer should be present. In all proceedings, every informal procedure for adjustment or resolution of conflicts must be exhausted before a formal proceeding is initiated.[25]

The key issue in grievance procedures is perhaps the question of the nature of the arbitration to be invoked. The *advisory* arbitration common throughout the Kennedy and Johnson years was not particularly successful, most notably in the case of the Post Office. Advisory arbitration lacks finality and decisiveness since it does not bind either the employee or the employer to an agreement. It places emphasis on cooperation and voluntary adherence, two values that are often lacking in many adverse action proceedings between labor and management, both within and without the public service.

[22] From Executive Order 10,988, cited in *The Civil Service Commission and its Publics: Annual Report, 1970*, Washington, D. C., U. S. Government Printing Office, 1971, p. 16.

[23] See also Cyrus F. Smythe, "Collective Bargaining Under Executive Order 10,988: Trends and Prospects," *Public Personnel Review*, Vol. 26 (October, 1965), pp. 199–201.

[24] *The Civil Service Commission and its Publics: Annual Report, 1970.*

[25] *Ibid.*

On the other hand, *binding* arbitration (as provided for in certain cases by the Nixon Orders) often contributes an effective incentive to negotiated settlements. Where both parties are confronted with the possibility of an imposed settlement, they sometimes display a greater tendency to resolve a contentious issue before arbitration so as to avoid an imposed decision unfavorable to both sides. When a dispute does go to binding arbitration, there can be no decision on the part of either party to ignore the settlement. The settlement is final and adherence is compulsory.

One can object to binding arbitration, of course, for several reasons. Unless the arbitration is completely neutral, there is always the possibility that prejudicial influences will affect the fairness of the decision and, accordingly, create distrust among the parties to the decision. To many people, binding arbitration represents a denial of individual freedom and an exercise of unwarranted authority. Indeed, in terms of constitutional law, there is some question as to legality of binding arbitration. Can a government which draws its authority from the people legally redelegate that authority to an outside third-party arbitrator for a binding decision?[26] This question of the source of an arbitrator's authority is difficult and raises many additional questions concerning the entire process of the redelegation of authority to independent agencies not directly responsible to the public. This issue is cited here not in the hope of providing a solution, but only to illustrate the pressing theoretical problems involved in binding arbitration.

DISMISSALS IN THE PUBLIC SERVICE

We turn next to the occasionally dramatic issue of removals in the civil service. There is a widely held belief that civil servants can neither be disciplined nor dismissed, except during their initial probationary stage. This is another example of a myth that has become a guide for thought and action, not because it is true but because individuals, including government supervisors, believe it to be true. As a matter of fact, it is quite possible to remove government employees, but the procedure required is often prolonged and embarrassing. A kind of due process has been built up which not only provides employees a necessary safeguard against arbitrary removal, but is widely viewed as leaning too far in that direction.

[26] See Paul D. Staudohar, "Public Employee Grievances and Arbitration: Some Unresolved Issues," *Public Personnel Review,* Vol. 33 (January, 1972), p. 58.

Obstacles to Dismissal

Governmental supervisors hesitate to dismiss an unsatisfactory employee chiefly because of the unpleasantness involved. Those who criticize government supervisors on this point should keep in mind that in industry too this task is avoided as long as possible. The difference in industry is that individual productivity becomes a survival factor sooner than in government. In those governmental agencies where the dismissed employee has no right to appeal for reinstatement, the supervisor hesitates to take action because of pressures brought to bear on him. These include the telephoned inquiries of a Congressman, the pressure of influential friends, the displeasure of fellow employees, whether organized or unorganized, and possible repercussions among social and fraternal groups such as the employee's lodge, church, or service men's club.

But the governmental supervisor is most apprehensive about appearing before a civil service dismissal hearing, which is always a trying experience. It has to be public to satisfy the requirements of due process, and it must meet rudimentary demands of legal procedure because the transcript of the evidence may become the basis for a court decision. Many lawsuits are brought by employees dissatisfied with civil service decisions and in states like New York, a large volume of such litigation occurs. This tendency to turn to the law illustrates again the legal flavor of public administration. In larger jurisdictions, one or more full-time attorneys advise the civil service commission. Indeed, some public personnel agencies have had to hire full-time referees to hear evidence because it is impossible for them to handle the volume.

The Hearing Procedure

Let us picture what goes on at a typical civil service hearing. Assume a state or local jurisdiction where the commissioners—lay, business, or professional people—hear all the evidence themselves. The commissioners, with the director of personnel and a stenographer, are grouped on one side of the conference table. On the other is the deputy attorney who handles the case for the employer; farther down the table sits the dismissed employee or his representative, with his attorney or a union agent, or both. Witnesses are sworn in as in a court of law, and every word is recorded. Witnesses for the employer are called first. Each is questioned by the lawyer for the city or state and then by the employee's attorney. The latter is ordinarily more accustomed to the rigor of court-room rules of evidence and, if an aggressive type, will try to confuse witnesses unfavorable to his client. The chairman of the commission may become irritated at such tactics and admonish the attorney that this is not a court of law but an administrative tribunal where considerable informality is permitted.

During the testimony of the employer's witnesses, there is often considerable tension. The first witnesses are usually supervisors who have participated in the dismissal, and the employee's lawyer may try to induce them to reveal personal animosity toward the discharged employee. Grasping every opportunity to embarrass the supervisors and employees who are the complainant's witnesses, he tries to make it appear that the supervisor responsible for the dismissal habitually fires people he does not like. This common impugning of the supervisor's motives has led to the quip that such hearings frequently result in the trial of the supervisor instead of the employee. Even civil service commissioners often reveal a certain sentimentality toward employees which they would not condone in their private affairs. They frequently seem to believe that their duty is to protect the employee rather than to provide an objective judgment.

The Fitzgerald Case

An example of the tortuous and difficult procedure involved in adversary hearings is the case of A. Ernest Fitzgerald, an Air Force cost analyst whose employment was terminated in 1970 under rather unusual circumstances.[27] Fitzgerald had testified before the Proxmire subcommittee which was investigating waste in the Defense Department. He indicated there that a 2 billion dollar "over-run" had been made by Lockheed Aircraft Corporation in its building of the C-5A, a giant military transport plane. Shortly thereafter, Fitzgerald was reassigned to the task of analyzing the operations of Air Force bowling alleys.[28] About a year after his testimony, he was retired, according to the Air Force, as a result of a "routine reorganization," in which his original position was eliminated.

Charging that he had been fired for telling the truth to a Congressional committee and that the White House itself had been involved in the action, Fitzgerald turned to the Civil Service Commission for a hearing on

---

[27] For a synopsis of the case, see Clark Mollenhoff, "Presidential Guile," *Harpers*, Vol. 246 (June, 1973), pp. 38–42.

[28] Of Fitzgerald's new post in Thailand, Air Force Secretary Robert C. Seamans remarked, "Proper supervision of recreation facilities is not to be taken lightly."

his situation. The Air Force, in turn, argued that his retirement had nothing to do with his testimony at the Proxmire hearings, and that contrary to his claims, the case had never been brought to the attention of the President. Meanwhile, investigations of Fitzgerald's background were being made, and some Congressmen who became interested in the case were told that the real reason for his termination was a matter that could not be revealed, but that it was of sufficient seriousness to warrant the Air Force's actions.

The subsequent hearings, begun in late 1971, illustrate dramatically the issues that may arise including, among others, questions of due process. Fitzgerald had asked for an open hearing, but this was initially denied by the chief hearing examiner for the Commission. Fitzgerald's lawyers then turned to the Federal District Court which upheld his plea and directed that the hearings be open. The Commission then turned to the Federal Court of Appeals, but here again the Court upheld the doctrine that an open hearing must be granted as a part of due process. The issue of bias also arose, and in the mind of Clark Mollenhoff, formerly a White House aide in the Nixon Administration but a career journalist with the *Des Moines Register,* the Commission's chief hearing examiner "indicated a clear bias in favor of the Air Force." Meanwhile, despite the tenacious efforts of Mollenhoff who interceded with the President and various aides as well as testified before the hearing, the case dragged on, and it has not yet been resolved. Mollenhoff's efforts, however, did reveal that earlier denials claiming the White House was involved were untrue. At a White House press conference, Mollenhoff pressed the issue with the President until the latter declared that he had indeed made the decision and accepted responsibility for it.

In its larger context, of course, this case entails a long-standing conflict between the executive and legislative branches. The separation of powers system virtually insures that such conflicts will arise. In the present context, it suggests the difficulties and inequities that can occur when individuals *qua* individuals find themselves opposed to the huge superstructures that characterize American society today.[29] One may assume that this realization is among the most compelling incentives for new departures in labor–management relations in the public service, including the right of collective bargaining and, ultimately, the right to strike, to which we now return.

---

[29] Here again is a vital and provocative issue in public administration, centering on the extent to which civil servants *should* defer to hierarchical authority and agency policy.

Strikes in the Public Service

At this point, we shall review in more detail the phenomenon of public service strikes and assess some of the implications, both positive and negative, that militancy among civil servants presents for the student of public administration.

Public service strikes are not entirely recent occurrences. Especially at the level of state and local governments, there exists a long history of strike action among government employees in this country. Indeed, as early as 1940, Ziskind conclusively showed that when public employees find the conditions of employment intolerable they will strike, in spite of laws forbidding such a step.[30] To be sure, strikes in the federal government have also occurred but, as noted, no nation-wide federal employees strike took place until 1969 when 200,000 postal workers left their jobs.

Some of the issues concerning public employees that have led to strike action can be illustrated by the recent experience of American teachers. At various points throughout the 1960's groups of teachers, traditionally a docile rather than aggressive element in the public service, left their jobs to protest low wages and unacceptable working conditions. The example of New York in 1962 is typical of the type of confrontation that has become more common in recent years. As Sterling D. Spero noted in an informative account of the event,[31] the immediate cause of the teachers' walkout was a dispute over salaries but the basic causes lay more deeply in the frustrations of public school employment, stemming from the authoritarian spirit which pervaded the school system from the administration through the principals to the teachers, and down ultimately to the children themselves. Here recently, protests against the rigidity of educational bureaucracies have been reinforced by popular issues regarding classroom size, participation by parents in demonstrations for revisions of curricula, and ideological dissent by teachers. Similarly, throughout the public service, labor claims have gone beyond traditional issues of wages and immediate conditions of work to concern with qualitative and normative aspects of public employment. Also included have been issues of participation, the employment of minority groups, government priorities in policy areas, the depersonalization of public hierarchies, and so on.

[30] David Ziskind, *One Thousand Strikes of Government Employees* (New York: Columbia University Press, 1940).

[31] "The New York Teachers' Strike," *Good Government*, Vol. 79 (Bulletin of the National Civil Service League), September, 1962.

As noted, 1970 brought the first truly national strikes, by postal workers and air controllers. Although the causes are varied, inflation and stressful conditions of work (among the air controllers especially) were probably the major reasons. In 1974, a strike of city employees in San Francisco caused widespread dislocation in city services, including transport and hospital facilities, all aggravated by an attending strike by the city's teachers. These events indicate that public servants will and do strike, when they come to regard conditions as inequitable, regardless of traditions and legislation to the contrary. Neither the opposition of their administrative superiors, elected officials, nor the inconvenienced public seems to deter them. For such reasons, it is important to discuss opposing views on this controversial issue.

Perhaps the most critical issue regarding strikes can be stated as follows: Can government employment be equated qualitatively with work in the private sector? If it can, should government workers have the same right to withdraw their labor to protest against low wages, poor working conditions, and related issues? Although this right is generally conceded to unionized labor in the private sector, it remains a moot point in public administration. Reactions are sharply divided. On one side are those who feel very strongly that public employment is different fundamentally from the private occupational world. One example of this "hard-line" view is provided by the United States Chamber of Commerce:

> To condone strikes is to facilitate disruption of essential services which ultimately could bring government to a stand-still. To condone strikes is to sanction putting the government employer, who lacks the weapons of his private counterpart, at the mercy of his organized workers. To condone strikes is to permit undermining the authority of government at a time when a growing majority of the American electorate feels that the symbols of governmental authority—if not the substance—are tattered and in need of mending. To condone government employee strikes is, in the final analysis, to reduce government to the level of just another corporate unit within our pluralistic society, and this is not conducive to a meaningful assessment of the nature, purpose, and basic functions of government in a democratic, representative system.[32]

This appreciation, which is reinforced of course by the vast subsidies provided business and industry through such mass employment services as the Post Office, probably represents a rather traditional view. But

[32] A report to the Advisory Commission on Intergovernmental Relations, September 1969, in *Strikes and the Public*, Chamber of Commerce of the United States, Washington, D. C., 1970, p. 30.

even the Advisory Commission on labor–management policies for state and local government, composed of a fairly representative cross-section of interests, took a "middle of the road" to "conservative" position on this issue, as indicated in one of their final recommendations:

> The Commission is convinced that these basic questions involving the freedoms of the individual worker and of employee organizations, as well as the necessary limits on these freedoms, should be treated in State legislation and should not be left to administrative or judicial determination or to the exigencies of a meet-and-confer or bargaining process. The time has long since passed when the argument could be made that public employees have no rights—yet the tenor of the times clearly indicates that an irrefutable case can *not* be made that the rights and privileges of public personnel are, in all major respects, comparable to and as comprehensive as those of their counterparts in the private sector. A balance must then be struck. . . .[33]

"Irrefutable" cases, of course, don't come along very often, and the Commission's disclosure that it was no longer *au courant* to argue that public servants have no rights is hardly news. Nevertheless, the Commission probably speaks for most Americans when it advises caution and the search for "balance" regarding the issue.

On the other hand, regarding the principle of free collective action, union leaders of public service organizations naturally advocate the extension of the right to strike. Also, a 70-man panel of well-known experts in several occupations, meeting under the auspices of the American Assembly, concluded that public employees should have a limited right to strike after "obligatory procedures" have been exhausted.[34] Some observers including Sterling Spero have made an attempt to distinguish between "vital" services and those that only "inconvenience" the public, concluding that strikes should be permitted by law in the latter areas.[35] Such a differentiation, however, has proved to be very difficult to make.

Speaking of *private* strikes that affect the public interest directly, George P. Schultz maintains that unhampered collective bargaining is a functional necessity for national development:

> . . . we must all realize, whether as members of "the public" or in our private capacities, that we have a tremendous stake and a great interest

---

[33] *Labor–Management Policies for State and Local Government, op. cit.,* p. 93. The Commission specifically recommends that state labor laws should "prohibit all public employees from engaging in strikes," p. 96. A similarly "conservative" stand was taken by the *New York Times* in editorial comments—see March 19, 1970, and March 26, 1970, pp. 1 and 46, respectively.

[34] See *New York Times,* November 1, 1971, p. 47.

[35] *Ibid.,* December 22, 1971, p. 35.

in the vitality of private parties and private processes. If you have a management that is moribund and is not doing anything, or if you have a union that is lazy and is not representing its workers adequately, you really do not have a healthy situation at all. We want, instead, companies and unions who are alert, energetic, driving—who are analyzing their interests and representing them vigorously. So we have a great stake, as the public, in having private parties who are vital in this sense. And if, because of our abhorrence of strikes, we take action that in effect takes the play away from private parties, we will sap their vitality, and wind up with a peaceful, stagnant inefficiency on both sides.[36]

The leap from private strikes affecting the public interest to strikes by public servants is a long one, yet it seems that the rationale used by Schultz could also apply to the public arena.[37] The argument that all government services are uniquely concerned with the public welfare is hard to defend. Medical doctors, nurses, milkmen, air line pilots, to name only a few, are surely as vital to public welfare as postal clarks and air controllers. In any event, as the record shows, civil servants *will* strike when they regard their conditions of work as intolerable. Moreover, if bureaucratic vitality is to be encouraged, perhaps there is considerable advantage to allowing its public members to improve the atmosphere of government employment and, as in the case of the Post Office, to promote innovation and change. Such latitude is probably bound to occur as part of the pervasive demand for fuller participation in their work role by individuals whose personal expectations and goals have changed in the recent past. Such expectations seem, moreover, to be attended by a growing preference for collective action, at the expense of the traditional competitive and individualistic definition of social life and occupational success. Such norms obviously have some disquieting aspects, in terms of net social productivity, but the main drift seems clear enough. The rapid emergence and articulateness of consumer, poverty, and protest types of groups provide dramatic evidence.[38]

[36] "Strikes: the Private Stake and the Public Interest," in *Labor–Management Policies for State and Local Government, op. cit.,* p. 4.

[37] For a fairly positive view regarding public strikes, see Robert Booth Fowler, "Normative Aspects of Public Employee Strikes," *Public Personnel Management,* Vol. 3 (March–April, 1974), pp. 129–37.

[38] For evidence indicating that this is an international trend, see Presthus (ed.), "Interest Groups in International Perspective," *Annals, American Academy of Political and Social Science,* Vol. 413 (May, 1974).

IV

FINANCIAL POLICY AND THE BUDGET PROCESS

14

Aspects of Financial Management

Students of public administration often regard financial management as a forbidding subject, to be avoided whenever possible. This attitude exists partly because this area has been associated almost exclusively with accounting and applied economics; it has been somewhat remote from the policy and the human sides of administration, which are more appealing to both citizens and students. This attitude also reflects the ambivalence toward numbers often characteristic of students of government. However, the concepts of "budgeting" and of "financial management" comprise much more than statistics and accounts. They are directly concerned with basic social and political issues. Today, only those of monumental insensitivity pretend that budgets are not based upon fairly patent normative assumptions.

THE IMPACT OF NATIONAL FISCAL POLICY

The earlier emphasis upon structure, accounting procedures, and control mechanisms is still important, but it is now linked with questions of national fiscal policy. As long ago as 1946 the Full Employment Act included the then novel idea of the use of the federal budget as a means of manipulating the national economy to accommodate an expected period of sharp post-war dislocation. The country was not yet ready for such a step during the Truman era. The Eisenhower Administration was dominated by orthodox economic ideas including the balanced budget, the end of deficit spending, and the stabilization of the national debt. Critics, however, claimed that this policy resulted in three avoidable depressions, each of which was amenable to efforts to "manage" the economy. Broadly speaking, the usual way of characterizing these efforts to control the economy has been "Keynesian," after John Maynard Keynes, a British economist and civil servant who advocated the frank and positive use of monetary and credit factors to counterbalance threatening movements in the national economy. The role of the President's Committee of Economic Advisors and the Federal Reserve Board provide well-known examples of such efforts.

Recent administrations have been especially sensitive to such policies, especially in the Johnson, Nixon, and Ford eras when vast military and foreign aid commitments and international investment by American firms brought a sharp disequilibrium in the American balance of payments. By 1970, the United States would have been unable to meet the demands for gold existing among dollar-holding nations, mainly in Western Europe. During the mid-1970's, a balance of payments structure that had usually showed a healthy credit balance turned into a serious deficit. Even before this, financial agencies and experts were obliged to become concerned with the effects of the public budget and its underlying policies on both national and international financial stability.[1] The energy crisis means that we have entered a period where national budget policy will be inseparably joined with issues regarding the health of the economy. The penetration of the budget process into the center of national and, indeed, international monetary policy has given financial administration a new intellectual dimension, the understanding of which involves intelligence of a high order. Students of public administration who have deplored its emphasis upon rather mundane processes, as contrasted with substance, should find satisfaction in this development.

Depth has also been added to the budget process by the growth of general systems theory and practice. Here again the emphasis is on major policy and decision-making, using information based upon electronic data gathering and analysis. The study of the "politics of budgeting" has also taken on new significance because of developments associ-

---

[1] See, for one example, *Hearings*, Subcommittee on Fiscal Policy, Joint Economic (Patman) Committee, 91st Congress, for October 7, 8, 9, 13, 14, 22, and 23, 1969 (Washington, D. C.: Government Printing Office, 1970). A review of this document will indicate the scope of inquiry now brought to federal fiscal policy.

ated with the huge Department of Defense budgets which have continued to expand, despite the end of the Vietnam conflict. A whole series of instruments and concepts for improving budgetary decisions as well as questions of military strategy and foreign affairs have emerged.[2] Although public budgets are intrinsically political, the budgetary process has at least developed a new potential for greater rationality, in part as a result of cost-benefit analysis and other data-based schemes. It is important to note, however, that such rationality remains essentially one of *means* rather than one of ends, and has had little effect upon the determination of larger national priorities. The latter, of course, have been sharply criticized in many quarters, but outside of a rather short-lived concern with poverty, job opportunity, and urban renewal, such priorities have not changed greatly.

IMPORTANCE OF BUDGETING

The budgetary process is central to administration because control of the purse is perhaps the most effective tool of *coordination*. The scope and nature of the entire governmental operation is determined by the allocation of appropriations to the various big programs, such as defense and social services. In this sense, budgeting is the generalist's sphere of action par excellence. His role is not limited to preparing estimates in a routine way; instead he must understand, evaluate, and justify proposed expenditures in a variety of areas, particularly if he is in a central staff agency. He becomes a management expert, often called upon to work closely with the chief executive, governor, or mayor, and to testify before appropriation committees. If he works for a line agency, he will play a similar role before the Office of Management and Budget. When not occupied with such work, the budget man often surveys administration in the operating departments, which provides him further insight into the program side of policy-making. In these ways, the budget process covers the whole spectrum of public affairs.

Financial administration is composed of three broad elements, each of which will be examined in detail in subsequent chapters. The most basic is *fiscal policy determination*, which concerns the role of political leaders in hammering out the broad outlines of programs and in authorizing appropriations to carry them out. This aspect includes problems

---

[2] *Cf.* Charles Hitch and Ronald N. McKean, *The Economics of Defense in the Nuclear Age* (Cambridge: Harvard University Press, 1960); and Charles Schultze *et al.*, *Setting National Priorities* (Washington, D. C.: Brookings Institution, 1972).

of employment, subsidies, taxation and revenue, deficit financing, etc.—problems that require more extensive discussion than can be given here. Instead, we shall assume that the revenues are available and that the initial problem is for legislatures and chief executives to allocate them among several program areas. A second element in financial administration is the broad problem of *accountability*, of insuring that money is spent wisely and honestly by political leaders and their administrative aides. Finally, there is the *management* element, which includes fiscal organization and the budget process.

DETERMINATION OF FISCAL POLICY

Although fiscal policy is obviously of signal importance, it is usually viewed as the province of political executives and legislators. "Policy" was defined earlier as "a definite course or method of action selected from among alternatives and in the light of given conditions to guide and usually determine present and future decisions." A critical example of one such national policy which has determined present and future decisions is the pervasive system of subsidies undertaken by the federal government. This example is especially useful in punctuating the normative element in policy-making and the extent to which such scientific apparatus as PPBS and systems analysis must work within a larger political context of precarious rationality.

FEDERAL SUBSIDY PROGRAMS

The congressional Joint Economic Committee defines a subsidy as any government financial assistance aimed at inducing particular private groups to alter their behavior in the marketplace.[3] Such assistance is usually awarded under the rationale that the interest concerned bears some special relation to the "public interest" and hence merits the subsidy. According to the Committee (1972), some $63 billion in subsidies is dispensed each year—about one-fourth of the total federal budget. Given problems of definition and scope, it is impossible to be very precise about the total. The beneficiaries are, however, infinitely varied and include virtually every sector of American society. Once a given interest begins to receive a subsidy, it seems virtually impossible to remove it

---

[3] See Taylor Branch, "Government Subsidies: Who Gets the 63 Billion," *Washington Monthly*, Vol. 4 (March, 1972), pp. 9–27.

from the favored list. One of the unanticipated and ironic consequences of the subsidy program is that, in most sections, the benefits tend to accrue disproportionately to its most affluent segments. Thus in agriculture, which enjoys about 5 billion per year in various types of subsidies, the wealthiest seven per cent of farm families receive $14,000 each, while the poorest 40 per cent receive only $300. The resulting net annual income of these two categories are $27,500 and $1,100, respectively.[4] A similar anomaly results in the oil industry where the depletion allowance subsidy enables some large companies to pay virtually no income tax.

The continuity and pervasiveness of the federal subsidy policy rests in part upon its relevance to the existing electoral system and the need for the parties to raise vast sums for campaign expenses. As Senator Fred Harris testified before the Joint Economic Committee, "Subsidies are to modern politics what patronage was to the politics of the 19th century. . . . Subsidies are the lifeblood of our electoral system, and this is precisely the reason it is so hard to eliminate them."[5] Such, in part, is the environment in which the budgetary process functions. As PPBS and systems analysis, it is obliged to accept as "givens" most of the larger political and normative conditions that account for the major priorities of public budgets. These conditions provide the "definite course of action selected from among alternatives" by political elites. They are the major constraints within which the real world of governmental budgeting exists.

PUBLIC BUDGETS AND THE NATIONAL ECONOMY

American budget agencies have for the most part given little consideration to the impact of government finance upon the entire economy. Their primary concern has been to find sources of revenue to meet the ever growing demands of the spending agencies. Thus municipal budget agencies have at times made studies of such matters as city income tax, business licensing, and distribution of gasoline taxes. But these have all had a single objective, namely, increasing municipal revenues. They

[4] From a study by Charles Schultze, former director of the federal budget, *Setting National Priorities*, 1973, cited in *ibid.*, p. 12. The economist Kenneth Boulding concludes similarly, "They [subsidies for agra-business] subsidize the rich farmer, drive the poor farmer out into the ghetto. That's why we have an urban problem." "Love, Fear, and the Economist," *Challenge* (July, 1973), p. 37.

[5] Cited in Boulding, *op. cit.*, p. 25.

have not been concerned with issues that interest the layman or the professional economist when he deals with taxes. Instead of asking who will ultimately pay the taxes and whether he can afford it, the main question has been how to get more revenue with the fewest protests.

American budgeting is still young, the major federal act having come in 1921. As in every new enterprise, the approach has been practical rather than scientific and theoretical. The first budget agencies were staffed by pragmatists with little experience and even less theory. There was no relevant American experience to build upon. We had gone along for a century and a half with governmental surpluses. Although state and municipal finances were not for the most part very well administered, crises did not appear until the 1920's. The causes include government deficits brought by war, the automobile, and unemployment. In the nineteenth century the economy could absorb small government without strain. When government on all levels takes about 40 per cent of the national income in taxes, as they do today, pragmatism must make room for planning.

Budget staffs, as a result, must pay more attention to the relation of government expenditure to the economy as a whole. Certainly this is desirable. One difficulty lies in the fact that here the economist is dealing with controversial material. As noted, John Maynard Keynes was perhaps most responsible for our greater sophistication regarding the role of government in the national economy.[6] He not only challenged the conventional economic wisdom; he urged on government a positive role in shaping the economy through the use of deficit financing to combat depression and unemployment. Needless to say, such viewpoints were once very controversial. When the President's Council of Economic Advisers was established in 1946, there was a widespread feeling that its advice would reflect the underlying social philosophy of the Administration in power rather than "sound" economic doctrine.[7] Indeed, one of its original members resigned because of his dissatisfaction with what he considered such a state of affairs. Although there is certainly a place for the trained economist in the budgetary process, the field is so inextricably bound up with value judgments regarding government's role in the econ-

---

[6] J. M. Keynes, *The General Theory of Employment, Interest and Money* (New York: Harcourt Brace Jovanovich, Inc., 1936); R. F. Harrod, *The Life of John Maynard Keynes* (New York: Harcourt Brace Jovanovich, Inc., 1951).

[7] See, among others, Edwin G. Nourse, *Economics in the Public Service: Administrative Aspects of the Employment Act* (New York: Harcourt Brace Jovanovich, Inc., 1953).

omy that such disagreements are bound to occur.[8] This points up again the difficult problem of harnessing scientific techniques to social values.

ACCOUNTABILITY

Perhaps the most important norm pressing upon the whole budgetary process is accountability. Here we are mainly concerned with its political and cultural origins, leaving for later chapters the institutional and mechanical checks used to achieve it.

Who is accountable to whom, and for what? In a certain sense everyone is accountable to someone, but we are concerned here with financial accountability for both money and property. Such accountability, which applies not only to high-status officials but also the rank-and-file, pervades all organizations where funds and property are involved, whether a family store, a giant corporation, or a government bureau. The journeyman is accountable to his supervisor for the proper use and custody of tools; the hospital pharmacist must account for his supply of narcotics; the cashier must balance his cash; the store manager must insure that his inventory conforms to the records.

Accountability is accomplished by a system of internal checks based upon record-keeping. When the journeyman wants to check out a diamond drill, he secures an order signed by his supervisor showing that he is authorized to use it. He presents the order to the toolkeeper, who requires him to sign a receipt. Thus the supervisor knows who was authorized to use the valuable instrument, and the toolkeeper is under constant audit by an equipment control unit. Private organizations use the same internal checks. Indeed there is a tremendous amount of record-keeping in all large organizations. Red tape is a function of size rather than of ownership. One early study indicates that manufacturing businesses evolve from one-man control to control by record when they have more than a hundred and fifty or two hundred employees.[9]

It is probably true, however, that government requires and tolerates

[8] Recent analyses dealing with the politics of budgeting include: D. J. and A. F. Ott, *Federal Budget Policy* (Washington, D. C.: Brookings Institution, 1969); C. Cohn and P. Wagner, Federal Budget Projections (Washington, D. C.: Brookings Institution, 1966); J. C. Anton, *The Politics of State Expenditure in Illinois* (Urbana: University of Illinois Press, 1966); I. Sharkansky, *Spending in the American States* (Chicago: Rand McNally Co., 1967); Schultze, *et al.*, *Setting National Priorities* (Washington, D. C.: Brookings Institution, 1972).

[9] Paul F. Lawler, *Records for the Control of Growing Manufacturing Enterprises* (Cambridge, Mass.: Harvard School of Business Administration, 1947), p. 12.

more record-keeping than business. Perhaps the primary reason is that government is more accountable to the public for its operations. The public business is everybody's business, whereas private business has enjoyed a considerable amount of autonomy. This situation, however, is changing very rapidly. The income tax, combined with increasing government regulation and the demands of consumer interests, are making private business more and more accountable to the public for the details of its operations. Nevertheless, the tendencies toward red tape are probably greater in government than in business. Several reasons explain this: many government records are required by law rather than by the needs of management; there may be more record-keeping for its own sake in government because of stratification and hierarchy, which in turn require more clearances before a decision can be made; one often senses a legal-accounting stereotype that makes government record-keeping a holy ritual. Because the rite has the sanction of time, only the sacrilegious would suggest its abolition; finally, a vested interest in record-keeping may be easier to defend in government.

But the prime function of fiscal accountability is to insure democratic responsibility to the public at large. The public official is subject to two types of such accountability: fiduciary accountability and accountability for the exercise of proper judgment in making fiscal decisions. "Fiduciary," which refers to faith, trust, and confidence, is the kind of quality expected of bankers, trustees, and treasurers. Such accountability looms largest in those areas where custodianship predominates: the work of treasurers and cashiers and in the investment of trust funds and warehousing. Loss in these areas is fairly well-guarded against by traditional bonding, auditing, record-keeping, reporting, and regulation by law.

The other type of accountability involves more discretion; it goes further than stewardship and enlists the policy-determining qualities of management. The decisions required during the budget process are illustrative. Should a hundred more police be hired or should such funds go toward building a juvenile detention building? Would money be saved by consolidating the park and recreation departments? Should the Veterans' Administration be required to abandon its own warehouses and use those of the General Services Administration? In other words, this kind of accountability asks whether fiscal officers are "good managers."

Myths of Accountability

It has long been an American myth that the way to get honesty in government is to divide power among many independent officers. Students of political science know that this myth gained support through the writings of Montesquieu and his description of eighteenth-century British practice. We now believe that Montesquieu misinterpreted the British system of checks and balances, and that our present constitutional pattern of accountability had not evolved and matured at that time. While we cannot speak for all students of government, it can be said that many regard the American interpretation and practice of separation of powers as dysfunctional, primarily because it diffuses leadership and prevents the assignment of responsibility (accountability).[10]

In financial administration the separation of power has clearly led to some abuses and weaknesses. It has led to the widespread *election* of chief fiscal officers on the state and local level. This in turn has often resulted in the selection of unqualified persons who have set up feudal domains rather than instrumentalities of fiscal coordination and control. It has also led to an irrational division of functions between the legislative and executive branches, as best illustrated by the perennial controversy over the federal Comptroller General, discussed elsewhere. In brief, this officer exercises powers of an executive rather than a legislative nature. The same can be said of many elective state comptrollers and municipal auditors.

Finally, this situation has blocked the introduction of modern systems of budgetary and accounting control because of its dispersion of power and authority. Even when power existed, effective accounting systems have not been installed largely because those responsible were not technically qualified to do so. In order to shield their inadequacies, they have laid down smokescreens of petty attention to auditing detail. They have been able to build up reputations as fiscal watchdogs, often gaining the approval of both legislature and public. This posture, however, reflects a frontier philosophy of democratic administration, which had some validity in the days when fiduciary accountability was a very real problem. But the opportunity for loss today is not in the fiduciary realm where the holes have been plugged by strict banking and trust laws. Losses are more likely to occur as the result of poor administration. Although honesty is always a matter of concern, governmental costs are now more sensitive to political irresponsibility and management ineptitude than to defalcation. Indeed, good management is one of the best defenses against dishonesty. The costs of contemporary government can be traced

---

[10] For one such viewpoint with special reference to administration, see Charles McKinley, "Federal Administrative Pathology and the Separation of Powers," *Public Administration Review*, Vol. 2 (Winter, 1951), pp. 17–25.

to overstaffing, incompetent personnel practices, poor motivation, unwise spending, poor accounting practices, unimaginative leadership, and pork-barrel appropriations. Yet the remedy too often suggested is negative prescriptions backed up by a paralyzing division of authority. The proper therapy lies instead in placing authority in administrative leaders and holding them accountable.

The Need for Standards

Perhaps the greatest need in this whole area of accountability lies in the area of standards. Precisely what are people to be held accountable for? The answer may seem obvious: for doing a good job. But what constitutes a good job? The answer is unclear because we do not have viable standards of performance in most activities. Scientific management, which has worked quite effectively in American industry, relies upon measured production. Yet in government a kind of defeatism has thwarted most efforts to develop standards. Changes for the better are occurring as the computer and related technologies, in effect, provide a vast increase in man's potential rationality. Time will tell whether computers will make a substantial contribution to management; but change cannot be put into effect without some form of work measurement,[11] based upon budgeting units of work and productivity rather than things to be bought and paid for. The theory is that the taxpayer can hold the bureaucrat more accountable when it is known that a given amount of money should buy x miles of street sweeping or y acres of soil conservation.

TYPICAL FINANCIAL FUNCTIONS

The Comptroller Function

The comptroller function is really carried out by the chief accounting officer, although some industrial comptrollers are much more than heads of accounting departments. A good comptroller, in addition to being a certified public accountant, is a member of top management and the most influential person in the area of financial policy. Government has generally failed to develop a unified approach to accounting, even though it is basic to all other fiscal activities. That is why accounting is men-

[11] For the pioneering study in this area, see Charles E. Ridley and Herbert A. Simon, *Measuring Municipal Activities* (Chicago: The International City Managers' Association, 1938).

tioned first in this inventory, rather than budgeting, which is of more interest to the generalist. Certain accounting activities have to be performed, and, indeed, one need not be a CPA to know whether they are being accomplished. The quality of the accounting process is one good index of the whole tone of financial administration.

The comptroller function in the federal government is undergoing a change, the eventual form of which is not yet entirely clear. The role of this officer in the Department of Defense gives some clue as to what is taking place.[12] He has become the Secretary of Defense's principal information resource person, and has a significant role in policy- and decision-making. As such he is more of an economist than accountant, more of a systems designer and analyst than a bookkeeper, and, above all, a department-wide coordinator.

The chief accounting officer maintains the data necessary to report on current status of funds and to maintain control. From a general administrative standpoint, his most important role is maintaining the appropriation and revenue control ledgers that reflect how money inputs compare with outputs. He also supervises the decentralized accounting systems maintained in other agencies; he has power to make them comply with over-all policies and to conform to departmental accounting practices. His relationship with other agencies, as with all other financial officers, is one of functional supervision rather than line-of-command control. Nevertheless, his latent authority often enables him to require compliance when necessary.

The accounting office maintains control accounts that furnish the program chiefs with up-to-date reports on spending. Proposals for expenditure are invariably routed to the accounting office to see whether money is available—a process known as the preaudit. This office also conducts the administrative audit, which is to be distinguished from the outside or legislative audit.

It is perfectly proper to have both an inside and outside audit; most industrial concerns find both necessary. The chief accounting office usually has a corps of traveling auditors who examine agency accounts periodically—another example of the internal checks that accompany tight financial management, and similar to the inspection function in decentralized personnel administration. The chief accounting officer also examines and certifies all payments into and out of the treasury, usually evidenced

[12] Charles J. Hitch, *Decision-making for Defense* (Berkeley: University of California Press, 1965). Hitch was Assistant Secretary and Comptroller in the Defense Department under McNamara.

by a paper called a "warrant." In federal practice a warrant is a blanket instrument covering many millions; when signed by the Comptroller General, it legalizes the transfer of funds from the treasury to the disbursing officer or from a collection agency into the treasury. In local government, a warrant is merely a check drawn upon a bank.

The Budget Bureau

The financial agency that appeals most to administrative generalists is undoubtedly the budget office. It reports directly to the chief executive or his director of finance, and acts as his financial staff arm. If it enjoys competent and imaginative leadership, the budget bureau can become the very center of day-to-day management. Through its power to allocate money and to reconcile budgetary conflicts among line agencies, it possesses tremendous "coordinating" influence. Often acting as a catalyst for management improvement, its principal function is the preparation of the annual budget which the President, governor, or mayor presents to the legislature, and which places such great policy·initiative in the hands of the chief executive. During the preparation of annual budgets, most budget agencies function under pressure, putting in considerable overtime. The effort to hammer out a final executive budget for presentation to the legislature is usually a hectic process.

In the off-budget season, staff members often carry out management improvement surveys. Indeed, it is now recognized that the budget agency should take a lead in stimulating the program departments and agencies to adopt better practices. Experience in a budget agency is a valuable item on one's employment record, not only because it affords personal contact with influential officials but also because it offers training in the art of coordination, the primary skill of the administrative generalist.

Revenue and Custody

The office of treasurer in American public administration is no longer as important as it was in the days of wildcat banking and unstable currency. Then the treasurer had the responsibility for guarding against a variety of losses that do not confront him today. (The chief present danger is inflation, about which the treasurer can do little.) His duties today are for the most part composed of routine compliance with law. His responsibilities as a custodian have been transferred to the banks, whose soundness is usually insured by such agencies as the Federal Reserve Board, the Comptroller of the Currency, and the Federal Deposit Insurance Corporation.

Essentially, the treasurer of a government jurisdiction is the official custodian of the bank books and deposit slips. To be sure, he may have important fiduciary tasks including the investment of surplus funds and administration of the public debt. But the really important revenue functions today are the assessment and collection of taxes. A quarter-century ago books on this subject would have been concerned with customs for the federal system. Today the administration of the income and sales taxes requires a virtual army of people whose supervision is an administrative problem of great moment. In public administration there is a tendency for separate agencies to be set up for the collection of each new tax. The best administrative thought, however, favors combining all revenue activities into an integrated unit.

The flow of money in and out of the treasury is subject to internal checks somewhat as follows: the revenue agency collects the taxes, the comptroller audits receipts, and if he finds them correct, he "covers" them into the treasury. While these official checks are going on, the money is usually deposited in a bank; large sums of cash are not ordinarily kept on hand. When an obligation has been incurred by a spending agency, payment is made by warrant drawn on the treasurer and countersigned by the comptroller. In the federal government the vastness of operations requires an additional step: the warrants are issued in lump sum to disbursing officers who make the detailed payments.

Auditing

The term "auditor" has often been misused in financial administration because of the tendency to regard this officer as the chief accountant. This is particularly true in state and local governments, but confusion has also existed at the federal level, as seen in the functions of the Comptroller General, who is an auditor rather than a comptroller. Strictly speaking, an auditor keeps no books of accounts; his primary duty is to examine the books of others. Every organization requires two types of audit—the current inside audit and the outside post-audit, which is regarded as a legislative function. Current administrative thought favors attaching an auditing office to the legislature. It should be noted, however, that the office of "legislative auditor," which has arisen in some states and cities, is a different kind of agency. It operates as a staff agency, advising the legislature on fiscal policy and expenditures, actually doing little or none of the detailed examination of books traditionally associated with auditing.

INTEGRATED FINANCIAL STRUCTURE

Expert opinion favors the integration of financial functions in state and local government under a director of finance reporting to the chief administrative officer. At the federal level, however, integration finds less favor. The task force report of the first Hoover Commission recommended the transfer of the then Bureau of the Budget to the Treasury Department and the establishment of a General Accountant in the Treasury. This would have made Treasury the focal point of federal financial administration. The recommendation, however, was not accepted by the Commission. Coordination of federal financial administration is in fact being achieved through the Joint Accounting Committee representing the Comptroller General, the Secretary of the Treasury, and the Director of the Bureau of Manpower and Budget.

The main argument for fiscal integration is that it makes for better management. Budgeting, accounting, and supply, along with personnel, are the cardinal management control activities. If they are well done, the program activities are also likely to be well run. In other words, program accomplishment correlates highly with the quality of administration. The chief function of administration is coordination, which in turn depends on budgeting, accounting, personnel, and supply. Personnel is mentioned here because personnel activities inevitably impinge on financial decisions, whether they are placed in a department of finance or not. Many budget agencies are in charge of wage analysis and salary administration. Moreover, legislative pressure for reduction of staffs has stimulated such agencies to launch programs that hope to motivate employees to be more productive.

The finance officer will usually supervise four or five bureaus including such activities as budgeting, accounting, taxation and revenue, treasury, and auxiliary services. There is some question whether the budget director should report directly to the chief political executive without going through the director of finance. Originally, the federal Bureau of the Budget was in the Treasury but was removed by presidential reorganization order. In states and cities there has been some favorable experience with the director of finance appointed by the governor, mayor, or manager. These officers tend, for all practical purposes, to exercise the most influence over the chief's budget decisions. Indeed, where the office of director of finance exists and where it has been given adequate power, it tends to become very influential.

THE BUDGET PROCESS

Although financial administration is mainly concerned with the functions discussed above, we have defined it broadly to include the wide policy framework within which the budget process is carried on. This helps dramatize the fact that budgeting is much more than a technical exercise. It is always affected by high-level political decisions, as well as by past patterns of authorization and spending. Such decisions involve allocating money in line with the major political objectives of the Administration in power. It is important to stress, however, that all Administrations are circumscribed by the "sunk costs" of ongoing programs, including interest on debts, subsidies, and long-term commitments for military and welfare expenditures. The budget process, which must fit within such objectives, includes the following major phases.

1. *Agency preparation of estimates for program activities.* At this point the budget is sometimes defined simply as "a device for securing money from a legislature." [13] But budget preparation involves much more than justifying an agency's requests for money. It is also a fiscal plan of an agency's operations, a way of coordinating work throughout the entire organization, and an inducement to improved administrative practices, such as increased cost-consciousness and better program evaluation. [14]

2. *Legislative authorization of the appropriations requests of the agencies.* This is a most critical phase in the budgetary process since it determines how well the agency's program is to be supported by public funds. Its outcome is anxiously watched by agency employees because the legislature's reaction is the best index of its opinion of the agency and its program, including the level at which the latter will be carried out. Here the agency's higher executives must enter the political arena, where even their expertise is not enough to save them from rough treatment by those legislators who are disenchanted with the agency for some reason.

3. *The final and less "political" phase in budgeting—the execution*

---

[13] Jesse Burkhead, *Government Budgeting* (New York: John Wiley, Inc., 1956), p. 246.
[14] *Ibid.*

stage. Here the big program decisions have been made, and the main question becomes one of spending the money according to a rational plan. The official is helped at this stage by numerous controls; these usually require, among other things, that money appropriated for one purpose not be spent for another (as noted elsewhere, however, chief executives are sometimes able to subvert legislative intent through the veto, with-holding funds, and related tactics) or that the money in an account be expended according to a schedule which prevents premature exhaustion of the account. A chapter is devoted to each of these three major phases.

15

The Budgetary Process: Preparation

In this chapter we turn to the preparation of the executive budget by the administrative branch for presentation to the legislature for authorization. Although the process is similar at all levels of government, we shall focus mainly on the federal system, since it is probably the most advanced in this area and it deals with problems on a vast scale, even compared with such huge states as New York and California. Coordinating the disparate requests of federal departments and agencies requires centralization to insure that they remain within estimated revenue and reflect generally the political preferences of the chief executive. This policy of presenting a synthesized executive budget is comparatively recent historically, and for this reason we turn first to a brief account of its development and main features.

THE REORGANIZATION MOVEMENT

Beginning about 1920, efforts were made to centralize federal fiscal planning, using various innovations. Before this time each of several departments and legislative committees proposed legislation that required appropriations. There was no single office to coordinate appropriations and weigh them against the demands of either politics or revenue.

Another unhappy condition was the absence of budgetary accounting, a process designed to gather and assimilate information upon which administrative decisions could be based. In the first decades of this century most governmental accounting systems failed to do this. At best, they gave an accurate report of how much cash had been taken in or paid out, but they often failed to meet even this limited objective. On the state and local levels, accounting activities were usually controlled by an officer who had been elected without much reference to qualifications. Nor were things much better at the national level. Indeed, federal budgetary accounting has only recently achieved full maturity. No one was charged with the responsibility of pulling expenditures together into a coordinated statement or report, let alone a plan. Under this system of legislative anarchy, there was no curb on lobbyists, the seekers of pork-barrel appropriations, or other apologists for special interests. Everyone except the unorganized public was represented. There was no over-all view which could say, "While this proposal for expenditure has its merits, the current condition of the Treasury does not justify it in the light of other obligations." The budgetary reforms of the 1920's sought to remedy such weaknesses through a system of structural and procedural changes.

One of the difficulties in bringing about change in the field of financial administration arises from the propensity of the American people to seek responsible government by dividing authority among several agencies. Such practices are the institutionalization of American political values and attending structural accommodations such as the separation of powers. Responsibility for federal accounting was rather ambiguously parcelled out among four different authorities: (1) the executive agencies themselves, (2) the Department of the Treasury, (3) the Bureau of the Budget, and (4) the General Accounting Office, headed by the Comptroller General. In 1949, an interdepartmental committee composed of representatives of these agencies—the Joint Program for Improved Accounting—was organized to try to bring about some coordination. This innovation proved so successful that it has been continued under the name of the Joint Financial Management Improvement Program. Before 1949 there had been considerable interagency friction because of the controversy surrounding the role of the Comptroller General, but apparently such tensions have been resolved as the result of the joint program.[1]

---

[1] Joint Financial Management Program, *15 Years of Progress* (1948–1963); Joint Financial Improvement Program, *Highlights of Progress* (1964); General Accounting Office, *The Functions of the General Accounting Office* (Committee on Government Operations, U. S. Senate, 1962); *Annual Report of the Comptroller General of the United States* (1972). (All of these publications issued by the Government Printing Office, Washington, D. C.)

The Executive Budget

Since the most serious weakness had been the absence of any collective financial plan, the major reform proposed an executive budget in which the chief executive would submit annually an all-inclusive fiscal plan to legislators. This plan was to be submitted early enough so that it could be scrutinized and authorized before the beginning of the coming fiscal year. The proposed executive budget was to include estimates for both revenues and expenditures, and, in principle at least, these were to balance. If deficits were to be incurred, they were to be planned for, and means of financing them were to be recommended by the chief executive.

A good example of such a comprehensive fiscal plan is Governor Carey's (New York) budget for 1975–76 (see Table 15–1). His message to the legislature begins with recognition of the "need for strong action to avert financial crisis," much of which is attributed to the budget inherited from the previous (Rockefeller) Administration which was "shaped by false (sic) illusions and wishful thinking." [2] The resulting deficit amounting to $271 billion, moreover, represents obligations written into law which must be assumed by the new Administration. To close the gap between expected revenue and proposed expenditures, the Governor first eliminated nearly $1 billion from the programs requested during 1974. Various agencies, commissions, and boards were to be merged or eliminated, reducing state employees by about 2,000. A hiring freeze was also introduced. In program terms, the only increase will be in support for the mentally disabled. These and other economies reduced State Purposes spending for the first time in recent history.

Despite such efforts, a gap of $656 million remained, and the Governor turned to revenue measures to fill this impressive gap. Ten cents per gallon is added to the gas tax; in addition to increasing revenue, the program will conserve energy resources. The basic tax on corporations is increased from 9 to 10 per cent; the franchise tax rate on banks is increased by a similar amount. The existing exemption from state taxes on unincorporated businesses enjoyed by professionals will be ended. Those who earn over $27 thousand per year will pay higher taxes, as will those who can afford "substantial luxuries" including presently exempted taxes on cosmetics and admissions to sporting events. Value is to be substituted for weight in determining auto taxes; chauffeurs, drivers, and learners license fees are to be doubled; and occupational licensing fees are to be

2 *New York Times*, January 31, 1975, p. 38.

TABLE 15-1. New York State Budget (1975-76)

	State Income	
	Amount	Percentage of Total
Personal Income Tax	$4,100,000,000	39%
User Taxes and Fees	3,955,300,000	37
Business Taxes	1,617,500,000	15
Other Income and Miscellaneous Receipts	625,200,000	6
Federal Revenue Sharing	241,000,000	2
Bonds	153,000,000	1

	State Expenditures	
	Amount	Percentage of Total
Local Assistance	$6,410,695,000	60%
State Purposes	3,346,497,000	31
Capital Construction	581,505,000	6
Debt Service	353,000,000	3

raised. In sum, these innovations will bring in about $806 million. As Table 15-1 shows, the principal sources of the state's revenue are personal income taxes, users' taxes and fees, plus business taxes, all providing just over 90 per cent of total income.

Turning to expenditures, the Governor emphasized his exacting and comprehensive review of overall state spending ("the first in at least 15 years") during the two-and-one half months between his election and the due date for the budget. Inflation, expanded work loads, state aid of various kinds, social security funding, debt service, and expanded services to the mentally ill are among the major areas requiring increased spending, in line with the Governor's aim "to provide funds where they will be needed the most—by local governments and the poor and unfortunate of our society." We turn next to another example of the budget reorganization movement.

Integrated Financial Structure

The second proposal for overcoming existing inadequacies was the establishment of an integrated financial structure in which financial activities were to be placed under a single director of finance. This was a reaction against the extreme diffusion of the financial function, which was often shared by several independent, elected officials. The proposed department of finance might include bureaus dealing with (1) budget planning, (2) accounting, (3) treasury functions, including tax collections, (4) purchase and supply, and (5) assessment.

Although this early concept of an integrated department of finance had influential advocates, and still commands favor, the widespread resistance to appointing comptrollers, auditors, and treasurers soon forced reformers to seek integration within the existing structure.[3] As a result, improvement in financial administration in the 1945–1975 period has resulted more from improved coordination than from integrated structure. Great progress has been made in establishing budget agencies under the chief executive, but the *accounting function* has often remained under some independent agency or has been divided among several agencies with ill-defined boundaries. An example is the situation in the federal government where (again because of cultural myths regarding the wisdom of the separation of powers) some accounting functions are placed in an agency responsible to Congress, the General Accounting Office, and others in the Treasury Department. Because neither of these agencies developed an effective accounting system, the Bureau of the Budget had to get into the act. This it did by tactfully organizing a committee of the three agencies, which over a period of years developed a coordinated approach to budgetary accounting. This device was recognized by Congress, which placed the responsibility for introducing budgetary accounting throughout the federal government in the Bureau of the Budget (now OMB).

BUREAU OF THE BUDGET

Until 1970 at the federal level, the staff agency for achieving the major objectives of the reformers has been the Bureau of the Budget, established in 1921. Located in the Executive Office of the President, the Bureau had two principal functions: to prepare the President's annual budget for presentation at the beginning of each session of Congress, and to encourage the entire administrative branch to improve its management practices. Under its first director the Bureau had a rather limited view of its role, restricting itself in the main to technical questions of economy and effi-

---

[3] For a careful account of an early attempt at federal reorganization, including fiscal and accounting methods, see Oscar Kraines, "The President Versus Congress: the Keep Commission," *Western Political Quarterly*, Vol. 23 (March, 1970), pp. 5–54; the early progress of financial reorganization in the states is outlined in *Reorganizing State Government* (Chicago: Council of State Governments, 1950), pp. 110–22.

ciency. As its first director said, "The Bureau of the Budget is concerned only with the humbler and routine business of government." [4] After 1937, however, the Bureau's role began to be more broadly conceived as a staff arm of the President, charged with the review of the *substantive* programs of the departments and agencies. Since then it has increased in both size and influence, as an analysis of its reorganization in 1952 and its role in program review will show.[5]

Reorganization of the Bureau

In 1925 a functional division of activities was used to bring about co-ordination and consultation between the "offices" and "divisions" of the bureau. The "divisions" were charged with broad general-purpose functions: International, Military, Resources and Civil Works, Commerce and Finance, and Labor and Welfare. The "offices" were set up to deal with such "process" activities as Legislative Reference, Management and Organization, Budget Review, and Statistical Standards. The Office of Accounting was added in 1956.

The Legislative Reference Office reflected the importance of the bureaucracy in the policy-making process. Originally set up to prevent the executive agencies from dealing directly with Congress without the President's knowledge or consent, it came to "review and co-ordinate" the executive agencies on legislative matters and maintains liaison between Congress and the President on most legislative items. It also coordinated the preparation and presentation of bureau testimony before congressional committees. The key words in the job descriptions for each of the offices were "coordinate" and "review." Thus the Office of Budget Review "coordinated the review of annual, supplemental and deficiency estimates." The Office of Management and Organization assisted the director in the formulation and coordination of programs for improving management in the executive branch. The Office of Statistical Standards coordinated the statistical activities of the government by reviewing questionnaires and statistical procedures.

The first Hoover Commission criticized the Bureau of the Budget rather sharply. Among other things, it was accused of poor relationships with Congress, departure from its role of neutrality in advocating partisan White House objectives, general bureaucratic inertia, and lack of leader-

---

[4] Charles G. Dawes, *The First Year of the Budget of the United States* (New York: Harper & Row, Inc., 1923), p. xi.

[5] For a review of the Bureau's history and organization, see Jesse Burkhead, *Government Budgeting* (New York: John Wiley, Inc., 1956), pp. 288–304.

ship. Whatever may have been the justice of these criticisms, the fact seems to be that the Bureau came to enjoy higher prestige in more recent years, as reflected by the leadership thrust upon it in carrying out the budgeting and accounting recommendations of the two Hoover reports. In the executive branch reorganizations of 1950 and 1956, Congress gave the Bureau a key role in bringing about the desired improvements. This new legislation called upon the head of each executive agency, in consultation with the Director of the Bureau, to do whatever was necessary to attain the following objectives:

1. Achieve consistency in accounting and budget classifications.
2. Bring about synchronization between accounting and budget classifications and organizational structure.
3. Provide information on performance and program costs to justify budget requests.

Agency heads were also instructed to insure, "as soon as practicable and in accordance with principles and standards prescribed by the Comptroller General, that their accounts be maintained on an accrual basis to show the resources, liabilities, and costs of operation . . . with a view toward facilitating the preparation of cost-based budgets. . . ." [6]

In 1956 the Bureau issued directives designed to carry out the above instructions by Congress. Legislation enacted in 1956 set the base for carrying out the recommendations of the second Hoover Commission. But the most significant development was the emerging management role of the Bureau.

Budget Bureau Leadership

The Bureau became the management staff arm of the federal government, both by default and by general consent. While the Bureau had long had an office of management and organization, it tended to regard its *modus operandi* as purely staff in nature. This was partly due to the venerable historical status of the Treasury, as well as the fact that the Budget and Accounting Act of 1921 charged the General Accounting Office with supervision of accounting. The Bureau was always hesitant about seeming to encroach upon the functions of these two agencies. Nevertheless, it was gradually realized that the federal government did not have an effective system of budgetary accounting and reporting, as pointed out by the task force of the first Hoover Commission.

---

[6] Bureau of the Budget, *Improvement of Financial Administration in the Federal Government* (Washington, D. C.: Government Printing Office, 1956).

The Commission pointed out that responsibility for accounting was dispersed among three agencies: the Treasury, responsible for fiscal accounts; the Comptroller General, with overall responsibility for administrative accounts; and the departments, which were almost autonomous regarding accounting. Thus the Commission recommended that an Accountant General be established in the Treasury with authority to prescribe accounting methods and to enforce accounting procedures, subject to the approval of the Comptroller General, within the powers conferred upon him by Congress. The Accountant General would take data from agency accounts and prepare reports for the President and Congress which would indicate the Government's current financial condition.

The second Hoover Commission re-emphasized these points but recommended that the Bureau of the Budget be given responsibility for budgetary accounting and reporting. The amendment to the Budget and Accounting Act in 1956 recognized the primacy of the Bureau while still retaining the Comptroller General's function of approving systems. That the Congress accepted (however reluctantly) the Bureau's leadership is suggested by reports of its committee's dealing with these matters.[7] In line with the second Hoover Commission's recommendations, an Office of Accounting was established in the Bureau of the Budget, and an assistant director (a professional accountant) was brought in from a firm specializing in industrial practice.

The Reorganization Plan of 1970

On July 1, 1970, one year before the fiftieth anniversary of its establishment, the United States Bureau of the Budget expired. Technically, responsibility for the functions that it had performed was transferred to the President who, in turn, redelegated (Executive Order 11,541) these functions to two new executive agencies, the Domestic Council and the Office of Management and Budget.

The Reorganization Plan designed by the Nixon administration held that the two basic functions centering in the President's office—that is, the functions of policy determination and of executive management—should be subsumed under two distinct, institutionalized agencies. In other words, management processes (including budgeting) should be structurally separated from the processes of policy formulation. Under this

---

[7] See particularly the Staff Report, Committee on Government Operations, *The Budget Process in the Federal Government*, H. R., 85th Cong., 1st sess (Washington, D. C.: Government Printing Office, 1957).

plan, the new Domestic Council would assume responsibility for the formulation and coordination of *policy* in the domestic arena in much the same way that the National Security Council was responsible for policy matters relating to foreign affairs and national defense. The Office of Management and Budget would become the principal executive tool for the exercise of presidential *managerial* functions.

The Domestic Council

Briefly, the Domestic Council was to be chaired by the President and would include as permanent members the Vice-President, the Secretaries of the Treasury, Interior, Agriculture, Commerce, Labor, Transportation, H.E.W., H.U.D., and the Attorney General. In effect therefore, the Domestic Council was a cabinet-level subcommittee whose membership could be supplemented at the discretion of the President by any other executive branch official. The Council was to be supported by a staff under the aegis of an Executive Director who was also a presidential assistant. Like the National Security Council, Domestic Council staff were to work in close coordination with the personal staff of the President but would retain an institutional hierarchy and identity of their own.

Formally, the functions of the Domestic Council were described as follows:

> Assessing national needs, collecting information and developing forecasts, for the purpose of defining national goals and objectives.
> Identifying alternate ways of achieving these objectives, and recommending consistent, integrated sets of policy choice.
> Providing rapid response to Presidential needs for policy advice on pressing domestic issues.
> Coordinating the establishment of national priorities for the allocation of available resources.
> Maintaining a continuous review of the conduct of ongoing programs from a policy standpoint, and proposing reforms as needed.[8]

In operational terms, the work of the Council was to be undertaken through temporary *ad hoc* committees employing, where necessary, additional staff support drawn from departmental and agency experts throughout the government.

---

[8] "Message from the President of the United States, Transmitting Reorganization Plan No. 2 of 1970," *Hearings* before a Subcommittee on Government Operations of the U. S. House of Representatives, 91st Congress, 2nd Session, April 28, 1970, Washington, D. C., U. S. Government Printing Office, 1970, p. 3.

Office of Management and the Budget

The second new agency, the Office of Management and Budget, was to retain most of the established structural instrumentalities of the old Bureau of the Budget. However, as its new name connotes, the OMB was to take on greater managerial responsibilities:

> While the budget function remains a vital tool of management, it will be strengthened by the great emphasis the new office will place on fiscal analysis. The budget function is only one of several important management tools that the President must now have. He must also have a substantially enhanced institutional staff capability in other areas of executive management—particularly in program evaluation and coordination, improvement of Executive Branch organization, information and management systems, and development of executive talent.[9]

In sum, the 1970 reorganization seems to represent a fundamental shift away from localizing primary coordinating functions in a single executive agency. With respect to the budget process itself, the OMB remains a very important central component but, at the stage of policy formulation and budget preparation, one must now also recognize the importance of the Domestic Council. As the new situation has been summarized:

> The Budget Bureau that was is not the Office of Management and Budget that will be. OMB will not be able to match its predecessor's position because it does not possess the monopoly held by the Budget Bureau over key presidential functions. The Domestic Council, however varied its experience will be under different Presidents, will be a rival of Managment and Budget for all of the great functions once housed in the Bureau. However, this does not mean that OMB should be written off as a major instrument of the Presidency. To be sure, the Bureau was downgraded by the 1970 reorganization, and the budget component of OMB was diminished in relation to the management work. But Management and Budget still will possess the longest institutional memory in the President's office and all future Presidents will rely on it for a variety of important chores.[10]

PREPARING THE EXECUTIVE BUDGET

Having traced the development and functions of the major budgetary agencies, we can now review the process of designing the chief executive's budget. This process, it should be emphasized, is very similar in most

[9] *Ibid.*, p. 4.

[10] Allen Schick, "The Budget Bureau That Was: Thoughts on the Rise, Decline, and Future of a Presidential Agency," *Law and Contemporary Problems*, Vol. 35 (Summer, 1970), pp. 538–39.

state administrative systems, as well as in major cities. The formal beginning of the federal budget cycle occurs well over a year before the start of the fiscal year to which the budget pertains. For example, the process by which the budget for fiscal year 1975 (July 1, 1974, to June 30, 1975) is established commences with the OMB's request for departmental and agency budget estimates in the spring of 1973. At this point, each agency

> . . . evaluates its programs, identifies policy issues, and makes budgetary projections, giving attention to important modifications, reforms and innovations in its programs, and to alternative long-range program plans.[11]

Agency estimates are often prepared on standard forms, known as the "green sheets," which contain the figures for the last completed fiscal year, the estimated amounts to be spent during the current year, the amounts requested for the coming fiscal year, and, frequently, rough estimates of expenditure levels several years into the future.

The method of computing estimates varies. In large "holding-company" departments such as Treasury or Health, Education, and Welfare, decentralization will go at least as far down as the bureaus—especially in those departments where bureaus enjoy considerable autonomy. Budget planning in some agencies will be decentralized to the regional offices and from there to the field stations. The more decentralized agencies set upper limits of expenditure for field units and ask them to develop plans within the stated amounts. In the centralized agencies, the detailed planning will go on almost entirely in Washington. In general, even though the existence of work-load standards in many federal agencies may facilitate budgetary decentralization, Washington is egocentric, and the dominant pulls are toward centralization, a trend which has almost certainly been accelerated by computer technology.

The Norm of Incrementalism

The bureaus and departments have their own fiscal and budget agencies, which do staff work for their chiefs. Actually, comparatively little is known about departmental budget planning. The literature of public administration has usually neglected budgeting at this level. Nevertheless, several observations concerning the actions of agency and departmental budget officials can be made. Clearly, despite the intent of the performance and program budgeting systems, it seems reasonable to as-

---

[11] Office of Management and Budget, *The United States Budget in Brief: Fiscal Year 1974*, Washington, D. C., U. S. Government Printing Office, 1973, p. 57.

sume that many agency budgets continue to be subject to various non-rational determinants. A budget official is often motivated by a desire to protect the position of his own agency, to obtain increments in the funds allocated to his agency, and to maintain felicitous relations with those government organs that exercise influence or control over various phases of the budget procedure. He realizes that very large, unprecedented requests for extensive funding are likely to be examined critically, so he often must temper his budget requests. On the other hand, he must seek sufficiently large amounts of money so that, if cuts are made, his agency will still receive adequate resources to carry out its responsibilities at least at their current level. Using the terms of Herbert Simon, budget officials do not try to maximize but, instead, they "satisfice" (satisfy and suffice).[12] Such behavior seems far removed from the thoughts of those who promote the highly rational, comprehensive criteria of systems analysis and program budgeting. Considerable evidence suggests that budget officials operate in a highly contingent universe, and that their ultimate appropriation requests are a *pot pourri* of convention, speculation, anticipatory responses to expected committee and OMB behavior, all larded with hope. There is apparently a tendency to inflate requests by a certain amount, in the experience-born expectation that committees will make "across the board" cuts.[13] Certain agencies, moreover, enjoy a favored status in budget politics. The FBI and CIA are well-known to have general congressional approval, contrasted with the independent regulatory commissions, toward whose policies many congressmen are ambivalent.

As a result and from a somewhat conservative perspective, agency budgeting has been characterized by several observers as "incremental," meaning that each year's proposals are essentially an extrapolation of those made in the years before. (It is hard, indeed, to conceive of any sector of human or technical activity in which this generalization does not hold.) As the Otts put it,

> Budgeting is incremental, not comprehensive. The beginning of wisdom about an agency's budget is that it is almost never actively reviewed as a whole every year in the sense of considering the value of

[12] *Models of Man* (New York: John Wiley, Inc., 1957), pp. 204–5.

[13] As a useful Brookings' study notes, "So in making decisions on programs and expenditures, agencies cannot, for strategic reasons, aim too high or too low. Their decision making will reflect seeking out and receiving clues and hints from the executive branch, Congress, clientele groups, and their own organizations. In this way they are able in most cases to get a rough idea of what will prove acceptable to the Budget Bureau, the President and his advisors, and the appropriations subcommittees in Congress." David J. Ott, and A. F. Ott, *Federal Budget Policy*, revised edition (Washington, D. C.: The Brookings Institution, 1969), p. 30.

all existing programs as compared to possible alternatives. Instead, it is based on last year's budget with special attention given to a narrow range of increases or decreases. Thus the men who make the budget are concerned with relatively small increments to an existing base. Their attention is focused on a small number of items over which the budgetary battle is fought.[14]

Clearly, the incrementalist approach does not fully explain some of the rational developments in federal budgeting that do exist, but it does present an important counterbalance to the proponents of the total relevance of technological analysis and systems procedures. On the other hand, it is "conservative" in the sense of encouraging an excessive empiricism.

Continuing with the preparation of the budget, after the estimates and evaluations are prepared by the agencies, they are sent for initial review to the Office of Management and Budget which, in turn, forwards the preliminary plans to the President. The President also receives projections on the nation's economic outlook and revenue estimates prepared by the Treasury Department, the Council of Economic Advisers, and the OMB. With this information and with the policy recommendations and studies carried out by his Domestic Council, the President establishes the general budget and fiscal policy guidelines for the fiscal year.[15]

At the same time, of course, Congress need not accept the President's fiscal leadership. Early in 1975, for example, President Ford's proposals to cut about $6.5 billion from the 1976 budget were "totally rejected" by a Democratically controlled Congress. Since some $5 billion of the proposed reduction depended upon changes in existing laws, the President's plan was negated. Meanwhile, forces beyond his control play a major role in shaping the budget. For 1976, for example, a rise in spending of about $30 billion reflected the following "uncontrollable" items: Social Security benefits, veterans' benefits, and debt service; the impact of inflation on defense and other programs; and the steep rise in unemployment compensation payments because of the recession.[16]

Throughout the fall and early winter, the OMB receives the agency

[14] *Ibid.*, p. 15. For a critique of the concept of incrementalism, see John J. Bailey and R. J. O'Connor, "Operationalizing Incrementalism," *Public Administration Review*, Vol. 35 (January–February, 1975), pp. 60–66.

[15] For further evidence that such guidelines are themselves the results of bargaining and compromise rather than the rational overall plan assumed (ideally at least) by advocates of executive budgets, see C. Schultze, *et al.*, *Setting National Priorities* (Washington, D. C.: Brookings Institution, 1972).

[16] *New York Times*, December 1, 1974, p. 13 and December 30, 1974, p. 10.

budgets. These budgets are given careful examination by OMB specialists assigned to the program area concerned. Soon thereafter, the OMB begins its own hearings with major financial officers of the agencies who come in to explain their budgets. What happens here is a sort of preliminary bout for the main event—the hearings before the legislative committees. The operating officials must justify their requests in the light of presidential policy. While the agency officials and the OMB examiners aim at consensus, major differences arise on occasion and are usually referred to higher levels. Substantive expertise is encouraged by the organization of OMB into several divisions, including budget review, legislative reference, executive development and labor relations, management and operations, national security and international affairs, human and community affairs, economics and government, and natural resources and science—all coordinated by a director's office.[17] Each division handles agency requests in its own area.

After final review by the Director's staff, the OMB forwards the budget data and recommendations to the President.

Department of Defense Budget

The budgetary procedure for the Department of Defense as developed under the leadership of Secretary Robert S. McNamara in the early 1960's set an example for budgeting not only in other federal departments, but for government in general in the years to follow. The experience of Planning, Programming, Budgeting Systems (PPBS) has been discussed in detail earlier. We have seen that DOD's success with program budgeting raised hopes that a new era of rationality could be achieved in federal budgeting but we have also noted that implementation of PPBS in other departments and state and local jurisdictions met with only mixed success.

The budget of the Defense Department continues to be influenced strongly by the procedures of program and systems budgeting. Clearly, the type of operations to which the Department is geared lends itself to extensive use of such analytical devices and rational criteria of evaluation. Combined with the immense size of the defense budget, these factors serve to distinguish DOD budgeting from that of civilian departments. Indeed even the relation between DOD and the OMB (or BOB before it) is somewhat different than the interaction that characterizes OMB-civilian department encounters.

[17] Office of Management and Budget, *United States Budget, 1975* (Washington, D. C.: Government Printing Office, 1974), pp. 64, 969, 1024.

It should be noted that the budget of the Department of Defense is handled somewhat differently from those of other agencies. The Bureau of the Budget participates with the financial officers of the Defense Department in a review of the requests of the various services for budgetary allowances, but its role here is not quite the same as with other agencies. It acts more as an adviser to the Secretary of Defense than as an arbiter; more decisions in this agency must be left for presidential action. In addition, final Defense budgetary decisions are made later than those of other agencies. Many of the crucial ones are held until late December.[18]

The President's Budget

In the last stage of the budget's preparation, the OMB pulls together the multitude of estimates and supporting documents into final form for printing and eventual presentation in late January to Congress and the legislative committees. The format of the President's budget has undergone very considerable change in recent years. It was formerly a volume about the size of a metropolitan telephone book, comprising over a thousand pages. It also contained considerable detail, known in budget vernacular as the "object" breakdown—meaning the "things" to be bought. Professional budgetary opinion has usually frowned upon including such detail, but legislators, whether city councilmen or congressmen, have tended to ask for it.[19] Today, the President's budget, a book-size volume set down in large readable type, contains less object breakdown but is accompanied by a supplement or appendix containing detailed statistics and information. The first third of the budget consists mainly of the President's budget message, interspersed with illustrative diagrams, tables, and charts.

Evaluation of the President's Budget. In comparison with the chaotic situation existing during the reform movement beginning about 1910, the present executive budget is much more precise and progressive, enabling the President to exercise major policy leadership, as he must in our system if leadership is to occur. This is because of the lack of party discipline, the traditional separatism and conflict between executive and legislature and the lack of strong central direction in our political parties, as well as the strong centrifugal effects of major interest groups demands. The President is, after all, the only nationally elected political leader; he alone is the representative of all the people. The executive budget

18 Ott and Ott, *op. cit.*, p. 23.
19 The larger "object" document is still available, but its distribution is confined to members of Congress and other insiders.

gives him a great psychological and strategic advantage in fulfilling this leadership role. It enables him to present a reasonably coherent political and financial program that Congress has found difficult to set aside. It also enables him to maintain some degree of order in his own administrative house, and to coordinate federal programs within the framework of larger national objectives.

The views of the leading student of budgetary matters suggest the extent to which corrective steps have been taken. Almost twenty years ago Professor Arthur Smithies raised questions regarding "the organization and structure of the government which seems to require an undue element of arbitrariness in major decisions concerning the defense budget." [20] Noting that the departmental approach to federal budgeting "interferes in important instances with effective programming at the Presidential level," he advocated instead reliance on a budget whereby the President would be given appropriations on a program basis which he could then allocate to the departments. This, however, would require extensive regrouping of functions among departments and agencies to ease duplication and overlapping. In the natural resource field, for example, he argued that "there is almost complete agreement by everyone concerned that no substantial change . . . is likely to occur without drastic organizational changes in the Executive Branch." [21] Here again, of course, one runs into the venerable problem of the "politics of reorganization," whereby departments and their legislative and clientele groups form "whirlpools of interest" that make such changes slow and extremely difficult.

An interesting criticism, which seems to conflict with the program type of budgeting just mentioned, is Smithies' conclusion that "the increase in the program emphasis in the budget has meant that the budget has become less useful for reviewing the efficiency of administration." [22] Even

[20] Smithies, *The Budgetary Process in the United States* (New York: McGraw-Hill Book Co., Inc., 1955), p. 129. A spate of books and reports has appeared recently concerning the budget process at the state and local levels, among which the following are representative: S. Kenneth Howard, *Changing State Budgeting* (Lexington, Ky.: Council of State Governments, 1973); Howard and G. Grizzle, *Whatever Happened to State Budgeting* (Lexington, Ky.: Council of State Governments, 1972); Robert D. Lee and R. W. Johnson, *Public Budgeting Systems* (Baltimore: University Park Press, 1973); Peter A. Pyhrr, *Zero-Base Budgeting* (New York: John Wiley, Inc., 1973); Donald Gerwin, *Budgeting Public Funds: The Decision Process in an Urban School District* (Madison: University of Wisconsin Press, 1969); Allen Schick, *Budgetary Innovations in the States* (Washington, D. C.: Brookings Institution, 1971).

[21] Smithies, *op. cit.*, p. 353.

[22] *Ibid.*, p. 107.

under the budget program, each activity is still broken down into "objects" such as personnel services and travel equipment, existing alongside the broad program classifications. In reality, the problem here is one of weighing the obvious advantages of the program system in increased simplicity and legislative understanding against the loss of detailed information that enables legislators to raise questions of administrative detail, which, it seems, is a major tendency under the present system.

Certainly, the process of preparing the executive budget has been vastly improved over the past two decades, perhaps especially among the more professionalized state governments. Centralization of final authority for the entire budget in staff agencies under the chief executive has provided order and continuity in this phase of the budgetary process. The major problems now existing involve the question of the priorities which political elites and chief executives bring to their shaping of the budget; the limited control that legislatures seem to have over such priorities and their dollar costs; the most effective meshing of federal and state–local programs; the revenue crisis and the attending decline in the quality of services in the great metropolitan centers; and finally, of course, the energy crisis and attending unprecedented problems of simultaneous inflation and recession. The ensuing tension between a Republican president and a Democratic Congress as to the best means of meeting the latter problems indicates again the inherently political nature (aggravated by the problem of conflicting advice from economic experts) of fiscal policy making.

Some efforts are being made to bring about a wider public knowledge and discussion of these issues,[23] but the size and scope of federal programs (and problems), as well as the uncoordinated claims of the great interest groups make rationalization difficult to achieve. Equally important in this period is the impact of uncontrollable foreign developments, such as the sharp rise in the price of oil and food. The consequences are explicit in the fact that whereas President Ford in his first message to Congress in August 1974 pledged to bring in a budget for 1976 lower than the $300 billion being spent in the current year, by December he was proposing a 1976 budget of $349.4 billion, an increase of 14 per cent over 1974 levels, and including a deficit in the area of $50 billion.

[23] Among others, see Schultze, et al., op. cit., Chap. 1; for problems of sharing programs and finances between the federal and state–local jurisdictions, see Michael Reagan, *The New Federalism* (New York: Oxford University Press, 1972), especially Chaps. 4, 5.

16

The Budgetary Process: Authorization

The budgetary process is essentially one of decision-making, and there are few branches in public administration where behavioral concepts find a better laboratory. Although capsule descriptions always entail oversimplification, we shall deal here with such concepts as rationality, values, and politics as critical elements in financial decision-making. The terms coined by Simon and Lindblom to symbolize the non-rational elements in the general process of decision-making are directly relevant to the budget area. Simon said, as noted, that the decision-maker "satisfices"; rather than choosing the best possible solution to a problem, he tends to select a suitable or satisfactory alternative.[1] Lindblom's concept of "muddling through" is obviously similar. What he calls the "comprehensive-rational approach," and what Nicolaidis refers to as "classical rationality"[2] cannot always apply in the administrative arena, not only because of its political context, but because of limitations of foresight, information, time, and what John Dewey, the American philosopher, called "the need for settled relationships." Man's tolerance for ambiguity is notoriously low, a condition that pushes him toward prompt rather than perfect decisions. Instead of the maximization of rationality, a succession of limited simulations occurs in which choices are made from a narrow range of alternatives

[1] Herbert A. Simon, *Administrative Behavior* (New York: The Macmillan Co., 1957), and *Models of Man* (New York: John Wiley, Inc., 1957).
[2] "Policy and Policy-Makers: an Empirical Analysis," *International Review of Administrative Sciences,* Vol. 29 (1963), pp. 1–10.

based upon "marginal" values.[3] Students need only ask themselves how much they knew about the university they now attend before they decided to attend it, in order to appreciate these strictures about human choice.

The subject of rationality is now a matter of great concern to behavioral science, particularly where engineers and social scientists have collaborated through their mutual interest in systems theory. Early budgetary theory, as we have seen, was characterized by the rationality of the reformers, who used the appeal of "efficiency" to fight corruption in government. Just as "reason" became the hallmark of the eighteenth-century revolutionaries, so did formal rationality provide the impetus for administrative reform. Today, a more sophisticated generation of scholars is re-examining old conceptions of rationality in the light of systems and decision theory.[4] Attempts have been made to introduce comprehensive scientific criteria into the budgetary process, especially regarding the relationship between the stated aims of the budget and its program achievements. The efforts and the mixed results of PPBS in this context have been noted elsewhere.[5]

HOW RATIONAL CAN BUDGET DECISIONS BE?

Communications technology has introduced a new element into human behavior. This may be called the greater *potential* for rational decision-making. (Insofar as it inhibits this potential, we have called the "incremental" school of budgeting essentially "conservative.") Theories of budgetary decision-making now seem to encompass a scale with complete rationality at one end and complete political bargaining at the other. The assumption is that the budget process can be moved further along toward the rational end of the scale using new technologies. No

---

[3] Charles E. Lindblom, "The Science of Muddling Through," *Public Administration Review*, Vol. 19 (Spring, 1959), pp. 79–88; D. Braybrooke and C. Lindblom, *A Strategy of Decision* (London: Macmillan-Collier, 1963).

[4] See among others, attempts to apply "consistency theory" and phenomenology to the question of how individuals conceptualize their worlds and choose among various courses of action, S. Feldman (ed.), *Cognitive Consistency: Motivational Antecedents and Behavioral Consequents* (New York: Academic Press, 1961); Alfred Schutz, *The Phenomenology of the Social World* (Evanston, Ill.: Nothwestern University Press, 1967) and his "On Phenomenology and Social Relations" in H. R. Wagner (ed.), (Chicago: University of Chicago Press, 1970); Kenneth Boulding, *The Image* (Ann Arbor: University of Michigan Press, 1956); Stanley H. Udy, "Administrative Rationality, Social Setting, and Organizational Development," in W. Cooper, *et al.* (eds.), *New Perspectives in Organizational Research* (New York: John Wiley, Inc., 1964), pp. 173–92.

[5] See pp. 79–86.

one argues that the process can become completely value-free or rational. A better conclusion is that budgets are neither wholly rational nor wholly political, but that the diminishing resources in surplus wealth and natural resources that now characterize the United States demand that the budget process be made more rational. The question is, How rational can budgeting become, given the limitations outlined earlier?

Insofar as fiscal policy, which provides the assumptions upon which budgets are designed, reflects either expert or public opinion, it is not always easy to find guidance. Economists do not always agree on the utility and consequences of certain measures such as tight money, price controls, or whether the so-called "law of supply and demand" has been rendered obsolete by monopoly control and administered prices. Equally eminent economists declare that the public sector has been starved, while others argue that this view is considerably exaggerated.[6] Presidents, moreover, tend to bring in advisers who reflect their own views, again illustrating the impact of politics upon disinterested decision-making.

Insofar as public opinion is concerned, survey research now provides some answers regarding the distribution of attitudes toward alternative policies among various groups. Findings now suggest that the willingness to pay taxes for all governmental programs generally rises with educational level.[7] Policy preferences also vary with income level. When "low" income is defined as those with under $3000 per year, it seems that people with such incomes are much more willing than those at the "high" level ($7,500 and over) to support hospital and medical care, unemployment benefits, help for the poor, and public works. Such information could be useful to a legislator or senior official who had doubts about popular reactions to different kinds of policy regarding the distribution of tax revenues. On the whole, this research raises some questions about the assumption that citizens are guided by a nice calculus of individual benefits in making such choices. It may be that the spread between "high" and "low" income categories was not great enough to provide a real test of the conventional belief that upper-income groups resist taxes more than their less affluent fellow-citizens.

The complexity of budget decision-making is again suggested by the

[6] A popular version of this view is J. K. Galbraith, *The Affluent Society* (Boston: Houghton Mifflin Co., 1958); for a rebuttal of this, see H. C. Wallich, "Public v. Private: Could Galbraith be Wrong?" in E. S. Phelps (ed.), *Private Wants and Public Needs* (New York: W. W. Norton, Inc., 1965), pp. 42–54.

[7] Eva Mueller, "Public Attitudes Toward Fiscal Programs," in R. Golembiewski (ed.), *Public Budgeting and Finance* (Itasca, Ill.: Peacock Publishers, 1968), pp. 161–63.

extent to which uncontrollable factors, such as world rises in food prices, impinge upon domestic fiscal calculations and programs. Greater inter-locking with and sensitivity to international economic organization and monetary fluctuations similarly affect the capacity of American budget officials to plan rationally.

Meanwhile, certain domestic political forces and conditions directly affect the budgetary process. One is the widespread assumption that the typical legislator (if such exists) is parochial, self-centered, and profligate with the taxpayers' money. To make any judgment about such claims, one might well begin with a consideration of the legislator's role and the constraints under which he operates. It may be wrong to conclude that legislators are rarely economy-minded; certainly, they often face an occu-pational dilemma: the simultaneous demands of their own constituents for economy—for everyone else—and for special expenditures for their own local projects.

As congressmen delight in pointing out, the Constitution gives them the major role in fiscal matters. Money bills must originate there, tax bills must be approved by them, and they alone can authorize the borrow-ing and the spending of money. In theory at least, the only limitation upon Congress' authorization power is that the period of military appro-priations can be for no more than two years. How Congress is equipped to handle these functions regarding the annual budget is the subject of this chapter. We have already suggested that congressional review of the huge executive budget is a superhuman task, and this problem will be touched upon here. We shall see that one of the main reasons for incomplete and sporadic legislative review is the diffusion of financial responsibility within Congress and we shall also find that the authoriza-tion phase of budget making is intensely political and that the authoriza-tion power is a means of implementing legislative values about particular programs.

THE LEGISLATIVE MIND

In considering the President's budget, legislators are buffeted by two opposing forces, one a highly articulate desire for economy and efficiency, the other the pressure of special interests for subsidies. A member of the House Appropriations Committee once stated that for "every member of Congress there are scores of pressure groups and lobbyists, including the government agencies, with conflicting objectives, eager to make a congressman's life easier by making his decisions for him." There is little question that some legislators genuinely desire to limit expenditures. On the other hand, legislators are keenly sensitive to appropriations for their own districts. Thus, if the Navy Department proposes to shut down an air base or a shipyard in his district, the local statesman is immediately bombarded by telegrams, letters, special delegations, and phone calls. His success as a congressman may be largely judged by whether he is able to keep the shipyard open. If the secular increase in governmental spending is an acceptable index, it seems that economy usually has a lower priority than political survival.[8]

In order to understand the legislative phase of budgeting, we must know something about the behavior and sentiments of legislators. They have certain reactions which, within limits, are predictable. In other words, a fairly consistent legislative belief system exists. This system is partly vocational in nature; that is, it is molded and conditioned by the legislative environment. The legislator also reacts as he does because he is conditioned by American cultural influences. What are some of the components of this belief system?

Parochialism

Among the most powerful legislative characteristics is parochialism; if the legislator is to stay in office, he must be something of a ward heeler. Let a professor write a book on political theory in which he decries the influence of sectionalism and advocates national, as against local, interests. Then let him be elected to Congress and sit on an appropriations subcommittee which threatens to cut out a half-million dollars for dredging the harbor in his home town. Will he tell the Chamber of Commerce that it is unethical for him to take a personal interest in the matter? Another conditioning factor is the local pressure group. If the legislator is from a seaport fishing constituency and the fishing fleet is idle and cannery workers are unemployed, will he vote against a tariff on fish imports? Suppose he is a Ph.D., with a major in economics and a minor in political science. He may have been conditioned to believe that international trade barriers are bad; yet his choice will often be to vote for the tariff on fish or to return to the classroom, a harsh fate indeed.

In addition, the American legislator is an individualist under little

---

[8] For differences between the attitudes and behavior of legislators, see Presthus, *Elites in the Policy Process* (New York: Cambridge University Press, 1974), Chap. 11.

party discipline; with his sources of power based locally, he must gain seniority if he is to become influential, yet he cannot very easily be sanctioned for failure to follow his party leaders. (Senior members of the committees on which he serves can, of course, bring both positive and negative sanctions to bear, often in the form of appropriations for pork-barrel projects in his home constituency.) On the whole, however, he enjoys considerable autonomy, which political scientists—who sometimes tend to have an uncritical admiration for the parliamentary system —have long regretted. They believe that more responsibility would be achieved by a genuine two-party system.[9] During much of recent history, they point out, the major committees in the federal system have been chaired by conservative Democrats from one-party states in the South who often openly opposed presidential policies, especially in the area of civil rights. This situation is often contrasted unfavorably with the Canadian or British system where individual MP's are virtually impotent because of rigorous party discipline and the sanctions that the party leaders can bring against MP's who deviate.[10]

Ambivalence Toward the Executive Branch

Another facet of the legislative mind is a somewhat critical attitude toward chief executives and their permanent aides in the bureaucracy. (At the same time, there is a great deal of respect shown for the *office* of the chief executive since it represents the most powerful and prestigeful role in the system.) Legislators want and need recognition and praise for their achievements, yet most of the publicity and credit in the mass media flow toward the chief executive. Since they tend to possess more than the average share of ego, legislators find this situation frustrating; they are not content to assume a passive role. Legislatures, moreover, tend to resemble a private club and an in-group, the ties of which cut across party lines. They may quarrel among themselves but they take collective offense at criticisms of the institution itself. This defensive ethos has been exacerbated recently by the popular impression of congressional subservience to the president, symbolized perhaps by the manner in which President Nixon impounded congressionally

---

[9] See, for example, Committee on Political Parties of the American Political Science Association, *Toward a More Responsible Two-Party System* (Washington, D. C., 1951); James M. Burns, *The Deadlock of Democracy* (Englewood Cliffs, N. J.: Prentice-Hall, Inc., 1963).

[10] For evidence regarding some limitations of the parliamentary system, see R. Presthus, *Elite Accommodation in Canadian Politics* (New York: Cambridge University Press, 1973).

approved funds, an issue to be covered in more detail later. This sensitivity is heightened when such highly emotional and politically sensitive issues as the Watergate Affair are current in the minds of legislators and the public.

Perhaps another pervasive trait of the legislative mind is its intuitive mistrust of bureaucrats and experts. This attitude toward bureaucrats flows partly from the fact that they are often allied with the executive branch and are therefore considered disciples of the chief executive. But bureaucrats are also to be classed with experts, and Americans have always been reluctant to give experts governmental power. Our institutions are based in part upon an assumption that there is a superior lay wisdom which should supersede expertise in the determination of public policy. Also present is Jacksonian egalitarianism. Congressmen resist the idea that their own lack of special knowledge vitiates their ability to make reasonable evaluations of complex programs. This attitude ties in with an ego drive which makes the legislator want to run things instead of merely engaging in passive deliberation or review, as often demanded by the authorization process, the complexities of modern government, and presidential initiative in public policy.

Political Values vs. Expertise

What has this discussion of legislative values to do with budgeting? Observers believe that legislative parochialism can be modified by internal reorganization of the legislature. All the reforms advocated in past years by the Hoover Commissions, the National Planning Association, and other reform-oriented groups had some bearing on the appropriation process. The first Hoover report recommended performance budgeting as a means of simplifying the appropriation process. The National Planning Association report stated, "Congress should place more emphasis on major policy and less emphasis on detail." The Legislative Reorganization Act of 1946 actually took steps to put some of these recommendations into practice. Political scientists urged reorganization of Congress in order to strengthen party responsibility and insure that committee chairmen, who exercise decisive influence over committee affairs, are in sympathy with the president's programs.[11]

[11] For authoritative studies of committees and the chairman's role, see Richard Bolling, *Power in the House* (New York: Dutton, 1972); John Manley, *The Politics of Finance: The House Ways and Means Committee* (Boston: Little, Brown, 1970); Richard Fenno, *The Power of the Purse: Appropriation Politics in Congress* (Boston: Little, Brown & Co., 1966).

Some of these recommendations have been accepted by Congress, only to be honored in the breach. Thus the Legislative Reorganization Act (1946) required that House and Senate revenue and appropriations committees meet, analyze the President's recommendations, and prepare a report for the whole Congress which would set ceilings "fixing the maximum amount to be appropriated in each year." This scheme was tried for one year and then abandoned, largely because the time schedule and the uncertainty of world events would not permit accurate prediction. The single-package appropriation bill was also tried for one year and allowed to lapse. It provided for substituting one omnibus appropriation bill for the dozen or so normally passed. In the year in which this was tried, appropriations were not authorized until August 4, some time after the beginning of the budget year. The single package put too great a burden on a few key legislators.

POLICY INFLUENCE OR MANAGERIAL CONTROL?

The usual conclusion drawn is that the mere enactment of reform measures will not alter behavioral patterns. Nevertheless, despite executive initiative and its own inadequacies, Congress can play an integral role in national fiscal policy-making, as suggested by the Revenue Sharing Act of 1971. Congressmen were ambivalent about the policy,[12] but they finally accepted it. Even though its impact is probably more symbolic than substantive (the annual estimated appropriation for the first year—1973—was only 3 billion, the legislation illustrates a policy innovation aimed at strengthening the role of local–state governments in the federal system. Earlier assumptions included the belief that close federal scrutiny of such grants-in-aid was required to insure probity and effectiveness in their use. Such assumptions persist, but congressional approval indicates that they have been substantially undercut. The legislation was passed only after intense lobbying by such groups as the Council of State Governments, the National Governors' Conference, the U.S. Con-

[12] Two statements by legislators suggest the basis for such reservations: "I think Congress can earmark money for these purposes more responsibly than the local politicians who would control these funds, men who are under heavy and direct pressure from special local interests." Again, "It is difficult for me to believe that state and local officials entrusted with the task of distributing tax dollars raised at the federal level could be as scrupulous as a federal official who has the prime responsibility for raising as well as spending that tax dollar." For evidence, however, that federal and state political elites are under roughly *equal* "heavy and direct pressure" from interest groups, see Presthus, *Elites in the Policy Process, op. cit.*, Chaps. 7 and 8.

ference of Mayors, and the National Legislative Conference. Equally important was the financial crisis among state and local governments (resting in good part upon citizen resistance to any further escalation of real property taxes).

Congressional ambivalence is further evident in the initial five-year limitation on the program, which will presumably allow its demise if such seems advisable. Over the prescribed period, some $30 billion will be allocated to about 38,000 jurisdictions, among which 50 states and 50 cities will receive two-thirds of the total. About two-thirds is allocated to cities, with the remainder to state governments. Very few federal controls over spending are prescribed, but they include a 2.5 billion ceiling on social service (i.e., welfare) programs during the five-year period, as well as periodic reports and surveillance by a team of federal auditors who will carry out periodic assessments on a sampling basis.[13]

Despite such examples of congressional sharing in fiscal policy determination, most reforms provide that legislatures should avoid considerations involving details and focus upon matters of broad policy. Given the size and scope of federal programs, this is probably accepting the inevitable. One need read only a few accounts of budget hearings to conclude that legislators are unable to exercise any control over specific aspects of agency programs. Their frustration at this condition is equally evident in the exchanges, some of which will be related in the chapter concerning legislative control of expenditures.

For these reasons, the principal theory underlying such innovations as performance budgeting is that legislators should be told that "it costs $1.19 per unit to provide police patrols; one hundred thousand units would cost x dollars, and two hundred thousand so much additional." They could then determine the answer to a policy question: What level of law enforcement should be introduced. Details such as the cost of gas, guns, handcuffs, patrol cars, and printing would be left to budget officials. The trouble is that the average legislator wants to know the details. In the past members of Congress have not always agreed with the concept that their proper role is one of deliberation on large policy issues. They have wanted a hand in actually running things. Despite this, legislators are still confronted with the problem of lack of details and expertise, both of which act as constraints upon their capacity to exercise a managerial role. As two observers put it:

Both the Senate and the House have committees on appropriations

[13] For a review of this program, see the special issue of *State Government*, Vol. 46 (Winter, 1973).

and subcommittees on particular areas of spending. One might expect expertise and partisan rationalizers to have developed in these committees. But a reading of the hearings . . . makes it clear that the committees themselves do very little analysis. They rely on the testimony of expert witnesses, frequently drawn from the operational agencies. Sometimes a legislator will enter into the record a critical newspaper article or letter from a constituent and ask the agency to respond.[14]

It is significant that the second Hoover Commission emphasized two themes: the need for better accounting and the "restoration of Congressional control of the purse." They proposed various means for increasing administrative accountability to Congress and the President, often of a technical, accounting nature, but understandable to most laymen. One of their main aims was to increase the *information* available to the legislator, to better enable him to evaluate administrative programs. On the second point, increasing congressional control of the purse, the Commission made the following proposals:

1. Continuing efforts to change from an object to a performance type of budget
2. Revamping the structure of the budget document and appropriation acts so as to reflect expenditures (instead of obligations) by programs
3. The use of accrual accounting which would reflect the resources available at the beginning of the year; goods and services received; the use of resources in relation to work performed; and liabilities at the end of the year
4. The adoption of cost or "business" type of accounting, whenever applicable.

In recent years, although some progress has been made toward implementing such proposals, Congress often continues to find itself lacking the procedures and information that would allow it to control effectively the expenditures and budget allocations for which it is responsible. Accordingly, reform measures continue to be suggested and, in some cases, implemented.[15] In examining the authorization and appropriations procedures in the following pages, we shall mention several of these reforms, proposed or achieved, which may aid Congress in its consideration of the budget.

[14] L. Merewitz and S. Sosnick, *The Budget's New Clothes* (Chicago: Markham, 1971), p. 77.

[15] See, for example, *Hearings*, Subcommittee on Budgeting, Management, and Expenditures, Committee on Government Operations, U. S. Senate, April 2, 9, 11, and 12, 1973 (Washington, D. C.: U. S. Government Printing Office, 1973).

THE AUTHORIZATION PROCESS

Until very recently, the most striking thing about the budget authorization phase has been that there was no *over-all* review of the budget by any committee or by either of the houses.[16] There was no formal debate in Congress on the whole budget nor was there joint consideration by the powerful appropriations and revenue committees. This condition reflected the dispersion of authority among several committees and subcommittees, which were usually organized on the basis of substantive interest and expertise. In each house there was a Ways and Means Committee (called Finance Committee in the Senate) responsible for finding the sources of revenue; an Appropriations Committee which reviewed and recommended appropriations; a Committee on Government Operations with authority to oversee executive management practices; a Joint Committee on Reduction of Nonessential Expenditures (which, parenthetically, must have been among the most frustrated of legislative agencies, since it has worked hard over the years to promote economy and efficiency without much headway); a Joint Committee on the Economic Report, whose work was outlined in the last chapter; and a Joint Committee on Internal Revenue Taxation.[17]

Although these structures remain basically intact (other than the Joint Committee on the Economic Report which has been incorporated in the Joint Economic Committee), several reforms have been initiated to provide Congress with a forum for a general overview of the budget. For example, the Legislative Reorganization Act of 1970 provided that the Appropriations Committees of the two Houses "shall hold hearings, early in each session on the budget as a whole, the transcripts of such hearings to be transmitted to every Member of the House." [18]

A more fundamental change, however, has been proposed in recent months to counter the fragmentation of the congressional budget process caused by the specialization and prolificacy of subcommittees involved in the appropriations process. A House–Senate study group has recommended several changes to eliminate the system whereby each of the thirteen annual appropriations bills is considered in a vacuum by subcommittees, with little or no attention paid to the overall appropriations

---

[16] Thus a Congressman who wanted to appraise the entire budget had to read some 25,000 pages of subcommittee hearings. See Arthur Smithies, *The Budgetary Process in the United States* (New York: McGraw-Hill Book Co., Inc., 1955), p. 131.

[17] *Ibid.*, pp. 131–33.

[18] House Committee on Rules, *Summary of H.R. 17654: The Legislative Reorganization Act of 1970* (Washington, D. C.: U. S. Government Printing Office, 1970).

total.[19] The most important reform suggested involves the vesting of the prime responsibility to set and enforce appropriations and expenditure ceilings and to allocate priorities within them in a single budget committee in both legislative chambers. The two respective committees would be comprised of members from the Appropriations Committees, the House Ways and Means or the Senate Finance Committee, and from other legislative committees. Submissions from all congressional committees or sub-committees having budget-making authority would be reviewed in the proposed budget committees in order to coordinate the appropriations process and establish clearer priorities and ceilings for expenditures. Sub-committee recommendations would no longer receive automatic approval in deference to their specialization; but a more centralized management function would be created in an attempt to eliminate parochialism and waste in the budget process and reassert congressional authority over expenditure patterns.

The Appropriations Committee

In the present system, major concern lies with the appropriations committees and their various subcommittees, each of which handles a particular aspect of the federal program such as Army, Air Force, or Agriculture. Although the Constitution provides that revenue bills must originate in the House, appropriations as well as revenue measures have also come to originate there. A kind of rough division of labor exists between the House and Senate committees, in which the former initiates such measures and the latter reviews them.

A brief description of the House Appropriations Committee and its work may be useful at this point. The Committee has fifty members, divided into several subcommittees including from three to six members each. The chairman, who serves ex officio on all subcommittees, also schedules the hearings for the subcommittees and, not surprisingly, exerts a powerful influence on them. Thirteen or fourteen appropriations bills are considered each year, and each subcommittee is responsible for reviewing one or two of them. Since members remain on the committees indefinitely, they build up considerable experience and knowledge in their respective program areas. The subcommittee hearings are *not* open to the public and are restricted to members of the government. The

[19] *Congressional Quarterly Weekly Report*, Vol. 31 (April 28, 1973), p. 1013. The recommendations of this report were introduced as a bill (H.R. 7130, S1641) in April, 1973.

work of the subcommittee is usually definitive, since the Appropriations Committee accepts its decision as binding.

Another relevant facet of the authorization process is that the departments and agencies sometimes present their own budgets to the committees without any participation by the White House Office of Management and Budget. Moreover, relations between Congress and the OMB, or the Bureau of the Budget before it, have been somewhat strained in recent years. Even a brief view of the hearings suggests that Congress has serious misgivings about their practice of apportioning money to the departments after it has been appropriated by Congress. As a House Appropriations Subcommittee member remarked:

> *Mr. Flood:* I see the language "The general apportionment was enacted on July 2; the Bureau of Budget apportionments were made on August 1." What does that mean? . . .
>
> *Mr. King:* I would like to explain what happens to July 2. We initiate our apportionments . . . for the Bureau of the Budget.
>
> *Mr. Flood:* Describe that for us. You pick up your briefcases and you take General Lawton (Director of Army Budget) and everybody down, and you go to the Bureau of the Budget with your hat in hand. Why?
>
> *Mr. King:* We have to rejustify to the Bureau of the Budget the requirement for the moneys appropriated on July 2.
>
> *Mr. Flood:* Do you hear that, Mr. Chairman? Now after Congress has enacted constitutionally, the President has signed the law, the Army must now get out its retinue of chauffeurs, automobiles, and the parade goes to the Bureau of the Budget. They go to the Taj Mahal where . . . they must rejustify what they have just done with the legislative branch of the Government.[20]

Often, it seems, legislators regard an office such as the OMB as a competitor that strengthens the President's part in budgetary preparation and control. This appreciation is illustrated further by the following exchange between the Director of OMB and the chairman of another subcommittee:

> *Senator Metcalf:* Now, of course, you and I are concerned with the allocation of various priorities so far as taxing the people of the United States and distributing it to the various existing governmental agencies, and that is what the Office of Management and Budget does. It determined some priorities and has, as I say, awesome responsibilities as to where our money is going to be allocated. You

---

[20] Subcommittee of the Committee on Appropriations, 85th Cong., 1st sess., *Hearings,* "Department of the Air Force, Appropriations for 1958" (Washington, D. C.: Government Printing Office, 1957), pp. 50–51.

are going to determine whether we are going to have education or bondage.

Mr. Weinberger: No, sir; we are determining what is the best recommendation for us to make to the President for him to submit as his proposal to Congress. The President cannot allocate any funds that have not been, as you know, appropriated by the Congress. He can—

Senator Metcalf: No, but you make determinations as to where the allocation of our various resources are going to be.

Mr. Weinberger: No, sir.

Senator Metcalf: You make recommendations as to whether or not we are going to buy a jet fighter.

Mr. Weinberger: No, sir; we make recommendations to the President for his proposal to the Congress.

Senator Metcalf: Yes.

Mr. Weinberger: And, there are some who regret that the President can't simply go out and buy a jet fighter when he feels it is needed.

Senator Metcalf: Because Congress does not appropriate the money.

Mr. Weinberger: His budget submission is simply a proposal to the Congress . . .

Senator Metcalf: Let's not get off the subject. Aren't we both agreed that there is a great deal of difference between the agencies, the independent agencies, that we are talking about and the agencies that are represented in the President's cabinet, and in other governmental organizations?

Mr. Weinberger: Not with respect to their budgets, I wouldn't agree, Mr. Chairman. I don't think there is any significant difference at all.

Senator Metcalf: I guess you and I are never going to come to an agreement.[21]

Subcommittee Hearings

Budget hearings before the subcommittees usually begin with a prepared statement by the department head outlining his program, its major assumptions, the money needed to carry it out, and the reasons for significant changes from the previous year. Once this has been done, the department head will often call upon his financial aides to present specific parts of the proposed budget. These men often know the subcommittee members well, and their introductory remarks may refer to their pleasure at appearing before the subcommittee again. The subcommittee's work and assistance is usually acknowledged by such officials, and often their compliments are returned by the subcommittee members who commend them on the detailed and comprehensive information given to the com-

[21] *Hearings* before a Subcommittee on Inter-governmental Relations of the Committee on Government Operations of the U. S. Senate, May 17, 1972, Washington, D.C.: U.S. Government Printing Office, 1972.

mittee. Such officials, in sum, combine technical skill with experience and political acumen.

It is generally agreed that, once the prepared statement is read by the department head, the hearings become highly random and the questioning may lead anywhere. As Arthur Smithies remarks, "Each subcommittee member has the right to question each department witness, and the questioning frequently fluctuates violently from basic policy issues to the most trivial detail." [22] Although legislators are helped by their continuing service on a given committee, it is extremely difficult for them to get a rounded view of the whole budget. Only rarely do they raise questions about the size and rationality of the whole budget; and such questions occur most frequently in the Senate, where, for example, Senator Paul Douglas from time to time questioned the defense budget.[23] That things change less than social scientists often assume is suggested by the fact that a quarter-century later, Senator William Proxmire, chairman of the Subcommittee on Economy in Government, was expressing similar judgments. The problem, however, extends to other substantive areas as well. Apparently the failure to debate the budget as a whole on the floor of Congress can lead to "frustration and cynicism on the part of members of Congress who are not directly involved in the appropriation process." [24]

Understandably, the subcommittees take a specialized view of their authorization role; they are not inclined to accept reductions in order that some other program element in the budget can receive more money. Thus they resist the coordinating efforts of the OMB and the President. The legislators become members of committees on the basis of their experience, interest, and the dominant economic character of the region they represent. It is well-known, for example, that members of the agricultural committees are from the major agricultural states. This condition, plus the difficulty of gaining any insight into the budget as a whole, results in a piecemeal approach to authorization on the part of Congress. Although there is a subcommittee on Full Defense which considers the military budget *en bloc*, there are also subcommittees for the three services, each of which has its advocates. The following comment of the Chairman of the House subcommittee on Army appropriations suggests the affinity between the members and their related service:

[22] *The Budgetary Process in the United States, op. cit.,* p. 133.

[23] For a summary of Douglas' experiences in this context, see his *Economy in the National Government* (Chicago: University of Chicago Press, 1952).

[24] Smithies, *The Budgetary Process in the United States, op. cit.,* p. 135.

> *Mr. Sikes:* We recognize the fact that we have a very serious responsi-
> bility this year in that there is a general demand for a more search-
> ing analysis of all budget requests. However, there is a belief that
> the Army has been cut more substantially in previous budgets than
> have other branches of the Service. We recognize the fact, too, that
> the Army has a very important job to do in the national defense . . .
> we must be careful that we do not cripple its effectiveness.[25]

Frequently, the discussion in defense-oriented appropriation subcommittees turns away from specific budgetary details and embraces more
abstract questions of American defense posture. On these occasions,
there is often animated verbal sparring between committee members and
representatives of the Defense Department:

> *Chairman Ellender:* Are you guessing that we are going to have a land
> war?
> *Admiral Moorer:* No, sir, I am not guessing anything.
> *Chairman Ellender:* I presume you picture Europe as the battlefield in
> the event we do have a land war?
> *Admiral Moorer:* I am dealing with capabilities, sir.
> *Chairman Ellender:* Is it the capability of the Soviet submarines to at-
> tack our fleet and our freighters when they are carrying supplies to
> our allies in Western Europe?
> *Admiral Moorer:* They would attack our ships in any ocean, including
> those ships coming to the United States with raw materials.
> *Chairman Ellender:* But your primary reason for saying what you have
> just stated is that you anticipate a conventional land war?
> *Admiral Moorer:* I do not; no, sir. That is not what I am saying. I want
> to emphasize that any war with the Soviet could not be fought in
> isolation between the United States and the U.S.S.R.
> *Defense Secretary Laird:* We are not trying to fight wars; we are trying
> to prevent wars . . .[26]

After the various subcommittees have reviewed the requests, they
prepare recommendations and a report covering the rationale for their
actions. These documents are then sent on to the appropriations committees of the House and Senate, where they are rarely considered in
detail. The subcommittees' decisions are binding in most cases; this
outcome is the result of necessity, tradition, and the pressure of time.
The consideration of the President's budget on the floor of Congress is
perfunctory, and the result is usually authorization of a budget figure very
close to that recommended initially by him. The bill finally goes on to

---

[25] *Hearings*, "Department of the Army Appropriations for 1958," *op. cit.*, p. 1.
[26] *Hearings* before a Subcommittee on Appropriations of the U. S. Senate, November 1, 1972, Washington, D. C.: U. S. Government Printing Office, 1972.

the President who, until the most recent years of the Nixon Administration, has rarely vetoed an appropriation bill.[27]

One result of this fragmentary procedure is that Congress rarely cuts the President's budget; even a 5 percent cut is the exception rather than the rule.[28] Indeed, the more frequent occurrence during the last years of Richard Nixon's tenure in office involved the inverse process; the President had cut congressionally approved appropriations in the expressed hope of reducing inflationary pressures on the economy.[29]

The House, which gets the appropriations bills first, has often made substantial cuts, but these are usually restored by the Senate, and the ensuing conference committee meeting between the two houses usually compromises on a figure very close to the President's original request. Thus, "At the appropriation stage, it is fair to state that the President is in a stronger position than the committees. This strength results in part from the fact that the committees are handicapped by lack of informaion. Neither the President's budget nor the extensive hearings provide them with a reasonable basis for differing from the President on major terms." [30]

IMPROVING CONGRESSIONAL REVIEW

This analysis indicates that legislative authorization is based to some extent on incomplete information reflecting the size and complexity of the budget, and is constrained by structural fragmentation of the authorization–appropriation mechanism of Congress itself. We noted earlier several suggestions to ease the dysfunctionalities of an uncoordinated subcommittee system in the budget process. A more basic informational problem was also mentioned—the difficulties that confront a legislator in examining great quantities of different budgetary information. Some attention has been paid recently to this second problem.

The Legislative Reorganization Act of 1970 called for rationalization and standardization of the presentation and processing of budget information.

[27] However, Franklin D. Roosevelt, when governor of New York, once vetoed an entire appropriation bill of $52,000,000, which in 1929 was a substantial sum. See James M. Burns, *Roosevelt: The Lion and the Fox* (New York: Harcourt Brace Jovanovich, Inc., 1956).

[28] Smithies, *The Budgetary Process in the United States, op. cit.,* p. 140.

[29] See the discussion of presidential impoundment of allocated funds in the following chapter.

[30] Smithies, *op. cit.,* pp. 140–41; see also pp. 163–67, for a summary of defects in both congressional and presidential budgetary activities.

The Secretary of the Treasury and the Director of the Office of Management and Budget, in cooperation with the Comptroller General of the United States, shall develop, establish, and maintain, insofar as practicable, a standardized information and data processing system for budgetary and fiscal data.[31]

Supplementing this requirement, the Act also makes several key recommendations to provide the legislator with more accurate budget information and assistance in interpreting budget requests. Among these provisions are the following:

1. The President is required to inform Congress in the annual budget of the amounts proposed for appropriation and expenditure in the ensuing fiscal year, and the estimated amounts for each of the ensuing four fiscal years on each of his proposals creating new programs or changing existing programs.
2. The President is required to submit a supplemental budget summary no later than June 1 reflecting for the ensuing fiscal year
   (a) all substantial alterations in or reappraisals of estimates of expenditures and receipts
   (b) all substantial obligations imposed on the Budget after its transmittal to Congress
   (c) current information relative to the estimated condition of the Treasury at the end of the ensuing fiscal year if the financial proposals contained in the Budget are adopted
3. The President is required to submit on or before June 1 summaries of estimated expenditures for four fiscal years following the fiscal year for which the Budget was transmitted in January.[32]

The implementation of these requirements has improved the situation of the legislator vis-à-vis the aggregation of budgetary data but it still remains extremely difficult for any legislator to comprehend the total impact of budget requests.

Another significant reform made in recent years concerns the introduction of a comprehensive unified budget. Following the recommendations of the President's Commission on Budget Concepts (1967), the 1969 budget was presented for the first time as a single, coordinated document. Prior to this event budgets had often come to Congress simultaneously in two or three different forms, each of which employed different terminology and pertained to a different scope of government

---

[31] *Legislative Reorganization Act of 1970* (84 Stat. 1140) section 201.

[32] Sections 221 a, b, and c as cited in *A Summary of the Major Provisions of the Legislative Reorganization Act of 1970,* prepared for the Senate Committee on Government Operations, Washington, D. C.: U. S. Government Printing Office, October, 1970, p. 8.

operations.[33] The new unified budget incorporated these earlier types of budget statements into one statement employing, for the most part, standardized accrual methodology. It fulfilled the Commission's hope that the budget should be presented as

> a broad financial plan, which includes appropriations, receipts, expenditures and lending transactions, the means of financing a budget deficit (or the use of a budget surplus), and information about the borrowing and loan programs of the government and its agencies.[34]

Several additional proposals on reform of the congressional budget process should be noted. Pointing out the continuing inability of Congress to pass appropriation bills before the beginning of the fiscal year to which they pertain, with resulting problems of retroactive funding, and recognizing the extreme constraints of time that confront legislators and sometimes prevent thorough consideration of budgetary measures (especially in the rush of the final days of a session), some observers have called for a complete reform of the congressional calendar. Beginning by changing the fiscal year so that it corresponds to the calendar year, they propose that the annual congressional session be divided into two separate periods: the first, extending from January until summer recess, to deal primarily with legislation, and the second, from September through December, to consider fiscal matters to come into force the following January with the commencement of the new fiscal year.[35]

Implementation of such a proposal presents several logistical problems, the most important of which is perhaps the question of fiscal coordination with state and local jurisdictions. Presently, all but three of the state governments operate with their fiscal years commencing on June 30 or July 1. Accordingly, change in the federal fiscal year without cor-

---

[33] The three types of budget statements most often used were:
  1) an "administrative budget" which did not include a large segment of government operations, notably the trust funds, and which stated expenditures on a checks-issued basis.
  2) a "consolidated cash budget" which included the trust funds and stated expenditures on a checks-paid basis.
  3) a "national income accounts budget" which included all government operations except loan transactions but stated expenditures on a mixed basis of accrual accounting and checks-issued. Ellsworth H. Morse, Jr., "Report of the President's Commission on Budget Concepts in Retrospect," *Public Administration Review*, Vol. 31 (July/August, 1971), pp. 443–50.

[34] *Ibid.*, p. 445.

[35] For further details and discussion, see Joint Committee on Congressional Operations, *Hearings*, June 14, 1971.

responding changes in those of the states could lead to considerable confusion, especially with respect to federal grants to state governments and revenue-sharing agreements; certainly the prospects for rapid and facile transformation of the fiscal calendars of such a large number of jurisdictions seem somewhat remote. If, however, such a change can be successfully accomplished and if the federal legislative chambers establish adequate procedural rules to insure that fiscal measures receive sufficient consideration before the beginning of the transformed fiscal year, many of the current congressional problems of lag and confusion in the budgetary cycle may be resolved.

Another proposal that warrants brief mention concerns reform of the relation between the authorization process and the appropriation process. Some critics have noted that a chief cause of delay in congressional analysis of the budget has been the recent tendency toward greater complexity in the authorization phase. Rather than merely representing approval of programs and stipulation of their general guidelines, authorizations have also come to contain specific references to expenditure ceilings, program operation, and budgetary details, matters which often involve considerable resources in time and man-hours. Essentially this process is repeated in detail at the appropriations stage. The question arises, therefore, whether there is need for such detailed examination at *both* the authorization and appropriation stage. In this respect, the OMB has suggested several basic changes:

> We therefore suggest that Congress make specific efforts—a "campaign," if you will—to synchronize the timing of the authorization process more closely with the need for a timely appropriation process. Specically, we would suggest that:
>
> All authorizations, with the possible exception of public works, be removed from the annual cycle and be made effective for longer periods of time, at least 2 years and preferably 5 years, or an indefinite period.
>
> A greater portion of the authorizing legislation be stated in program terms instead of in dollar amounts, leaving the amount of dollars to be determined by the Congress when it acts on the appropriations.
>
> All authorizing legislation which expires in any one calendar year be received and renewals enacted (if Congress decides that there should be renewals) at the session of the year preceding. In other words, renewals and extensions would be enacted at the 1972 session for the legislation which expires in calendar 1973.
>
> Where authorization renewals are not acted upon in a timely manner, either affirmatively or negatively, the rules of Congress be amended to make it possible for appropriations to be considered, and a simple 1-year

extension of the authorizing legislation to be accomplished, if necessary, in an appropriation bill.[36]

At this point, most of these proposals have been embodied in enabling legislation (e.g., Senate Bills 40, 565, 846, 905, 1030, and 1213), indicating that changing attitudes regarding congressional budget procedures (i.e., the gradual process of seeking greater rationality) are now being institutionalized. Huge federal deficits, an unprecedented unfavorable balance of payments, attending inflation—all accompanied by economic recession—have provided the major impetus for such changes.

[36] George P. Schultz, Director of the Office of Management and Budget, *Hearings*, Joint Committee on Congressional Operations, June 14, 1971. See also, Stephen Horn, *Unused Power: The Work of the Senate Committee on Appropriations* (Washington, D. C.: Brookings, 1970), Chap. 7.

17

The Budgetary Process: Execution and Control

We now turn to the final phase of budgeting: execution and control. On the one hand, this phase can be defined negatively as the process whereby the chief executive and the legislature keep the departments honest. On the other hand, it can be regarded as the stage in which the money needed to carry out programs is made available in the most positive and flexible way possible. Both aspects will be considered here because both can be seen at work in most agencies. One should also note at the outset that execution is not a discrete phase in the budget process but is closely interwoven with both the preparation and authorization phases, and particularly with the latter, which often includes measures attempting to control expenditures. Execution and control are carried out at three fairly distinct levels—chief executive, legislative, and departmental. Each is considered separately, after a review of the major objectives of execution.

LIMITS ON BUDGETARY CONTROL

It is important at the outset to emphasize the sharply limited parameters of control available at the federal level to Congress and the President. The main reason is that existing and ongoing commitments assume so large a share of the national budget. As Elmer B. Staats, the Comptroller General says, "Nearly *three-quarters* of the President's budget is beyond his control as it is fixed by previous legislation; i.e., earlier decisions which cause money to be spent for veterans' pensions, Medicare, farm subsidies, and urban renewal, or to pay for completion of defense contracts." [1] The Tax Foundation concludes similarly: "It is certainly true that a large and growing portion of budget outlays is beyond annual control through regular budget processes, barring major changes in statutory requirements." [2]

A similar situation exists at state and local levels where governmental expenditures have been rising at an even faster rate than in the federal system. Since the end of World War II, such expenditures have increased 12 times, compared with a federal rise of about 4 times. [3] The point is that despite the expressed aims of legislators for economy and improved fiscal and auditing procedures, control of governmental budgets in its largest sense seems virtually impossible to achieve. As we saw earlier, the generalized acceptance of the multiple claims of articulate interest groups and the derivative benefits accruing to legislators, the Presidency, and the bureaucracy, as well as the attending lack of central planning and evaluation of such claims tend to result in governmental hypertension. [4] Any analysis of budgetary control must be understood in this large and essentially political context. As observers conclude, regarding the Defense budget,

> The defense budget, while susceptible to rational analysis, remains a matter of political resolution. Choices of this order can be made in only one place: the political arena. There the relative importance of values can be decided by the relative power brought to bear on their behalf. There the distribution of power can decide matters that the distribution of fact and insight cannot. [5]

The subject matter of this chapter—execution and control—has been in transition in recent years. Indeed, it has become a dynamic area

---

[1] "A Perspective on Intergovernmental Fiscal Relations," *State Government*, Vol. 46 (Winter, 1973), p. 25, italics added.

[2] *The Federal Budget for Fiscal Year 1973: Future Implications*, New York, 1972, p. 19.

[3] *Ibid.*

[4] The monumental weight of such imperatives is perhaps illustrated by the experience of Richard Nixon who assumed the Presidency determined to reverse the trend toward an overconcentration of power in Washington (see, for example, his letter to Speaker R. S. Smith of Kentucky, December 20, 1972, cited in *State Government, ibid.*, pp. 5–6) yet incurred the largest non-wartime deficits in federal history, amounting to $23 billion in 1971 and 1972 and rising to about $30 billion in 1973.

[5] Warner R. Schilling, P. Y. Hammond, G. H. Snyder, *Strategy, Politics and Defense Budgets* (New York: Columbia University Press, 1962), p. 15.

whose developments mirror at least three trends: the evolution of the comptroller's job; the adjustment of control operations to computer technology; and the transformation from line-item control to program control. The comptroller has had to "abandon the cozy isolation of the counting room and forget about his spread sheet and calculating toys." [6] In the Department of Defense he has become an assistant secretary with his hands in decision-making at the strategic policy level. [7] In the civilian departments, the comptroller function has also come increasingly to take on greater policy dimensions.

BUDGETARY EXECUTION

Because of such recent changes, it is difficult to write definitively about the control function. Changes continue to occur in such areas as the installation of accrual accounting and standardized classification of accounts. The decentralization of budget control to the agencies is an ongoing process and the application of computer technology to control mechanisms continues to alter and, in some cases, revolutionize the budget execution phase. Thus what is said here must be read with the understanding that the process of change begun in the mid-1960's has not yet completely ended nor is it likely to end entirely if the control and execution phase is to adapt itself to our evolving social and technological environment.

The Objectives of Execution

Most commentators believe that the execution stage should aim for a nice balance between legislative intent and administrative flexibility. From what we have seen, however, it seems that the budget in recent years has more often been an index of executive than legislative intent. Clearly, it has been the executive branch, spearheaded by such agencies as the Office of Management and Budget or the Budget Bureau before it, that has taken the initiative in the budget process, both at the preparation and execution stages. The legislature does continue to play a role in the defining of budget objectives and the delineation of guidelines and limits for governmental expenditures; yet, in many instances,

---

[6] *Highlights of Progress: Joint Financial Improvement Program, Fiscal Year, 1964* (Washington, D. C.: Government Printing Office, 1965), p. 20.

[7] See Charles J. Hitch, *Decision-making for Defense* (Berkeley: University of California Press, 1965). The comptroller in Defense, however, had some of his powers curtailed after Hitch left the federal service.

these functions appear to have been conducted more often in the spirit of an endorsement of executive initiatives than of critical evaluation or fiscal policy initiation by Congress in its own right.

This imbalance, however, seems to be changing. Congress has come to react strongly against the concentration of inordinate fiscal power in the executive branch, and, more specifically, has sought to reassert its rights in matters of expenditure allocation. Part of the reason for its slow reaction has been the fact that presidential hegemony in financial affairs has followed mainly from his traditionally accepted dominant role in foreign affairs. In recent months, Congress has, for the first time since the commencement of American involvement in Indo-China, voted decisively to cut off all funding to the executive branch for *military operations* in South-East Asia. Congress has objected vocally to presidential invocation of "pocket vetoes" and the use of impoundment procedures, of which we will have more to say later in this chapter. In sum, Congress now seeks a confrontation with the executive branch from which it hopes a better balance between legislative and executive roles in the budget process can be re-established.

The essential objective of execution is the observance of any financial limitations set down by the legislature. This objective falls within the "control" context mentioned earlier. Today the acceptance of deficiency appropriations is quite general, and indeed, they are regarded as necessary and proper. For quite a time it has been felt that deficiency appropriations "can strengthen rather than weaken Congressional control." [8] This is because, assuming that deficiencies were prohibited, regular appropriations would have to be more "liberal" than at present. The burden of proof is, moreover, shifted to the executive branch to show that it really needs a supplemental grant.[9] One less acceptable aspect of deficiencies, however, is their use to hide major increases in the President's initial budget.[10]

The final objective is maintaining flexibility so that the administration can meet the demands of change and emergency. As one observer says,

[8] Arthur Smithies, *The Budgetary Process in the United States* (New York: McGraw-Hill Book Co., Inc., 1955), p. 149.

[9] *Ibid.*

[10] In December 1966, for example, some of the luster of the Johnson Administration's much-bruited financial expertise was dulled by the announcement that the costs of the Vietnam war had been underestimated by some $10 billion. As Robert Maynard Hutchins said, "How did we get a budget of $140 billion? Only a couple of years ago the President was assuring us that expenditures would be kept under $100 billion. . . . How can an administration that boasts of a computerized, "cost-effective" Defense Department make a mistake of $10 billion in estimating the outlays required by a relatively small war?" (*Los Angeles Times*, December 19, 1966).

"The ability of a budget execution system to cope with these changes depends in large measure on the way in which budget authorizations are written by the legislature." [11] An exceptional but instructive example occurred during World War II when an appropriations measure included a provision that funds of any act of Congress were not to be used to pay the salaries of Messrs. Lovett, Watson, and Dodd, three FCC officials accused of subversive activities.[12] Efforts to limit deficiencies, to prescribe the number of personnel specialists per x number of federal employees, to fix the total amount of money that may be spent during any given fiscal year—all have been tried without much success. Apparently, if expenditures are to be kept within the limits initially authorized, it is the administrative branch that must do it.

THE PRESIDENT'S ROLE IN EXECUTION

Apportionment

A major instrument of presidential control is the right to apportion the rate at which appropriated funds are spent. In addition, if the need arises, the president can require the departments to withhold unneeded funds as reserves. The president assumed this power under the Budget and Accounting Act of 1921, and in 1950 the General Appropriation Act specifically confirmed his authority to do so. Perhaps the most dramatic use of this power in recent times occurred in 1947 when President Truman impounded an $875 million appropriation for the Air Force which provided for a 70-group air arm when he had recommended a 55-group arm.

"The apportionments may be considered the first stage of budget execution." [13] This process of setting up the schedule and the amounts to be spent for given programs is also sometimes called "funding" or "financial planning." The main distinction between this process and the initial budget is that funding involves the *operational* aspects of the budget; it "provide(s) an operating plan for the execution of the budget." [14] The initial budget is a statement of "requirements," while funding is concerned with "capabilities."

[11] Jesse Burkhead, *Government Budgeting* (New York: John Wiley, Inc., 1956), p. 345.

[12] *United States v. Lovett* (328 U. S. 303, 1946).

[13] Frederick C. Mosher, *Program Budgeting Theory and Practice* (Chicago: Public Administration Service, 1954), p. 185.

[14] *Ibid.*, p. 186.

An outline of apportionment in the Defense Department suggests its character and the president's influence over it, usually exercised through his political aides at the secretarial level. The president participates through the OMB, which holds hearings on the apportionment requests of the military departments. Representatives of the Secretary of Defense attend such hearings, after which "advices of apportionment" are issued by the OMB, "usually authorizing the obligation of funds for each of the first three quarters of the fiscal year within each appropriation." [15] Before these authorizations go to the three service heads, they are reviewed and certified by the Secretary of Defense, who can limit or reserve the use of funds. In important matters he will do this at the direction of the President.

It should be noted that apportionment is also a mechanism for *internal* departmental control by agency and department heads. This aspect is considered later when budget execution at this level is discussed.

Impoundment: President vs. Congress

One of the most pressing issues involving the execution of appropriations and budget authority centers around the issue of the president's "right," mentioned above, to reserve or impound funds previously approved by Congress. Briefly stated, the process of impoundment refers to an action taken by or on behalf of the president to prevent the expenditure of funds to meet given obligations for which congressional authorization and budget authority has already been given. Impoundment usually involves the "reserves," or amounts of money withheld from an agency or department's budget by the executive branch

> . . . to provide for contingencies, or to effect savings whenever savings are made possible by or through changes in requirements, greater efficiency of operation, or other developments subsequent to the date on which such appropriation was made available.[16]

The Constitution does not clearly stipulate whether the president is legally required to spend funds appropriated by Congress or whether he can exercise independent, discretionary authority over the timing and need for federal spending.[17] This constitutional ambiguity has given rise to recurring executive–legislative conflicts over the issue of

[15] *Ibid.*

[16] 64 Stat. L. 595, Sec. 1211, as cited in Smithies, *The Budgetary Process in the United States*, p. 150.

[17] See for example, J. D. Williams, *The Impounding of Funds by the Bureau of the Budget* (University: University of Alabama Press, 1955).

presidential control of the apportionment of federal funds. Since the beginning of the Republic, various presidents have withheld or impounded funds but this tendency has increased significantly since the New Deal in accordance with the exponential growth in government spending and greater budgetary complexity. On one occasion during his administration President Truman, as has been mentioned, impounded $725 million that Congress had voted to use to increase the size of the Air Force. Eisenhower acted similarly several years later when he set aside $137 million previously appropriated by Congress to buy Nike-Zeus anti-missile system hardware.[18] Both Kennedy and Johnson also exercised executive impoundment procedures during their regimes. Johnson, for example, set aside almost $5.3 billion (including $1.1 billion in highway funds and $760 million for housing and urban development) in 1966 to combat the inflationary impact of the Vietnamese war.[19] In mid-February 1975, President Ford released $2 billion of funds for highway construction impounded by successive administrations. The funds, released in an effort to reduce unemployment which had risen to the highest level in over three decades, were only a small part of the $11 billion of such funds impounded over the years by previous administrations.[20]

Concern over the legitimacy of presidential impoundment tactics however, has only recently reached critical levels. In the last two or three years of the Nixon administration, a growing number of congressional spending bills were vetoed by the President and very significant amounts of appropriations approved by the legislative branch have been impounded. The expressed justification for these actions has been the President's commitment to limit the inflationary effects of increased governmental spending but there is widespread feeling, especially among liberal Democrats, that these measures reflect an unprecedented presidential attempt to impose executive priorities on congressional appraisal of the budget. This concern for presidential infringement on the prerogatives of Congress has been reinforced and given greater emotional content by the spectacular revelations about the mis-use of executive power arising out of the Watergate affair, thereby effectively pushing into the public spotlight a budgetary issue that remained latent during previous administrations.

To illustrate the current legislative–executive conflict over the im-

---

[18] *Congressional Quarterly Weekly Report,* Vol. 31 (February 3, 1973), p. 213.
[19] *Ibid.*
[20] *New York Times,* February 15, 1975, pp. 1, 30.

poundment issue, several recent congressional actions can be noted. Shortly before the close of the 1972 session, President Nixon asked Congress to impose a $250 billion limit on spending for fiscal year 1973 and to grant him the authority to make whatever spending cuts he deemed necessary to hold expenditures to that level.[21] The House of Representatives approved the ceiling but, by a substantial margin (46–28), the Senate effectively negated the ceiling by adopting an amendment to a debt limit bill (PL 92-591) that imposed limitations on executive spending cuts. A compromise proposal worked out later by a conference committee, imposing less stringent restrictions on the President's authority to cut spending, was subsequently also rejected by the Senate, thus indicating the depth of feeling of many of its members on the issue.

More recently, the Senate has again shown its conviction that congressional authority over appropriations must be reinforced. On April 5, 1973, the Senate adopted an amendment to the gold devaluation bill (S929) that imposed a limit of $268 billion on spending for fiscal year 1974, authorized the President to make cuts to insure that expenditures conform to that level, but also stipulated that the President may not reduce appropriations beyond that point. Two days earlier, the Government Operations Committee of the Senate had reported an anti-impoundment bill (S373) that would require explicit congressional consent to the impoundment of any funds for a period exceeding approximately two months.[22] The President would be legally obliged to report to Congress within 10 days of the impoundment of any appropriated funds and would be required to obtain a concurrent resolution from both the House of Representatives and the Senate to ratify the impoundment within 60 days of the original report to Congress. An identical bill (S2581) introduced a year earlier (which died at the end of that session) drew strong criticism from the executive branch through the Office of Management and Budget.

> The bill would fundamentally alter the long-established relationships between the Legislative and Executive branches of the Government and would constitute a serious infringement upon the Executive's responsibility to "execute" the laws enacted by Congress. The establishment of reserves, within appropriations, and their release, is an action of an administrative nature, fully consistent with the President's constitutional duty to "take care that the laws be faithfully executed." [23]

[21] *Congressional Quarterly Weekly Report*, Vol. 31 (April 7, 1973), p. 1014.
[22] *Congressional Quarterly Weekly Report*, Vol. 31 (April 28, 1973), p. 788.
[23] U. S. Senate Committee on Appropriations, *Hearings*, February, 1972, p. 126. For an excellent discussion and interpretation of the constitutional provision requir-

The position promoted by the Nixon administration to justify the use of impoundment procedures and reserves by the executive is elaborated in the following remarks by Caspar Weinberger, director of OMB:

> In addition to (the) specific statutory authority provided by the Antideficiency Act, authority for the President to establish reserves (i.e., to impound funds) is derived basically from the constitutional provisions which vest the executive power in the President . . . we believe the power to withhold appropriated funds is implicit in them.[24]

A 1972 OMB press release also stated:

> The reasons for witholding or deferring the apportionment of available funds usually are concerned with routine financial administration. They have to do with the effective and prudent use of the financial resources made available by Congress.

The argument against executive powers of impoundment and reserve is thus founded in part on the doctrine of the separation of powers. As explained by Senator Sam Ervin,

> The power of the purse is one of the most basic powers of the legislative branch, and if it is not exercised in a decisive and fiscally responsive manner, the Congress itself may rightfully be accused of abrogating its role under the separation of power doctrine.[25]

Supreme Court Justice William N. Rehnquist has agreed with the Ervin position. In an opinion written while he was still assistant attorney-general, Rehnquist stated:

> With respect to the suggestion that the President has a constitutional power to decline to spend appropriate funds, we must conclude that existence of such a broad power is supported by neither reason nor precedent. There is, of course, no question that an appropriation act permits but does not require the executive branch to spend funds. But this is basically a rule of construction, and does not meet the question

---

ing that the President insure that laws are "faithfully executed" as it relates to the execution of appropriations, see Robert E. Goostree, "The Power of the President to Impound Appropriated Funds: With Special Reference to Grants-in-aid to Segregated Activities" in Wildavsky, ed., *The Presidency* (Boston: Little, Brown and Co., 1969), pp. 727–41. He argues, for example, that "The President cannot dispense with the execution of the laws, under the duty to see that they are executed. To hold otherwise would be to vest completely the legislative power in the President or to confer upon him a veto power over laws duly passed and enrolled. To accord discretion to a President as to what laws should be enforced and how much would enable him to interpose a veto retroactively, perhaps even upon legislation in full force and effect for decades" (p. 732).

[24] *Congressional Quarterly Weekly Report*, Vol. 31 (February 3, 1973), p. 214.

[25] *Ibid.*, p. 215.

whether the President has authority to refuse to spend where the appropriations act or the substantive legislation, fairly construed, require such action.[26]

A definitive legal resolution of the issue occurred in 1975 when the Supreme Court ruled unanimously that President Nixon had improperly withheld funds that Congress had earmarked in 1972 for water-pollution control programs. The nature of that decision, however, was perhaps foreshadowed by a ruling delivered April 2, 1973, by the Eighth U.S. Circuit Court of Appeals which held that the Administration had acted illegally in withholding construction money apportioned to the State of Missouri under the 1956 Highway Trust Fund. The court maintained that funds appropriated by Congress "are not to be withheld from obligation for purposes totally unrelated to the highway programs" [27]—that is, merely on the ground that such an expenditure would be inflationary.

OFFICE OF MANAGEMENT AND BUDGET

Another useful instrument of presidential control is through the division of the Office of Management and Budget concerned with improving management practices throughout the federal government. Although this agency has never quite achieved the active influence hoped for, its influence in this area has increased in the past few years, especially since 1970 when it was reorganized out of the old Bureau of the Budget, mainly as a result of Hoover Commission recommendations and increased acceptance of its role by Congress.[28]

The Joint Accounting Program illustrates how this agency became influential in financial matters. For many years, accounting functions in the federal government were divided among several agencies, including the Comptroller General, who was regarded as the watchdog of Congress. During World War II, however, the Comptroller, the Budget Bureau, and the Treasury began informal cooperation, largely on the basis of personal rapport among their top officials. In 1950 Congress formalized this arrangement in the Budget and Accounting Act, which was amended in 1956 to further shift power and initiative from the General Accounting Office to the Bureau.

26 *Ibid.*
27 *Congressional Quarterly Weekly Report* (April 7, 1973), p. 788.
28 *Cf.* A. Schick, "The Budget Bureau that Was: Thoughts on the Rise, Decline and Future of a Presidential Agency," *Law and Contemporary Problems*, Vol. 35 (Summer, 1970), pp. 519–39.

In all this, there has been a gradual change from defining accounting as a negative control instrument to one of positive direction. A new program charged the Comptroller General with encouraging the development of better accounting, disbursement, collection, and reporting practices. The extent of the changes is suggested by the fact that the General Accounting Office has almost completely decentralized accounting to the departments and agencies. In a way similar to the Civil Service Commission, its main role is to encourage the operating agencies to improve their own practices and programs.[29]

Insofar as complete reporting is essential to presidential control, the recommendations of the second Hoover Commission were most important. The Commission proposed that the Bureau of the Budget be empowered to require annual "performance" reports from the heads of all operating agencies. These in turn would permit the President to make an annual report on administrative performance in the executive branch. When set alongside the Commission's recommendations for central financial reporting, this suggests a trend toward accepting the need to centralize leadership for management improvement. However, the Bureau itself was reluctant to add to existing demands for reports from the operating agencies, and suggested that for the present it confine itself to developing central reports on financial matters.[30] While declaring its "firm intention to take all possible measures to bring Bureau staff into closer contact with agency operations and employees. . . ," the Bureau suggested that the trend toward reducing its staff while constantly adding new functions ought to be reversed. In its brief history, the OMB has had to face similar questions as it refines the tasks formerly charged to the BOB.

President's Fund for Management Improvement

The federal budget contains a small appropriation for "expenses necessary to assist the President in improving the management of executive agencies and in obtaining greater economy and efficiency through the establishment of *business* methods in Government operations. . . ."[31]

---

[29] For detailed information, see Frank L. Lewis and F. G. Zarb, "Federal Program Evaluation from the OMB Perspective," *Public Administration Review,* Vol. 34 (July–August, 1974), pp. 308–17.

[30] Bureau of the Budget, *Improvement of Financial Management in the Federal Government* (Washington, D. C.: Government Printing Office, 1956), pp. 25–26.

[31] *U. S. Budget for 1966,* p. 179. For some of the problems encountered by the Bureau of the Budget as a central agency in the federal budgetary process, see Schick, "The Budget Bureau That Was: Thoughts on the Rise, Decline, and Future of a Presidential Agency," *op. cit.*

In 1975, $500,000 was appropriated to the President for these purposes.[32] This enables him to bring in consultants or have the agencies themselves survey their methods under general OMB direction. Here again, the President has an opportunity to control and reshape financial practices.

Although the President through the Office of Management and Budget and his political control of department heads can exert important controls during the execution process, the authority and responsibility for long-run management effectiveness must rest upon the departments and the agencies themselves. Neither the President nor Congress can exercise a continuous scrutiny of their programs in day-to-day terms. Nor has the Comptroller General been able to gain full support for his annual recommendations for improvement. We turn now to the question of legislative control during the execution phase.

LEGISLATIVE OVERSIGHT

Control by Appropriation

The close relationship among the three major budgetary phases is suggested by the fact that the main form of legislative control is through appropriations, by which legislatures sometimes try to limit the discretion of the executive agencies. Examples include specific provisions against the transfer of funds from the appropriated account to some other program. This proscription is quite common among state legislatures and occurs also in many city governments. In the federal government "the tradition has long been to permit no transfer among agencies and very little within agencies, except on specific occasions and for specific purposes, as stated in annual appropriation acts; for example, a department might be permitted to transfer 5 per cent from one title to another." [33] Legislators are very reluctant to grant transfer authority to the agencies; yet the trend is clearly in this direction, as indicated by the lump-sum appropriations that characterize the federal budget.

Another traditional instrument of control is the line-item appropriation, which makes it difficult to transfer money from one item to another and results in a rigidity that some observers deplore.[34] Line-items control expenditure by a line in the budget document, such as x typist clerks at $6,000 per year or x automobile tires at $27,000. An interesting ex-

[32] See *The Budget of the United States Government, Fiscal Year 1974*, Washington, D. C., U. S. Government Printing Office, 1973, p. 184.

[33] Burkhead, *Government Budget, op. cit.*, p. 349.

[34] *Ibid.*, pp. 128, 355.

ample of congressional efforts to control expenditures is the Whitten amendment to the Supplemental Appropriations Act of 1952, which attempted to prevent expansion of the federal payroll during emergencies, with resulting strains when people were let go following the emergency.[35] Limitations were placed on promotions and the opportunities for people to gain civil service tenure. Most personnel officers opposed the amendment, and even the Civil Service Commission was accused of dragging its feet in supporting it. This seemingly inherent tendency of bureaucracies to expand has, of course, been delightfully caricatured by Professor Parkinson, who showed among other things that the smaller the number of capital ships in the British Navy, the larger the number of civilian personnel in the Naval Establishment.[36] Legislators everywhere suspect that Parkinson's "law" is valid, and some of them, like the late Senator Byrd, have spent decades trying unsuccessfully to curtail the growth of the federal bureaucracy.[37]

It is easy to understand the efforts of the legislature to control expenditures by such means as "ceilings" on personnel and limiting the number of budget items and determining their costs. Here it seems is something definite to which an agency can be held. By contrast, the program budgeting concept seems strange, and as we have seen, it does limit the legislator's ability to evaluate administrative practices by limiting the amount of detailed information he receives. This posture is also encouraged by the fact that many legislators are small-town lawyers or businessmen with little experience in big organizations where cost-centered approaches to accountability have been more common.

The Comptroller General's Role

Since the Comptroller General is usually regarded as a servant of Congress, it seems appropriate to review his activities here. The Budget and Accounting Act of 1921 established the Comptroller General as head of the new General Accounting Office. The position is filled through appointment by the President, with Senate Approval, for a term of fifteen

[35] *Report of the Committee on Post Office and Civil Service*, 84th Cong., 2d sess., House Report No. 1855 (March 1, 1956), p. 11.

[36] C. Northcote Parkinson, *Parkinson's Law* (New York: Harper & Row, Inc., 1957), p. 33.

[37] For example, a federal budget which in 1960 had been $75 billion had risen to $350 billion by 1975–76. The budget seems to grow steadily with GNP, remaining at about 16 per cent of GNP since the end of World War II. Although defenders of this rate of growth often cite this condition, critics such as Edwin L. Dale, Jr., point out that federal spending is rising much faster than the *actual volume of production,* which is the "real" GNP. *New York Times,* December 1, 1974, p. 13.

years, no incumbent being allowed to succeed himself. The following powers and duties were imposed: (1) devising and installing improved accounting procedures, (2) covering monies into and out of the treasury by signing payment and covering warrants, (3) auditing of accounts, and (4) acting as financial adviser to Congress.

Recently, the General Accounting Office has re-stated the functions assigned to it by law: (1) assisting Congress in its legislative and over-sight activities, (2) providing legal services to Congress, (3) auditing the programs and operations of Federal departments and agencies, (4) assisting in the improvement of Federal agency financial systems, and (5) settling claims and collecting debts.[38] Behind these functions, two important purposes for the activities of the GAO can be discerned; they are to

> . . . provide as much assistance to Congress, its committees, and Members as it can, consistent with its responsibilities as an inde-pendent nonpolitical agency

and, to stimulate

> . . . constructive actions that contribute to making Government operations more effective and more efficient.[39]

An example suggests the role of the Comptroller General as the "watchdog" of Congress. In mid-1959, at the same time that appro-priations for the Administration's foreign aid program were being con-sidered, the Comptroller General testified before a House Appropria-tions subcommittee that waste, inefficiency, and lax administration ran "throughout the entire complex" of the foreign aid program.[40] He re-ferred to programs in Korea and Pakistan where "serious deficiencies" existed. United States aid to Pakistan, he insisted, had been beyond Pakistan's "technical and financial capacity," while in Korea vast stores of military supplies were lying about unused. He also criticized the Defense Department and the then International Cooperation Adminis-tration for keeping records secret from his agency.

Currently, the Comptroller General cites in detail many cases of pervasive waste and inefficiency in Government operations. He claims that the actions of the GAO in uncovering such instances led ultimately to

---

[38] *Annual Report of the Comptroller General of the United States, 1972*, Wash-ington, D. C., U. S. Government Printing Office, 1973, p. 1.

[39] *Ibid.*

[40] *The New York Times*, July 24, 1959, pp. 1, 6.

a savings of $292 millions in fiscal year 1972.[41] Two cases drawn from his report illustrate the type of potential waste that GAO actions prevented: In the first case, the Army had planned to replace certain heavy equipment but, at the insistence of the GAO, was compelled to repair equipment on hand instead. The estimated savings was $131.2 million. In the second case, the GAO persuaded American armed forces units in Europe to rebuild vehicle tires rather than purchase new ones as they had intended—at estimated savings of $9.3 million. The sobering thought, however, is that such instances probably represent the few exceptional cases where waste is prevented by prior action rather than discovered and ventilated *post facto* by the Comptroller General.

The most visible function of the GAO remains its auditing role:

> The primary purposes of our audits are (1) to evaluate the efficiency, economy, legality, and effectiveness with which Federal agencies discharge their financial, management, and program responsibilities and (2) to provide the Congress and Federal Agency officials with significant and objective information, conclusions, and recommendations which will aid them in carrying out their responsibilities.[42]

During fiscal year 1972, the GAO carried out 1,838 audits in the United States and in 50 other countries where American personnel were stationed.[43]

The Comptroller General, in addition to the tasks to which he is normally assigned, has recently been delegated an important new responsibility that, although it does not pertain directly to the budget process, is interesting to note here. The Presidential Election Campaign Fund Act (title VIII, Pl. 92–178, approved December 10, 1971) and the Federal Election Campaign Act of 1971 (Pl. 92–225, approved February 7, 1972) ascribe to the Comptroller General various tasks concerning the conduct and regulation of election campaign activities, with specific emphasis on campaign funding. The former requires the Comptroller General to audit and report expenses incurred during presidential and

---

[41] *Appendix to the Annual Report of the Comptroller General of the United States, 1972,* Washington, D. C., U. S. Government Printing Office, 1973, p. 157.

[42] *Annual Report, 1972, op. cit.,* p. 51.

[43] These audits can be classified as follows:
1. audits of civil agency programs—703
2. audits of defense programs—790
3. audits of international programs—196
4. audits of government-wide and multi-agency programs—149
   Total—1,838

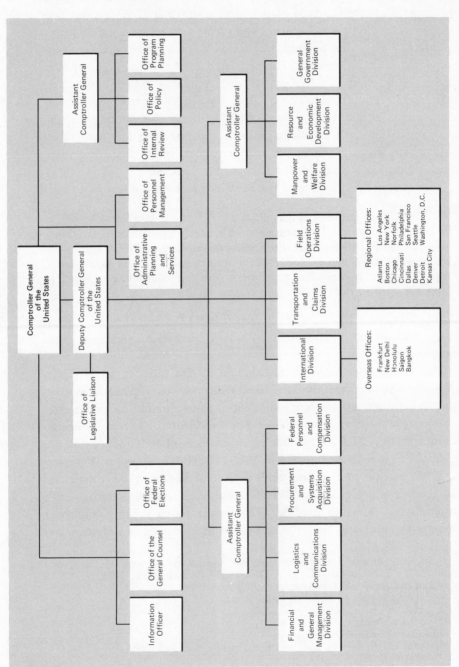

Fig. 17-1. Organizational structure of the General Accounting Office. Source: *Annual Report of the Comp-*

vice-presidential campaigns, to report to Congress on payments made to political parties, and to audit a checkoff procedure by which, commencing in the presidential election of 1976, a taxpaper may allocate $1. of his tax payment to a political party.

The second Act (effective April 7, 1972) gives the Comptroller General responsibility for administering various provisions pertaining to the campaigns for president and vice-president, including limits to the amounts which candidates may spend to use communication media during their campaigns, and compulsory reporting of all campaign expenditures and receipts. Similar responsibilities are given to the Clerk of the House of Representatives and the Secretary of the Senate, for House candidates and Senate candidates respectively. In order to discharge these new responsibilities, an Office of Federal Elections was established during reorganization of the GAO in 1972 (see Figure 17-1).[44]

The Need for More Information

Congress' main problem in the execution phase has been a lack of information necessary for adequate review. Several developments suggest that improved congressional participation is possible, and we shall now outline some of the recommendations made by students of budgeting. Arthur Smithies has suggested that Congress' role will not be much improved until a distinction is made between the policy side and the management side of the federal budget.[45] To improve policy evaluation, he recommends first that the reports made by the Appropriations Committees to Congress should include judgments as to what effects proposed legislation will have on "the controllability of the budget." Second, he suggests that the Committees be given power to propose amendments to such legislation if this will bring better balance to the entire budget. In these ways, attempts to bypass the appropriations stage by using other means of financing, such as contract authorizations or the use of public-debt transactions,[46] would be made known to Congress.

At the same time, there is some evidence that Congress has sometimes abdicated its role of policy evaluation. This is particularly evident regarding military spending. As Richard Barnet says, "Since 1946 the

[44] For more details on the election campaign responsibilities of the GAO, see *ibid.*, pp. 27–29.

[45] *The Budget Process in the United States, op. cit.*, pp. 175–78.

[46] Contract authorizations commit Congress automatically once the initial program is begun; public-debt transactions enable the agencies to borrow from the Treasury and thereby avoid legislative scrutiny.

taxpayers have been asked to contribute more than one trillion dollars for national security. Each year the federal government spends more than 70 cents of every budget dollar on past, present, and future wars. The American people are devoting more resources to the war machine than is spent by all federal, state, and local governments on health and hospitals, education, old-age and retirement benefits, public assistance and relief, unemployment and social security, housing and community development, and the support of agriculture. Out of every tax dollar there is about 11 cents to build American society." [47] The dysfunctional consequences have included unbalanced priorities, inflation, and lowered consumer expenditures. In the immediate context, how effective has Congress's surveillance of such policy commitments been?

Authoritative answers are available. In an exchange between Senator William Fulbright and Budget Director Charles Schultze, the following comments occurred:

> *Fulbright:* Last year (1969) is the first time since I have been in Congress that there has been any serious questioning of the military budget.
> *Schultze:* That is correct; yes sir.
> *Fulbright:* Any serious questioning. Before that it went through with just a nod.
> *Schultze:* That is correct; yes sir.[48]

Senator William Proxmire, chairman of the Subcommittee on Economy in Government, commented similarly, "For years, Congress has been a pushover for the Pentagon. It had gone along with the military's wishes, and a protective network of practices and traditions had grown up around the military procurement and appropriation bills, the members of the Armed Services and Appropriations Committees who handle them, and the relationship of the Pentagon to members of both Houses of Congress." [49] For a variety of reasons, including the Department of Defense's mastery of the language and the techniques of systems theory and the emotional appeal of programs couched in terms of national security, Congress and the committees concerned have rarely exercised much control of the largest single element in the federal budget. And it appears

---

[47] *The Economy of Death* (New York: Atheneum Publishers, 1969), p. 5, cited in Stephen W. Hartman, "Impact of Defense Expenditures on the Domestic American Economy 1946–72," *Public Administration Review*, Vol. 33 (July/August, 1973), pp. 379–90.

[48] *Hearings*, Committee on Foreign Relations, Senate (April 28, 1970), p. 231.

[49] Hartman, *op. cit.*, p. 381.

that even the criticism which has been made of military spending and waste during the recent past has failed to change the situation. "Measured in dollars of constant purchasing power, the 1972 defense budget for purposes other than Vietnam will be about the same as it was in 1968." [50] Such evidence suggests that, in addition to the problems raised by inadequate staff and information, which could be remedied by Congress there is a lack of will insofar as the critical review of defense policy is concerned.

Here again, the explanation must include political factors, including the natural desire of legislators not to be put in the position of denying the military establishment whatever arms it feels are necessary for national security. At other times, legislators are faced with a *fait accompli*, as in the case of Vietnam where successive presidents increased American commitments without much consultation with congressional leaders, after which requests for increased spending occurred. There is also a notable tendency for legislators to use defense appropriations to shore up economic conditions in their home state, while at the same time gaining personal political advantages from their ability to provide such contracts for their constituents. Certain Southern states, whose congressment often hold senior positions on the Armed Services Committee due to their seniority, enjoy special benefits from defense spending. Lip service is paid to efforts to limit military spending, but congressmen are naturally reluctant to have it begin in their own states.

To some extent, such political-economic realities make the contemporary emphasis upon rational policy-making, the use of such instruments as performance budgeting, and recommendations for more adequate congressional surveillance somewhat Quixotic. Nevertheless, part of Congress' inability to control spending stems from procedural inadequacies, and we now turn again to this subject.

PERFORMANCE BUDGETING

We have been thrust into a bureaucratically organized society so rapidly that we are only now developing yardsticks with which to evaluate our huge institutions. We often try to deny that they exist, to revert to attitudes and thinking characteristic of a simpler nineteenth-century environment while demanding the services which only a bu-

[50] Schultze, *et al.*, *Setting National Priorities*, *op. cit.*, p. 1.

reaucratic society can bring us. As we gradually assimilate this change, however, we are beginning to attack the real problem: the need for social control of bureaucracy through modern instruments designed for that purpose. Performance budgeting is one such device.[51]

Performance budgeting stresses the gathering of statistical information, such as man-hours worked or number of miles flown. Performance budgeting may be regarded as one aspect of the PBB system. The first Hoover Commission (1949) popularized the concept of performance budgeting and the Second Hoover Commission (1955) stressed the need for more accounting information. Particular emphasis was placed upon "accrual accounting," a term that needs some explanation because the Commission seemed to use it synonymously with "annuality of appropriations"; much of the opposition encountered in Congress flowed from this interpretation. Perhaps a discussion of the matter should be preceded by a note on commercial accounting. Once again, recent history is useful in explaining contemporary developments.

Recent administrations have brought in at the highest political appointment levels (class I–V) many businessmen with an affinity for corporate practices. Although the attending trend toward the use of business accounting in government has inspired some controversy, there was a certain timeliness in its revival during the 1950's. Corporate business had in general vastly improved its own accounting practices by then. The urgent need for up-to-date procedures had been brought home to industry by the Ford Motor Company's experience. In the Ford case, a financial crisis was precipitated largely because the only information available on its financial condition was the balances in the numerous bank accounts which the senior Henry Ford had established. When these began to get alarmingly low, the corporation was forced to reorganize both management and accounting in order to provide the information needed to pinpoint weaknesses.[52]

This example is mentioned in a discussion of legislative control to illustrate the following points: first, the sophistication of accounting and the availability of information have increased vastly in recent years. Second, there is often a resistance to the introduction of new accounting

[51] For relevant information, see David Novick, *Program Budgeting: Program Analysis and the Federal Budget* (Cambridge, Mass.: Harvard University Press, 1965).
[52] William B. Harris, "Ford's Fight for First," *Fortune*, Vol. 50 (September, 1954), pp. 123, 126; for an account by a Ford official, see R. E. Roberts, "Ford's Reorganization: The Management Story," *Advanced Management*, Vol. 19 (May, 1954), pp. 9–12.

procedures, even from top management itself. Third, this maturation of the theory and practice of accounting calls for a re-evaluation of its applicability to government. Finally, any emphasis on program budgeting calls for a new type of accounting information.

Until recently governmental accounting was mainly concerned with accountability for cash, along with maintaining fidelity and probity. While business accounting is also interested in keeping people honest, it has been more concerned with providing information that management could use in *making decisions* and in evaluating management results. This orientation is often symbolized by the term "managerial accounting." There is no inherent conflict between fidelity accounting and this approach. Indeed, the best way to maintain honesty is to create a record of all transactions. Managerial accounting, however, provides more meaningful records than a mere accounting of cash receipts and disbursements. It calls for information about the results of operations, supported by data related to such results. The main evaluation document in a business enterprise is the profit-and-loss statement; and the fact that this datum does not apply to government has led to the assumption that business accounting practices are generally inapplicable. But certain aspects of business accounting do apply to government, especially those activities amenable to performance budgeting.

Accrual Accounting

One such practice is accrual accounting. The distinction between accrual and cash accounting lies in the fact that, under the latter, accumulated totals can be supplied only for cash paid out or taken in. Accrual accounting, on the other hand, can tell one how much cash is due and what obligations have been incurred but not yet paid for. Accrual accounting is not new, having been advocated by budget specialists for many decades; indeed, it has been practiced in progressive agencies for some time.

The second Hoover Commission's recommendations for accrual accounting were concerned with the same principle but with a slightly different application. Expenditures for many government projects such as flood control or military aircraft procurement often extend over more than a single fiscal year. The result is that money appropriated for a particular year will not be "spent" until two or three years later. It thus becomes impossible to furnish a budgetary statement showing at any particular time the true status of expenditures because bills accumulated from prior years are always being paid.

The Hoover Commission sought to correct this by requiring that appropriations for each long-term project be reappropriated in each annual budget. Thus the annual budget would show not only the "new" spending for that year but also the obligations from previous years expected to be spent during that year. Appropriation accounts could thus reflect at any time an accurate report on current expenditures as well as the status of "accrued" obligations. This would insure an accurate picture of the status of appropriations and expenditures. In 1958, after long hearings, Congress passed a watered-down amendment to the Budget and Accounting Act of 1921 [53] authorizing the President to take steps in this direction. In the years since 1958 accrual accounting procedures have gained general acceptance in the federal service.

The New Budgeting Theory

While the concept of performance budgeting was popularized by the first Hoover Commission, a working theory explaining how to operate it remained to be developed. This fell to the Rand Corporation under contract with the Department of Defense. While the term "program budgeting" has come into general use, this should not be interpreted to mean abandonment of the concept of "performance" because the two are inseparably related. A program budget must ultimately be based on detailed performance data. The designation that became popular in federal circles was "Planning-Programming Budgeting."

The development and implications of PPBS were discussed in some detail in a previous chapter, but it is useful to reiterate a few brief points here. The original developmental and conceptual efforts at Rand resulted in the publication of what is usually regarded as a classic statement of the new budgetary theory.[54] The key figures in this episode moved into the Department of Defense and were requested by Secretary McNamara to put their theories into operation.[55] As noted earlier, President Johnson and the Bureau of the Budget tried to install the concept of program budgeting in the civilian agencies but with only mixed

[53] USC 11; 42 Stat. 20.
[54] Charles Hitch and R. M. McKean, *The Economics of Defense in the Nuclear Age* (Cambridge, Mass.: Harvard University Press, 1959).
[55] See Hitch, *Decision-making for Defense* (Berkeley: University of California Press, 1965).

success.[56] Today, as noted earlier, there is some evidence that PPB has lost favor in the federal government, but it would be inaccurate to assert that the emphasis on "performance" has also come to an end. Indeed, the experience of PPB has indicated that performance and program orientations in federal budgeting have many benefits. Problems arise, however, when advocates of this type of approach fail to take into account the non-rational and non-quantifiable aspects of fiscal policy determination in their attempts to introduce technological rationality into the budget process.[57]

The theory of cybernetics, which is based on the fundamental concept of the message as the atom of organization, is also relevant here. As originally applied to electrical machines, it involved the concept of feedback, the process whereby the behavior of an organism or machine is modified by reinserting into it information resulting from its own performance. Thus an organization is a communication network in which messages are constantly interacting with each other; mutual reacting occurs as one message modifies the meaningful content of others. A message is a datum or piece of information, and such data constitute the lifeblood of control. Hence it is a natural stage in the evolution of budgetary history that the concept of general systems should emerge, not only as the basic device to control missiles in the air, but also to control budgetary operations.

SOCIAL BUDGETING

The National Commission of Technology, Automation, and Economic Projects was an impressive body composed of industrial executives, professors, and labor leaders. The general tone of its recommendations was forward-looking and many of them would have been regarded as radical

[56] A symposium by various Rand employees is reported in Novick, *Program Budgeting: Program Analyses and the Federal Budget, op. cit.* Developments in federal budgeting are traced in A. Wildavsky and A. Hammond, "Comprehensive Versus Incremental Budgeting in the Department of Agriculture," *Administrative Science Quarterly,* Vol. 11 (December, 1965), pp. 321–46.

[57] Among other useful analyses and critiques of PPB and similar innovations, see Leonard Merewitz and Stephen Sosnick, *The Bulget's New Clothes* (Chicago: Markham Publishing Co., 1971); Allan Schick, *Budget Innovations in the States* (Washington, D.C.: Brookings Institution, 1971); David Ott and A. Ott, *Federal Budget Policy* (Washington, D. C.: Brookings Institution, 1969); *International Social Science Journal* "Innovation in Public Administration," Vol. 21 (November, 1969), pp. 9–134. For an illuminating critique of the application of systems theory to the study of international relations, see John Weltman, "The Processes of a Systematist," *Journal of Politics,* Vol. 34 (May, 1972), pp. 592–611.

by persons of similar status only a generation or so ago.[58] For example, it recommended a system of "income maintenance" which would assure everyone a minimal income even though not employed. From the standpoint of governmental budgeting, perhaps the most remarkable proposal was the extension of the concept of performance budgeting to the quality of human living itself.

The point was made that the Depression of the 1930's had produced many social reforms which had resulted in a demand for information about the national economy, gradually leading to the development of a variety of economic data hitherto not available. Thus today we have such measures of economic health as the gross national product. But we do not have a system of social accounts which will furnish the same kind of data relative to the quality of social living.[59] What is needed is a set of social indices indicating the relationships between economic investments and the quality of living. Acknowledging the difficulty of devising measurements and indices, the Commission nevertheless urged vigorous exploration and experiment because the need was so great. That the concept is not altogether new is indicated by the reference above to the attempt to establish measurement of social variables in cost-benefit analysis.[60]

The theoretical groundwork continues to be laid for a national network of social data systems comparable to the comparatively mature data systems existing in the areas of economics and production. Many cities have experimented with computer installations which, although often directed largely toward providing financial and physical data, will inevitably include social information. This movement has been hastened by the exigencies of the Poverty Program, minority unrest, education of the poor, and related social problems that require policy-makers to demand answers which can flow only from data. An example of such a step was the state of California's contracts with the aerospace industry to apply systems approaches to the solution of the state's problems. Thus one corporation has produced a comprehensive plan for dealing with the problem of crime and delinquency based on the establishment of interconnected information systems and an experimental approach.[61]

[58] *Technology and the American Economy*, Vol. I (Washington, D. C.: Government Printing Office, 1966).

[59] *Ibid.*, pp. 55 ff.

[60] See Novick, *Program Budgeting, op. cit.*

[61] Space-General Corporation, *Final Report: Prevention of Crime and Delinquency.* (El Monte, Calif.: The Corporation, 1965.) For further discussion of "social indicators" as they apply to general policy-making, see pp. 88–89.

EXECUTION AND CONTROL IN THE DEPARTMENTS

We have seen that the responsibility for effective execution often rests largely in the departments and agencies. What are the ways used by operating officials to carry out and control the spending phase? We touched first upon the traditional "control" instruments that insure honesty and regularity in financial practices. Within the broad framework of administration policy, the agency head has considerable freedom of action. He has the responsibility for setting up effective internal systems of accounting and reporting. Generally his guide is the objectives set down in the Budgeting and Accounting Act of 1950, as amended in 1956, which include full disclosure of financial activities and providing information that will encourage management improvement. Deficiency appropriations provide an example. When needed, they must be submitted to Congress for authorization. Since such appropriations always occur in response to emergencies of one kind or another, and since agencies may otherwise be inclined to exhaust their appropriations before the end of the fiscal year, central control of their use is an important factor within the departments.

Transfer of funds appropriated for one item to another is another area in which agency discretion is circumscribed by the Office of Management and Budget and the President, and even their authority to make such transfers is limited. The President has only the authority specifically granted to him in the appropriations act for the program concerned. Sometimes the Act will set a figure, usually 5 or 10 per cent, within which the Executive may transfer funds from one kind of expenditure to another. However, Congress seems jealous of its authorization power and resists executive transfer of funds. As noted earlier, the struggle for control over appropriations between the executive and the legislative branches has reached a critical stage. How far the President will go in pressing his authority is uncertain but, whatever steps he takes, he must always be cognizant of the fact that he will have to return to Congress each year to secure authorization for his spending program.

V

SEEKING ADMINISTRATIVE RESPONSIBILITY

18

Executive Control
of Administration

Any discussion of administrative responsibility requires a brief note on party government in the United States. According to traditional conceptions of democratic theory, bureaucracy's role is essentially ministerial—i.e., it is charged with simply carrying out policies set down by the parties and broadly endorsed by the electorate. The essence of political responsibility lies in the capacity to make this principle work in practice. Responsible democratic government can occur only when elected officials and their politically appointed aides are able to direct the bureaucracy along the policy lines for which they have received a popular mandate.

Such a scheme of party and bureaucratic responsibility, however, is somewhat tenuous in the United States. Our separation-of-powers system, local and state election of congressmen, the staggered calendar term, as well as the great extent to which spending programs are committed over time and cannot be controlled, all militate against responsible party government. Moreover, even when the President or Governor enjoys a legislative majority, he cannot typically count on its support, since, once elections are over, the temporary unity of the party is shattered by other powerful claims to the legislator's loyalty. Among the most pressing of such claims is that of articulate interest groups which, as we have seen,[1] enjoy many points of access in our political system and a sustained, direct role in policy-making.

BUREAUCRATIC EXPERTISE AND AUTONOMY

These facets of the American political system aggravate the problem of control, but it almost seems that bureaucracy has an autonomous quality, which puts it beyond human control. Part of the explanation lies in official expertise and the extent to which bureaucratic processes remain unknown to the outsider, including legislators. As Max Weber says,

> The power position of the fully developed bureaucracy is always great, under normal conditions overtowering. The political 'master' always finds himself vis-à-vis the trained official, in the position of the dilettante facing the expert. This holds whether the 'master', whom the bureaucracy serves, is the 'people' equipped with the weapons of legislative initiative, referendum, and the right to remove officials; or a parliament elected on a more aristocratic or more democratic b﹍is and equipped with the right or the *de facto* power to vote a lack of confidence; or an aristocratic collegial body, legally or actually based on self-recruitment; or a popularly elected president or an 'absolute' or 'constitutional' hereditary monarch.[2]

EXECUTIVE CONTROL

Clearly, control of administration by higher executives is a central requisite of democratic government. If this responsibility is to be made good, they must be able to control the bureaucracy which is charged with carrying out their policy.[3] The President especially needs authority and assistance equal to the responsibilities of his office. Such needs for

[1] See Chapter 7 for a detailed account; see also Presthus, *Elites in the Policy Process* (New York: Cambridge University Press, 1974).

[2] *Economy and Society,* Vol. 3 (New York: Bedminster Press, 1968), pp. 991–92, pp. 990–1003, *passim.* Weber's remarks here, by the way, indicate that he was specifically including American society in these generalizations. A useful critique of Weber's ideal-type model is Arun Sahay (ed.), *Max Weber and Modern Sociology* (London: Routledge and Kegan Paul, 1971). For an authoritative account of Weber's pragmatic approach to and participation in politics of his time, see Ilse Dronberger, *The Political Philosophy of Max Weber: In Quest of Statesmanship* (New York: Appleton-Century-Crofts, 1971).

[3] One problem with such generalizations is that there are often striking exceptions. In this case, one thinks immediately of Sweden, among the most democratic societies in the world, yet where "we have no doctrine of ministerial responsibility for decisions made by civil servants. Ministries are small and serve only as advisory units for the ministers. The bulk of administrative work is carried out by "autonomous authorities." Ulf Christoffersson, *Higher Civil Servants in Sweden* (Goteborg: University of Goteborg, Institute of Political Science, 1973 (mimeo.), p. 2.

responsible administration have not always been adequately emphasized, perhaps because we tend to define the bureaucracy as an instrument for achieving public policy, forgetting that it is sometimes an impediment. The civil service develops precedents which sometimes make the acceptance of new policy and programs difficult. During the New Deal, for example, party leaders were sometimes obliged to bypass old-line agencies. The British Labour government after 1945 met some resistance from a conservative administrative class, and the counterrevolutionary role of the German civil service during the Weimer Republic is well known. It is wise, therefore, to review the means for controlling bureaucracy.

It is very difficult for chief executives to control the huge and complex administrative systems now existing in national, state, and many local governments. Not only is the number and size of agencies awe-inspiring, but they are often in conflict. Many seek to strengthen their position *vis-à-vis* the executive by alliances with legislatures and pressure groups, as well as by appeals to the public. One motivation for such behavior is the agencies' perception of the executive as a temporary figure, contrasted with their own permanent status.

In addition, they develop vested interests not only in program areas but in established procedures which enhance their power. Any change that threatens this equilibrium is often resisted. For these reasons, although the bureaucracy is often an aggressive contender for new power, it can also be a conservative force. Indeed, so great an admirer of bureaucracy as Max Weber believed that only charismatic political leaders could galvanize it into change-oriented action.

The issue of control of the civil service was dramatized during the Eisenhower Administration. Some department heads did not feel able to carry out their policies with personnel who had served under the Roosevelt and Truman Administrations; yet most of the department staffs, including many top personnel, had civil service tenure. At least one department head found even his number two man under civil service.[4] As a result, Eisenhower directed the Civil Service Commission to re-examine all classified jobs with a view to removing from civil service protection those "of a confidential or policy-determining character." This "Schedule C" category illustrates well the instruments of control available to the chief executive. Apparently its intended impact was considerably less than anticipated, however, since by the end of January, 1954, only

[4] Herman M. Somers, "The Federal Bureaucracy and the Change of Administration," *American Political Science Review*, Vol. 53 (March, 1954), p. 141.

879 positions had been approved by the Commission, which rejected 929 agency requests for Schedule C positions.[5] Whether "confidential or policy-making" positions can be defined precisely, and whether the bad impact on civil service élan of such orders outweighs the benefits, are moot points. They do show that presidential efforts at control can have limited effects.

Power of Appointment

The President relies mainly upon high-level politically appointed officials to give direction and inspiration to the civil service.[6] These officials influence the broad outlines of public policy and the general objectives of the bureaucracy, and they also guide the implementation of such policy. The power of appointment rests upon the constitutional mandate which charges the President to insure "that the laws be faithfully executed."[7] In the case of major officials, such as department heads, members of the regulatory commissions, Supreme Court justices, ambassadors, ministers, and consuls, the President's appointing power is, of course, shared with the Senate. His appointing power is also shared with special interest groups. Organizations that have considerable political power, such as the Farm Bureau Federation, the AFL-CIO, the National Association of Manufacturers, and the Air Force Association, often play an active role in the appointment of top officials in their respective areas. The President cannot avoid being influenced by them. Often their influence is exerted through the Senate which sometimes rejects controversial nominations.

The practice of "senatorial courtesy," whereby appointments to positions in a state are in effect made by the congressmen from that state, is another limitation on the President's appointive power. The appointment of "inferior" officials, however, is usually vested entirely in the President, the courts of law, and department heads. At the state and local levels, the appointing power of the chief executive is much more limited. In several states, for example, almost all top-level executive positions are elective. In these cases, officials are virtually independent of the chief executive and develop political machines of their own which give them independence and extended tenure.

Despite these various limitations, the appointing power clearly gives

[5] *Ibid.*, p. 143.

[6] Although this chapter relates primarily to presidential controls, the observations apply in most cases to governors and mayors as well.

[7] Edward S. Corwin, *The President: Office and Powers*, 4th ed. (New York: New York University Press, Inc., 1957), pp. 82–83; chap. 31, *passim.*

the President vast potential influence over the bureaucracy. By selecting strong prestigeful cabinet heads, who share his own point of view about government and the economy, he can make his will felt. In the regulatory agencies, he is also able, given time, to determine broadly whether an agency will have a "consumer" or a "producer" orientation. President Johnson's decision in 1965 not to reappoint Joseph Swidler, a vigorous advocate for consumer interests, as Chairman of the Federal Power Commission provides an illustration. In a larger context, appointments to the Supreme Court can be structured to increase the probabilities that certain administration policies and programs will receive judicial legitimization if and when they are challenged by disenchanted publics. The efficacy of many high-level political appointments is undercut by relatively brief tenure and the difficulty that many business executives have in operating in the highly political Washington environment.[8] Nevertheless, as an exceptional appointment such as that of Secretary of Defense MacNamara indicates, even so powerful an interest as the military establishment can be brought under some control by inspired presidential appointments.

Appointments can also be used to create a certain desired presidential and Administration image. President Kennedy's recruitment of Ivy League professors, for example, reinforced both United States and world perceptions of him as a President with a dignified, intellectual style and an historical appreciation of the presidency. Whereas Eisenhower's Under-Secretary of the Interior could boast publicly that he "had kicked out a group of Ph.D's. from Harvard and Columbia," [9] Kennedy preferred to bring them back in. Johnson, on the other hand, tended to rely somewhat more upon professional politicians for his close advisers. Nixon, meanwhile, also brought in appointees who shared his own values and policy orientations. Despite some rejections, he was able to strongly affect the political complexion of the Supreme Court by a number of "conservative" appointments. The Watergate investigations revealed perhaps more completely than ever before the operational assumptions and considerable discretion possessed by the members of the White House staff who numbered 400, in mid-1973, only a few of whom had direct access to the President. President Ford's appointments tend, it seems, to symbolize his own essentially conservative business values, particularly

---

[8] For a careful analysis of such appointments, see Dean E. Mann, and Jameson W. Doig, *The Assistant Secretaries: Problems and Processes of Appointment* (Washington, D.C.: The Brookings Institution, 1965).

[9] *Washington Post*, September 29, 1953.

regarding Nelson Rockefeller and the members of his Council of Economic Advisers. At the same time, he has shown an appreciation of changing popular values, among half his constituency, at least, by appointing a woman Cabinet member, Ms. Carla A. Hills. In effect, the tone of an Administration can be both set and seem to be set by the President's appointments, which in turn tend to closely reflect his own social and political values.

Power of Removal

When administrators fail, the President has broad powers of removal. The problem of delineating the scope of this power brought about the first major constitutional debate in our history, centering about a bill originally authorizing the President to remove the Secretary of "Foreign Affairs" without the concurrence of the Senate. The controversy ended in a narrow victory for the advocates of unrestricted presidential removal power over department heads.[10] This power enables the President to discipline important officials who fail to carry out their duties properly, as defined by him. Insofar as executive officials are concerned, moreover, his removal power is not subject to judicial review.[11]

Because removals often appear in the guise of "resignations," the significance of the removal power tends to be underestimated. In fact, high officials are removed as a result of inadequate performance, insubordination, or as a concession to unfavorable public opinion. Examples are plentiful. Since John Adams removed his Secretary of State, Timothy Pickering, because of his opposition to the President's second French mission and other policies, presidents have not hesitated to remove their subordinates. During Jackson's war on the Bank of the United States, which he regarded as both unsafe and undemocratic, he ordered the Secretary of the Treasury, William J. Duane, to remove all federal funds from the Bank. Duane refused and was immediately removed; his successor, Roger B. Taney, carried out the President's order. Franklin D. Roosevelt removed Arthur E. Morgan as Chairman of the TVA, and Harry Truman fired Secretary of Commerce Wallace in 1946 following a speech in which the Secretary took sharp issue with the Administration's foreign policy. Eisenhower removed Secretary of the Air Force Talbot when the latter used his position to promote business for his own company. He also removed Arthur Larsen as Director of the U.S. Informa-

---

[10] See Leonard D. White, *The Federalists* (New York: The Macmillan Co., 1948), pp. 17–25.

[11] *Myers v. U.S.* (302 U.S. 379).

tion Agency when Larsen revealed a lack of political acumen in working with Congress. Kennedy removed Secretary of the Navy Fred Korth on a conflict-of-interest issue involving the TFX aircraft contract. President Johnson fired George Reedy, his press secretary, Richard Nixon removed his personal aides John D. Ehrlichman and Harry R. (Bob) Haldeman in connection with the Watergate scandal, and President Ford removed John H. Powell as head of the Equal Employment Opportunity Commission.

Presidential Law Making

The extension of administration into technical areas and the need for prompt action have resulted in increased delegation of law-making power to the President by Congress. He, in turn, subdelegates much of this power to the administrative arm. The orders and regulations by which this is done provide the President with an important means of controlling the sprawling administrative structure. Such powers must in every case be vested in the executive by the Constitution, treaties, or statutes. Increasingly, however, Congress has been content to state its objectives in very broad terms, permitting the President to "fill in the details" through sublegislation. In this way, he can issue directions concerning specific programs, the action of officials in given cases, and the powers of particular agencies.

Control over Official Information

The power of the President over administration in the higher bureaucracy also includes specific directions to officials. While it is well known that officials reveal information in committee hearings and "leak" information to the press, the information they release is subject to some control by the President. The 1947 loyalty order provides an example. In March 1948, President Truman issued an order forbidding all departments and agencies to furnish information concerning the loyalty of any employee to congressional committees or to the courts. This move followed demands of the House Un-American Activities Committee that Secretary of Commerce Averill Harriman surrender an FBI report on Dr. Edward Condon, whom the Committee, with typical hyperbole, termed "one of the weakest links in our atomic security" program. By direct order of the President, Harriman refused to comply. Rather than cite the Secretary for contempt, which logically it should have done,[12] the Com-

---

[12] Corwin, *The President: Office and Power, op. cit.,* p. 142.

mittee waited for reinforcements, which soon came in the form of a House resolution ordering the President to release the Condon file. The President's "freeze order" of March 15 followed. During subsequent hearings, a State Department official, complying with the order, refused to disclose certain information concerning persons handled under the department's loyalty proceedings:

> Senator [Joseph] McCarthy: Who were the other 11?
>
> Mr. Humelsine: The other 11 cases, Senator, I could not give. I could not answer that.
>
> Senator McCarthy: On what theory can you not give them—under the Presidential order?
>
> Mr. Humelsine: Under the Presidential order.[13]

The Watergate Cover-up

A dramatic example of presidential denial of information occurred during the Senate Hearings regarding the Watergate affair (1973), when President Nixon refused to turn over to the Ervin Select Subcommittee on Political Activities tape recordings of his conversations with various members of his staff, the Cabinet, and the Republican Campaign organization, which the Committee argued would provide evidence concerning the ultimate locus of responsibility for the authorization and attempted cover-up of the buggings, break-ins, subsequent pay-offs, and offers of immunity associated with the 1972 presidential election and the Watergate and Los Angeles break-ins by individuals commissioned by members of the White House office. The constitutional basis for the President's refusal was the privacy of presidential papers, his power to take whatever measures seemed required to preserve national security, as well as a separation of powers doctrine which provided several precedents for presidential refusals to release information and documents to Congress when these involve the executive prerogative in such fields as foreign affairs and national defense. As the President said in a letter to Judge John Sirica of the U.S. District Court, "The independence of the three branches of our government is at the very heart of our constitutional system. It would be wholly inadmissible for the president to seek to compel some particular action by the courts. It is equally inadmissible for the courts to seek to compel some particular action from the president."

The Committee in turn appealed to the court for a subpoena that

---

[13] Subcommittee of the Senate Committee on Appropriations, 82d. Cong., 2d sess., *Hearings* on the Appropriation for the Department of State (Washington, D.C.: Government Printing Office, 1952), pp. 404–5.

would force the President to release the tapes, which the Committee insisted were central to its efforts to determine the facts regarding Watergate. Despite the fact that the issue was a melange of political rivalry between the Presidency and Congress, Democratic urges to discredit the party in power, personal motivations to avoid prosecution, seek revenge, and gain publicity, it does provide a dramatic example of presidential denial of information to Congress and the courts, not to mention the public. It is quite clear that the testimony of high-level aides, such as John Dean and John Erlichman, was prepared in a way that sought to reinforce the claims of executive autonomy and privilege in areas putatively dealing with national security.

EXERCISING EXECUTIVE CONTROL

Chief executives have numerous agencies and instruments that help them check on the huge administrative machines for which they are constitutionally accountable. Personal staffs not only provide eyes and ears through which they can scrutinize bureaucratic activities, they can also be used to galvanize particular agencies into action in response to the demands of policy and politics. It is impressive, given the conventional and entirely reasonable accounts of presidential overload, to find that President Nixon could handle so many matters of detail, as shown for example by his direct intervention in the Fitzgerald case, mentioned earlier. We turn next to the kinds of staff agencies available to chief executives.

Executive Staff Agencies

The President, for example, has several such agencies, in part as a result of recommendations by advisory commissions, beginning with the President's Committee on Administrative Management (1937), and followed in post World War II years by the two Hoover Commissions and other experts. Both advocated more staff help for the President, upon whom "falls the crushing burden of bringing all the units of the executive branch into harmony." His main staff aid is the Executive Office of the President, which comprises the White House Office (including several special assistants to the president), the Office of Management and Budget, Council of Economic Advisers, National Security Council, the National Security Resources Board, the Office of Defense and Civilian Mobilization, and the Federal Domestic Council, which is the most recent addition, along with the reorganized Budget Bureau.

The Domestic Council (1970) has the broad purpose of designing, coordinating and reviewing all policy initiatives in the domestic arena. To do this, it works through a number of sub-committees covering both program areas and ad hoc issues. Chaired by the president, it includes the heads of the premier departments, the Vice-president, and the chairman of the Council of Economic Advisers. The director of OMB and his deputy-director are also members. In effect, the traditional weak coordinating role of the Cabinet can be strengthened by this new mechanism. Its relative newness makes any evaluation difficult, although clearly the Council's utility will depend mainly upon the president's willingness to use it.

The OMB is among the most important of these agencies, enabling the president to act as chief fiscal planner, within the limitations noted elsewhere. OMB acts as the President's agent in coordinating policy and in improving procedures of the entire federal administrative operation. To do this, it relies principally upon the budget estimates process, which permits a broad overview of the executive program, gained primarily through discussions between the Office's estimates and fiscal units and the budget officers of the various departments. Subsequently, the director of OMB meets with cabinet officers and the heads of the independent agencies to discuss their programs and set them in the framework of presidential policy. Detailed budgets are then submitted by the departments and agencies and justified before Office examiners. Finally, the President and the director meet, review the broad outlines of agency programs, and make final decisions regarding the figures to be presented to congressional appropriation committees.

The terms of reference of this fiscal evaluation include a broad estimate of tax revenues, the economic outlook, the urgency and level of defense preparations, and the main elements of the President's legislative program. The policies and programs of the bureaucracy are fitted into these larger objectives and expressed in quantitative terms. OMB has the unpopular task of keeping proposed agency expenditures in line with the overall policy of the chief executive. We shall see later that it withheld millions of dollars from HUD.

The OMB also attempts to coordinate non-fiscal legislation originating in the executive branch by requiring its advice on all proposed measures. Although measures opposed by the President are sometimes sent to Congress, independent agency action is discouraged by OMB's close association with the President and its power of recommending approval or disapproval of bills before the President signs them. All these instruments facilitate presidential management, but the record shows that the size and scope of federal administration (as well as that of state and big city governments) make sustained control by the chief executive virtually impossible.

Personal Assistants

Although presidents vary in their use of trusted aides to influence a reluctant bureaucracy, the practice of employing them has been common since Federalist times. Certain presidential assistants, located either in the White House office or without official portfolio, are used as "convincers." Armed with the prestige of the White House, having both the ear and confidence of the president, they penetrate the bureaucracy, often with little regard for the formal chain of command while pressing hard for action on matters of vital importance to their chief. At other times, they may serve as sources of information on existing programs or on the building of new ones. Thus in recent foreign affairs crises, such as Vietnam and the Dominican Republic, President Johnson often bypassed State Department officials and sent his own man (usually Lawrence O'Brien) to the scene to negotiate and bring back first-hand reports. Events such as the Bay of Pigs fiasco, in which the new President, John Fitzgerald Kennedy, received questionable advice and information from within the bureaucracy—mainly the Central Intelligence Agency and the Pentagon—suggest why presidents are wary of depending entirely upon official bureaucratic sources in handling major policy issues.

Another explanation for bypassing the bureaucracy is its tendency to resist and water down innovation through a complex and slow interdepartmental committee process. Thus strong presidents such as Franklin Roosevelt used personal assistants widely and created organizations such as the Securities and Exchange Commission and the TVA to carry out new programs, rather than entrust them to old-line departments. On the other hand, hold-the-line presidents, such as Dwight Eisenhower, tended to rely much more on the established departments and agencies for recommending and carrying out policy. In addition to the personality and experience of the chief executive, it is important to remember that such divergent postures are greatly conditioned by larger events. In periods of crisis, presidents will be more likely and more able to discard so-called administrative principles. In times of economic prosperity and relatively tranquil international conditions, the incentive and latitude for experiment are obviously less compelling.

As noted, since World War II, largely because of huge armament expenditures and the need for central planning to insure better management in government, three important agencies have been added to the President's executive staff. These are the Domestic Council, the Council of Economic Advisers, and the National Security Council.[14] In brief, the Advisers seek to assist the President in forming national economic policy by providing expert analyses of economic developments which form the basis for his annual Economic Report. The Security Council has broader terms of reference; it seeks to ". . . advise the President with respect to the integration of domestic, foreign, and military sources and the other departments and agencies of the Government to cooperate more effectively in matters involving the national security."

White House Office

Members of the President's White House Office staff occupy positions of special importance for executive control. Inside observers have estimated that only two or three Cabinet members rival the 'President's Men' in influence and authority.[15] This staff is probably the major instrument for keeping the bureaucracy in line with presidential policies. Kennedy's staff has been described as "not a pyramid but a wheel figuring a network of bilateral relations between the President and his aides."[16] Among the 22 men heading up the staff, two were "all-purpose" types, involved in recruitment or "head-hunting" and liaison between the President, the United Nations, the State Department, and the intellectual community. Five of the 22 were assigned precise functional tasks, including such White House administrative chores as appointments with the President; special counsel to the President; the special assistant for national security affairs; the assistant for congressional relations; and the Press Secretary. The annual budget (1975) of the office amounts to about $5 million.

Issues, of course, often cut across functional areas, so that two or three of these aides often worked together on a given issue. Apparently, there

14 On these agencies, see Edward S. Flash, Jr., *Economic Advice and Presidential Leadership: The Council of Economic Advisers* (New York: Columbia University Press, 1965), Chaps. 8–9; Henry M. Jackson (ed.), *The National Security Council* (New York: Frederick A. Praeger, Inc., 1965).

15 Joseph Kraft, "Kennedy's Working Staff" *Harper's Magazine* (December, 1962), pp. 29–36.

16 *Ibid.*

existed a quasi-military terseness and brevity among staff members and in their relations with Kennedy. This norm apparently led to some tension between the "Irish Mafia," comprised of tough-minded, politically experienced members of the staff and its "Harvard" component which operated in a rather different style. The staff's capacity to handle the bureaucracy got off to a bad start with the Bay of Pigs affair, in which the President received somewhat inadequate advice and intelligence from the military and the CIA. "At that point," according to one of the aides, "we just didn't have the confidence to tell the veterans of the bureaucracy,[17] 'Look, you're crazy.'" In other areas, the administration was quite successful in working with both the bureaucracy and Congress.

Executive Office of the President

Much larger than the White House Office, although with occasional overlapping, is the Executive Office of the President which under Lyndon Johnson numbered about 1,500, comprised of nine major elements: the White House Office (376 employees), Management and Budget Office (485 employees), Council of Economic Advisers (57), National Security Council (43), Office of Emergency Planning (406), Central Intelligence Agency (no employment figures available), National Aeronautics and Space Council (28), Office of Science and Technology (48), and the Office of the Special Representative for Trade Negotiations (30). An index of the salience of this agency is the size of its budget, estimated at $102 million for 1975. "This super-organization of the presidential office has been accompanied by the amplification, consolidation and exercise of presidential power. The authority that men like Lincoln and Theodore Roosevelt have exercised in times of crisis, real or assumed, has become a stable, dependable, and predictable basis for the exercise of presidential authority." [18]

Such authority is activated by the various powers and benefits that a president can allocate. As James McGregor Burns concludes, "The presidential politicians in power hold a commanding position in the vast political arena. The White House is a superb command post from which to conduct day-to-day presidential politics. It is also a 'bully pulpit' from which Presidents can hurl political thunderbolts and moral judgments. Day after day the nation's politicians, legislators, group leaders, and freewheeling VIP's troop into the west wing as steadily as the tourists trudge

[17] Cited in *ibid.*, p. 31.
[18] James McGregor Burns, *Presidential Government: The Crucible of Leadership* (Boston: Houghton Mifflin, Inc., 1966).

through the east wing and the mansion. The White House is a round-the-clock, round-the-year campaign headquarters."

Its political resources are enormous. Even aside from the President's constitutional power in determining "who gets what, when, and how," he has a reservoir of specific favors that whet any politician's appetite. The host of appointments, including the most prestigious such as ambassadorial ones, are only the more obvious kind of favors. The presidential politicians can grant access to the President, obtain a letter or photograph from him, and arrange special forms of recognition, such as an invitation to a state dinner. An interest group can be favored with a special White House conference on a problem it wishes spotlighted. Presidential commissions can be established to focus attention on an issue, and membership on the commission is another form of patronage. Presidential acceptance of invitations to speak is an important kind of patronage. Such presidential favors may seem to the outside observer to be rather freely and loosely distributed; actually there are few given out that are not schemed and struggled for, and they are granted only after the presidential politicians have carefully calculated the advantages to the President.

The presidential party at the center is a highly centralized and disciplined political organization. Political decisions are made on the basis of one criterion: what is best for the political standing, prestige, reputation, and re-electibility of the *President*. The Chief Executive's almost absolute control over his staff is as crucial politically as it is administratively. Anyone below the President is expendable. Men must be willing to take the gaff for errors; they must be able to cope with the disappointed politicos who may be left out of presidential favor and who vent their wrath on "the White House gang" or the "inner circle" which, they feel, have cut them off from the President.[19]

Reorganization Power

Insofar as his control is increased by a rational division of authority and responsibility within an agency, the President's reorganization power is an important instrument of bureaucratic control. Beginning with the Reorganization Acts of 1939 and 1949, he has been given power to design and submit reorganization schemes to Congress. While exemption of certain agencies has restricted such action, the most recent statute (1949) included no exemptions and extended somewhat the two-year time limit

[19] *Ibid.*, pp. 167–68.

during which the President must act. Under this statute, President Truman submitted some forty reorganization plans in an effort, in his words, "to achieve a more responsible and efficient administration of Federal programs." The vast majority of these plans, which go into effect automatically in sixty days if not negated by a majority vote of House or Senate, were accepted by Congress.[20]

President Eisenhower also used the reorganization power, as indicated by his letter accompanying Reorganization Plan No. 1 of 1958, which merged the civil defense establishment with the office of defense mobilization: "I transmit herewith Reorganization Plan No. 1 of 1958, prepared in accordance with the Reorganization Act of 1949, as amended. The reorganization plan provides new arrangements for the conduct of Federal defense mobilization and civil defense functions. In formulating Reorganization Plan No. 1, I have had the benefit of several studies made by the Executive Branch as well as those conducted by the Congress."

The reorganization transferred to the President the functions of the Civil Defense Administration and the Office of Defense Mobilization, establishing a single agency for the two somewhat related functions. A new Office of Defense and Civilian Mobilization was set up in the Executive Office of the President. The main reasons for the President's action are suggested by his concluding statement:

> The taking effect of the reorganization included in Reorganization Plan No. 1 of 1958 will immediately reduce the number of Federal agencies by one and, by providing sounder organizational arrangements for the administration of the affected functions, should promote the increased economy and effectiveness of the Federal expenditures concerned. It is, however, impracticable to itemize at this time the reduction of expenditures which it is probable will be brought about by such taking effect. I urge that the Congress allow the reorganization plan to become effective.

The second Hoover Commission, reporting in 1955, brought public opinion to bear by its recommendations for further reorganization. Indeed, the national chairman of its Citizens Committee maintained that "a national ground swell of public sentiment for Federal economy and efficiency is gaining strength daily and is now close to the surface." [21] Despite this ground swell, the President was soon obliged to ask for an abrogation of the existing federal debt limit, suggesting that those who

---

[20] Senate Committee on Expenditures in the Executive Departments, 82d Cong., 2d Sess., *Reorganization of the Federal Government* (Washington, D.C.: Government Printing Office, 1952).

[21] Clarence Francis, as quoted in *Congressional Quarterly* (April 4, 1958), p. 436.

emphasized the economy aspect of reorganization must have experienced some frustration. Nevertheless, the Commission's record with Congress was impressive. In 1959 the second Hoover Commission had made 167 recommendations for reorganization that required legislative action. Of these, 55 were carried out by the 84th Congress, while the 85th Congress passed laws "consistent with 11 recommendations."

Another example of the successful use of presidential reorganization power occurred in 1970 when Nixon presented a plan to establish the OMB and Domestic Council, while ending the Bureau of Budget. The President used the argument of "greater efficiency," as did Eisenhower regarding the ODCM during his regime. "While this plan will result in a modest increase in direct expenditures, its strengthening of the Executive Office of the President will bring significant indirect savings, and at the same time will help ensure that people actually receive the return they deserve for every dollar the Government spends. The savings will result from the improved efficiency these changes will provide throughout the Executive Branch—and also from curtailing the waste that results when programs simply fail to achieve their objectives." [22]

Appeals to Public Opinion

His position as political leader of his party, general manager of the executive branch, and Commander in Chief obviously give the President great influence over public opinion, enabling him to focus national attention upon great issues and to generate support for his policies. While this influence is most dramatically illustrated in his relations with a reluctant Congress, the President can also use his position to tune up the administrative machine. The public opinion the chief executive creates on policy issues not only defines more clearly for the agency the "public interest" insofar as it relates to these issues, it also helps the agency resist the claims of special groups. When faced with a particular issue, administrators often have difficulty in identifying the public interest. Presidential emphasis upon an issue, reinforced by public discussion, can provide both a criterion for administrative action and a base of support. The emphasis here upon the "public interest" and the tacit assumption

[22] "Message from the President of the United States Transmitting Reorganization Plan No. 2 of 1970," *Hearings* before the Subcommittee on Executive Reorganization and Government Research of the Committee on Government Operations, United States Senate, 91st Congress, 2nd session (May 8, 1970), Washington, D. C.: U. S. Government Printing Office, 1970, p. 8.

that it can sometimes be identified are perhaps warranted by the fact that the big issues upon which the President takes a stand usually involve interests clearly broader than those of any single group or constellation of groups.

It is important to add, however, that the effectiveness of appeals to public opinion is largely a function of the personality of the President and his conception of the office itself. Franklin D. Roosevelt, for example, used the presidency as a forum for vigorous leadership. Dwight D. Eisenhower, on the other hand, played a reluctant role, reflecting his preference for a legislative dominated federal government. John Fitzgerald Kennedy was also reluctant to appeal directly to the public when Congress refused to support him on such vital programs as medicare and federal aid to higher education. Richard Nixon tended to have very limited interaction and rapport with the mass media, which restricted the utility as well as the use of broad appeals to public opinion. By contrast, President Ford has used the mass media more intensely, in part because of the harsh economic problems confronting his Administration. Organizationally, such diverse conceptions are reflected in different degrees of dependence upon staff aides. Whereas Truman, Johnson, and Roosevelt tended to act independently on vital issues, Eisenhower, Nixon, and Ford preferred to delegate considerable authority to their aides.

Three Vital Speeches

Among the most effective appeals to national opinion are the statements of policy comprising the three principal speeches made by the President each year. The State of the Union Message, for example, given at the opening session of each Congress, sets down very generally the President's main objectives. Cabinet members and key officials participate in drafting the message, indicating major domestic and foreign problems and the Administration's plan for attacking them. Thus the issues are placed before the nation, Congress, and the bureaucracy. The Economic Report, which consists of a detailed analysis of current economic problems and prospects for the immediate future, provides a second opportunity to outline Administration policy and mobilize public support for it. Prepared with the aid of the Council of Economic Advisers, the report recommends legislation to meet existing or anticipated problems. Finally, the President's Budget Message provides a means of planning and controlling administration by outlining the programs and financial requirements of the entire federal establishment, as prepared by the Office of Management and Budget. Included in this message is a statement of the legislation which the various agencies have requested.

These instruments of presidential leadership not only enable the President to focus public attention upon critical problems and his proposed solutions but they also serve as a challenge to Congress and the bureaucracy. The President in effect says, "Here is my program; this is what I need in the way of legislation, money, and administrative skill." Given the representative character of the presidency and the political independence the President normally enjoys because of his national constituency, this demand can have great weight. The presidency, moreover, possesses a unity of intent and purpose, as well as a capacity for decisive action, denied Congress by its collective nature. Unlike any given administrator hedged about by specific pressures and programs, the President has freedom to speak in terms of the "public interest." This combination of constitutional and strategic power gives him a peculiar advantage in focusing public opinion upon the bureaucracy, an opinion to which it, as part of a democratic society, will sometimes respond.

CONTROL REMAINS INADEQUATE

Despite these powers, the President usually finds his control of the administrative arm less than adequate. While he may have been exaggerating somewhat for effect, we have the word of Harry Truman, expressed regarding his successor, Dwight Eisenhower: "He will come in, sit behind this desk and give orders, and nothing will happen." The inertia and resistance of departments and agencies, many of which have their own external sources of political strength, the sheer magnitude of the federal program, the opposition of Congress to measures strengthening executive control—an important obstacle to executive reorganization plans, for example, has been the contest for power between the President and the Congress—the peculiar position of the regulatory commissions, and the brief tenure of many of his top political aides are among the major factors inhibiting effective control by the chief administrator. He can, it is true, appoint his major aides and remove them. He can dispatch trusted aides to break administrative log-jams. He can appeal to the nation, dramatizing issues which Congress and the bureaucracy must accept. By Executive Orders, directives to key officials, and reports from agencies, he can guide administrative policies and programs. The reorganization power, moreover, enables him to improve the structure and operation of the bureaucracy. His staff offices, particularly the Office of Management and Budget and the National Security Council, also assist him in coordinating the economic and military resources of the nation.

But the task of supervising and controlling about one hundred departments and agencies that "report" to the President is too great. Despite some conflicting evidence the divided commitments and loyalties of a competitive bureaucracy (sometimes called the last vestige of free enterprise in our society) and their alliances with legislative and producer elites create "whirlpools of interest" beyond the sustained control of any chief executive, despite the political and administrative weapons at his command.

19

Legislative Oversight of Administration

Although his impact is probably somewhat greater and certainly more direct, the President's influence over the bureaucracy is shared with Congress, which shapes the broad objectives of administration and authorizes the funds required to achieve them. Routine activities of the bureaucracy are open to legislative scrutiny through committee hearings. At other times, individual legislators may develop an exhaustive interest in a particular agency, seeking evidence of dereliction. Such excursions are often of value and appear to have become an accepted part of legislative activity. It should not be forgotten, meanwhile, that the mere possibility of legislative intervention has some influence on the behavior of administrators.

MEDIA OF OVERSIGHT [1]

Legislatures, of course, have a vital role in setting the main objectives of administration. That the chief executive and the bureaucracy participate in policy-making does not alter the fact that legislatures pass the laws and appropriate the money which make administration possible.

---

[1] The term "oversight" is used instead of "control" to emphasize that the legislative role in this context is typically *post hoc* and that "control" is probably too strong a concept to accurately describe the process.

They also determine the structure of agencies and sometimes concern themselves with the minutiae of their internal operations and organization. Had Congress, for example, refused to accept executive recommendations that NASA be designed as an independent agency, enjoying certain freedoms which departments do not enjoy, it probably could not have earned international acclaim in the area of space research and technology. On the other hand, official discretion can be limited and routine decisions controlled through detailed legislative prescriptions as seen in the allocation of Agency for International Development funds and the limiting of presidential discretion in reciprocal tariff agreements.

Legislatures exercise the most decisive control over administration through their powers of appropriation and law making. They may, as they occasionally do, abolish an agency or cripple it through limiting the funds necessary to support its programs. Through *ex parte* representation they can influence an agency's policy in specific cases. They can check the achievements and routine work of agencies through hearings before which officials appear. Investigation may reveal how well the bureaucracy is carrying out its legal obligations. Legislatures also participate in the appointment of public officials, and thus shape administration through their powers of confirmation and rejection. These various measures will now be considered in turn.

The Appropriation Process: Some Limitations

Legislatures control the purse strings and hence, it would seem, the very existence of the bureaucracy and its programs. It is generally agreed that appropriation committees are the main instrument of legislative scrutiny and control of administration. In issues of striking importance or in instances where the lawmakers' wrath has been stirred by official misbehavior, legislatures can and do punish offenders by slashing their appropriations. But in many cases legislatures (especially Congress, given the huge sums and programs involved) are not competent to evaluate administrative requests for funds. In the first place, executive budgets have grown to enormous proportions. The annual federal budget, for example, now totals $300 billion; its programs for some one hundred departments and agencies comprise fourteen hundred pages. Congress does not have the time to analyze this huge budget, partially because of the late date at which it is received. Congressmen, moreover, are laymen; they cannot be expected to command the technical knowledge or experience required to evaluate the requests of scores of agencies charged with a bewildering variety of programs. They must rely on the experts, the bureaucracy.

Not only is careful appropriations analysis often beyond the temporal and technical resources of congressmen; they have, for reasons which are not very clear, often failed to provide themselves with the staff necessary to gain the specific information required to control government functions. The dilemma of Congress here is explicit in the words of Senator Paul Douglas, a well-known economist: "I shall never forget my gasp of surprise when I discovered that the Senate Appropriations Committee had only *one* professional man to help evaluate a $61 billion appropriation bill for the Department of Defense." The words of Congressman Meader, member of a House subcommittee on military appropriations, are even more suggestive.

> The Committee and the House are dealing with this huge and difficult task without adequate tools. Seven men almost with their bare hands are standing up to a huge organization with thousands of officials, both civilian and military, devoting their full time to the presentation of self-serving statements and documents, and inundating the committee with a plethora of testimony and charts and statistics which the committee is unable to digest, to say nothing of challenging. The Congress is at the mercy of the executive. . . . What if they had asked for eighty billion instead of fifty-six billion? Would the committee have been able to challenge and resist the request? [2]

Some quarter-century later, the situation had not changed very much. As Congressman Les Aspin (Wisconsin) concludes,

> Congressmen are rarely experts on anything except how their constituents are reacting to the current political, social, and economic state of affairs. Sometimes, as a result of this, congressmen develop a passing expertise on domestic matters. Rarely, however, does a member of Congress turn into an expert on defense or foreign policy, much of which is either highly technical or exotic or both. On these subjects, particularly, the congressman is painfully aware that the "experts" (scientists, economists, generals) are working for the executive branch. For Congress to stand up to the Executive on a major issue requires that over half of the congressmen are confident enough to declare, in effect, that they know more about a particular issue than the so-called experts. But probably no more than a relative handful of members of the House of Representatives knows enough about any given weapons system, for example, to vote for or against it on its merit. No wonder the Pentagon hardly ever loses.[3]

[2] Cited in "Has Congress Failed?" *Fortune* (February, 1952), p. 222.
[3] Les Aspin, "Why Doesn't Congress Do Something?" *Foreign Policy*, Vol. 15, (Summer 1974), p. 73.

The problem is aggravated, moreover, by the fact that budget esti-mates are distributed among several subcommittees of the appropriations committees; each proceeds independently with little communication with the others. Although the recommendations of each sub-committee are reviewed by the parent committee, little time is left for careful analysis, and the expertise which the sub-committees develop in their given areas means that their decisions have great influence. Shared expertise, more-over, may develop into empathy. Committee members may become too sympathetic toward the programs with which they are concerned. Some observers do not agree that Congress does not handle appropriations analysis adequately, but the weight of opinion supports this conclusion.

Some analysts have a happier view of congressional capacity to con-trol military expenditures: "Congress in the 1960's did not docilely accept and ratify the defense policy decisions of the executive. On the con-trary, it played a relatively lively role in particular policies, an activism whose level seemed to be associated with a perceived inadequacy of presidential decisions and actions. Congress can influence in the future, as it has influenced in the past, the *content* of defense policy by means of control of appropriations."[4] The size of federal deficits and the well-known waste in military spending raise strong doubts about this gen-eralization.

Certain means of legislative control of spending do exist. One is the attachment of riders to appropriations bills in an attempt to control future executive programs. This does not always work. In June 1965, for ex-ample, President Johnson vetoed a $70 million flood relief bill because certain projected activities could be carried out only with subsequent and specific approval of certain House committees. Calling the provision a violation "of the spirit of the division of powers between the executive and legislative branches," he vetoed the measure. He did, however, in-dicate that he would sign it if Congress would delete the offending pro-vision, which it promptly did.

The essentially *post hoc* nature of much legislative control is suggested by the conclusions of a sub-committee of the House Armed Services Committee. In late 1965, the sub-committee charged that the Air Force's "think factory," the Aerospace Corporation, had engaged in a number of extravagant spending practices. Challenging the Corporation's man-agement concepts and the Air Force's acceptance of them, the sub-

---

[4] Arnold Kanter, "Congress and the Defense Budget: 1960–1970," *The American Political Science Review*, Vol. 66 (March, 1972), p. 142.

committee cited the spending of $22 million for land and new buildings in California when unused government property was available and criticized as well "frivolous spending" for country club memberships for Aerospace executives; "unusually high starting salaries . . . with unlimited sick leave and excellent relocation allowances." Such investigations undoubtedly result in some tightening up of agency spending, but Congress has great difficulty in maintaining any sustained *pre-spending* scrutiny of the vast bureaucratic apparatus.

The Comptroller General as Arm of Congress

Perhaps the most incisive scrutiny of management practices is carried out by the Comptroller General though the General Accounting Office, established in 1921 as a "Congressional watchdog." Although he issues periodic reports regarding waste in the military establishment, the Comptroller General's penumbra is much broader, extending to all government agencies (save CIA and, presumably, the FBI as well), including those abroad.[5] In 1964, for example, investigations were made at almost three thousand different places, including forty-one foreign countries. Regarding the Department of Defense—our largest spender—the Comptroller had a great deal to say.[6] Figure 19–1 is one of fourteen pages of similarly detailed analyses of poor military management and attending overspending.

In all, the Comptroller claimed that he had saved the taxpayer $292 million during 1972 [7] by his audits and investigations. Here again, there is little doubt that the Comptroller's disclosures, which are passed on to Congress and hence to the interested public, have some effect on administrative spending. At the same time, we are told by the Comptroller that federal agencies do not always heed the good advice he gives them. And once again, such inquiries are *post hoc*. The disclosures appear only after the waste has occurred.

The GAO has other limitations. According to Joseph Harris, the Comptroller General tends to encroach upon policy matters involving

---

[5] See, for example, Comptroller General of the United States, *Report to the Congress of the United States: Review of the Administration of the Economic and Technical Assistance Program for Vietnam* (Washington, D.C.: Government Printing Office, 1964).

[6] Comptroller General of the United States, *Annual Report* (Washington, D.C.: Government Printing Office, 1964), pp. 341–55.

[7] *Appendix to the Annual Report of the Comptroller General of the United States, 1972,* Washington, D. C.: U. S. Government Printing Office, 1973, p. 157.

Title	Waste and mismanagement	Estimated unnecessary costs and losses
Unnecessary procurement initiated for 9,000 B.t.u. air conditioners, Department of the Army, B–146807, Jan. 16, 1964.	The Army initiated a procurement for 214 air conditioners for which firm requirements did not exist. The Signal Corps failed to advise the Corps of Engineers in a timely manner that the units were not needed.	$161,500.
Unnecessary cost incurred in the procurement of AN/ARN 21C TACAN radio components through failure to accept option offer, Department of the Air Force, B–146836, Jan. 24, 1964.	Air Force incurred unnecessary costs of over $1,000,000 by its failure to incorporate into a contract an option offered by the supplier of TACAN radio components to furnish additional quantities at the original contract price.	$1,000,000.
Unnecessary costs relating to reassignment of management responsibility for tool sets, Department of the Army and Defense Supply Agency, B–146856, Jan. 28, 1964.	The Defense General Supply Center (DGSC), under the Defense Supply Agency, had in process or planned unnecessary procurement of $261,000 worth of hand tools and $13,000 worth of needed tools were disposed of as a result of failure to transfer $1,200,000 worth of excess Army hand tools to the DGSC. Moreover, the cost of complete tool sets purchased by DGSC could have been reduced by $82,000 if DGSC had furnished its contractors some of the tools needed which were available from the excess stocks.	$356,000.
Overbuying and unnecessary overhaul costs resulting from the failure of the Army to follow the Navy's practice of separating accessories from spare reciprocating aircraft engines, Department of the Army, B–132989, Jan. 30, 1964.	The Army bought aircraft engine accessories costing $1,014,000 during the 6-year period ended Dec. 31, 1962, and incurred overhaul costs estimated at $421,000 during fiscal years 1961 and 1962 that could have been avoided by following the Navy's practice of removing accessories from spare engines.	$1,435,000.
Excessive charges for components for M-60 tanks under contract with Chrysler Corp., Detroit, Mich., Department of the Army, B–133295, Jan. 31, 1964.	The revised final contract price for M-60 tanks under Department of the Army contract with Chrysler Corp., contained duplicate and excessive costs which increased the contract price by about $315,200 for components made at certain of the contractor's plants. The procuring agency (1) failed to obtain a certification on the cost data, despite a contract requirement for such a certificate, and (2) accepted the summary cost data submitted without an adequate review.	$315,200.
Increased costs incurred for ammonium perchlorate purchased during 1961 for solid-propellant missile motors, Department of the Air Force, B–146843, Jan. 31, 1964.	The Government incurred increased costs, estimated to be $500,000 in 1961, in procuring its requirement of ammonium perchlorate because prices paid by Air Force contractors generally were higher than prices paid by the Navy under contracts negotiated directly with one of the principal suppliers.	$500,000.
Overpricing of ship propulsion boilers purchased under fixed-price contract NObs-76301 negotiated with Foster Wheeler Corp., New York, N.Y., Department of the Navy, B–146733, Jan. 31, 1964.	The price that the Bureau of Ships negotiated with Foster Wheeler for boilers amounting to $1,722,300, was at least $132,200 greater than the costs Foster Wheeler could reasonably expect to incur plus profit at the rate of 10 percent of such costs, the rate used in Foster Wheeler's price proposal.	$132,200.
Excessive stocks at selected bases of U.S. 5th Air Force in Japan and Korea, Department of the Air Force, B–146844, Jan. 31, 1964.	Over $4,300,000 worth of excess stocks were on hand or on order from U.S. depots. The excesses accumulated because of failure to appropriately consider (1) prior usage, (2) large number of items on hand in maintenance shops, and (3) available substitute or reparable items.	$4,300,000.
Overpricing of nuclear reactor components purchased from Westinghouse Electric Corp., Pittsburgh, Pa., under cost-plus - a - fixed - fee contracts awarded by the Bureau of Ships, Department of the Navy, B–146733, Feb. 6, 1964.	Plant Apparatus Division, Westinghouse, under Navy cost-plus-a-fixed-fee contracts, awarded a subcontract for 35 pumps and 16 casings to Atomic Equipment Division, Westinghouse, without obtaining AED's estimated cost of performance or information as to actual incurred costs in prior production of similar components.	$705,000.
Unnecessary costs resulting from Government production of M-14 rifle repair parts rather than procurement from commercial sources, Department of the Army, B–146848, Feb. 7, 1964.	The Government incurred unnecessary costs of $216,000 because the Army Weapons Command placed orders for certain repair parts for M-14 rifles with Springfield Armory without first comparing costs to be incurred by the armory with prices it was currently paying to commercial sources for the same parts.	$216,000.

¹ Exclusive of international operations listed separately.

Fig. 19–1. Comptroller General's audit of military overspending.

economic and military judgments in which the GAO has no special competence.[8] In 1959, for example, loan criteria of the Development Loan Fund were criticized; in 1962 the Comptroller General informed Congress that the testing and control measures used by the National Institutes of Health ought to conform with those of the Food and Drug Administration, even though different kinds of drugs were involved. In the process, traditional conflicts between the legislative and executive branches tend to be exacerbated. On the whole, however, it seems that the GAO performs a vitally necessary function of ventilating administrative errors, which might otherwise remain unknown.

Committee Hearings

Hearings on appropriation requests provide a reasonably effective means for legislators to acquaint administrators with their values and objectives. Committee members and the officials who appear before them often retain their respective posts over a long period of time, which means that each will come to know the other's mind. At times, legislators will single out a certain agency for criticism, making the appearance of its officials a trying experience. At the same time, of course, there are agencies, such as the Federal Bureau of Investigation, the Army Corps of Engineers, and the Passport Division of the State Department, which enjoy the full confidence of Congress.

Congressional attitudes and the detailed influence exerted through committee hearings are suggested by the following testimony before a Senate subcommittee on government operations concerning a bill to regulate the outside employment of civil servants. The major basis for the discussion was a report by the General Accounting Office showing that certain employees involved in map making had formed dummy corporations to carry out contracts with federal agencies. The GAO stated that one hundred and twenty-five federal employees had worked for local map-making companies during the period 1953–1956, and that some of them had financial interests in the companies. The report also revealed that only four of these one hundred and twenty-five employees had informed their superiors that they were engaged in outside work. Another background datum is that all the government agencies appearing before the committee opposed the proposed legislation on the basis that they already had sufficient authority to control personnel activities.

---

[8] *Congressional Control of Administration, op. cit.*, pp. 150–52.

The inquiry was initiated by Senator George D. Aiken of Vermont on the basis of complaints received from one of his constituents. As the Senator remarked before the sub-committee:

> I want to tell you why this bill, S 2259, has been introduced by me. It was drafted to end abuses which first came to my attention approximately 4 years ago. Between 1954 and 1957 I received repeated complaints from the National Survey, a map-making concern located at Chester, Vt. These complaints alleged that much of the Government map-making work was being done by fly-by-night companies located in the Washington metropolitan area. The president of The National Survey told me that these companies were hiring Government employees in their spare time to do map work under Government contracts to local concerns, and that bidding was done by Government employees on Government contracts through strawmen or dummy companies.[9]

Another example illustrates the extent to which congressmen can make officials aware of their own preferences:

> *Mr. Flynt:* In the future, after the war in Vietnam which most of these deserters and draft evaders have evaded, at that time do you think a general amnesty law would be in the best interests of future manpower requirements in view of the many thousands killed and wounded and maimed for life?
>
> *Secretary Laird:* I can only say that in the history of our country, our Commander in Chief has always considered the question of amnesty only after—
>
> *Mr. Flynt:* I am talking about after.
>
> *Secretary Laird:* That would be under those terms. I do not think it serves a helpful purpose right now to get into the kinds of recommendations or the kinds of programs that might be worked out which would temper our system of justice with the degree of mercy that is needed and necessary as far as our society is concerned. I would not want to make that kind of recommendation now.
>
> *Mr. Flynt:* I would like to add, in the form of an observation rather than a question, that as one member of this committee, I would certainly oppose any general amnesty legislation, because I feel that in view of the excessive number of draft evasions and desertions during the past 8 years, if a general amnesty law were to be enacted, this coun-

---

[9] Subcommittee of the Senate Committee on Government Operations, 85th Cong., 2d sess., *Hearings* on the Bill To Regulate Outside Employment of Federal Employees (Washington, D.C.: Government Printing Office, 1958), p. 7. It should be noted that the initiation of this inquiry actually came from the public, i.e., from the President of the National Survey.

try would never again be able to fulfill its manpower requirements under a Selective Service Act.

Secretary Laird: That concern is shared by me. . . .[10]

An exchange between Representative George W. Andrews of Alabama and Lt. Gen. A. D. Starbird, U.S. Army, suggests the kind of detailed information congressmen can elicit in hearings:

> *Mr. Andrews:* General Starbird, if I understand correctly, the purpose of this Safeguard system is to protect our retaliatory forces, not our cities.
>
> *Gen. Starbird:* This is correct; and to protect against the Chinese type attack, should that develop.
>
> *Mr. Andrews:* Protect what against the Chinese?
>
> *Gen. Starbird:* Even the cities.
>
> *Mr. Andrews:* All of them?
>
> *Gen. Starbird:* All of continental United States.
>
> *Mr. Andrews:* Why do you say protect against the Chinese rather than the Russians? Because the Chinese do not have as great a capability?
>
> *Gen. Starbird:* That is correct.
>
> *Mr. Andrews:* You mean, if you had these sites out in the Midwest, and these other places that you propose to protect, all the cities on the east coast, the west coast, and the middle United States, it would do so against the Chinese attack?
>
> *Gen. Starbird:* Right, sir; against the Chinese type attack . . .
>
> *Mr. Andrews:* Suppose you had a double-barrelled attack from the Chinese and the Russians, where would you be?
>
> *Gen. Starbird:* Then the Russians would overwhelm it insofar as protecting cities are concerned.
>
> *Mr. Andrews:* But you still can protect our missile sites?
>
> *Gen. Starbird:* Our deterrent; right.[11]

While this example reveals the detail into which legislators may go in questioning officials, and also the kind of information they receive from such individuals, one gets the impression that legislators are sometimes rather frustrated by their lack of knowledge of administrative policy and action. The time available to cover the vast scope of administrative operations is also limited.

Hearings can be used to implement legislative control in still another way. They provide legislators an opportunity to give directions to of-

---

[10] See exchange between Representative John J. Flynt, Jr., of Georgia and Melvin R. Laird, Secretary of Defense, *Hearings* before a Subcommittee of the Committee on Appropriations, House of Representatives, 92nd Congrss, 2nd session, Washington, U.S. Government Printing Office, 1972, p. 517.

[11] *Hearings* before a Subcommittee of the Committee on Appropriations, House of Representatives, 91st Congress, 1st session, Washington, U.S. Government Printing Office, 1969, Part 6, pp. 202–3.

ficials concerning specific programs. The effectiveness of this technique is suggested by former Senator McCarran's comments regarding security measures:

> I will tell you something coming from the heart of the Chairman. If the policy of the State Department would be to carry out the spirit and intent of the Internal Security Act, you will get a lot of sympathy from one member of this committee. I would like to see it carried out more rigidly and more emphatically than I think it has been carried out. . . .[12]

Limitations on the Effectiveness of Hearings.   As noted, committee hearings on legislative proposals enable Congress to influence administrative behavior. The attitudes of committee members and their interpretation of the objectives of a particular bill are often made patent. When the bill becomes law, officials responsible for its implementation will be fully aware of the legislature's will and can make it known through directives and general supervision. Hearings, in sum, provide a means of inquiry into proposed measures, the reasons for their introduction, the bases of their support, and the objectives their sponsors seek. But here again their effectiveness as a control measure has several limitations.

Hearings are sometimes partisan encounters in which witnesses present selected data supporting only their own point of view. In some cases, moreover, committee members themselves do not bring an open mind to the hearing. They have already decided whether or not they favor a particular bill and will often bend the questions and testimony to justify their preconceptions.[13] Testimony from the Senate (Kefauver) sub-committee hearings on the drug industry indicates the intensity of such differences. Senator Dirksen, who opposed legislation extending control over prices, production, and nomenclature of pharmaceuticals, commented following a summary of the committee's findings by Senator Kefauver who had advocated stronger controls:

> First. I think I ought to correct you about the source of new drugs, when you said Germany was the great source. I thought the record showed that two-thirds of all the new, effective ethical drugs were initiated in the United States, and one-third in the rest of the world.

---

[12] Subcommittee of the Senate Committee on Appropriations, 82d Cong., 2d sess., *Hearings* on the Appropriation for the Department of State (Washington, D.C.: Government Printing Office, 1952), pp. 36–37.

[13] Harris, for example, concludes, "Congressional investigations of administration . . . are seldom free of partisanship." *Congressional Control of Administration, op. cit.*, pp. 292–93.

What you read is a summary of the majority report, and as you know, we wrote a rather extensive minority report, and I think we refuted every one of the contentions you made with respect to prices, lack of competition, profits and cost structure, and permanent control of the market, and this whole question of patents and everything else.[14]

Special Investigating Committees

The work of regular standing committees must be differentiated from special investigations by select committees. Although the use of such committees can degenerate into a scramble for publicity, some of these investigations have been valuable and, if properly used, provide a useful means of control. During the 1920's Congress investigated corruption in the Harding Administration; during the 1930's the Temporary National Economic Committee carried out a broad-gauged inquiry into the growing concentration of economic power in the United States. The evidence and recommendations of the TNEC had considerable impact. Certainly, some of the differences between economic theory and practice in our economy were dramatized.

During the New Deal, the scope of the investigatory power to control administration was expanded by its use to dramatize the need for social change. Investigations were nicely timed to coincide with presidential recommendations for important legislation. The inquiry into lobbying in 1935, for example, opened the way for laws restraining utility holding companies, while the enactment of the Securities and Exchange Act of 1935 was undoubtedly made easier by committee revelations of questionable exchange and banking practices which contributed to the 1929 debacle.[15]

During the 1940's, major investigations of war expenditures carried on by the Truman Committee were effective in encouraging agencies to adopt improved procedures. The Committee's methods were exemplary. A bipartisan approach promoted objectivity, witnesses were well-treated, and responsible officials were allowed to read and evaluate the Committee's reports before their release. During the post-war period, the scrutiny of military expenditures has been continued by several congressional committees which have revealed some instances of maladminis-

---

[14] Senate Subcommittee on Antitrust and Monopoly, 87th Cong., 1st sess., *Hearings* pursuant to S. Res. 52 on S. 1552 (Washington, D.C.: Government Printing Office, 1962), pp. 15–16.

[15] M. N. McGeary, *Development of Congressional Investigation Power* (New York: Columbia University Press, 1940), pp. 37–45.

tration. Perhaps the most effective have been Senator E. C. Johnson's preparedness sub-committee and that of Congressman Hardy, who after an on-the-scene investigation branded the North African air base construction program a "fiasco" in which some $50 million had been wasted.

In 1957–1958, a sub-committee on legislative oversight made some important revelations about certain questionable policies and practices of officials. Senator Kefauver's investigation of the drug industry (1962), aided by the tragic consequences of the use of thalidomide, resulted in improved legislation in a vital area. The investigation of the Watergate affair by a Senate Select Committee on Presidential Campaign Activities during 1973 provides an even more dramatic example of the operation of such committees. Watergate, in turn, inspired the creation of other special investigations by congressional committees, including an inquiry into the operations and accountability of the CIA and the Internal Revenue Service.

Senate Confirmation of Appointments

In major appointments, of course, the President's power is shared with the Senate, which enables it to participate directly in selecting high officials who play an important role in directing the bureaucracy. Appointments often have an immediate effect on the implementation of legislation. Even when the Senate confirms an appointee, the hearing gives Senators an opportunity to influence administration by expressing their values and expectations in regard to the operation of the agency concerned. This aspect of control is nicely illustrated in the nomination of Richard Kleindienst as Attorney General:

> Senator Bayh: If you have someone out there who is about to overthrow the Government or you have reason to believe that there is this kind of conspiracy, I think you ought to put the hammer on him, you ought to go to court, get a warrant, tap, get him if you can, and if that leads to prosecution, that is fine. But to go on this kind of fishing expedition where you really do not have prosecution in mind, this is the big brotherism type of thing that a lot of us feel interferes with our operating as a free country.
>
> Mr. Kleindienst: If I am confirmed by the Senate, I understand that I am to have imposed on me this awesome responsibility. The first amendment to me is the most precious right that an American citizen has. The use of electronic eavesdropping devices on an American citizen without a warrant to me should be an exceptional act by the President of the United States and his Attorney General. And I can assure you that none will be authorized in the Department of

Justice without my personal signature, and I can assure you that they will be operated and instituted sparely and with the most sensitive regard for the fundamental rights of citizens in this country.

Senator Bayh: You will make this decision personally?

Mr. Kleindienst: I shall personally.

Senator Bayh: Will you review it periodically?

Mr. Kleindienst: I will. They will be made personally by me, they will not be delegated to anybody else, and I will accept and assume the full responsibility for each and every one of them.

Senator Bayh: Do you have any objections to a request by this committee that you provide this information to us in confidence, what you review periodically, the type of bug, the information gathered, without naming names?

Mr. Kleindienst: I would certainly be amenable to a dialogue with the Congress with appropriate safeguards to protect both the national security and innocent persons to do that. I believe the Director of the Federal Bureau of Investigation from time to time does provide that information to appropriate committees of the Congress on a confidential basis and has for many years.

Senator Bayh: Then you would have no objection to this committee having a confidence, anyhow, a regular report of the number of taps, the reason for the taps, if you are not getting a warrant? Is the FBI doing that now?

Mr. Kleindienst: I think the FBI is doing that now, Senator Bayh.

Senator Bayh: You would have no objection to that.

Mr. Kleindienst: I would have no objection to that continuing.[16]

Senate confirmation has long been a means of enhancing legislative control over both domestic and foreign policy. From Washington's administration on, the Senate has used this instrument to advance its views on foreign affairs. In 1809 non-confirmation was used as a means of denying the very need for foreign missions. By refusing to confirm two nominees of President Jefferson—William Short and John Quincy Adams —as envoys to Russia, the Senate expressed its disapproval of the President's policy of representation. In neither case was the character of the nominee questioned.

Although the Senate's role in controlling foreign policy through such

---

[16] An exchange between Senator Birch Bayh of Indiana and Richard G. Kleindienst, Attorney General designate, *Hearings* before the Committee on the Judiciary, United States Senate, 92nd Congress, 2nd session, on "Nomination of Richard G. Kleindienst, of Arizona, to be Attorney General," Washington, U.S. Government Printing Office, 1972, pp. 19–20. For a famous case where Senate confirmation of an appointment was withheld, see "Nomination of Clement F. Haynsworth, Jr., of South Carolina, to be Associate Justice of the Supreme Court of the United States," *Hearings,* Committee on the Judiciary, United States Senate, 91st Congress, 1st session, Washington, U.S. Government Printing Office, 1969.

power has steadily diminished, new demands for wider participation occurred after World War II, signalized by Senate power to confirm all appointments to the various European Aid missions. A related example was the refusal of a Senate subcommittee to confirm Philip C. Jessup as United States representative to the General Assembly of the United Nations, mainly because some committee members felt that he was "soft" toward communism and he had been a member of several groups which later came to be classified as "un-American" by the Attorney General.[17]

The Senate also refused to confirm Lewis Strauss as Secretary of Commerce, mainly because of his role in the *Dixon-Yates* case and his strained personal relations with several members of the Senate, including Clinton Anderson of New Mexico, who had been chairman of the Joint Committee on Atomic Energy, which had experienced considerable difficulty in getting information from Strauss during its hearings on the Dixon-Yates contract.

The Legislative Veto

In the past few years Congress has added another measure which enables it to make or control administrative policy. This is the so-called legislative veto, whereby certain administrative decisions must be submitted to Congress before going into effect. An example is the requirement that presidential reorganization plans be laid before Congress for sixty days *before* the proposed action takes effect. During this period, Congress can disapprove such proposals by a concurrent resolution, by the action of its standing committees, or by a simple resolution of either House.[18] For students of administration, this is perhaps the most interesting use of the legislative veto. The Reorganization Acts of 1939, 1945, and 1949 gave Congress power to nullify such proposals. Shortly after the 1949 Act was passed, Congress rejected President Truman's proposal for a Department of Welfare. Similar resolutions may also be used to terminate executive action in international agreements, such as the Greek-Turkish Aid pact and the Mutual Defense Assistance Act. Another interesting use is intervention in executive appointments; for example, in the case of the TVA, board members may be removed by a concurrent resolution of the House and Senate.

The requirement of "prior approval" by legislative committees of ad-

---

[17] Subcommittee of Senate Committee on Foreign Relations, *Hearings* on the Sixth General Assembly of the United Nations (Washington, D.C.: Government Printing Office, 1971).

[18] Harris, *Congressional Control of Administration, op. cit.,* pp. 204–48, 282–84.

ministrative action is illustrated in a law (H.R. 4914) concerning naval and military installations, whereby the Secretaries of the Navy, Army, and Air Force must "come into agreement" with the Senate and House Armed Services Committees with respect to the purchase, transfer, or lease of land for such purposes. The Atomic Energy Act (1946) also requires congressional approval of administrative actions; for example, the Atomic Energy Commission is required to report all contractual arrangements with private and public agencies to the Joint Committee on Atomic Energy, which has a thirty-day period in which to scrutinize them. While one may question such legislative intervention, it is well to remember that in some cases, notably the Dixon-Yates affair, this requirement led to the termination of a contract which seemed clearly against the "public interest." At the same time, for administrators to argue that such interventions violate the separation-of-powers principle seems somewhat strained, since this "principle" is of limited relevance to political and administrative realities.

Anticipatory Responses by the Bureaucracy

A final avenue of control is provided by the effort of departments and agencies to maintain productive relationships with Congressmen by responding quickly and affirmatively to their requests for information and services. While such behaviors have the defect of being essentially *ad hoc* and remedial, they do constitute another means of legislative control over the bureaucracy. The following example indicates the extent to which such policies can be consciously followed:

Memorandum: Department of Health, Education and Welfare
             Office of the Secretary

To: Assistant Secretaries and Agency Heads

From: The Secretary

Subject: Apologies for Delays in Congressional Responses

Since overdue letters to Members of Congress undermine our efforts to work effectively with the legislative branch, I am requesting your participation in a new effort to repair the badly damaged relationships which result from HEW's negligence in failing to acknowledge or respond promptly to Congressional inquiries.

Hereafter, when your office is responsible for a long overdue letter either because you have failed to prepare the response accurately by the due date or because you have held it up during the clearance process,

I will be asking you to call the offended Congressman personally and apologize to him for the *wanton disrespect* for the legislative branch which occurred in your office.

The following talking points are suggested for such a telephone conversation:

1. Secretary Richardson has reminded me of the fact that I have been negligent in failing to acknowledge your inquiry of   (date)   about   (subject)   and I am calling at the Secretary's request to personally apologize to you for my failure to respond in a timely and comprehensive manner.

2. I know how important your work in Congress is to the effectiveness of this Department. Your work determines what we can do, what resources we have for achieving our objectives, and, to a large extent, how we do it. Therefore, I know that your inquiries should receive our highest priority attention. My failure to see that this attention was given to your letter of   (date)   is inexcusable, and I want you to know that I will make every effort to see that it does not happen again.

3. The reason why we have not been able to respond completely so far is as follows   (here insert the reasons such as (a) although the letter was sent forward to the Secretary, I had misspelled your name, (b) although the letter I sent forward was quite long, it did not respond to your questions, etc.)

4. I have told Secretary Richardson that we will reply to your inquiry by   (date)   . At that time, we will provide you with a complete and responsive report on   (subject)   .

When I request you to make a telephone call of apology, please be sure to call within 48 hours since I have instructed the Congressional Liaison Office to call the Congressman 48 hours after my request to you to make sure that (1) the Congressman has talked to you personally and (2) he is satisfied with your response.

You can avoid the need for these calls if you prepare an interim acknowledgment which tells the Congressman when a complete response will be prepared. Of course, it is important that you follow through to make sure that the due date is met.

When the delay is a result of failure of an OS office to clear a letter expeditiously, I will ask the appropriate Assistant Secretary to make the apology. In those few cases where an Assistant Secretary cannot clear a letter because of the need for OMB approval or other circumstances beyond his control, the Assistant Secretary should prepare an immediate interim acknowledgment even though the action was not originally assigned to his office.[19]

[19] "Memo of the Month" series, *Washington Monthly*, Vol. 3 (December, 1971), p. 27, italics added.

EFFECTIVENESS OF LEGISLATIVE CONTROL

On the surface, it appears that Congress has adequate means of controlling administration through its powers of lawmaking, appropriation, and investigation. Yet, as we have seen, its attempts at control are spasmodic and *post hoc,* and only rarely does it assume the initiative in policy-making. Largely in response to the demands of constituents for service, interest group activity, the complexity of modern legislation, the initiative enjoyed by the chief executive, and centrifugal political forces within Congress, its role has shifted from one of policy initiation to the screening, sifting, and authorizing of policy usually set before it by others. Congress, moreover, has extreme difficulty in exercising an incisive review of appropriations. Finally, the use of committees as an investigatory instrument has inherent defects. It is spotty, transitory, and remedial rather than preventive. Thus for several reasons, many of which spring from the atomization of members' time and energy, legislative control often seems to be of limited effectiveness.

The evidence in support of this conclusion is convincing. Senator Paul Douglas, an eminent economist by profession, has shown that Congress is almost helpless in considering the validity of Department of Defense budget requests, which represent by far the largest share of present expenditures: "Because of the technical knowledge of military men, we are reluctant to criticize them or their budget." Senator William Proxmire's subcommittee on government economy has revealed a succession of defense spending extravagances, but it is not clear that these have had any impact upon either Congress or the military.

There is a real question moreover about the strength of Congress' desire to control spending, as shown by its conduct in the House Office Building affair. This elephantine building, which covers fifty acres of floor space, contains one swimming pool (cost, by *Fortune's* estimate, $300,000), 30 elevators, 23 escalators, and thousands of offices with 13 foot, 9 inch ceilings, was apparently the personal project of Speaker Sam Rayburn. Beginning about a decade ago with an exploratory appropriation of $25,000, present costs total $86,400,000, with additional developments slated to bring total costs to some $150,000,000. Allied with the House Office Building Commission—a three-man group charged with planning and supervising the architecture and construction—Rayburn pushed the project through the committees concerned with a minimum amount of scrutiny. For example, the Chairman of the subcommittee for legislative appropriations, Tom Stead of Oklahoma, says, "As far as I know, the Rayburn Building project was the only item our subcommittee had no control over. It was carried out under a blank check approved by the House Office Building Commission, and we had to abide by their decisions." [20]

The Comptroller General has an audit of the entire project underway, but here again, scrutiny is occurring only *after* the money has been spent. Some minor corrections will apparently be made, including legislation providing for proper standards for the position of Architect of the Capitol, who under present requirements need not have an architecture degree and whose influence is much greater than his essential role, largely House Office maintenance work, merits. As Senator Paul Douglas said in frustration on the Senate floor, "The present Architect of the Capitol is the most expensive, the most wasteful, most incompetent architect we could possibly engage." The appointment, however, is a political one and the incumbent, who has an engineering degree from the University of Delaware, is a former Congressman and a long-time friend of influential House members such as Rayburn and Vinson.

In 1972, the management of the Kennedy Center for the Performing Arts came under similar criticism from the General Accounting Office for its inadequate internal budgetary and accounting practices, revealing among other things that some stage-hands were being paid $1500 per week and that the Center's parking lot, built at a cost of $20 million, had failed to pay its way, as promised by the Center's managers. [21] Although the Center is apparently a resounding artistic success, it has been forced to ask Congress for annual subsidies, in addition to the initial cost of $72 million, most of which came from federal funds. Such events suggest that Congress' presumed concern with overspending has, like Mark Twain's death, been somewhat exaggerated.

Improving Legislative Surveillance

The means to improve legislative control are well known, but they fly in the face of constitutional prescription, the weight of tradition, and the demands of political survival. Party responsibility is probably a basic requirement, but given the separation-of-powers system, the localism, and divided loyalty that accompany our method of electing United States legislatures, party responsibility is extremely difficult to achieve. Im-

[20] *Fortune*, Vol. 71 (March, 1965), p. 176.
[21] Among others, see *Newsweek*, Vol. 80 (September 11, 1972), pp. 74–75.

proving the committee system by curbing committee autonomy and abolishing seniority as the basis for appointment and influence are widely recommended, but here again political realities have usually proved an insurmountable barrier. Although not everywhere accepted as desirable, the recommendation of more staff aid for congressional committees is often cited and is slowly being followed. Meanwhile the legislator's time will continue to be devoted mainly to the essential requirements of political survival, political fence-building, and constituent demands. Politics remains a vocation in which priorities must be carefully weighed. Although the means to more adequate control are no secret, rational solutions are not always applicable in the political arena. Once again, it is clear that the impact of "facts" and the admonitions of experts are always limited by conflicting economic and political interests.

Allied with presidential difficulties of adequate control mentioned earlier, this conclusion emphasizes again the need to reinforce existing measures of control with a more positive instrument. Perhaps one such recourse is an appeal to the ethical and professional standards of public officials, to which we will turn after a consideration of judicial control of administrative discretion.

20

Judicial Control
of Administration
Decisions

Although we tend to think of judicial review as essentially *ex post facto* in that individuals typically seek it only after being disadvantaged, it may also be conceptualized as a salient means of controlling administrators by establishing guidelines for subsequent administrative conduct through a series of court decisions. Indeed, such case law is perhaps the major basis for determining existing policy and procedures in various areas.[1] This fact punctuates the role of judicial review in administration and explains the inclusion of courts among the means of controlling administrative behavior. Although the decisions of all government agencies and departments are open to review, we shall focus on federal regulatory bodies which provide a dramatic context for the confrontation between the needs of the state and the rights of the individual. To make judicial control meaningful, it is useful to begin with some definitions and generalizations about the regulatory process, including the amount of finality or conclusiveness usually accorded administrative decisions by the courts.

[1] See, for example, W. J. Baumol and A. G. Walton, "Full Costing, Competition and Regulatory Practice," *Yale Law Review*, Vol. 82 (March, 1973), pp. 639–55 where an analysis of the use of such criteria as competition in rate-setting by the ICC, FTC, and CAB is based almost exclusively upon precedents set down in judicial decisions.

FINALITY OF ADMINISTRATIVE DECISIONS

Theoretically at least, there is almost no limit upon the right of courts in the United States to review the decisions of administrative agencies. Our doctrine of constitutional limitations permits the judiciary to question almost every administrative act. Legislatures occasionally insulate agencies against review by including clauses in statutes that specifically prevent review. But even if a state constitution, for example, did set up an administrative agency whose acts were not reviewable by state courts, judicial review could almost certainly be obtained in the federal courts under the due-process clause of the Fourteenth Amendment. Speaking very generally and subject to many exceptions, one may summarize the situation as follows:

1. The courts may in theory review to the extent they feel desirable
2. There is no method of determining whether they will or will not review in given cases
3. Administrative decisions are to some undefined extent final.

The Supreme Court has permitted a large degree of finality in old and tested fields where accepted principles and techniques of regulation prevail, and it has even been responsible for the acquisition of certain new powers by the regulatory commissions.[2] As Chief Justice Warren said in *Federal Trade Commission v. Colgate-Palmolive Company* (1965), "This Court has frequently stated that the Commission's judgment is to be given great weight by reviewing courts." Again, "as an administrative agency which deals continually with cases in the area, the Commission is often in a better position than are the courts to determine when a practice [TV advertising in this case] is 'deceptive' within the meaning of the Act." In the area of military decisions especially, the Courts have traditionally allowed a great deal of latitude, presumably because of the stringent circumstances under which such decisions are made.

Nevertheless, the courts maintain a watchful eye over even such venerable agencies as the Interstate Commerce Commission. Although they have consistently upheld administrative decisions in the tried and tested area of railroad regulation[3] they have reversed a Commission order in

---

[2] "The Function of the Supreme Court in the Development and Acquisition of Power by Administrative Agencies," *Minnesota Law Review*, Vol. 42 (December, 1957).

[3] *Chicago, P.M., & O. Ry. v. U.S.* (322 U.S. 1, 1944); *Interstate Commerce Commission v. Jersey City* (322 U.S. 503, 1944).

the relatively new field of truck transportation on the ground that both the record and proof were inadequate.[4] A U.S. District Court negated an ICC order permitting a merger between two Florida railroads, Atlantic Coast Lines and Seaboard Air Line.[5] The Court held, in effect, that the proposed merger would violate the Clayton Antitrust Act by reducing competition in the area served by the corporations. Antitrust policy, the Court held, "must be measured in terms of criteria that have been developed by Congress and the courts." The ICC's findings were not sufficient to sustain its argument that the merger would not restrict competition among various forms of transportation in the Southeast.

At the same time, judicial recognition of administrative expertise was nicely expressed in a part of the decision which rejected the government's request that the merger be permanently enjoined. This, the Court concluded, "would require that we invade the long-established province of the commission. Resolving such considerations is a complex task which requires extensive facilities, expert judgment, and considerable knowledge of the transportation industry. The wisdom and experience of the Commission, not of the courts, must determine whether the proposed consolidation is consistent with the public interest." In effect, the Court said, "We won't accept your argument supporting the merger at the present time, but we will not foreclose the possibility that you may find that future conditions justify it."

Students of administrative procedures agree that there are certain areas of discretion and fact in which the courts should and do give the regulatory agencies considerable latitude. The courts have long recognized the importance of the specialized experience and technical competence of these administrative bodies and the need for uniformity of regulation. On the whole the courts—and especially the federal judiciary—welcome the relief afforded by the growth of administrative adjudication in the last few years. Without this aid their dockets would have been so crowded that some other solution would have been required. Many lawyers, on the other hand, maintain a running battle against administrative adjudication, under the banner of individual rights such as due process.[6]

The courts have, on balance, been reluctant to relinquish their right to a final review of administrative action. The Administrative Procedure

[4] *Eastern Central Assn. v. U.S.* (321 U.S. 194, 1944).
[5] *Florida East Coast R. Co. v. U.S. and Interstate Commerce Commission* No. 34-64-Civ. J., filed May 13, 1965.
[6] For ideological and personal factors in judicial policy-making, see G. Schubert, *The Judicial Mind Revisited* (New York: Oxford University Press, 1975).

Act (1946 as amended) provides a broad basis for judicial review and the following generalizations suggest the basis upon which the courts have authorized it.

Exhausting Administrative Remedies

One cannot ordinarily resort to the courts until he has exhausted all administrative remedies, i.e., until he has fully sought an accommodation with the agency handling his particular grievance. This is quite proper, since to have earlier recourse to the courts would deprive the administrative process of the speed which is one of its assumed virtues. Section 10 of the Administrative Procedure Act, however, has a provision for "interim relief" which apparently aims at undercutting this doctrine of the exhaustion of administrative remedies. To avoid "irreparable harm," every reviewing court is authorized to issue orders postponing the effective date of agency action or preserving individual status or rights until the review proceedings have ended. This provision makes it easier for individuals to go to the courts for declaratory judgments or orders before exhausting the remedies available through administrative action.

The American Bar Association would further increase the scope of judicial review by substituting for the present "substantial evidence" test the standard now used by the U.S. Courts of Appeal in reviewing findings of fact by district courts. This change would encourage the courts to substitute their own judgment for that of the agency in determining the validity of facts in a given case.[7] The proposed code would also allow the courts to reverse any agency action that seems a "clearly unwarranted exercise of discretion," even though Section 10(e) of the Administrative Procedure Act already guards against such abuses. This change would also permit injunctions to be sought at any stage of the agency proceeding, undercutting the rule that all administrative remedies must be exhausted before the individual turns to the courts. In commenting upon these changes, an attorney for the Atchison, Topeka and Santa Fe Railway Company concludes, "this represents a complete departure from the philosophy of regulation that has evolved through experience over the course of the last fifty years . . . [the] existing relationship between the courts and the independent regulatory commissions in this field is in a reasonably satisfactory state of balance." [8]

[7] *Ibid.*
[8] *Ibid.*, pp. 523–24.

Questions of Law and of Fact

Courts have usually not examined questions of fact unless they also involve questions of law or questions of constitutional authority.[9] When a hearing is held, it is the responsibility of the agency to determine the facts upon which the agency's decision rests. Judicial control is usually limited to whether there is substantial evidence. Under the provisions of the Johnson Act,[10] for example, a federal district court cannot issue an injunction against a state administrative order when such an order (1) affects rates chargeable by a public utility, (2) does not interfere with interstate commerce, (3) has been made after reasonable notice and hearing, and (4) provides a plain, speedy, and efficient remedy that may be had at law or in equity in the courts of the state.[11] As applied to judicial review of tax errors, where there has been a failure to resort to administrative remedies, this doctrine has expanded administrative finality.[12] This is due to the judicial tendency to refuse the right to attack tax administrators through the courts for mere irregularities. There must instead be a showing of fraud to merit a judicial remedy.

As a general rule, then, courts have attempted to distinguish between questions of law and fact and have reviewed the former but not the latter. As all generalizations, however, this one must be qualified. In a recent case, a federal district court held that the ICC had not presented sufficient evidence and specifically directed it to include in its record the costs of owner–operators (hired by a carrier on a subcontracting basis) in a decision regulating the rates charged by the carrier.[13] In effect, the court held that the ICC could not properly determine whether a carrier's rates were "just and reasonable" without having before it the costs charged by such owner–operators, who themselves were not subject to the Commission's jurisdiction.

---

[9] Louis J. Jaffe, "Judicial Review: Questions of Law," *Harvard Law Review*, Vol. 69 (1955), p. 239. For a general analysis, see that article and Jaffe, "Judicial Review: Question of Fact," *Harvard Law Review*, Vol. 69 (1956) and "Judicial Review: Constitutional and Jurisdictional Fact," *Harvard Law Review*, Vol. 70 (1957).

[10] 48 Stat. 775, 28 U.S.C.A. (May 14, 1934).

[11] "The Johnson Act—a Return to State Independence," *Illinois Law Review*, Vol. 30 (1935), p. 215; "Limitation of Lower Federal Courts' Jurisdiction over Public Utility Rate Cases," *Yale Law Journal*, Vol. 44 (November, 1934), p. 119.

[12] *Dobson v. Commissioner* (320 U.S. 489, 1943).

[13] *Eastern Central Motor Carriers Assn. Inc., et al. v. United States of America and Interstate Commerce Commission* (No. 12, 34–64), March 26, 1965.

The fulsome attitude of the court toward its review powers is punctuated by the following item from its opinion:

> This court is bound to inquire into every aspect of the proceedings below wherein it may appear that the Commission has otherwise applied an erroneous standard of law, or has made arbitrary findings, or has reached ultimate conclusions without adequate subordinate facts, or has failed *in any other way* to observe those procedures of investigation and elaboration which have become the hallmark of *proper* administrative determination.[14]

A related exception to administrative finality in the area of facts is in rate-fixing cases in which confiscation is alleged; here, the Supreme Court has stated that the appellate courts will grant a trial *de novo*.[15] In findings of fact, however, there must be evidence sufficient to support the decision. This provision actually vitiates the hypothesis. In deciding whether a given set of facts is *sufficient* to support administrative findings, the court is establishing a precedent that will guide future cases, since such a decision formulates a given set of facts into a legal measure of the sufficiency of evidence. Under such conditions the distinction between questions of law and questions of fact tends to break down. As John Dickinson once put it, "matters of law grow downward into roots of fact, and matters of fact reach upward, without a break, into matters of law." [16]

The distinction between fact and law therefore provides only limited guidance toward a rule as to when the courts will review. This generalization is reinforced by the Administrative Procedure Act, which clearly extends the power of the courts to review matters of fact, insofar as they bear upon questions of agency jurisdiction. The "substantial evidence" requirement also brings the courts into the area of administrative fact finding. The Supreme Court, moreover, has insisted that findings necessary to determine the *jurisdiction* of an agency or the *constitutionality* of its decisions must be reviewed *de novo* by the courts. Dickinson's early conclusion is still useful: "When the courts are willing to review, they are tempted to explain by the easy device of calling the question one of 'fact'; and when otherwise disposed, they say that it is a question of 'law.'" [17]

---

[14] *Ibid.*, emphasis added. See also Raoul Berger, "Administrative Arbitrariness and Judicial Review," *Columbia Law Review*, Vol. 65 (January, 1965).

[15] *Ohio Valley Water Co., v. Ben Avon Borough* (253 U.S. 287, 1920); *St. Joseph Stock Yards Co. v. U. S.* (298 U. S. 38, 1936).

[16] *Administrative Justice and the Supremacy of the Law* (Cambridge, Mass.: Harvard University Press, 1927), p. 38.

[17] *Ibid.*, p. 55.

Jurisdictional Facts

Another difficulty exists in attempting to distinguish between law and fact. The decision in a celebrated Supreme Court case [18] presents the doctrine of "jurisdictional fact," also referred to as a basic or constitutional fact. Briefly, this doctrine states that when a fact is the constitutional basis for the exercise of administrative power, the court itself must make a finding as to the fact.[19] A federal statute gives the U. S. Employees' Compensation Commission authority to make awards to certain persons. Among other things, however, the relation of employer and employee must exist before the Commission has jurisdiction to make an award. Since the fact of the employer–employee relationship is the one that determines the jurisdiction of the Commission, it is referred to as a jurisdictional fact, which raises a question of law.

In *Crowell v. Benson,* the Commission decided that such a relation existed and made an award to the injured employee. The employer appealed and the Supreme Court held that the Commission had no authority to make an award unless the injured party actually was an employee. Since the fact was a jurisdictional one, the Commission should not be permitted to decide unilaterally, for to do so would be to allow the Commission to decide for itself whether it had jurisdiction. In deciding against the Commission, the court held that the person seeking the award was not in fact an employee, and hence its ruling prevented the enforcement of the award. The majority held that the question of the existence of the jurisdictional fact must be determined by evidence presented in a court.

The practical result of the doctrine of jurisdictional fact is to permit a complete judicial reexamination, or trial *de novo,* of facts that otherwise would have been conclusively determined by the administrative agency. Yet, a decision of the Interstate Commerce Commission, made after a formal hearing and protected by procedural safeguards, should be considered differently from a decision of fact made by a meat inspector that impure food must be destroyed. In the former case, there are no strong reasons for applying the doctrine of jurisdictional fact. Where a case can be tried again on new evidence before another tribunal, thus delaying the final set-

---

[18] *Crowell v. Benson* (295 U. S. 22, 1932). See also *Producers Transportation Co. v. Railroad Commission* (176 Cal. 499; 169 Pac. 59, 1917); *People v. Lang Transportation Co.* (217 Cal. 166; 17 Pac. (2d) 721, 1932); "Finality of Administrative Findings of Fact Since Cromwell vs. Benson," *Virginia Law Review,* Vol. 24 (January, 1933), p. 478.
[19] Jaffe, "Judicial Review: Constitutional and Jurisdictional Fact," *op. cit.,* p. 953.

tlement, the result is to deprive the administrative authority of its potential advantage of speed. It also tends to make the agency appear ineffectual. Nevertheless, the *Crowell v. Benson* doctrine has never been specifically abandoned by the Supreme Court, although subsequent decisions have restricted its scope.[20]

On the other hand, the courts seem to recognize the need to fight delay by accepting the expertise of the commissions, perhaps because delay is one of their own major problems. In the *Colgate-Palmolive* case, both the Circuit and Supreme Courts accepted the FTC's findings that a certain Rapid Shave advertisement constituted misrepresentation of the product's qualities. "This Court has frequently stated that the Commission's judgment is to be given great weight by reviewing courts."[21] The Circuit Court, however, negated the accompanying FTC order which seemed to attempt to prohibit the future use of all similar props. As Chief Justice Earl Warren said, "The breadth of the Commission's [first] order was potentially limitless, apparently establishing a *per se* rule prohibiting the use of simulated props in all television commercials."[22] A revised FTC order was then upheld by the Supreme Court, which thus reversed the decision of the Court of Appeals.

In the opinion, the Court again enunciated its attitude toward administrative expertise. The FTC argued that the Rapid Shave commercial made representations that (1) sandpaper could be shaved by Rapid Shave, (2) an experiment had been conducted verifying this claim, and (3) the viewer was actually seeing this experiment. Colgate-Palmolive insisted that only the first two representations were being made. The FTC, however, found that all three were being claimed. In accepting the FTC position, the Supreme Court held that, "Since this is a matter of fact resting on an inference that could reasonably be drawn from the commercials themselves, the Commission's finding should be sustained . . . the focus of our consideration is on the third [representation] which was clearly false."[23]

Other Factors Affecting Administrative Finality

The adequacy of an administrative hearing also determine whether the courts will review. If there has been no hearing, the courts frequently

---

[20] Schwartz, "Does the Ghost of Crowell v. Benson Still Walk?" *University of Pennsylvania Law Review*, Vol. 98 (December, 1949), pp. 163–82.
[21] *Federal Trade Commission v. Colgate-Palmolive Co., et al.*, p. 10.
[22] *Ibid.*, pp. 5–6.
[23] *Ibid.*, p. 11.

review, since hearing is essential to due process.[24] Adequacy is also tied up with the question of whether the hearing satisfies due process. Although, for example, the courts will normally refuse to interfere with immigration orders for deportation, they will set aside such orders if they are based on an arbitrary hearing. In general, procedural due process has been emphasized to the extent that a full hearing is usually required, and the administrative process moves more slowly as a result.[25]

Probably the safest guide as to whether the courts will review is the nature of the subject matter. It is necessary here to distinguish between a legal right that is a privilege and one that is not clearly so. In the former instance, including chiefly cases where an individual has sought some benefit from the government such as a grant of public land, the courts have been reluctant to review. Similarly, they have usually refused to reverse Post Office Department fraud orders because, here again, the government is performing a business service to individuals on favorable terms. This distinction, however, is not very useful because of the difficulty of distinguishing between "rights" and "privileges." [26]

Even these tentative generalizations have been challenged by developments in which judicial review has been concerned with requirements of due process in cases involving personal freedom, foreign travel, personal security, military discharge, immigration, and deportation.[27] In several cases, for example, doctors who refused to sign loyalty oaths were inducted as army privates under a law permitting the drafting of physicians and dentists. They were granted review, and following an amendment to the law, the lower courts held that the army could not retain them in a non-commissioned status.[28] The view that "privileges" fare less well in court than "rights" has also been challenged. For example, after a New York City school teacher had been discharged for pleading the Fifth Amendment before an investigating committee, the Supreme Court held that the discharge was arbitrary and therefore void.[29] Thus, although there is no constitutionally guaranteed right to be a school teacher, the court has declared that even "privileged occupations" may not be taken away without due process.

[24] "Judicial Review of Administrative Adjudicatory Action Taken Without a Hearing," *Harvard Law Review*, Vol. 70 (February, 1957), pp. 698–708.
[25] N. L. Nathanson, "Law and the Future: Administrative Law," *Northwestern University Law Review*, Vol. 51 (May–June, 1956), p. 174.
[26] C. F. *Slochower v. Board of Higher Education* (24 U.S.L. Week 4178, 1956).
[27] Nathanson, "Law and the Future," *op. cit.*
[28] *Nelson v. Peckham* (210 F. 2 & 574; 4th Cir., 1954); *Levin v. Gillespie* (121 F., Supp. 239; N.D. Cal. 1954).
[29] *Slochower v. Board of Education* (350 U. S. 551, 1956).

Federal and state "loyalty-security" programs have been similarly regarded by the Supreme Court. A state law holding that membership in a proscribed organization prevented individuals from holding public employment was held to violate due process, since there was no requirement that the individual had to have been aware of the subversive purposes of the organization.[30] At the federal level, the Supreme Court in the *Peters*[31] case found that the action of the Loyalty Review Board in removing Peters, a physician in the Department of Health, Education and Welfare, exceeded the authority of Executive Order No. 9835, President Truman's original "loyalty" order of March, 1947. It held the board's action properly belonged to the Secretary of Health, Education, and Welfare, to whom Peters was responsible. In the *Cole*[32] case the Court found that Executive Order No. 10450, which extended the basic "security" act of 1950 (64 Stat. 4765 U.S.C.A.) to all civilian employees of the federal government, was *ultra vires*. The Court held that the 1950 statute related only to "sensitive" jobs, whereas the security order attempted to cover *all* employees.[33]

Another area in which review has restructured administrative policy involves situations where the Secretary of State has denied passports to persons whose political views would allegedly make foreign travel inimical to the national interest. This issue was treated by the Circuit Court in *Briehl v. Dulles*,[34] where the Secretary's power to deny the passport was upheld because Briehl, a psychiatrist who wanted to attend conferences in Geneva and Istanbul, refused to sign an affidavit concerning membership in the Communist party. While this prerogative is based upon the inherent power of the executive to act independently in foreign affairs, the courts have begun to question it on due-process grounds and on the premise that foreign travel is a fundamental personal liberty.[35] Thus a "quasi-judicial" hearing is now required when a passport is denied, certain grounds of refusal are subject to judicial review, and passport issuances are no longer solely a matter of executive discretion.[36]

---

[30] *Wieman v. Updegraff* (344 U.S. 551, 1956).

[31] *Peters v. Hobby* (349 U.S. 331, 338; June, 1955).

[32] *Cole v. Young* (351 U.S. 536, 1956).

[33] For an analysis of judicial review of presidential action affecting the civil service, see Glendon Schubert, *The Presidency in the Courts* (Minneapolis: University of Minnesota Press, 1957), Chap. 2.

[34] 248 F. 2 & 561 (D. C. Cir. 1957).

[35] "Authority of the Secretary of State to Deny Passports," *University of Pennsylvania Law Review*, Vol. 106 (January, 1958), pp. 420–36.

[36] See, for example, *Aptheker v. Secretary of State* (378 U.S. 500, Sup. Ct. 1964), which in effect invalidated the Briehl decision; see also *Schachtman v. Dulles* (225 F. 2 & 983; D.C. Cir. 1955); *Dulles v. Nathan* (225 F. 2 & 29; D.C. Cir.

The Due-Process Clauses

In effect, the due-process clauses of the Fourteenth and the Fifth Amendments are frequently used to question or nullify administrative acts. One of the fundamental elements of due process is representation by counsel, and this applies to administrative proceedings as well as to judicial, after it has been determined that a right to a hearing exists. The doctrine has been stated as follows: "The rule generally formulated is that a formal hearing, presumably including the right to counsel, is necessary to satisfy due process requirements when the agency is acting in an adjudicatory (quasi-judicial) capacity, and when the interest involved is regarded as a substantive right and not as a mere privilege." [37] The right to counsel rests upon three bases: by *statute*, in which legislation, such as the Administrative Procedure Act, Section 6(a), guarantees the right; by *implication*, in which the right to a hearing subsumes representation; and by *constitutional* right.[38]

Our courts, moreover, sometimes interpret due process to include matters of substantive law as well as procedure. It is under this guise that judges sometimes express disapproval of new social and economic concepts by reading their own philosophy into a provision of the Constitution originally designed to protect freed Negro slaves. As noted earlier, the section of the Fourteenth Amendment which says that no state shall "deprive any person of life, liberty, or property, without due process of law" has been interpreted as a bar to arbitrary government in general. Toward the end of the nineteenth century the Supreme Court began to use this clause to nullify administrative acts and legislation which seemed to it contrary to "proper" social and economic policy. Judicial review under this clause has had a widespread impact upon administrative practice and findings.

Other Avenues of Appeal

An administrative action may be brought before a court for review in several ways. An aggrieved party may bring an action for damages.

1955); *Boudin v. Dulles* (136 F. Supp. 218; D.D.C. 1955); *Bauer v. Acheson* (106 Supp. 445; D.D.C. 1951); "Passports: The Executive's Discretion over Foreign Affairs as a Basis for Passport Denial," *University of Pittsburgh Law Review*, Vol. 19 (Spring, 1958), pp. 661–66.

[37] "Representation by Counsel in Administrative Proceedings," *Columbia Law Review*, Vol. 58 (March, 1958), pp. 396–97.

[38] *Ibid.*, pp. 403–7.

Sometimes, as in the case of the Federal Trade Commission, the administrative agency must resort to the courts to enforce its orders. The so-called extraordinary writs also serve to bring administrative acts before the regular courts. These include certiorari, prohibition, mandamus, injunction, and habeas corpus. In addition, there are also express statutory provisions for appeal; for instance, the provision allowing appeal from the California Railroad Commission direct to the state supreme court. Another opportunity for judicial review occurs when an agency is permitted by statute to sue for the expense of executing an order after its non-observance. The question of the validity of the order may be raised in such a suit.

As noted, under our system of law, courts have the power to review administrative acts to the extent that they deem desirable. There are no ironclad rules, however, that enable one to forecast how far a court will review in a given case. James M. Landis, perhaps the leading authority on administration law, would determine the basis of judicial review or administrative finality upon such factors as competence and expertness. He would leave questions involving strictly legal interpretation to the courts, whereas matters of technology would rest with official experts in that field. Difficulties have arisen in the past because the courts have sometimes cloaked themselves in an aura of expertness "in matters of industrial health, utility engineering, railroad management, even bread making." [39] According to Landis, formerly Chairman of the CAB and SEC, they should instead retreat from fields of expertness in which they have no claim to fitness and leave final determination of such problems to administrators.

APPEALS TO JUDICIAL REVIEW BY DISADVANTAGED GROUPS

An example of how disadvantaged groups can obtain redress is seen in a series of recent cases brought by Local Housing Authority corporations against the federal Housing and Urban Development agency.[40] The financing of public housing (along with various other facets of the "poverty programs") is in disarray. Low rentals and rising operating

[39] Landis, *The Administrative Process* (New Haven, Conn.: Yale University Press, 1938), p. 155.

[40] Among others, see Robert Pozen, "The Financing of Local Housing Authorities: A Contract Approach for Public Corporations," *Yale Law Journal*, Vol. 82 (May, 1973), pp. 1208–26.

costs have resulted in large operating deficits for LHA's, but Congress has not appropriated sufficient funds to meet their deficits. Apparently, neither HUD nor the Office of Management and Budget have pushed strongly for funds which might ease their burden.[41] Given these conditions, local housing authorities and tenants have turned to the courts to find some solution. Their efforts have taken two forms: attempts by LHA's to secure writs of mandamus which would force HUD to provide larger operating subsidies, and suits by tenants against the LHA's for statutory violations. A major case in the latter context is *Barber v. White* (41 USLW 2301–02) in which tenants sued the New Haven LHA for exceeding legal rent limits and were upheld on the ground that the state law which set the rents was subordinate to federal law. The judge concluded that if the LHA were unable to operate under federal limitations, it had the choice of going out of business: "nothing in the Act nor any judgment of this Court enforcing the Act requires the NHHA to continue its operation." [42]

Related kinds of court action have been brought by welfare recipients, against individual states and HEW. Often at issue is the failure of most states to meet their own "full standard" criterion for adequate monthly welfare payments. Only 13 states meet this standard,[43] and some of the wealthiest states, mainly in the Southwest and far West, pay only about one-half of their own estimated cost-of-living expenses for families of four.[44] Interestingly, the four states which were designated as targets by the Nixon Administration (1971) for achieving compliance were all Republican strongholds—Arizona, California, Indiana, and Nebraska. Federal officials launched a program of "compliance hearings" with state officials, attended by somewhat symbolic threats of a cut-off of federal welfare funds. Partly because congressmen have little incentive to encourage state compliance, welfare organizations and individuals concerned have tended to turn to the courts. Perhaps another inducement to litigation is the vast number of federal welfare regulations, as suggested by the following comment of Senator Clifford Case who, having asked for HEW's public assistance handbook, declared, "I was

---

[41] *Ibid.*, p. 1211. The role and the influence of OMB are suggested by the fact that it held back (in 1972) 44 million dollars of funds which would apparently have met LHA demands.

[42] *Ibid.*, cited at p. 1216.

[43] For a report on this problem in intergovernmental relations, see J. K. Iglehart "Welfare Report: HEW Pushes Regulation Compliance," *National Journal* (February, 1971), pp. 401–9.

[44] *Ibid.*, p. 401.

appalled to receive a package of regulations weighing almost six pounds, as thick as the Washington, D.C. telephone directory." [45] State welfare directors naturally have a difficult time honoring all such regulations, which provides a basis for suits. Finally, and ironically, the National Welfare Rights Organization maintains that there is some evidence that the turn to the courts produces faster action than the administrative process in inducing state compliance.[46] At the same time, one of the effects of such suits has been to spur HEW to faster action.

The cases cover a variety of issues, from those involving the size and speed of payment of welfare benefits to the larger question of state compliance with federal welfare targets, and we can only cite one random example here, which is useful among other reasons because it indicates that disadvantaged individuals can have their day in the highest court in the United States. *Rosado v. Wyman* (397 U.S. 1970) involved a challenge by a New York state welfare recipient of the state's policy of "ratable reduction," a formula whereby states can lower their payments below their own standard of need by setting some proportion of that standard as the maximum amount they are prepared to pay. Although the Johnson Administration had recommended that states be required to raise their payments to their maximum standard annually, Congress, for mixed ideological and political reasons, refused to require states to comply.[47] In the *Rosado* case, a class action against the New York State Commissioner of Social Services, plaintiffs argued that the state's action had abrogated federal requirements by reducing by 20 per cent their welfare payments, and that its amended law providing for the change violated the equal protection clause of the 14th Amendment because recipients in Nassau County received lower benefits than similarly conditioned recipients in New York City.[48] A three-man District Court passed the case to the District Court, which issued an injunction against the enforcement of the amendment—i.e., it decided for the plaintiffs. Moreover, following a reversal by the Court of Appeals, the Supreme Court reversed the Court of Appeals, and "found that New York state had redefined its *standard* of need in such a manner that it had circumvented the previously noted federal requirement for increases to reflect changes in the cost of living." [49] If New York were allowed to redefine

---

45 *Ibid.,* p. 403.
46 *Ibid.,* p. 409.
47 *Ibid.,* p. 408.
48 Notes, *American University Law Review,* Vol. 21, pp. 209–13.
49 *Ibid.,* p. 210, italics in original. For a case in which the courts decided otherwise, see *Jefferson v. Hackney* (304 Fed. Supp. 1332, 1969).

its standard, it would "render the cost-of-living reappraisal (of the Social Security Act), a futile, hollow, and indeed, a deceptive gesture. . . ." [50]

Appeals by Women Against Air Force Regulations

Among military regulations governing female personnel is one which provides for the discharge of those who become pregnant, whether married or single. This regulation has been challenged regarding the Air Force on the grounds that it violates constitutional guarantees against the denial of privacy and equal protection. First Lieutenant Mary Gutierrez was an unmarried officer stationed in Turkey, who had not served the three-year probation period and presumably had no right of appeal against involuntary discharge.[51] After being discharged, she turned to the Federal district court, arguing that both her discharge and the subsequent denial of a hearing by the Air Force Secretary were unconstitutional. The Court issued a preliminary injunction against the discharge, but granted the Government's motion for summary judgment. Lieutenant Gutierrez then filed an appeal with the Court of Appeals, whereupon the Air Force nullified her discharge. Such cases are unusual because the Courts have long been reluctant to review military decisions.[52]

Congressman Moss v. the Civil Aeronautics Board

Late in 1969, the CAB permitted certain airlines to charge increased fares pending an investigation of fare schedules proposed by a number of trunk airlines. Shortly thereafter, Congressman John Moss and other legislators began attempts to require the airlines involved to remit to passengers alleged overcharges resulting from the Board's decision, which covered a 54-week period during 1969–1970. Finally, Moss and his colleagues appealed the Board's decision to the U.S. Court of Appeals, which invalidated the Board's action on the ground that it had engaged in ratemaking without conducting the public hearing required by law. The fares based on the Board's Order were therefore declared illegal, and the Court handed the case back to the CAB for further proceedings. The fare increases involved amounted to $265 million. In a subsequent decision, which will almost surely be appealed, the Board held that the

---

[50] *Ibid.* For further detail, see *National Journal* (April, 1970), p. 774.

[51] Notes, "Pregnancy Discharges in the Military: The Air Force Experience," *Harvard Law Review*, Vol. 86 (January, 1973), pp. 568–94.

[52] Notes, "God, the Army, and Judicial Review," *California Law Review*, Vol. 56 (1968), pp. 413–38.

disputed fares and the revenues accruing from them were neither unreasonable nor excessive. "The carriers were not unjustly enriched . . . and it would be inequitable to compel them to make restitution to all fare payers." [53]

Here, as in cases cited earlier, individuals turn to the Courts to challenge administrative decisions thought to be illegal or arbitrary. The problems of judicial review are apparent in the fact that the Board's final decision, on an issue begun in 1969, was made on July 13, 1973. Moreover, it is highly probable that more litigation will be involved before the matter is finally reconciled. But the main point here is the example of judicial review of decisions by administrative agencies. Disenchanted by the slowness, expense, and difficulty of attempts to obtain redress by judicial means, some observers have suggested other alternatives, to which we turn next.

ALTERNATIVES TO JUDICIAL REVIEW

Despite such opportunities for judicial review, it is probably true that the vast majority of individuals who feel disadvantaged by an administrative determination do not carry the issue further. In many cases, they are unaware of their rights; in others, they doubt that they can secure redress through the courts. More important, perhaps, are the time and expense required to bring suit. Such considerations have led to various suggestions for alternative institutions and procedures, usually patterned after European experience. The most common of these include the introduction of a system of administrative courts and, more recently, the use of an Ombudsman as a special defender of citizen rights vis-à-vis government.

Administrative Courts

Such courts provide for special review of the decisions of administrative agencies, patterned after the French, Italian, Swiss, and German systems, in which two independent legal apparatuses exist: the ordinary judiciary and the administrative. In France, for example, an independent Tribunal of Conflicts determines the appropriate jurisdiction when necessary. Although some observers have criticized the French courts on the ground that they give the government official a privileged position, legal

[53] Civil Aeronautics Board, *Release*, July 13, 1973.

scholars believe that they offer both expertise and adequate protection of individual rights. Perhaps the basic reason for the administrative court system is French acceptance of state responsibility for private damages arising from its torts or those of its agents. In America and England, although change has been rapid during the past decade, the concept of state liability has been relatively limited by comparison.

The cases that come before continental administrative courts include tort liability, violation of contracts, controversies arising out of rank, salary and pension awards in the civil service and the military, and *ultra vires* proceedings. French *droit administratif* is case law, developed mainly during the last half-century. Although the Fifth Republic is characterized by a loosely written constitution and a very powerful executive and legislative branch, the Council of State (the supreme administrative court) can nullify the acts of the executive. It can not declare statutes unconstitutional, but it can vitiate administrative ordinances that are legislative in character; even the decrees of the President can be voided. In sum, the French system provides forceful, expert, and yet judicial-like review of administrative actions. Problems arising in America from conflict between administrators and lawyers, and the difficulty of obtaining a sympathetic review of administrative action, have led some observers to recommend a similar system here. Here again, the courts have not escaped the pervasive challenge of established authority. Their shortcomings have been dramatized, especially the problem of delay.[54] Still, at this writing, it seems that the idea of a system of administrative courts has little chance of being put into practice in the United States.

The Ombudsman

Another instrument, again of European origin, for controlling the discretion of administrative agencies has received considerable attention in the United States. This is the office of ombudsman, which dates back some three centuries in Scandinavian countries and provides essentially

---

[54] This problem is largely the result of the increasing litigiousness of consumer and poverty groups, as well as the general challenge to traditional authority. As one observer noted in 1972, "In the last four years, cases docketed in the District Courts rose from 104,000 to 145,000, with few new judgeships. In the last decade, cases in the Court of Appeals grew staggeringly, from 4,200 to 14,500, while the Supreme Court's docketed cases nearly doubled from 2,585 to 4,533." Mark W. Cannon, "Can the Federal Judiciary be an Innovative System," *Public Administration Review*, Vol. 33 (January–February, 1973), p. 74.

for a government official who assumes the task of protecting the public against abuses of power by administrative agencies, including the court system. This aspect of the ombudsman's role apparently began during the late nineteenth century with the rise of democratic government. According to Brian Chapman, most of this official's cases arise through periodic inspections and incidents aired in the daily press.[55] Such offenses cover both procedural errors and substantive disadvantage. In most cases, the ombudsman merely brings the offense to the attention of the offending agency, with the expectation that it will be made right. He may also, however, bring the official concerned into court. The latter may be fined a small amount or in severe cases even be removed from office. In all cases, the ombudsman may demand evidence and documents, and he may question whomever he wishes. Most observers feel this office has been fairly successful in helping maintain citizen feelings of efficacy in the countries concerned. By 1972, the office existed in about 21 countries, of which France was the most recent major state to adopt it (1972).[56] Some cities, including Zurich, some states, such as Hawaii, and about 100 universities have also adopted the plan.

In a comprehensive analysis of the system, Donald Rowat summarizes its major inadequacies as including the fact that too often the ombudsman is an agent of the *executive* branch of government, which undercuts the independence of his role. All governments have apparently been rather stingy with the funds and other resources provided for the office, thereby limiting the scope of their influence. Moreover, in some systems, including the Danish, the ombudsman's jurisdiction does not extend to the courts or judges, nor in others can he act without a formal complaint, in writing, which again tends to inhibit the extent of his influence.

Certainly, any instrument that helps ease pervasive rank-and-file feelings of remoteness and inefficacy *vis-à-vis* government is useful, and in this sense the ombudsman system is a welcome addition to the controls mentioned elsewhere. To some extent, the rise of consumer and protest

---

[55] *The Profession of Government* (London: George Allen & Unwin, 1959), pp. 245–59; see also A. H. Rosenthal, "The Ombudsman—Swedish 'Grievance Man,'" *Public Administration Review*, Vol. 24, (December, 1964), pp. 226–30; H. Reuss, and S. V. Anderson, "The Ombudsman: Tribune of the People," *Annals of the American Academy of Political and Social Science*, Vol. 363 (January, 1966), pp. 44–51; S. V. Anderson, "The Ombudsman: Public Defender Against Maladministration," *Public Affairs Report*, Vol. 6, (1965); "The Swedish *Justifieombudsman, American Journal of Comparative Law*, Vol. 11, (Spring, 1962), pp. 225–38.

[56] Donald Rowat, *The Ombudsman Plan* (Toronto: McClelland Stewart, 1973); also a "State Statute to Create the Office of Ombudsman as Liaison between City, Agency and Legislator," *Harvard Journal of Legislation*, Vol. 2 (June, 1965), pp. 213–38.

groups, again an international phenomenon, has reduced the need for such officials. Moreover, insofar as they tend to work within the official system, they might as history suggests, tend to be co-opted by those who provide their resources. Governments seem to react essentially to *publicity* and the work of the ombudsman hardly has the appeal to the mass media of the dramatic and provocative tactics used by protest-consumer groups.

21

Responsibility of
the Administrator

Executive, legislative, and judicial control are augmented by another factor of a quite different kind. Whereas the former are highly institutionalized, we turn here to certain personal, ethical, and professional standards that may guide public officials. In addition to their conception of the "public interest," such prescriptions include the standards of performance instilled by their extensive education and the democratic socialization that most higher public officials have had. These influences probably tend to increase their sensitivity to community expectations of reasonable equity, disinterest, expertise, and service. Given the scope and complexity of governmental programs, they are probably the most practical means of controlling our huge public bureaucracies. As we have seen, legislative oversight is apt to be spectacular but spotty. Political executives similarly have a hard time managing the far-flung activities for which they are in theory responsible. Judicial remedies are *post hoc* by definition and court dockets are overloaded. Despite some violence to democratic theories of responsibility, we are in truth forced to rely upon officials themselves for responsible public administration.

WHAT IS RESPONSIBILITY?

Although "responsibility," like the "public interest," is a nebulous, often honorific term, it is a basic democratic ideal, bound up with the idea of one's obligation to some external body or standard of behavior.[1] Public administrators, for example, are responsible to the rule-of-law doctrine, which provides a fairly effective standard for judging some administrative decisions. Political responsibility is similarly involved with the idea of government's control by public opinion, political parties, and the community. Responsibility is also commonly used to denote the obligation of an individual to behave according to certain ethical and technical norms. In public administration, responsibility has often had a negative connotation: we have usually been satisfied if the official is kept from doing wrong.

Responsibility and Accountability

"Responsibility" and "accountability" should be differentiated. Accountability refers to the hierarchical or legal locus of responsibility. Responsibility, on the other hand, has personal, moral connotations and is not necessarily related to formal role, status, or power, although it is probably true that greater power brings greater responsibility. Thus a department head is *accountable* for the actions of all his subordinates, although in actual fact he is not *responsible* for their use of the power which he must delegate to them. This, in part, is the basis upon which President Nixon defended his position regarding the Watergate affair.

On the other hand, in exercising discretion every official is morally responsible for his decisions, although he is often not legally accountable. In practice, responsibility must be shared; it percolates throughout the entire administrative apparatus. Accountability, which concerns the formal relationships among and within the executive, legislative, and judicial branches, can never be shared. The bureaucracy is regarded as being accountable to elected representatives and to the courts who apply the rule-of-law doctrine. Within the executive branch, accountability is sought through a hierarchy of offices and duties that seems to make possible a "line of command" from the top to bottom. The heads of the various departments must answer to the President as general manager. Bureau, section, and division chiefs are legally accountable in turn to department heads. Upon the President (as well as governors and mayors) falls the monumental job of coordinating and directing the whole executive branch, under the constitutional mandate that gives him "execu-

---

[1] Problems of ethics and responsibility in government are considered in Emmette S. Redford, *Democracy in the Administrative State* (New York: Oxford University Press, 1969); see also "Ethics in America: Norms and Deviations," *Annals of the American Academy of Political and Social Science,* Vol. 363 (January, 1966), pp. 12–43.

tive power," and directs him to insure that "the laws are faithfully executed."

This appreciation of accountability, however, is formalistic and misleading. Although senior executives appoint subordinates and thus exercise some control over their character and behavior, in specific cases they exercise little or no control. The President's control is limited by the vast size and conflicting loyalties of the bureaucracy, as well as by the diffusion of power in our political system. He cannot hope to be aware of, much less supervise, all the activities of the some one hundred agencies for which he is constitutionally accountable. Executives at many levels face a similar problem. As a result, legal accountability often becomes a mere façade, like the "public interest" rhetoric of a regulatory agency commissioner who is in fact the captive of his most vocal clientele group. In such cases, the authority and prestige of the state are bent to the service of private groups, and responsibility to the public and the chief executive becomes tenuous. As we have seen, this situation is encouraged by the size and scope of government, by the whirlpools of power that form in our political system, and by the unofficial representative apparatus provided by private interest groups.[2]

Administrative Discretion

Responsibility is also bound up with discretion. When an official has no power to choose among alternatives, he cannot be held personally responsible because he has exercised no choice. In modern administration, however, it is clear that officials do have considerable discretion. Responsibility is now diffused throughout the bureaucracy and traditional measures of popular control suffer accordingly. The resulting necessity of relying on the moral and professional ethics of the official is complicated by the fact that he is often not only legally unaccountable, but anonymous. In practice, this means that his legally accountable chief must often assume a burden of moral responsibility that properly belongs to his subordinate. Thus the President may be held responsible for unethical conduct anywhere in the civil service. This possibility suggests

---

[2] Here again is a critical issue for students of public administration: *should* interest groups, despite their unofficial status in the political system, play the generally legitimated and pervasive role they now exert in shaping public policy? In effect, is the "public interest" merely the sum of the realized claims of great, organized, and usually producer interests? Indeed, can the very concept "the public interest" be operationalized?

why many executives are reluctant to delegate; if a subordinate errs, they are held responsible.

In effect, traditional concepts of administrative responsibility tend to be somewhat unrealistic and vastly oversimplified. They fail to recognize the highly institutionalized nature of administrative decisions. Most decisions are a product of many minds, with a resultant diffusion of responsibility. Meanwhile, the failure of our political parties to provide clear guidelines of public policy tends to create a power vacuum into which administrators, interest groups, and other wielders of informal power move. There are also psychological differences that cause one official to grasp authority while his colleague shrinks from it. Sometimes, in an effort to rationalize democratic theory, officials are viewed as mere automatons who passively follow the dictates of higher reason, presumably supplied by elected elites.

RESPONSIBILITY TO WHOM?

Despite such complexities, there are a few rough standards that help determine the locus of an agency's administrative responsibility. One concerns its ultimate loyalty: To whom does an agency answer? Whose objectives and values does its program really reflect? It is hardly adequate to say that agencies are responsible to the "people" at large through their elected representatives. One must analyze particular agencies in particular situations and build generalizations about their conception of responsibility from their behavior. It is clear that an agency must often compromise between several interests, but by checking its decisions and policies over time in cases where the issues are fairly well defined, it is possible to determine where its responsibility really lies. Such a determination, however, is obviously complicated by the fact that agency loci of responsibility change over time as new administrations and new administrators bring new preferences to bear. The various publics influenced by an agency will have also different points of view about its "proper" role. Interest groups sometimes regard regulatory agencies as service units. Research indicates that most administrators also regard themselves as guardians of the particular interest represented by their agency.[3] Consumers, on the other hand, tend to regard them as defenders of the public interest over against such groups.

[3] Cf. Presthus, *Elites in the Policy Process* (New York: Cambridge University Press, 1974), pp. 294, 296.

DEFINING THE "PUBLIC INTEREST"

Since the "public interest" is so often cited as an honorific symbol and a presumably operational guide to administrative decisions, it is useful to analyze it further. In effect, we must ask, Is the public interest a useful guide for governmental policy, or is it merely a shibboleth enlisted by interest groups and agencies to rationalize their own limited claims?

Broadly, it seems that two discrete concepts of the public interest exist. One defines it as a moral imperative resting on the assumption that some collective, over-arching community or national good exists.[4] Rousseau's ideal of the *volonté générale* is relevant here, as well as the doctrines of natural law.

The second broad conception regards the public interest essentially as a *process*, rather than a substantive reality. The "public interest," in effect, results from the accommodation of a multiplicity of competing interests. The final result of group struggle *is* the public interest. Most group theorists, following Arthur Bentley, hold this point of view, which has the advantage of legitimating the practical consequences of the existing political system. Let us consider these opposing views in turn.

It must be conceded at once that the public interest is a spook-like concept. Philosophers Wayne A. R. Leys and Charner Perry, for example, following a survey of the opinions of seventy-five philosophers, political scientists, and men of affairs, conclude, "It is quite possible that the 'public interest' has only a limited usefulness and that it is now being overworked."[5] Indeed, the poverty of political philosophy is suggested by its inability to define this common concept in other than generalities. Walter Lippmann, for example, offers the following vignette: "The public interest may be what men would choose if they saw clearly, thought rationally, acted disinterestedly and benevolently."[6] Perhaps the main problem with this Platonic view is the difficulty of deciding just *whose* conception of the public good should rule. The thorny problem of operationalization remains. Those who believe in philosopher kings have little

---

[4] See, among others, Ernest S. Griffith, "Ethical Foundations of the Public Interest," in C. Friedrich (ed.), *The Public Interest* (New York: Atherton Press, 1962), pp. 24–25; Anthony Downs, "The Public Interest: Its Meaning in a Democracy," *Social Research*, Vol. 29 (Spring, 1962), pp. 28–29.

[5] *Philosophy and the Public Interest* (Chicago: Committee to Advance Original Work in Philosophy, 1959), p. 14; see also Jacob, *Policy and Bureaucracy*, pp. 192–201.

[6] *The Public Philosophy* (Boston: Little, Brown & Co., 1955), p. 42.

difficulty answering the question, but those with a more tragic view of history are less sure.

The "process" advocates, impressed by the limitations of an imperfect political world, say in effect that the "public interest" is what emerges after the contestants in a given issue have compromised their claims and arrived at an acceptable decision.[7] There is a latent and often unfounded assumption of relatively equal group access and influence in policy decisions.[8] It is also assumed that no national interest, apart from or superior to, those of the interest groups, exist. To such observers the public interest is a political myth, occasionally useful as a manipulative device, but only a myth nevertheless.

Glendon Schubert believes that neither of these broad prescriptions offers much help to the policy-maker. Indeed, after a careful study of the literature, he concludes, "It may be somewhat difficult for some readers to accept the conclusion that there is no public interest theory worthy of the name."[9] Again, "I would also argue . . . that if the public interest concept makes no operational sense, notwithstanding the efforts of a generation of capable scholars, then political scientists might better spend their time nurturing concepts that offer greater promise of becoming useful tools in the scientific study of political responsibility."[10]

On the other hand, some careful observers, such as E. H. Carr, regard the public interest as something more than mere myth. Government is seen as the major agent for achieving it.

> Every modern state has intervened, first, to protect employers against trade unions, and, later, to protect the rights of the unions. If we wish to get a correct picture of the structure of the modern world, we must think not of a number of individuals . . . but of a number of large and powerful groups, sometimes competing, sometimes cooperating, in the pursuit of their group interests, and a state *constantly impelled* to increase the strength and scope of its authority in order to maintain the necessary minimum of cohesion in the social fabric. . . . The issue is whether to allow social action to depend on the haphazard outcome of a struggle

---

[7] David Truman, *The Governmental Process* (New York: Alfred A. Knopf, Inc., 1951), p. 50.

[8] For evidence from random samples that only about one-fourth to one-third of all types of interest groups are highly active politically, when this is defined as interacting with governmental elites, see Presthus, *Elites in the Policy Process, op. cit.,* p. 178; "Among both American and Canadian directors, almost three quarters spend only one-tenth to one-third of their work time in personal contact with members of the governmental elite," p. 176.

[9] *The Public Interest* (New York: The Free Press of Glencoe, Inc., 1959), p. 223.

[10] *Ibid.,* p. 224.

between interest groups or to control and coordinate the activities of these groups in the interest of the community.[11]

Class

Carr, however, assumes a questionable dichotomy between "government" and "interest groups." In fact, government and the major institutional sectors are symbiotically intertwined. Most of the time they are engaged in a highly beneficial exchange of valued currencies. As long as vast sums are required for political campaigns, and for government subsidies, this situation is likely to continue.

A Hierarchy of Values

In considering the premises that guide the public administrator, it seems worthwhile to pose the idea of a hierarchy of values. This view recognizes that many values affect his policy choices but assumes that they are assigned different weights in his calculus of behavior in a given situation. Three possible elements of this value hierarchy may be suggested: the official's professional standards; the values of his dominant clientele group; and his conception of the "public interest." While the administrator will no doubt weigh all these in making up his mind, we assume that he will not weight them all equally. The problem, of course, is that one cannot generalize as to how administrators will evaluate such values in given cases, since this will vary in terms of the situation, the administrator's personality, the prestige and independence of his agency, the power and status of the individual or group whose interest is at stake, and several other factors. We can only generalize that in the decision-making process, the administrator will consider several variables which will be assigned different weights according to his own personality, values, and the peculiar conditions impinging upon the given situation. In some cases, his definition of the "public interest" will have the highest priority; in others, the welfare of his major client groups; sometimes, depending upon his role, his professional standards will carry more weight.

As we saw in the chapters on policy-making, careful studies of representative decisions are required in order to determine the factors and the values that affect decision-making. It may be possible eventually to predict results as certain categories of decisions are analyzed and both the procedure and the criteria of relevance become more standardized.

[11] E. H. Carr, *The Conditions of Peace* (New York: The Macmillan Co., 1962), pp. 74–75; italics added.

This latter condition suggests why the search for objective procedures and standards is so eagerly pressed by those who want to operationalize and objectify the decision-making process. At present we cannot do much more than emphasize the complexity and variability of decisions. However, we have enough empirical evidence from civil servants, politicians, and students of administration to conclude safely that such values as professionalization, the public interest, and clientele interests do influence the administrator when he exercises discretion.

Impact of Democratic Theory

The public official, it seems, cannot avoid being influenced to some extent by the dominant political thought of the society in which he lives. In the United States such thought now strongly reflects a majoritarian ethic. The official knows (in normative theory at least) that ultimate political authority rests in all the people. The authority to act must necessarily be delegated to elected representatives and appointed officials— to legislatures and chief executives, and to the administrative officials who reflect and mold their policy. But this imperative does not change the fact that popular sovereignty and majority rule are the essential ideals of government.

In the liberal democratic view, the state is widely regarded as a means of extending both individual and community freedom, rather than as an instrument for curbing an arbitrary majority. Government is no longer, as Madison would have it, devoted mainly to the preservation of that "diversity in the faculties of men from which the rights of property originate." Instead, government is also a means of preventing economic dislocation and insuring social, economic, and political equality. On the whole, this view of government has been increasingly realized in practice in democratic countries during the twentieth century. In the process, an inversion of government's historic role has occurred. As Carl Becker says:

> In the eighteenth century the most obvious oppressions from which men suffered derived from governmental restraints on the free activity of the individual. Liberty was therefore naturally conceived in terms of the emancipation of the individual from such restraints. In the economic realm this meant the elimination of governmental restraints on the individual in choosing his occupation, in contracting for the acquisition and disposal of property, and the purchase and sale of personal services. But in our time, as a result of the growing complexities of a technological society, the emancipation of the individual from government restraint

in his economic activities has created new oppressions, so that for the majority of men liberty can be achieved only by an extension of governmental regulation of competitive business enterprise.[12]

Extending Individual Opportunity

In the United States, the main political drift has been toward majoritarian government. It seems impossible, moreover, to separate individual gains from community gain; to insist, in effect, that a majority-oriented government must *necessarily* deny or harm individual or minority interests to achieve community ends. Instead, contemporary democracy has often sought to extend privilege beyond a limited group, thereby adding to the sum of individual opportunity and freedom. It should not be forgotten that the strength of liberal democracy in the eighteenth and nineteenth centuries came from its devotion to freedoms which transcended class lines—freedom of speech and religion, and freedom from oppressive administration. Economic freedom alone, on the other hand, can never command such widespread support because of the conflict between the economic interests of social groups.

In this ideal sense, the public interest is often held to be bound up with the majority or the community interest. Aristotle made the need for such a community feeling clear in his claim that any form of government was acceptable, provided its rules aimed at the good of all rather than at the good of only certain classes. Lord Bryce, similarly, in describing democracy said, "The average citizen . . . will try to comprehend the main issues of policy, bringing to them an independent and impartial mind, which thinks first not of its own but the general interest." This "general interest" *ideal* runs throughout much of western democratic political theory. At the same time, of course, individual liberty has been a constant factor, and since the McCarthy and Watergate eras, we are all unhappily aware of how government can subvert individual freedoms in the name of national security.

The Operational Significance of the Public Interest

The analysis of responsible administration and the public interest is bound up with the pluralism of American society. Ours is a political system in which many groups and associations compete and cooperate to achieve their ends. Most of them, moreover, rationalize these ends in terms of the public interest. They seek to gain popular approval by

[12] *Modern Democracy* (New Haven, Conn.: Yale University Press, 1941), p. 34.

identifying with approved values. Labor unions, corporations, governments, and universities, however self-centered their goals, commonly indulge in procedural and rhetorical obeisance to the community welfare. Such efforts suggest the *operational significance* of value propositions such as the public interest.

Faced by the ethical devaluation attending this competition for respectability, some observers insist that no collective interest distinct from the interest of such groups exists. This group thesis of politics is suggestive, for individual objectives in our complex society are usually attained through group action, and the great influence of interest groups in our system is well established.[13] The thesis leads, however, to the following realistic but questionable proposition: that public administration should be responsible primarily to organized client groups, since they are part of the public interest and are the only groups which systematically make their wishes known. In a word, agencies are responsible if they meet the demands of their client groups. Undoubtedly, such a criterion encourages organizational survival in our system, but its effect on responsibility and the attempt to achieve a broader "public interest" is less clear. Indeed, one could argue that an agency's *resistance* to the demands of its clientele groups provides a better index of its responsibility, since in the case of the regulatory agencies, at least, their statutory obligation is to enhance the broader public interest, convenience, and necessity.

Under the theory of functional representation, moreover, the bureaucracy presumably spends its time merely referending the power of organized groups. Administrative behavior becomes merely a reflection of the existing distribution of economic and social power. Finally, the group thesis accepts the mechanistic notion that competition among special interests culminates in the general interest. In this sense it is a philosophy of frustration with little place for the larger community objectives that government in a politically sophisticated society must seek. Democratic government, it seems, survives by its ability to compromise special interests, not merely among themselves, but in the larger public interest.

As we have seen, the public interest is not systematically defined because it is often impossible to identify in any specific instance. It would, of course, be most helpful if the administrator faced with a vital decision

[13] The theory of "functional representation" was first expressed in C. M. Wiltse, "The Representative Function of Bureaucracy," *American Political Science Review*, Vol. 35 (June, 1941), pp. 510–15.

could determine objectively the public interest and act accordingly. However, even if such a reality existed in a given case, it is rarely possible to isolate it. Definition of the public interest thus becomes largely a matter of values of the particular individual or group defining it.

Why, then, our concern with the concept? *Because it is a powerful social myth which shapes some unknown amount of administrative behavior.* As I. W. Thomas said, "If situations are defined as real, they are real in their consequences." Actually we are not speaking of the public interest, but rather of the *conception* of it that administrators may have in a democratic society. For example, it is often maintained that there is some inherent opposition between special interests and the general interest. Whether this is objectively true or not, some officials *believe* it to be true and act accordingly. Fully one-half of our sample of higher civil servants in the U.S. and Canada (N=471) state that the "public interest" is the major single factor guiding their own decision-making.[14] This suggests again the pervasive thrust of the "public interest." In a democracy, majority is, over time and with many aberrations, the ultimate criterion. The public official will sometimes be guided by such values. He may believe, for example, that it is "right" for the government to assume a major role in reducing the disparity between democratic theory and practice, as for example in the case of the Negro or the urban poor. He may believe that "the public interest is not the mere sum of the special interests, and it is certainly not the sum of the organized special interests. Nor is it an automatic consequence of the struggle of the special interests."[15] Operationally, the "public interest" may be defined as a normative myth that sometimes helps officials to achieve a working compromise between the claims of various publics, without sacrificing the interest of the inarticulate, unorganized majority.

REPRESENTATIVE ROLE OF BUREAUCRACY

This strategic role of administrators in mediating group claims means that bureaucracy has a representative function. In cases involving regulatory activity, for example, administrators give precise meaning to broad legislative declarations of public policy. In advancing the social objectives of the community, they sometimes develop a rough index of the public interest, which is occasionally applied when decisions are

[14] Presthus, *Elites in the Policy Process, op. cit.,* p. 290.
[15] E. E. Schattschneider, "Political Parties and the Public Interest," *Annals of the American Academy of Political and Social Science,* Vol. 280 (March, 1952), p. 22.

made. The bureaucracy, in effect, shares with the legislature the task of insuring a reasonable amount of equity in the allocation of public resources.

In selecting among alternative policies, in extending or denying consent, the administrator necessarily works in a value context. Often, the perceived factors impinging upon a decision are isolated and assayed in line with what the official thinks is both "right" and "feasible." In some cases, the public interest will be an element in this process. This criterion is neither scientific nor quantitative. Nor is it necessarily based upon majority will because this cannot usually be known, concerned with, nor in many cases, affected by the particular issue at hand. It is often not clearly rationalized in the official's mind as a conscious influence. Instead, his feeling for the public interest is an emotive force, bound up with the administrator's personal code of behavior.

Positive Role of Administration

In the modern democratic state, in effect, government is expected to do more than merely adjudicate the claims of organized groups. Public policy no longer merely reflects haphazard shifts in power relations among such groups. Instead, the state has been granted a moral sanction to act as arbiter. As Reinhold Niebuhr insisted:

> Social life, when not consciously managed and manipulated, does not develop perfect equilibria of power. Its capricious disproportions of power generate various forms of domination and enslavement. Human society therefore requires a conscious control and manipulation of the various equilibria which exist in it. There must be an organizing center within a given field of social vitalities. This center must arbitrate conflicts from a more impartial perspective than is available to any party of a given conflict; it must manage and manipulate the processes of mutual support so that the tensions inherent in them will not erupt into conflict; it must coerce submission to the social process by superior power whenever the instruments of arbitrating and composing conflicts do not suffice; and finally it must seek to redress the disproportions of power by conscious shifts of the balances whenever they make for injustice. [16]

This view is sometimes challenged on the ground that it allows officials to "play God," to assume that they know what the public interest is in any instance. The presumed neutrality of the civil service is violated. Nevertheless, delegated legislative authority and decision-making power

[16] *The Nature and Destiny of Man,* Vol. II (New York: Charles Scribner's Sons, 1948), p. 266.

in our complex political system have made policy choices by administrators inevitable. Officials must act, and their behavior reflects certain premises about the "public interest." How they arrive at such decisions is an infinitely complicated process, involving personal values, professional standards, needs for security, agency programs, and the most recent election returns. Regardless of the buffeting that government's legitimacy has suffered from the Vietnam war and Watergate, it alone has the resources and the mandate to reconcile group demands. Administrators, as government agents, must adjudicate among the conflicting demands of the groups representing the various institutional sectors of American society. In the process, they cannot easily avoid some concern about the interests of the unorganized consumer. This concern evokes considerations of the public interest. However variable and subjective this conception is, it probably has considerable influence. As Lloyd Warner and his colleagues found, the belief that they were serving some larger community interest was a common source of good morale and satisfaction among higher civil servants.[17]

At the same time, the recent problems of the Nixon Administration, as well as the disenchantments of poverty and consumer groups, suggest that we cannot rely upon democratic values to insure that public officials are sensitive to the kinds of issues raised here. Instead, a self-consciously didactic process of education seems to be required. Here, hopefully, the new thrust toward extended education and training for public officials will include the patent consideration of normative issues, under some such rubric as "ethics in administration."

[17] The American Federal Executive, *op. cit.*, pp. 248–50.

Index